SpringBoard®

Level 5

English Textual Power™

THE COLLEGE BOARD
inspiring minds™

About the College Board

The College Board is a mission-driven not-for-profit organization that connects students to college success and opportunity. Founded in 1900, the College Board was created to expand access to higher education. Today, the membership association is made up of more than 5,900 of the nation's leading educational institutions and is dedicated to promoting excellence and equity in education. Each year, the College Board helps more than seven million students prepare for a successful transition to college through programs and services in college readiness and college success — including the SAT® and the Advanced Placement Program®. The organization also serves the education community through research and advocacy on behalf of students, educators and schools.

For further information, visit www.collegeboard.com.

ISBN: 0-87447-916-9
ISBN: 978-0-87447-916-4

7 8   16 17 18
Printed in the United States of America

Acknowledgments

The College Board gratefully acknowledges the outstanding work of the classroom teachers and writers who have been integral to the development of this revised program. The end product is testimony to their expertise, understanding of student learning needs, and dedication to rigorous but accessible language arts education.

Susie Challancin
English Teacher
Bellevue School District 405
Bellevue, Washington

Paul De Maret
English Teacher
Poudre School District
Fort Collins, Colorado

Suzie Doss
District English/ Language Arts
    Coordinator
Hobbs Municipal Schools
Hobbs, New Mexico

John Golden
English Teacher
Grant High School
Portland, Oregon

Nancy Gray
English Teacher
West Shore Junior/Senior High School
Melbourne, Florida

Ellen Greig
English Teacher, Consultant
Charlotte, North Carolina

Karen Hanson
Exceptional Student Teacher
Volusia Public Schools
DeLand, Florida

Cheryl Harris
English Teacher Consultant
Bedford, Texas

Susie Lowry
English Teacher
Volusia Public Schools
DeLand, Florida

Julie Manley
Middle School Language Arts
    Tech-Curriculum Coach and
    Humanities Teacher
Bellevue School District 405
Bellevue, Washington

Joely Negedly
Secondary Reading and
    Language Arts Specialists
Volusia Public Schools
DeLand, Florida

JoEllen Victoreen
Instructional Specialist,
    SpringBoard
San Jose, California

Douglas Waugh
Administrative Coach,
    SpringBoard
Bellevue, Washington

Nina Wooldridge
Instructional Specialist,
    SpringBoard
Los Angeles, California

Advisors, Reviewers, Special Feature Writers

The following teachers and writers provided invaluable assistance in creating special features and reviewing manuscript. We gratefully acknowledge their contributions to this revised edition.

Gary Cowan
English/Language Arts Coordinator
Metro Nashville Public Schools
Nashville, Tennessee

Nicki Junkins
Administrative Coach,
    SpringBoard
DeLand, Florida

Jeanneine Jones
Professor, Departments of Middle,
    Secondary, and K-12 Education
University of North Carolina
Charlotte, North Carolina

William McBride
Emeritus Professor of English
Colorado State University
Fort Collins, Colorado

Daniel Millet
English Teacher
Weld county School District
    Re-8
Fort Lupton, Colorado

Melanie Sangalli
English Teacher
Irving Public Schools
Irving, Texas

Special Acknowledgments

The College Board wishes especially to acknowledge the writers of the original *Pacesetter* program. Much of their work continues in use today. The result of their efforts was a program that helped both teachers and students succeed. With its roots in Pacesetter, the current program had an excellent foundation on which to build.

Willie Mae Crews
Educator
Birmingham, Alabama

R. Steven Green, Ed.D.
Educator
Kansas City, Missouri

Ellen Greenblatt
University High School
San Francisco, California

Alice Kawazoe
Educational Consultant, California Academic
    Partnership Program
San Carlos, California

Jenny Oren Krugman
Vice President, Southern Region
College Board
Miami, Florida

William McBride, Ph.D.
Emeritus Professor of English
Colorado State University
Fort Collins, Colorado

Robert Scholes, Ph.D.
Research Professor, Brown University
Providence, Rhode Island

In addition, we wish to acknowledge the educators and writers whose work on prior editions helped to continue the *Pacesetter* excellence and to establish the high expectations for which the College Board's SpringBoard program is known.

Lance Balla
Bellevue, Washington

Bryant Crisp
Charlotte, North Carolina

Nancy Elrod
Atlanta, Georgia

Ann Foster
Melbourne, Florida

Ana Gandara
Edinburg, Texas

Alex Gordin
Portland, Oregon

Kenyatta Graves
Washington, DC

Don Keagy
Poultney, Vermont

Don Kirk
Poultney, Vermont

Dana Mebane
Baltimore, Maryland

Bob Messinger
Providence, Rhode Island

Debi Miller
Miami, Florida

Melanie Ross Mitchell
Atlanta, Georgia

Lisa Rehm
DeLand, Florida

Penny Riffe
Palm Bay, Florida

Rick Robb
Clarksville, Maryland

Sue Rodriguez
Miami, Florida

Research and Planning Advisors

We also wish to thank the members of our SpringBoard Advisory Council, the SpringBoard Language Arts Trainers, and the many educators who gave generously of their time and their ideas as we conducted research for the program. Their suggestions and reactions to ideas helped immeasurably as we planned the revisions. We gratefully acknowledge the teachers and administrators in the following districts:

Broward County Public Schools
Fort Lauderdale, Florida

Cherry Creek School District
Cherry Creek, Colorado

Chicago Public Schools
Chicago, Illinois

DeKalb County School System
DeKalb County, Georgia

Duval County Public Schools
Jacksonville, Florida

Guilford County Schools
Greensboro, North Carolina

Hillsborough County Public Schools
Tampa, Florida

Hobbs Municipal Schools
Hobbs, New Mexico

Indianapolis Public Schools
Indianapolis, Indiana

Miami-Dade County Public Schools
Miami, Florida

Metropolitan Nashville Public Schools
Nashville, Tennessee

The City School District of New Rochelle
New Rochelle, New York

Orange County Public Schools
Orlando, Florida

School District of Palm Beach County
Palm Beach, Florida

Peninsula School District
Gig Harbor, Washington

Pinellas County Schools
Largo, Florida

San Antonio Independent School District
San Antonio, Texas

Spokane Public Schools
Spokane, Washington

Volusia County Schools
DeLand, Florida

Editorial Leadership

The College Board gratefully acknowledges the expertise, time, and commitment of the language arts editorial manager.

Betty Barnett
Educational Publishing Consultant

Level 5 Contents

To the Student

Welcome to the SpringBoard program. We hope you will discover how SpringBoard can help you achieve high academic standards, reach your learning goals, and prepare for success in your study of literature and language arts. The program has been created with you in mind: the content you need to learn, the tools to help you learn, and the critical-thinking skills that help you build confidence in your own knowledge and skills.

The College Board publishes the SpringBoard program as a complete language arts curriculum that prepares you for Advanced Placement and college-level study. SpringBoard maps out what successful students should know and be able to do at each grade level to develop the language, reading, writing, and communication skills needed for success. College Board also publishes the SAT and Advanced Placement exams—exams that you are likely to encounter in your high school years.

Connection to Advanced Placement

The College Board's Advanced Placement program provides the opportunity to complete college-level courses while in high school. In addition to receiving college credits, participation in AP courses helps you develop the skills and knowledge that add to your confidence and ease the transition from high school to college.

The SpringBoard program assists you in preparing for AP-level courses in several ways:

- ▶ Exposing you to the same types of tasks as on the AP Language and Literature exams; for example, close reading of fiction and nonfiction texts, responding to writing prompts, writing under timed conditions, and writing for multiple purposes (persuasion, argumentation, literary analysis, and synthesis).
- ▶ Introducing you to AP strategies, such as TP-CASTT and SOAPSTone, that help you analyze literary and other texts, giving you the tools you need to independently analyze any text.
- ▶ Preparing you for higher-order skills and behaviors required for college-level work through ongoing practice in key skills such as generating and organizing ideas, analysis of different types of texts, synthesis and explanation of concepts, and original writing in a variety of modes.

What Is the Foundation for SpringBoard?

The foundation of SpringBoard is the College Board Standards for College Success, which set out the knowledge and critical-thinking skills you should acquire to succeed in high school and in future college-level work.

The English Language Arts College Board Standards are divided into five categories: reading, writing, speaking, listening, and media literacy.

Your success as a **reader** depends on many factors, including your interest and motivation to read, the amount of time you spend reading, understanding the purpose for reading, knowledge about a topic, and knowledge about how to read different kinds of text.

Your success as a **writer** depends on learning many words and how to use those words effectively to communicate a story or information for others to read and understand. Successful writers determine their purpose for writing, such as to explore, inform, express an opinion, persuade, entertain, or to share an experience or emotion. As they write, they also consider their audiences and choose the language that will help them communicate with that audience. Writing is a process that involves several steps, and you will have many opportunities in this program to learn the process and to improve your own writing.

Your success as a **speaker** is based on how well you communicate orally. What is your message, what words will best communicate it, how do you prepare, or rehearse, for a speech? Good speakers also consider the audience and what they know about a specific topic. They can then deliver a message that uses a shared understanding, or develops one based on common knowledge, with their listeners.

Being a good **listener** is the other part of effective communication. Communication includes the speaker, listener, message, feedback, and noise (the conditions surrounding the communication). You'll have opportunities throughout the program to practice both your speaking and listening skills.

Finally, being **media literate** means that you can interpret, analyze, and evaluate the messages you receive daily from various types of media. Being media literate also means that you can use the information you gain to express or support a point of view and influence others.

As you complete the activities in this text, you will develop your skills and knowledge in all of these areas.

How Is SpringBoard Unique?

SpringBoard is unique because it provides instruction with hands-on participation that involves you and your classmates in daily discussions and analysis of what you're reading and learning. The book is organized into multiple activities that invite participation by providing adequate space for taking notes and writing your own thoughts and analyses about texts you're reading or questions you're answering. Among the key features that make SpringBoard a unique learning experience are:

- ▶ Activities that thoroughly develop topics, leading to deep understanding of the concepts and enabling you to apply learning in multiple situations.
- ▶ Extensive opportunities to explore a variety of texts—both fiction and nonfiction—that introduce you to many different ways of thinking, writing, and communicating.
- ▶ Questions that help you examine writing from the perspective of a reader and a writer and the techniques that good writers use to communicate their messages effectively.
- ▶ Built-in class discussions and collaborative work that help you explore and express your own ideas while integrating the ideas of others into your base of knowledge.
- ▶ Integrated performance-based assessments that give you practice in showing what you know and can do, not just repeating what you've read.
- ▶ Assessments that help you decipher tasks and plan how to accomplish those tasks in timed situations like those for standardized tests.

Strategies for Learning

As you complete the activities in this text, you will work on many reading, writing, and oral presentation assignments. You will often work in groups and pairs. To help you do your best, you and your teacher will use a variety of reading, writing, and collaborative learning strategies.

Reading strategies give you specific tools to help you improve your skills in reading and making meaning from text. These strategies will help you improve your ability to analyze text by developing skills in using context clues, finding meaning for unfamiliar words, or organizing your responses to what you read. As you learn to use different reading strategies, it's important to think about which ones work best for you and why.

Writing strategies help you focus on your purpose for writing and the message you want to communicate to your readers. Using writing strategies will help you analyze your own writing for specific purposes and identify how to improve that writing using better word choices or punctuating differently or using sentence structure in different ways.

You and your classmates will use *collaborative strategies* to explore concepts and answer text-related questions as you work in pairs or in groups to discuss the work you're doing and to learn from each other.

Performance Portfolio

You will learn to use language in both written and spoken forms in this course. You are encouraged to keep your work in a Working Folder from which you can choose examples to show where you started and how you are growing in your skills and knowledge during the year. Presenting your best work in a Portfolio not only helps you evaluate your own work and improvement, but also helps you explore your unique style and analyze how your work can best represent you.

Presenting your portfolio provides direction as you revisit, revise, and reflect on your work throughout the year. Your teacher will guide you as you include items in your portfolio that illustrate a wide range of work, including examples of reading, writing, oral literacy, and collaborative activities. As you progress through the course, you will have opportunities to revisit prior work, revise it based on new learning, and reflect on the learning strategies and activities that help you be successful. The portfolio:

▶ Gives you a specific place to feature your work and a way to share it with others.

▶ Provides an organized, focused way to view your progress throughout the year.

▶ Allows you to reflect on the new skills and strategies you are learning.

▶ Enables you to measure your growth as a reader, writer, speaker, and performer.

▶ Encourages you to revise pieces of work to incorporate new skills.

As you move through each unit, your teacher will instruct you to include certain items in your portfolio. Strong portfolios will include a variety of work from each unit, such as first drafts, final drafts, quickwrites, notes, reading logs, audio and video examples, and graphics that represent a wide variety of genre, forms, and media created for a variety of purposes.

We hope you enjoy using the SpringBoard program. It will give you many opportunities to explore your own and others' ideas about becoming effective readers, writers, and communicators.

How to Use This Book

English Textual Power, Level 5, focuses on the theme of culture and how our personal cultures help to shape us as individuals. This year you will explore cultural identity through texts written from different cultural perspectives. You will also look at a different culture through reading the novel, *Things Fall Apart*. Finally, you'll look at how different cultures view justice and how cultural clashes often lead to conflict in the world.

Preview the Unit

Essential Questions pose questions to help you think about the "big ideas" and make connections between what you learn and how you apply that learning.

Unit Overview sets the stage by:

▶ Providing a bridge from what you know to what you'll be learning in the unit.

▶ Outlining the big ideas in the unit and how the book's theme is connected from unit to unit.

Unit Contents give a snapshot of the unit activities and identify the texts and genres you'll explore in the unit.

▶ **Goals**—skills and knowledge you'll learn in the unit.

▶ **Academic Vocabulary**—key terms you'll use in the unit and to help you gain the vocabulary needed for AP courses and college.

Unit 4

Justice

Essential Questions

? What is the nature of justice?

? How does one construct a persuasive argument?

Unit Overview

Everyone must deal with issues of justice. What is a fair consequence for breaking a rule in class? Do students have freedom of speech in school? Should the principal be allowed to search lockers randomly? You have examined culture through many lenses. You can define a culture by its beliefs about what is right and wrong—its sense of justice. Different cultures may have different standards and methods for arriving at justice, but every society has to ask the questions about what is right and fair. Unit 4 presents nonfiction, drama, and art from around the world and across time that ask the key question: What is justice?

197

Unit 4 Justice

Contents

Goals

▶ To examine perspectives of justice across cultures and over time
▶ To recognize effective elements of persuasion
▶ To create a persuasive piece
▶ To rehearse and present a dramatic interpretation

ACADEMIC VOCABULARY

Justice
Chorus

Preparing for Learning

Learning Focus connects what you already know with what you'll learn in the unit and why it's important.

▶ Highlights key terms.

▶ Connects learning from unit to unit.

▶ Introduces concepts for the unit.

Previewing the Unit helps you: identify the expectations for knowledge and skills you'll need to learn in the unit by asking you to read and respond to:

▶ **Essential Questions**

▶ **Unit Overview–Learning Focus**

▶ **Embedded Assessment and Scoring Guide**

Starting with the End in Mind

Graphic organizer helps you:

▶ Map out the skills and knowledge you'll need for the Embedded Assessments.

▶ Read the assignment and the Scoring Guide (see page xvi) and outline what you'll need to do.

▶ Identify skills and knowledge to be assessed.

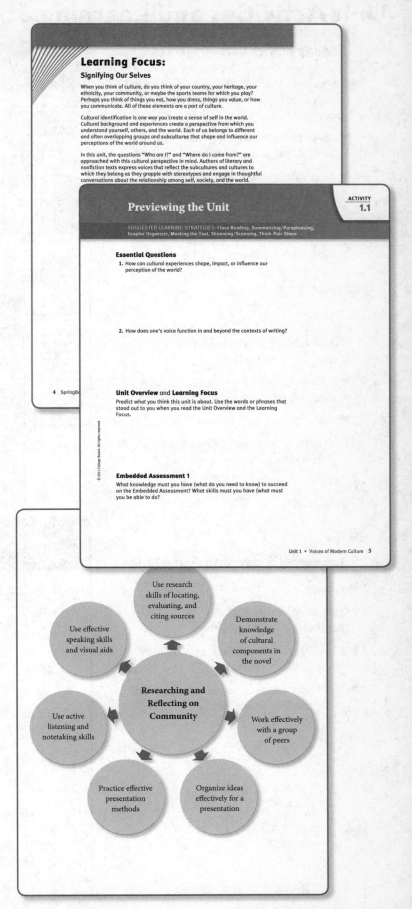

Unit Activities and Learning Strategies

Literary and Other Texts

from classic to contemporary introduce you to a variety of writers, stories, themes, and perspectives to help you interact with all types of writing.

▶ **About the Author** provides author's background and insights about the text.

▶ **Texts** include examples from a variety of genres, including poetry, film, autobiography, essay, print and online articles, folk tales, myths, fables, memoir, short stories, novel excerpts, interviews, Informational text, and drama.

My Notes provides space for you to interact with the text by:

▶ Jotting down your thoughts and ideas as you read.

▶ Using the space to analyze text.

▶ Writing notes about literary elements in texts.

Suggested Learning Strategies

▶ Clearly listed at the top of the page.

▶ Suggest strategies that are most appropriate for the activity.

▶ Over the course of the year, you'll learn which strategies work best for you.

▶ You'll find these strategies consistent with those used in AP courses.

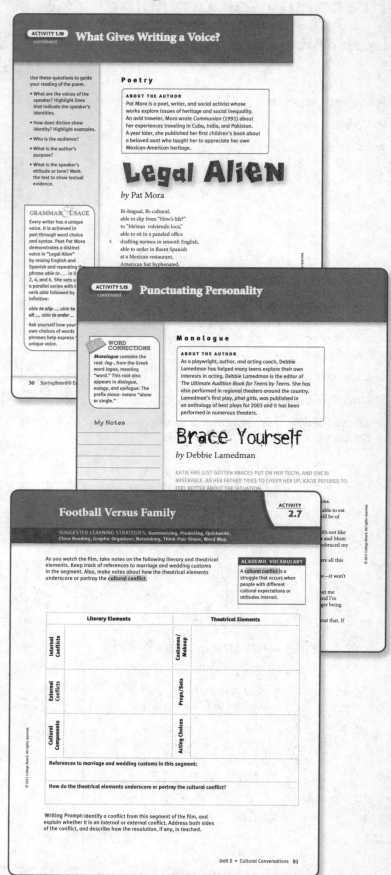

Integrated Language Skills

Vocabulary and Word Study

▶ **Academic Vocabulary** highlights key words you'll need to know for the unit and to expand your vocabulary for AP and college.

▶ **Literary Terms** define key words as you encounter them in your reading and analysis of text.

▶ **Word Connections** help you use context clues from Latin and other roots, understand analogies, and identify words with multiple meanings.

Grammar & Usage

▶ Offers tips about points of grammar and how to avoid common errors.

▶ Shows how writers use various grammatical constructions to clarify their text and to convey meaning for readers.

▶ Helps both speakers <u>and</u> writers use grammar to make their text or message more effective.

ACTIVITY 2.5

Family Perspectives: Neighbors

SUGGESTED LEARNING STRATEGIES: Quickwrite, Marking the Text, Paraphrasing, Word Map

ACADEMIC VOCABULARY

Humor is the quality of being amusing.

Satire is a type of writing that pokes fun at or ridicules an individual, a group of people, a behavior or attitude, or a cultural or social institution by pointing out weaknesses in a humorous way.

LITERARY TERMS

Exaggeration represents something as larger, better, or worse than it really is.

Irony is a literary device that exploits reader's expectations; irony occurs when what is expected turns out to be quite different from what actually happens.

Understatement is the representation of something as smaller or less significant than it really is; the opposite of exaggeration.

What Makes Something Funny?

ACTIVITY 2.13 *continued*

Identify all the parts in the four prompts below. You may use different colored markers to highlight different parts in each prompt. The first prompt may be done together as a class. Afterward, complete the remaining prompts.

Prompt 1: Think of something at your school that you would like to change in order to create a more positive learning environment. The change could affect anything from a policy or procedure to an attitude or tradition. In a well-organized persuasive letter, write to an adult at your school presenting the problem, your solution to that problem, and why the environment would change.

Subject:

Speaker:

WORD CONNECTIONS

Synthesis contains the root *-thes-*, from the Greek word *thesis* meaning "put, place, or set." This root also appears in *hypothesis*, *photosynthesis*, and *antithesis*. *Syn-* is a prefix, meaning "with or together."

72 SpringBoard® En...

Essay

ACTIVITY 2.16 *continued*

An Indian Father's Plea

by Robert Lake

ABOUT THE AUTHOR
Robert Lake, also known as Bobby Lake-Thom and Medicine Grizzly Bear, is a descendent of three Native American tribes. He has written numerous articles and two books on Native American culture and spirituality.

Wind-Wolf knows the names and migration patterns of more than 40 birds. He knows there are 13 tail feathers on a perfectly balanced eagle. What he needs is a teacher who knows his full measure.

Dear teacher, I would like to introduce you to my son, Wind-Wolf. He is probably what you would consider a typical Indian kid. He was born and raised on the reservation. He has black hair, dark brown eyes, and an olive complexion. And like so many Indian children his age, he is shy and quiet in the classroom. He is 5 years old, in kindergarten, and I can't understand why you have already labeled him a "slow learner."

At the age of 5, he has already been through quite an education compared with his peers in Western society. As his first introduction into this world, he was bonded to his mother and to the Mother Earth in a traditional native childbirth ceremony. And he has been continuously cared for by his mother, father, sisters, cousins, aunts, uncles, grandparents, and extended tribal family since this ceremony.

From his mother's warm and loving arms, Wind-Wolf was placed in a secure and specially designed Indian baby basket. His father and the medicine elders conducted another ceremony with him that served to bond him with the essence of his genetic father, the Great Spirit, the Grandfather Sun, and the Grandmother Moon. This was all done in order to introduce him properly into the new and natural world, not the world of artificiality, and to protect his sensitive and delicate soul. It is our people's way of showing the newborn respect, ensuring that he starts his life on the path of spirituality.

The traditional Indian baby basket became his "turtle's shell" and served as the first seat for his classroom. He was strapped in for safety, protected from injury by the willow roots and hazel wood construction. The basket was made by a tribal elder who had gathered her materials with prayer and in a ceremonial way. It is the same kind of basket that our people have used for thousands of years. It is specially designed to provide the child with the kind of knowledge and experience he will need in order to survive in his culture and environment.

GRAMMAR USAGE

Verbs do important work in sentences. They show time (**tense**), voice (**active or passive**), and action or being (action and linking verbs). Therefore, *a writer's choice of verbs is very important*.

Notice the tense and voice of the verbs (action verbs) in this sentence:

The basket **was made** (past tense, passive voice) by a tribal elder who **had gathered** (past perfect tense, active voice) her materials with prayer....

The passive voice gives attention to the subject, *basket*. The past perfect tense indicates that the action was completed in the past before another past action (making the basket).

Unit 2 • Cultural Conversations **109**

ACTIVITY 2.13

Deconstructing a Prompt

SUGGESTED LEARNING STRATEGIES: Marking the Text, Graphic Organizer, Word Map, Think-Pair-Share

Writing prompts often contain many details but little direction. It is easy to get caught up in the details and forget the main task. You may write an excellent response with flawless syntax, but if you do not respond to the prompt, you will not receive a high score. This activity offers guidance in deconstructing—or reading, analyzing, and understanding—writing prompts.

When considering any prompt, look for five basic parts. Most if not all the parts will be present. Finding as many as you can will help you figure out what you need to do and how to respond to the prompt correctly.

Five Parts to Look for in a Writing Prompt

1. **Subject:** What is the subject you need to write about? A well-written prompt will identify the subject, but it may be vague. For example, a prompt might tell you to think of a childhood experience. What common themes or ideas (either implicit or explicit) are associated with the subject?

ACADEMIC VOCABULARY

Synthesis is the act of combining ideas from different sources to create, express, or support a new idea.

2. **Speaker:** Who is writing the answer? (You are, but are you writing it as a student, a citizen, an authority?) The prompt should tell you who you are as the writer.

3. **Type of Essay:** What kind of response are you writing—expository, persuasive, **synthesis**, personal narrative? An effective prompt must tell you the type of writing you need to do. It may give you a choice. Choose wisely.

4. **Task:** What is the prompt asking you to do? For example, your task may be to take a stand on an issue and write a five-paragraph persuasive essay. Read the details carefully to identify exactly what you need to do.

5. **Hints:** Does the prompt give you suggestions to get started? The prompt may suggest ideas to think about or literary devices to identify and analyze.

Writing

▶**Writing Process** is defined and practiced through opportunities to draft, revise, edit, and prepare publishable writing.

▶ **Writing Prompts & Timed Writings** provide practice in identifying specific writing tasks and writing under timed conditions.

▶ **Portfolios** are encouraged to collect your writing throughout the year to show your progress.

Performance-Based Assessment

▶ **Embedded Assessments** provide opportunities to demonstrate your knowledge and your skills in applying that knowledge in a variety of assessments.

▶ **Scoring Guide** walks you through the expectations for performance.

- Descriptions under Exemplary, Proficient, and Emerging describe the level of work required and set the expectations for what you need to know and do <u>before</u> you start the Embedded Assessment.

- Using the descriptions for Exemplary, Proficient, and Emerging, you decide what you'll do and take responsibility for your performance.

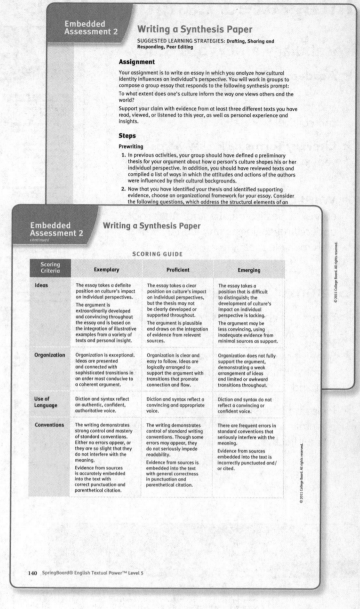

Embedded Assessment 2

Writing a Synthesis Paper

SUGGESTED LEARNING STRATEGIES: Drafting, Sharing and Responding, Peer Editing

Assignment

Your assignment is to write an essay in which you analyze how cultural identity influences an individual's perspective. You will work in groups to compose a group essay that responds to the following synthesis prompt:

To what extent does one's culture inform the way one views others and the world?

Support your claim with evidence from at least three different texts you have read, viewed, or listened to this year, as well as personal experience and insights.

Steps

Prewriting

1. In previous activities, your group should have defined a preliminary thesis for your argument about how a person's culture shapes his or her individual perspective. In addition, you should have reviewed texts and compiled a list of ways in which the attitudes and actions of the authors were influenced by their cultural backgrounds.

2. Now that you have identified your thesis and identified supporting evidence, choose an organizational framework for your essay. Consider the following questions, which address the structural elements of an

Embedded Assessment 2 *continued*

Writing a Synthesis Paper

SCORING GUIDE

Scoring Criteria	Exemplary	Proficient	Emerging
Ideas	The essay takes a definite position on culture's impact on individual perspectives. The argument is extraordinarily developed and convincing throughout the essay and is based on the integration of illustrative examples from a variety of texts and personal insight.	The essay takes a clear position on culture's impact on individual perspectives, but the thesis may not be clearly developed or supported throughout. The argument is plausible and draws on the integration of evidence from relevant sources.	The essay takes a position that is difficult to distinguish; the development of culture's impact on individual perspective is lacking. The argument may be less convincing, using inadequate evidence from minimal sources as support.
Organization	Organization is exceptional. Ideas are presented and connected with sophisticated transitions in an order most conducive to a coherent argument.	Organization is clear and easy to follow. Ideas are logically arranged to support the argument with transitions that promote connection and flow.	Organization does not fully support the argument, demonstrating a weak arrangement of ideas and limited or awkward transitions throughout.
Use of Language	Diction and syntax reflect an authentic, confident, authoritative voice.	Diction and syntax reflect a convincing and appropriate voice.	Diction and syntax do not reflect a convincing or confident voice.
Conventions	The writing demonstrates strong control and mastery of standard conventions. Either no errors appear, or they are so slight that they do not interfere with the meaning. Evidence from sources is accurately embedded into the text with correct punctuation and parenthetical citation.	The writing demonstrates control of standard writing conventions. Though some errors may appear, they do not seriously impede readability. Evidence from sources is embedded into the text with general correctness in punctuation and parenthetical citation.	There are frequent errors in standard conventions that seriously interfere with the meaning. Evidence from sources embedded into the text is incorrectly punctuated and/or cited.

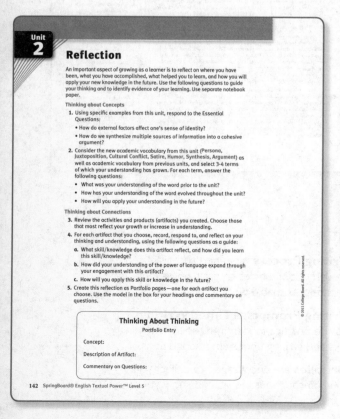

Unit 2

Reflection

An important aspect of growing as a learner is to reflect on where you have been, what you have accomplished, what helped you to learn, and how you will apply your new knowledge in the future. Use the following questions to guide your thinking and to identify evidence of your learning. Use separate notebook paper.

Thinking about Concepts

1. Using specific examples from this unit, respond to the Essential Questions:
   - How do external factors affect one's sense of identity?
   - How do we synthesize multiple sources of information into a cohesive argument?

2. Consider the new academic vocabulary from this unit (Persona, Juxtaposition, Cultural Conflict, Satire, Humor, Synthesis, Argument) as well as academic vocabulary from previous units, and select 3-4 terms of which your understanding has grown. For each term, answer the following questions:
   - What was your understanding of the word prior to the unit?
   - How has your understanding of the word evolved throughout the unit?
   - How will you apply your understanding in the future?

Thinking about Connections

3. Review the activities and products (artifacts) you created. Choose those that most reflect your growth or increase in understanding.

4. For each artifact that you choose, record, respond to, and reflect on your thinking and understanding, using the following questions as a guide:
   a. What skill/knowledge does this artifact reflect, and how did you learn this skill/knowledge?
   b. How did your understanding of the power of language expand through your engagement with this artifact?
   c. How will you apply this skill or knowledge in the future?

5. Create this reflection as Portfolio pages—one for each artifact you choose. Use the model in the box for your headings and commentary on questions.

> **Thinking About Thinking**
> Portfolio Entry
>
> Concept:
>
> Description of Artifact:
>
> Commentary on Questions:

Unit Reflection helps you to take ownership of your learning by stopping at regular points to think about:

▶ What you've learned.

▶ What strategies and tools helped you learn.

▶ What you still need to work on in the future.

Voices of
Modern Culture

Essential Questions

? How can cultural experiences shape, impact, or influence our perception of the world?

? How does voice function in and beyond the contexts of writing?

Unit Overview

Culture is often difficult to define, but it influences everything from who you are as an individual to how you relate to other people at home and around the world. Just what is culture, and how does it contribute to the way you see the world? In this unit, you will explore these questions by investigating factors that affect your personal and cultural identities. You will learn about the concept of voice, or how you express identity in written, spoken, or artistic forms. By engaging with and constructing different types of print and nonprint texts, you will discover how writers and speakers use voice to express cultural ideas and personal identities.

Unit 1

Voices of Modern Culture
Contents

Goals

▶ To examine a variety of voices writers and speakers use and the reasons they use them (audience, purpose, context, and genre)

▶ To apply analytical, critical, creative, and reflective strategies to published, personal, and peer-generated texts

▶ To develop speaking and listening skills that build capacity for effective communication

ACADEMIC VOCABULARY

Culture

Subculture

Symbol

Perspective

Stereotype

Texts not included in these materials.

Learning Focus:

Signifying Our Selves

When you think of culture, do you think of your country, your heritage, your ethnicity, your community, or maybe the sports teams for which you play? Perhaps you think of things you eat, how you dress, things you value, or how you communicate. All of these elements are a part of culture.

Cultural identification is one way you create a sense of self in the world. Cultural background and experiences create a **perspective** from which you understand yourself, others, and the world. Each of us belongs to different and often overlapping groups and **subcultures** that shape and influence our perceptions of the world around us.

In this unit, the questions "Who am I?" and "Where do I come from?" are approached with this cultural **perspective** in mind. Authors of literary and nonfiction texts express voices that reflect the subcultures and cultures to which they belong as they grapple with stereotypes and engage in thoughtful conversations about the relationships between self, society, and the world.

Voice is the unique style by which we express our identity in speaking and writing. Voice conveys attitude, personality, and experiences. We all have many voices that are influenced by the cultures with which we identify. Since language is the primary means by which writers share their perspectives and create a distinctive cultural voice, a deep understanding of **diction, syntax, imagery, symbol,** and **tone** enhances your ability to analyze the voices expressed by others and create your own distinctive voice in writing. As you begin to consider how your own voice is shaped by your cultural identities and personal experiences, you will be better able to make stylistic and language choices that express your distinctive voice.

Independent Reading: In this unit, you will read several texts that focus on voice and culture. For independent reading, look for a novel, memoir, collection of essays, or short stories that focus on voice and culture.

Previewing the Unit

SUGGESTED LEARNING STRATEGIES: Close Reading, Summarizing/Paraphrasing, Graphic Organizer, Marking the Text, Skimming/Scanning, Think-Pair-Share

Essential Questions

1. How can cultural experiences shape, impact, or influence our perception of the world?

2. How does one's voice function in and beyond the contexts of writing?

Unit Overview and Learning Focus

Predict what you think this unit is about. Use the words or phrases that stood out to you when you read the Unit Overview and the Learning Focus.

Embedded Assessment 1

What knowledge must you have (what do you need to know) to succeed on the Embedded Assessment? What skills must you have (what must you be able to do)?

Class Culture Quilt

WORD CONNECTIONS

Artifact contains the roots *-art-* and *-fac-*, from the Latin words *ars*, which means "to join or fit," and *facere*, which means "to make or do." These roots also appear in *artisan, article, factory, manufacturing,* and *benefactor*.

Add circles to create a word web around the word *Quilting*. Write words or phrases that you associate with quilting. Draw lines to connect the new circles to the one shown below.

Brainstorm a list of images, artifacts, objects, memories, and experiences from your childhood that reveal who you are as a person.

	Image, Artifact, Object, Memory, and/or Experience	Explanation of Significance to You
1.		
2.		
3.		
4.		
5.		
6.		
7.		
8.		

MY MOTHER PIECED QUILTS

by Teresa Paloma Acosta

ABOUT THE AUTHOR

Born in 1949 in McGregor, Texas, poet Teresa Paloma Acosta grew up listening to family stories about working in and living near cotton fields. She came from a family of hardworking men and women. The women were known particularly for their sewing skills. Paloma Acosta combines her love for her Mexican heritage and her family's quilting and storytelling abilities in her poem "My Mother Pieced Quilts."

My Notes

they were just meant as covers
in winters
as weapons
against pounding january winds

but it was just that every morning I awoke to these   5
october ripened canvases
passed my hand across their cloth faces
and began to wonder how you pieced
all these together
these strips of gentle communion cotton and flannel
         nightgowns   10
wedding organdies
dime store velvets

how you shaped patterns square and oblong and round
positioned
balanced   15
then cemented them
with your thread
a steel needle
a thimble

how the thread darted in and out   20
galloping along the frayed edges, tucking them in
as you did us at night
oh how you stretched and turned and rearranged

your michigan spring faded curtain pieces
25 my father's santa fe work shirt
the summer denims, the tweeds of fall

in the evening you sat at your canvas
—our cracked linoleum floor the drawing board
me lounging on your arm
30 and you staking out the plan:
whether to put the lilac purple of easter against the red
      plaid of winter-going-
into-spring
whether to mix a yellow with blue and white and paint the
corpus christi noon when my father held your hand
35 whether to shape a five-point star from the
somber black silk you wore to grandmother's funeral

you were the river current
carrying the roaring notes . . .
forming them into pictures of a little boy reclining
40 a swallow flying
you were the caravan master at the reins
driving your thread needle artillery across the mosaic cloth bridges
delivering yourself in separate testimonies

oh mother you plunged me sobbing and laughing
45 into our past
into the river crossing at five
into the spinach fields
into the plainview cotton rows
into tuberculosis wards
50 into braids and muslin dresses
sewn hard and taut to withstand the thrashings of twenty-five years

stretched out they lay
armed/ready/shouting/celebrating

knotted with love
55 the quilts sing on

Imagery and Diction

Novelist Robert Newton Peck once said, "A good author makes a camera out of a pen." An author creates imagery through his or her **diction**. Imagery is language that appeals to the senses. Writers use it to describe an experience and evoke a feeling.

1. Review Acosta's poem and identify two **images**. Explain why the images appeal to you.

2. Next, consider the topic, purpose, and occasion of Acosta's poem. How might they shape her diction or choice of words?

3. The power of a sentence or a line of poetry to produce a reaction in the reader lies mainly in the **connotations** (the suggested meaning) of words. Consider the final image in the poem, "knotted with love the quilts sing on." What are the denotations of the words *knotted* and *sing*? What are their connotations? Discuss the connotations of the words *knotted* and *sing*.

4. Consider what would happen if the author's *diction* were different. For example, suppose instead of "knotted," she had used "entangled," "mixed up," or "tied together." How might a different word or phrase affect the reader's perception of the final line in the poem?

LITERARY TERMS

Images help create pictures or ideas in the reader's mind. Most images appeal to the sense of sight.

Connotation is the emotional feeling attached to a word. A connotation may be positive, negative, or neutral.

Denotation is the literal meaning of a word.

Diction is the writer's choice of words.

WORD CONNECTIONS

In this poem, the patches of the quilt represent pieces of the author's life. The patch-quilt analogy has also been used to describe the make-up of the U.S. population. Explain the meaning of this analogy.

Contemplating Culture

SUGGESTED LEARNING STRATEGIES: **Word Map, Graphic Organizer, Discussion Groups, Think-Pair-Share, Visualizing**

Add circles to create a word web around the word **Culture**. Write words or phrases that you associate with culture. Draw lines to connect the new circles to the one shown below.

Use your prior knowledge and what you have learned in the unit to write a definition of culture in the box below.

Culture is...

Discuss your definition with a small group of peers. Revise your definition to include any new ideas you have about culture.

Culture Word Sort

Your teacher will provide you with a set of index cards. Each card contains a word that describes some element of culture. You will work in groups to sort the words into stacks of words that are related. After placing all the words in stacks, your group will choose a category to describe each of your stacks.

Culture Vocabulary

You will next work in groups to describe the meaning of one of the following words relating to culture. Your teacher will assign each group a word. On separate paper, work with your group to define your term. Draw an illustration that represents the key ideas in your word.

customs	diversity	ethnocentrism
assimilation	stereotypes	cultural norms

SUGGESTED LEARNING STRATEGIES: Marking the Text, Notetaking, Think-Pair-Share

Memoir

ABOUT THE AUTHOR

Born in Abadan, Iran, writer Firoozeh Dumas spent much of her childhood living in California. She credits her father, a Fulbright scholar and engineer who attended Texas A&M University, and his fondness for humorous storytelling, for inspiring her to write stories of her own. After the events of September 11, 2001, friends urged Dumas to publish her stories as a way to remind readers of the humor and humanity of Middle Eastern cultures.

from Funny in Farsi

by Firoozeh Dumas

When I was seven, my parents, my fourteen-year-old brother, Farshid, and I moved from Abadan, Iran, to Whittier, California. Farid, the older of my two brothers, had been sent to Philadelphia the year before to attend high school. Like most Iranian youths, he had always dreamed of attending college abroad and, despite my mother's tears, had left us to live with my uncle and his American wife. I, too, had been sad at Farid's departure, but my sorrow soon faded—not coincidentally, with the receipt of a package from him. Suddenly, having my brother on a different continent seemed like a small price to pay for owning a Barbie complete with a carrying case and four outfits, including the rain gear and mini umbrella.

Our move to Whittier was temporary. My father, Kazem, an engineer with the National Iranian Oil Company, had been assigned to consult for an American firm for about two years. Having spent several years in Texas and California as a graduate student, my father often spoke about America with the eloquence and wonder normally reserved for a first love. To him, America was a place where anyone, no matter how humble his background, could become an important person. It was a kind and orderly nation full of clean bathrooms, a land where traffic laws were obeyed and where whales jumped through hoops. It was the Promised Land. For me, it was where I could buy more outfits for Barbie.

We arrived in Whittier shortly after the start of second grade; my father enrolled me in Leffingwell Elementary School. To facilitate my adjustment, the principal arranged for us to meet my new teacher, Mrs. Sandberg, a few days before I started school. Since my mother and I did not speak English,

WORD CONNECTIONS

Eloquence contains the root *-loqu-*, from the Latin word *loqui*, meaning "to speak." This root also appears in *loquacious* and *colloquial*. The suffix *-ence* indicates that the word is a noun.

My Notes

the meeting consisted of a dialogue between my father and Mrs. Sandberg. My father carefully explained that I had attended a prestigious kindergarten where all the children were taught English. Eager to impress Mrs. Sandherg, he asked me to demonstrate my knowledge of the English language. I stood up straight and proudly recited all that I knew: "White, yellow, orange, red, purple, blue, green."

The following Monday, my father drove my mother and me to school. He had decided that it would be a good idea for my mother to attend school with me for a few weeks. I could not understand why two people not speaking English would be better than one, but I was seven, and my opinion didn't matter much.

Until my first day at Leffingwell Elementary School, I had never thought of my mother as an embarrassment, but the sight of all the kids in the school staring at us before the bell rang was enough to make me pretend I didn't know her. The bell finally rang and Mrs. Sandberg came and escorted us to class. Fortunately, she had figured out that we were precisely the kind of people who would need help finding the right classroom.

My mother and I sat in the back while all the children took their assigned seats. Everyone continued to stare at us. Mrs. Sandberg wrote my name on the board: F-l-R-O-O-Z-E-H. Under my name, she wrote "I-R-A-N." She then pulled down a map of the world and said something to my mom. My mom looked at me and asked me what she had said. I told her that the teachers probably wanted her to find Iran on the map.

The problem was that my mother, like most women of her generation, had been only briefly educated. In her era, a girl's sole purpose in life was to find a husband. Having an education ranked far below more desirable attributes such as the ability to serve tea or prepare baklava. Before her marriage, my mother, Nazireh, had dreamed of becoming a midwife. Her father, a fairly progressive man, had even refused the two earlier suitors who had come for her so that his daughter could pursue her dream. My mother planned to obtain her diploma, then go to Tabriz to learn midwifery from a teacher whom my grandfather knew. Sadly, the teacher died unexpectedly, and my mother's dreams had to be buried as well.

Bachelor No. 3 was my father. Like the other suitors, he had never spoken to my mother, but one of his cousins knew someone who knew my mother's sister, so that was enough. More important, my mother fit my father's physical requirements for a wife. Like most Iranians, my father preferred a fair-skinned woman with straight, light-colored hair. Having spent a year in America as a Fulbright scholar, he had returned with a photo of a woman he found attractive and asked his older sister, Sedigeh, to find someone who resembled her. Sedigeh had asked around, and that is how at age seventeen my mother officially gave up her dreams, married my father, and had a child by the end of the year.

As the students continued staring at us, Mrs. Sandberg gestured to my mother to come up to the board. My mother reluctantly obeyed. I cringed. Mrs. Sandberg, using a combination of hand gestures, started pointing to the map and saying, "Iran? Iran? Iran?" Clearly, Mrs. Sandberg had planned on incorporating us into the day's lesson. I only wished she had told us that earlier so we could have stayed home.

After a few awkward attempts by my mother to find Iran on the map, Mrs. Sandberg finally understood that it wasn't my mother's lack of English that was causing a problem, but rather her lack of world geography. Smiling graciously, she pointed my mother back to her seat. Mrs. Sandberg then showed everyone, including my mother and me, where Iran was on the map. My mother nodded her head, acting as if she had known the location all along but had preferred to keep it a secret. Now all the students stared at us, not just because I had come to school with my mother, not because we couldn't speak their language, but because we were stupid. I was especially mad at my mother, because she had negated the positive impression I had made previously by reciting the color wheel. I decided that starting the next day, she would have to stay home.

The bell finally rang and it was time for us to leave. Leffingwell Elementary was just a few blocks from our house and my father, grossly underestimating our ability to get lost, had assumed that my mother and I would be able to find our way home. She and I wandered aimlessly, perhaps hoping for a shooting star or a talking animal to help guide us back. None of the streets or houses looked familiar. As we stood pondering our predicament, an enthusiastic young girl came leaping out of her house and said something. Unable to understand her, we did what we had done all day: we smiled. The girl's mother joined us, then gestured for us to follow her inside. I assumed that the girl, who appeared to be the same age as I, was a student at Leffingwell Elementary; having us inside her house was probably akin to having the circus make a personal visit.

Her mother handed us a telephone, and my mother, who had, thankfully, memorized my father's work number, called him and explained our situation. My father then spoke to the American woman and gave her our address. This kind stranger agreed to take us back to our house.

Perhaps fearing that we might show up at their doorstep again, the woman and her daughter walked us all the way to our front porch and even helped my mother unlock the unfamiliar door. After making one last futile attempt at communication, they waved good-bye. Unable to thank them in words, we smiled even more broadly.

After spending an entire day in America, surrounded by Americans, I realized that my father's description of America had been correct. The bathrooms were clean and the people were very, very kind.

My Notes

Components of Effective Communication

Take notes as the class brainstorms the meaning of communication.

Read the text below. Then fill in the graphic organizer.

Facts About Conversations

Every conversation must have both a sender and a receiver of information. When the sender sends the information to the receiver, the receiver must first filter that information through his or her past experiences or frame of reference. For example, when you are asked to draw a dog, you probably think about dogs you have seen. The same process occurs in discussions of more complex ideas and issues. The message from the sender must be translated by the receiver in order to be understood.

Label each shape in the graphic organizer with terms introduced in the paragraph above.

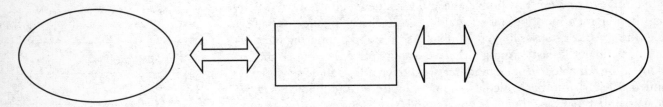

Discussion: Observe your classmates as they attempt to communicate a simple or complex task. Use these questions to discuss the process of communication.

1. Was there ever a point at which communication broke down because the two individiuals did not identify things in the same way?

2. What variables appear to affect one-on-one communication?

3. Explain how the sender was conscious of the need to be clear and to connect with the receiver's past experiences.

4. What strategies might be used to minimize barriers and improve communication?

Creating Group Norms

The quotations that follow reflect how people act when they communicate with each other. Read the quotations and make inferences about how to best communicate with others.

"The problem with communication . . . is the *illusion* that it has been accomplished." *George Bernard Shaw*

"The newest computer can merely compound, at speed, the oldest problem in the relations between human beings, and in the end the communicator will be confronted with the old problem, of what to say and how to say it." *Edward R. Murrow*

"The greatest compliment that was ever paid me was when someone asked me what I thought, and attended to my answer." *Henry David Thoreau*

"Most conversations are simply monologues delivered in the presence of a witness." *Margaret Miller*

"I like to listen. I have learned a great deal from listening carefully. Most people never listen." *Ernest Hemingway*

"I remind myself every morning: Nothing I say this day will teach me anything. So if I'm going to learn, I must do it by listening." *Larry King*

"If speaking is silver, then listening is gold." *Turkish Proverb*

> GRAMMAR&USAGE
>
> Notice the **reciprocal pronoun** of *each other* in the second line. Reciprocal pronouns show a two-way action, as in two people communicating. *Each other* is used to describe actions between two people. *One another* is also a reciprocal pronoun and is used to describe actions between more than two people, as in students in the class communicating with one another.

Identify two to three norms (guidelines) you and your fellow students can follow to communicate effectively when you work with partners or in groups.

1.

2.

3.

What Contributes to Our Perceptions of the World?

SUGGESTED LEARNING STRATEGIES: **Brainstorming, Quickwrite, Graphic Organizer, Think-Pair-Share**

After looking at the images your teacher provides, record in the organizer below the meanings and associations evoked by the images.

Image	My First Associations	Responses from Peers

Quickwrite: Respond to the Essential Question, "How can cultural experiences shape, impact, or influence our perception of the world?"

ACADEMIC VOCABULARY

A **symbol** is a thing that represents or stands for something else. For example, a flag is a symbol of a country; a dove is a symbol of peace.

Brainstorm at least five artifacts that serve as **symbols** for you, your life, and your culture that you could include in a "Perception Box" of your own. What do the objects reveal about you and your culture?

Culture and Art

Use the image or artwork provided by your teacher to complete the graphic organizer below.

Title of Artwork:	
Author:	
See What details do you observe in the artwork?	I see . . . I notice . . .
Mean What might these details mean? (Hint: Consider connotative associations that may be symbolic.) Consider color, shapes, and objects you see.	
Matter To whom does the image matter, and why? What conclusions can you draw about the creator of the image? What can you say about the purpose or effect of the image?	
Interpretive or Thematic Statement:	

Culture and Literature

My Notes

While reading, examine how the text features of this poem (for example, indentation, stanzas, italics, and single lines) advance the author's theme and voice.

Poetry

ABOUT THE AUTHOR

Langston Hughes (1902–1967) is one of the great African American poets of the twentieth century. While working as a busboy in a Washington, D.C., hotel, Hughes offered his writing to poet Vachel Lindsay, who was so impressed that he helped launch Hughes's career. Over the next fifty years, Hughes wrote poetry, plays, and translations, and edited anthologies that voiced the concerns and experiences of black Americans.

Theme for **English B**

by Langston Hughes

The instructor said,

> *Go home and write*
> *a page tonight.*
> *And let that page come out of you —*
5 > *Then, it will be true.*

I wonder if it's that simple?
I am twenty-two, colored, born in Winston-Salem.
I went to school there, then Durham, then here
to this college on the hill above Harlem.
10 I am the only colored student in my class.
The steps from the hill lead down to Harlem,
through a park, then I cross St. Nicholas,
Eighth Avenue, Seventh, and I come to the Y,
the Harlem Branch Y, where I take the elevator
15 up to my room, sit down, and write this page:

It's not easy to know what is true for you or me

at twenty-two, my age. But I guess I'm what

I feel and see and hear. Harlem, I hear you:

hear you, hear me — we two — you, me talk on this page.

(I hear New York, too.) Me — who?   20

Well, I like to eat, sleep, drink, and be in love.

I like to work, read, learn, and understand life.

I like a pipe for a Christmas present,

or records — Bessie, bop, or Bach.

I guess being colored doesn't make me not like   25

the same things other folks like who are other races.

So will my page be colored that I write?

Being me, it will not be white.

But it will be

a part of you, instructor.   30

You are white —

yet a part of me, as I am a part of you.

That's American.

Sometimes perhaps you don't want to be a part of me.

Nor do I often want to be a part of you.   35

But we are, that's true!

As I learn from you,

I guess you learn from me —

although you're older — and white —

and somewhat more free.   40

This is my page for English B.

TWIST	Response	Textual Support
Tone: the attitude of the speaker toward the subject		
Word Choice: the specific words and their connotations, associations, or emotional impact		
Imagery: the sense impressions (sound, smell, sight, taste, and touch)		
Style: the author's use of language, including figurative language and poetic devices such as repetition, rhyme, and rhythm		
Theme: the author's insight about life		
Thesis Statement:		

Circles of Influence

SUGGESTED LEARNING STRATEGIES: Graphic Organizer, Close Reading, Marking the Text, Rereading, Drafting, Revisit Prior Work, Think-Pair-Share

The graphic organizer below identifies several **subcultures** in this country. Think about your experiences as members of each subculture. Then identify images or ideas that reflect each. Write those words or images in the appropriate circle.

ACADEMIC VOCABULARY

A **subculture** is a smaller subsection of a culture; for example, the artsy students are a subculture within the culture of a high school.

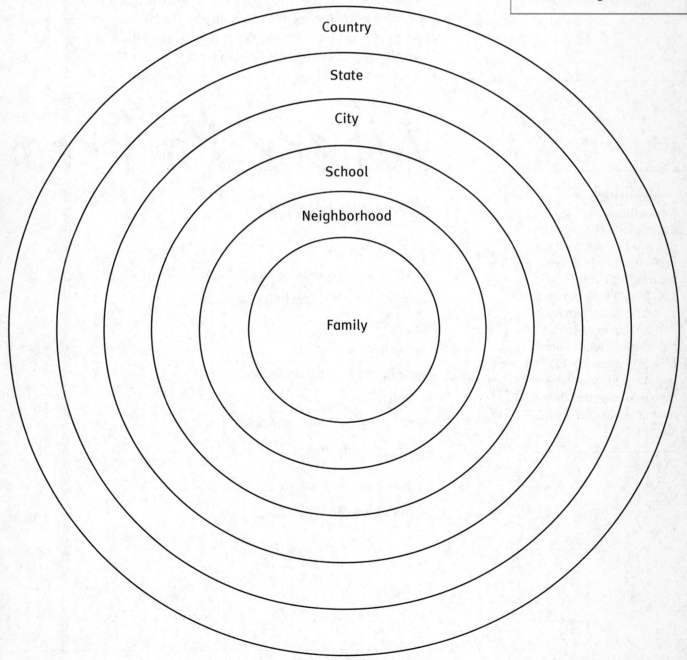

My Notes

Poetry

ABOUT THE AUTHOR
George Ella Lyon is the author of award-winning children's books, including *Catalpa*, a book of poetry that won the Appalachian Book of the Year Award, and the novel *With a Hammer for My Heart*. Lyon is often asked about her unusual first name. On her Website, she explains that she was named after her uncle George and her aunt Ella.

Where I'm From

by George Ella Lyon

I am from clothes-pins
from Clorox and carbon-tetrachloride.[1]
I am from the dirt under the back porch.
(Black, glistening,
5   it tasted like beets.)
I am from the forsythia bush,
the Dutch Elm
whose long gone limbs I remember
as if they were my own.

10   I'm from fudge and eyeglasses,
      from Imogene and Alafair.

[1] **carbon tetrachloride,** *n.*, chemical used for dry cleaning

I'm from the know-it-alls

    and the pass-it-ons,

from Perk up! and Pipe down!

I'm from He restoreth my soul   15

    with a cottonball lamb

    and ten verses I can say myself.

I'm from Artemus and Billie's Branch,

fried corn and strong coffee.

From the finger my grandfather lost   20

    to the auger,[2]

the eye my father shut to keep his sight.

Under my bed was a dress box

spilling old pictures,

a sift of lost faces   25

to drift beneath my dreams.

I am from those moments—

snapped before I budded—

leaf-fall from the family tree.

Writing Prompt: Write your own "Where I'm From" poem emulating the style of George Ella Lyon. Consider using anaphora to create rhythm and an effective pattern to convey aspects of your culture.

---

[2] **auger**, *n.*, a hand tool used to dig holes in wood or dirt

Creating an Artistic Representation of My Culture

SUGGESTED LEARNING STRATEGIES: **Graphic Organizer, Drafting, Self-Editing**

Assignment

Your assignment is to create a three-dimensional artistic representation of your culture and compose a written text that explains the significance of two of the symbols you have chosen to represent yourself.

Steps

Planning

1. Use the graphic organizer on the next page (or one that you create) to generate a list of symbols that represent the cultures with which you identify. You may also draw on the "Where I'm From" poem you wrote for Activity 1.9.

2. Select two symbols from each category (a total of ten) and think of an artistic method for making each symbol. You may use painting, sculpture, collage, found materials, watercolors, cut paper, ink, pastels, and/or actual artifacts or souvenirs, and so on. Remember that your final product must be three-dimensional, not a flat surface.

Creating

3. Collect and/or create the objects for your artistic representation.

4. Then choose two symbols from the ten you created that are especially meaningful to you. Write one or two paragraphs that explain the significance of the two symbols.

Refining

5. Experiment with various arrangements until you find a way to display the ten objects that is aesthetically pleasing and engages your audience.

6. As you look at your artistic representation, try to anticipate questions that your audience might have. Practice answering the questions aloud.

7. When you revise your written explanation of the significance of your symbols, try to incorporate answers to those anticipated questions into your explanation. Include in your draft an explanation of how you organized your artistic representation and why you chose to map it in that order. As you revise, carefully consider your word choice and revise as needed based on your purpose, audience, and genre.

8. Edit your written explanation using the tools available to you to present a technically sound document.

9. Be prepared to share and explain your artistic representation of your culture to a small group or in a gallery walk setting.

10. End-of-Task Reflection: Did people read my symbols in the way that I thought they would? Explain. How might I map, or organize, my artistic representation differently to better communicate my ideas?

Review the detailed lists that you made for the Circles of Influence activity (Activity 1.9). Consider those details as well as new ones that come to mind as you list objects or artifacts that represent your culture or cultures. List as many details or items as you can in each box. You may want to add additional categories.

Family	Sports or Hobbies	Clothing	Education
Food	**Music or Art**	**Religion**	**Gender Roles**

Highlight the five categories on the organizer that most strongly identify and define you culturally. Choose two items from each category to include in your project. (Remember, you have to represent them artistically.)

Then choose two items that you feel represent you in a significant way and explain how they symbolize you culturally.

Creating an Artistic Representation of My Culture

SCORING GUIDE

Scoring Criteria	Exemplary	Proficient	Emerging
Artistic Representation	The three-dimensional art form can be characterized as unique, thought provoking, and visually engaging. The representation demonstrates an extensive effort to include an assortment of symbols from a variety of categories and to organize them in a way that enables the audience to make sense of the piece as a whole.	The three-dimensional art form can be characterized as interesting and visually pleasing. The representation demonstrates an effort to include symbols from different categories that are organized in a logical way.	The three-dimensional art form is attempted, yet it may be characterized as confusing or visually distracting. The representation demonstrates little effort to include symbols from different categories, and the symbols may be disorganized.
Explanatory Text	The explanatory text clearly and thoroughly explains the meaning of two symbols from the artistic representation, including their relationship to the artist's culture(s), as well as the significance of the artistic method chosen to portray each symbol. The explanation demonstrates the author's keen ability to anticipate viewers' questions.	The explanatory text discusses the meaning of two symbols from the artistic representation, including the relationship to the artist's culture(s), as well as the significance of the artistic method chosen to portray each symbol. The explanation demonstrates the author's basic ability to anticipate viewers' questions.	The explanatory text attempts to discuss the meaning of two symbols from the artistic representation but may not adequately show the relationship to the artist's culture(s) or the significance of the artistic method chosen to portray each symbol. The explanation does not demonstrate the author's ability to anticipate viewers' questions.

SCORING GUIDE

Scoring Criteria	Exemplary	Proficient	Emerging
Evidence of the Writing Process	There is extensive evidence that the explanatory text reflects the various stages of the writing process.	There is evidence that the explanatory text reflects stages of the writing process.	There is little or no evidence that the explanatory text has undergone stages of the writing process.
Reflection	The reflection shows a thorough metacognitive analysis describing viewers' and readers' reactions to the artist's representation and how revisions could be made accordingly.	The reflection adequately shows a metacognitive analysis explaining and describing viewers' and readers' reactions and how revisions could be made accordingly.	The reflection attempts to show some metacognitive analysis describing viewers' and readers' reactions but not thoroughly enough to explain how revisions could be made accordingly.
Additional Criteria			

Comments: _____

_____

_____

_____

_____

_____

Learning Focus:

You Have Great Voice

After watching the latest person audition on a television show, your friend turns to you and says, "That dude's got a great voice." The meaning of *voice* in this context seems pretty clear; but what would it mean if, after reading a new story in class, your friend turned to you and said, "Wow, I love the writer's voice in this poem"? Or what if your teacher asked you, "How does your voice change in different social situations"? These last two questions are central to the idea that "voice" is a deliberate creation, an expression of who you are.

It is clear that there are many different factors that shape who you are. Your family, the social roles you play, and the groups or subcultures you belong to all represent different areas or contexts that influence how you think and act and speak. They affect how you talk and what you talk about—in short, your voice. You probably talk and act differently in different contexts or roles. These differences help explain the concept of voice.

Modifying your voice—what you talk about, the words you use to express yourself, and the manner in which you deliver your words—is something you do every day in speaking about different subjects to different audiences. You trade information with your friends differently than you persuade the adults in your life to do what you want.

In writing, as in speaking, voice is conveyed by the choices you make in subject matter, in diction, syntax, and punctuation. Crafting your writing deliberately to communicate a certain voice illustrates the power written and spoken language has to entertain, persuade, complain, censure, praise, and amuse. Your ability to manipulate language to convey voice is central to your success as a writer, as a communicator, and as an individual.

Voice and Writing

Excerpted from *Pacesetter English:*
Voices of Modern Culture

What gives writing a **"voice"**? The metaphor on which the term is built incorporates two things associated with the human voice—the articulation of personality, individuality, and the speaking out, the emerging from silence into speech.

"Voice" in writing seems to imply distinctive qualities, uniqueness, that which makes writing personal—not mainly in terms of content (though WHAT is said is believed to bring about writing with a "strong voice") . . . but in terms of style. Writing "with a strong voice" characterizes the writer, both confirming and projecting his or her identity.

"Voice" also implies a speaking out, a refusal to be without language. Often, this quality is associated with the social voices of writers who are in some sense oppressed or who are denied the opportunity to speak their experiences by a dominating "mainstream," but a writer's connection to a social group can take other forms as well. This social aspect of "voice" is more than psychological; it presents itself within a cultural context, claims a space within a conversation. To do this, such writing needs to represent not just an individual but also a kind of experience that has resonance for some people besides the writer, members of some group whose identity AS A GROUP matters. That group could be any group: a recognized ethnic or racial population or a subgroup of the high school student population, such as female athletes, musicians, working students, etc.

These two shades of meaning in the word *voice* seem to be on a collision course: one looks for the qualities of an individual style, the other at how a piece of writing articulates a cultural perspective shared by more than one person. Our criteria need to account for writing that does both, that is both distinctive and culturally powerful.

Essential Question

How does voice function in and beyond the contexts of writing?

> ### LITERARY TERMS
>
> **Style** is the distinctive way a writer uses language. It is characterized by elements such as diction, syntax, imagery, and use of literary devices.

> ### WORD CONNECTIONS
>
> *Psychological* contains two roots, *-psych-* and *-logy-*, from the Greek words *psyche*, meaning "soul or breath," and *logos*, meaning "word." The roots also appear in *psychic, psychotic, biology,* and *logical*. The suffix *-al* indicates that the word is an adjective.

> ### ACADEMIC VOCABULARY
>
> A **perspective** is one's attitude or way of looking at the world.

Use these questions to guide your reading of the poem.

- What are the voices of the speaker? Highlight lines that indicate the speaker's identities.

- How does diction show identity? Highlight examples.

- Who is the audience?

- What is the author's purpose?

- What is the speaker's attitude or tone? Mark the text to show textual evidence.

GRAMMAR & USAGE

Every writer has a unique voice. It is achieved in part through word choice and syntax. Poet Pat Mora demonstrates a distinct voice in "Legal Alien" by mixing English and Spanish and repeating the phrase *able to . . .* in lines 2, 4, and 6. She sets up a parallel series with the verb *able* followed by an infinitive:

*able **to slip** ..., able **to sit** ..., able **to order** ...*

Ask yourself how your own choices of words and phrases help express your unique voice.

Poetry

ABOUT THE AUTHOR
Pat Mora is a poet, writer, and social activist whose works explore issues of heritage and social inequality. An avid traveler, Mora wrote *Communion* (1991) about her experiences traveling in Cuba, India, and Pakistan. A year later, she published her first children's book about a beloved aunt who taught her to appreciate her own Mexican-American heritage.

Legal Alien

by Pat Mora

Bi-lingual, Bi-cultural,
able to slip from "How's life?"
to "Me'stan volviendo loca,"
able to sit in a paneled office
5   drafting memos in smooth English,
able to order in fluent Spanish
at a Mexican restaurant,
American but hyphenated,
viewed by Anglos as perhaps exotic,
10   perhaps inferior, definitely different,
viewed by Mexicans as alien,
(their eyes say, "You may speak
Spanish but you're not like me")
an American to Mexicans
15   a Mexican to Americans
a handy token
sliding back and forth
between the fringes of both worlds
by smiling
20   by masking the discomfort
of being pre-judged
Bi-laterally.

Analyzing Components of Voice

SUGGESTED LEARNING STRATEGIES: Graphic Organizer,
Notetaking, Drafting, Think-Pair-Share

As you watch the short clip from the film *Grease*, note how John Travolta's character, Danny, changes in the scene. Record the verbal and nonverbal details that characterize his two voices.

T-Bird Danny	Sandy's Danny

In what ways does Danny's voice change in the scene? Why?

1. Write an e-mail to the principal explaining why you were late to school.

2. Write an e-mail to your best friend explaining why you were late to school.

3. What differences do you notice in your voice? Explain.

4. In your emails, how did your diction express a unique voice, and how did it change from one audience to the other?

Voice and Style

Mad Talk Quickwrite	Reflection on Syntax, Diction, and Tone
Soft Talk Quickwrite	Reflection on Syntax, Diction, and Tone
Fast Talk Quickwrite	Reflection on Syntax, Diction, and Tone

LITERARY TERMS

Tone is a writer's attitude toward his or her subject or audience.

Syntax is the way in which words are put together to make meaningful elements, such as phrases, clauses, and sentences.

Diction is the writer's choice of words.

Now choose one of these voices to present orally to your classmates. Use facial expressions, eye contact, and tone to convey emotion.

What differences do you notice among the voices in other presentations?

What factors explain the differences between the voices?

Experimenting with Tone

SUGGESTED LEARNING STRATEGIES: **Close Reading, Marking the Text, Revisiting Prior Work, Brainstorming, Think-Pair-Share**

Select a tone word and use a thesaurus to create an array of related words.

My Notes

TONE ARRAY

←————→ ←————→ ←————→

_____ _____ _____ _____

Song Lyrics

> **ABOUT THE AUTHOR**
> John Lennon (1940–1980) is best known as one of the founding members of the pop group The Beatles. Lennon's song "Imagine" reflects the singer's beliefs in the power of peaceful action. Lennon was assassinated on December 8, 1980.

by John Lennon

Imagine there's no heaven,
It's easy if you try,
No hell below us,
Above us only sky,
Imagine all the people   5
living for today. . .

Imagine there's no countries,
It isn't hard to do,
Nothing to kill or die for,
No religion too,   10
Imagine all the people
Living life in peace. . .

Imagine no possessions,
I wonder if you can,
No need for greed or hunger,   15
A brotherhood of man,
Imagine all the people
Sharing all the world. . .

You may say I'm a dreamer,
but I'm not the only one,   20
I hope some day you'll join us,
And the world will live as one.

Contrasting Voices

Prewriting

Drafting

Persona Voice #1

Persona Voice #2

What changes do you notice between the two voices? What explains these differences?

Punctuating Personality

SUGGESTED LEARNING STRATEGIES: Quickwrite, Graphic Organizer,
SOAPSTone, Close Reading, Marking the Text, Think-Pair-Share, Adding

Using a grammar handbook, identify the punctuation marks below and
describe their function.

Mark	Name	Purpose/Function
*		
!		
.		
?		
,		
;		
:		
--		
()		
[ ]		
" "		
/		

Think about how you use punctuation to express yourself. Then
complete the sentence frame below.

I identify myself as a _____ because _____.
          (punctuation mark)

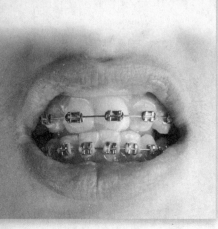

WORD CONNECTIONS

Monologue contains the root *-log-*, from the Greek word *logos*, meaning "word." This root also appears in *dialogue*, *eulogy*, and *epilogue*. The prefix *mono-* means "alone or single."

My Notes

Monologue

ABOUT THE AUTHOR

As a playwright, author, and acting coach, Debbie Lamedman has helped many teens explore their own interests in acting. Debbie Lamedman is the editor of *The Ultimate Audition Book for Teens by Teens*. She has also performed in regional theaters around the country. Lamedman's first play, *phat girls*, was published in an anthology of best plays for 2003 and it has been performed in numerous theaters.

Brace Yourself

by Debbie Lamedman

KATIE HAS JUST GOTTEN BRACES PUT ON HER TEETH, AND SHE IS MISERABLE. AS HER FATHER TRIES TO CHEER HER UP, KATIE REFUSES TO FEEL BETTER ABOUT THE SITUATION.

KATIE: Don't look at me…and don't make me laugh…I look hideous.

I don't care if everyone I know has them. I care that I won't be able to eat solid food for the next two years. I care that every school picture will be of some FREAK.

What do you mean it'll be worth it? My teeth weren't so bad—it's not like I had this huge overbite or anything. I could have lived with it. You and Mom always taught me to embrace the differences—well I would have embraced my crooked teeth, if only you had let me.

But now they're going to be perfect and straight and I'm not sure all this suffering is worth it, Dad…plus I'm in a lot of pain…

Well, I guess a chocolate milkshake would taste good right now—it won't involve chewing. (*Pause.*)

Okay, I'll let you buy me one…but don't think that's going to put me in a good mood. I plan on being miserable for the next two years and I'm not gonna smile until these things are off and my teeth and no longer being held hostage.

And Dad…you say one day I'll thank you, but we'll just see about that. If that day comes…I'll buy you a milkshake.

Monologue

The Crush

by Debbie Lamedman

NICOLE CONFRONTS ANDREW, A GUY SHE'S ADMIRED FROM AFAR, AND TELLS HIM HOW SHE FEELS ABOUT HIM.

NICOLE: My friend Janet has a zoom lens on her camera so she took your picture when you weren't looking. I got it blown up and it's hanging over my bed. I hope you don't think that's weird, but I think you're…gorgeous. I mean, you look like a movie star or something. (*Pause.*) Oh God, I'm totally humiliating myself, aren't I?

I don't know how I got the nerve to come talk to you, but I just couldn't stand it anymore. I had to tell you how I feel.

Yeah…I know I don't even know you, but I'd like to get to know you. I guess what I'm trying to do is ask you out on a date. Maybe you think the guy is the one who is supposed to ask, but let's face it—you didn't even know I existed until two minutes ago so I thought I'd better make the first move.

I'm freaking you out? Why?

Oh, the picture thing? Hey, I'm harmless—look I have a crush on you—what's the big deal? You should be flattered.

I'm not a stalker!

Well you don't have to be such a jerk about it. I don't think I'd go out with you now even if you begged me. And you're not as good-looking as I thought you were.

(*Calling after him as he walks away.*) And I'm definitely taking your picture off my wall. (*Pause.*) Men!

My Notes

Monologue

THE JOB INTERVIEW

by Debbie Lamedman

HEATHER IS INTERVIEWING FOR HER FIRST JOB AS A WAITRESS AT A LOCAL RESTAURANT.

HEATHER: Well, no…I don't have any experience, but how hard could it possibly be, right? You take an order—when it's ready you bring it to them. I do that all the time at home. My family is constantly ordering me to bring them things.

Tray service? You mean carrying food out on one of those big trays? (Pause.)

Yeah! I could do that. I'm really strong. I may not look it, but I did five chin-ups for the physical fitness test at school—that's like a record.

You want to hire me? That's great!

Okay, what's my schedule? Let's see…well, I can't work on Friday or Saturday nights because I just got a boyfriend and well…ya know…I gotta have a social life. I really can't work weeknights because I'll have homework, and my parents wouldn't like it too much if I was working late.

(*Thinking.*) Um…Sunday is family day so that's out. I'm finished with school by 2:30 but I'll need to eat and destress from the day, so I could probably start my shift at 3:30 or 4 and work until 6 or 6:30-7 at the absolute latest. I could work Monday, Tuesday, and Wednesday afternoons, but sometimes I have after-school activities so you'll need to be flexible….

But otherwise, I'm totally available. So…when would you like me to start?

Monologue

The Date

by Debbie Lamedman

JOHNNY IS INTERESTED IN DATING MARIE. HOWEVER, HE IS FORCED TO DEAL WITH HER BROTHER FRANK TO GET HIS PERMISSION.

JOHNNY: If I knew Marie was your sister, I would have never asked her out. Nothing's wrong with her. She's great. That's why I want to go out with her. But I don't need any more enemies, so if you'd rather I didn't date her, I won't.

Wait a minute, first you get on me for wanting to take her out, and now you're on me for not wanting to? What are you trying to do, drive me crazy?

Yes. I want to take out your sister. I didn't realize I needed to ask your permission. But here goes…

Frank, may I have the honor of taking out your sister Marie this Saturday night?

I solemnly swear that I am not a pervert and I will be a perfect gentleman and have her home by one. Okay…twelve. Eleven? Don't ya think that's kinda early for a weekend?

Okay, okay. I'll have her home by—how's eleven thirty—that's a nice compromise, right? Good. Okay. Thanks, Frank. Thanks a lot. Thanks for letting me date your sister.

(*Aside.*) Jeez, I'm surprised he didn't make me sign a contract. I hope he doesn't put out a contract—on me!

My Notes

My Notes

Monologue

OFF THE COURT

by Debbie Lamedman

CHRIS EXPLAINS TO HIS FATHER THAT HE IS NOT INTERESTED IN PLAYING ON THE BASKETBALL TEAM HIS FATHER IS COACHING AND HE WOULD MUCH RATHER BE A MUSICIAN.

CHRIS: Look Dad, I don't know how to tell you this…so I'm just gonna say it—I think it's great that you're coaching the basketball team. I think you'll be a great coach, but…I don't want to be on the team.

No! It has nothing to do with you! See—that's what I'm talking about. YOU want me to be on the team. YOU want me to be a great basketball player, but you never asked me what I want. I don't even like basketball. I'm not good at it and I probably never will be. You've never asked me what I'm good at. Just because you're good at sports doesn't mean I am. And what I really want to do is study music. That's what I'm good at, Dad, and that's what I want to do.

I want to play piano—classical or jazz—any kind of music, really. I just want to get really, really good at it. I want to be the best piano player there ever was and I want to compose my own stuff and play concerts and everything…

C'mon Dad—don't be mad. You wouldn't be proud of a son who was lousy on the court, but think how proud you'll be when you see me playing at Carnegie Hall.

WORD CONNECTIONS

Understanding both the denotation and connotation of words can help you use and understand analogies. For example, colors are often used to describe emotion. Think about using "blue" to describe someone who is sad. Complete the following analogy.

red : angry ::
yellow : _____

a. death
b. happy
c. flower
d. funny

Monologue

Dinner Guest

by Debbie Lamedman

My Notes

GREG IS HAVING DINNER AT HIS GIRLFRIEND CINDY'S HOUSE. CINDY HAS PREPARED A MEAL THAT IS ABSOLUTELY AWFUL. GREG TRIES TO BE AS POLITE AND TACTFUL AS POSSIBLE REGARDING CINDY'S COOKING BECAUSE HE WANTS TO CONTINUE DATING HER.

GREG: So…Cindy…this is really good. Seriously, I had no idea you were such a great cook. You could probably become a famous chef or something—that's how good you are.

I never really ate anything like this before. What do you call this dish again?

Ohhhh. "Cindy's Experiment." Ohhhh. So, what's in it? I mean, how did you get it to be this sort of greenish color?

I see…that's your little secret…not gonna share the recipe with anybody. Okay.

What? Oh no, no thanks. No seconds for me—I'm so full I couldn't eat another bite. I want to, but I ate a really big lunch, and I'm really *stuffed*. But thanks, anyway.

Oh—there's dessert? Well, that's cool. I love dessert—I suppose I could make room for that. What did you make for dessert? Chocolate cake? Apple pie?

You call it "Cindy's Surprise?" Wow. It looks…wow…it's really sort of purple, isn't it? (*Pause.*)

Not too big of a piece now…remember, I'm really full. But it looks great. Just great. I can't wait to taste it.

Punctuating Personality

A Close Reading of Text

SOAPSTone	Response	Textual Support
Speaker: Who is the speaker?		
Occasion: What is the social, cultural, historical, geographical context of the text?		
Audience: Who is the target audience?		
Purpose: What is the message of the text? Why was it written?		
Subject: What is the text about? What is the theme?		
Tone: What is the speaker's attitude towards the subject?		

Voices Against Stereotypes

SUGGESTED LEARNING STRATEGIES: **SOAPSTone**, **Brainstorming**, **Close Reading**, **Marking the Text**, **Rereading**, **Word Map**, **Drafting**

What is a stereotype?

A stereotype is generally based on assumptions about a group of people based on race, gender, location, behavior, or physical traits. For example, many jokes and movies focus on the stereotype of the "dumb blonde" or the clueless "nerd" with glasses.

Stereotypes have been around a long time. They reflect the ideas that people have about others who are not like them in some way. When you hear someone describe a classmate as a "nerd" or a "jock," you're hearing a stereotype that is assigning that person to a category based on a label.

Stereotypes are not all negative; for example, "nerdy kids are smart" or "girls are better at intuition than guys" are positive stereotypes. Using either negative or positive stereotypes to describe people ignores the uniqueness of people by mischaracterizing who they are and what they think and believe as individuals.

ACADEMIC VOCABULARY

A **stereotype** is a fixed, oversimplified image of a person, group, or idea, or something conforming to that image.

 WORD CONNECTIONS

Uniqueness contains the root *-uni-*, from the Latin word *unicus* or *unus*, meaning "single or one." This root also appears in *unison*, *unicorn*, *unicycle*, and *university*. The suffix *-ness* indicates that the word is a noun.

My Notes

Poetry

ABOUT THE AUTHOR

Diane Burns (1957–2006) published only one book of poetry, *Riding the One-Eyed Ford* (1981), but she was a vivid presence in the New York City poetry scene in the 1980s. Admiring critics have described her poetry as "fierce," "witty," and "sardonic."

Read the poem below and then complete the SOAPSTone activity that follows.

Sure You Can Ask Me a Personal Question

Diane Burns
(Lac Courte Oreilles-Chemehuevi)

How do you do?
No, I am not Chinese.
No, not Spanish.
No, I am American Indi—uh, Native American.

5   No, not from India
No, not Apache
No, not Navajo.
No, not Sioux.
No, we are not extinct.
10   Yes, Indian.

Oh?
So that's where you got those high cheekbones.
Your great grandmother, huh?
An Indian Princess, huh?
Hair down to there?   15
Let me guess. Cherokee?

Oh, so you've had an Indian friend?
That close?

Oh, so you've had an Indian servant?
That much?   20

Yeah, it was awful what you guys did to us.
It's real decent of you to apologize.
No, I don't know where you can get peyote.
No, I don't know where you can get Navajo rugs real cheap.
No, I didn't make this. I bought it at Bloomingdales.   25

Thank you. I like your hair too.
I don't know if anyone knows whether or not Cher is really Indian.
No, I didn't make it rain tonight.

Yeah. Uh-huh. Spirituality.
Uh-huh. Yeah. Spirituality. Uh-huh. Mother   30
Earth. Yeah. Uh-huh. Uh-huh. Spirituality.

No, I didn't major in archery.
Yeah, a lot of us drink too much.
Some of us can't drink enough.

This ain't no stoic[1] look.
This is my face.   35

---

[1] **stoic**, *adj.*, unaffected by emotions in the midst of adversity

My Notes

Voices Against Stereotypes

A Close Reading of Text

SOAPSTone	Response	Textual Support
Speaker: Who is the speaker?		
Occasion: What is the social, cultural, historical, geographical context of the text?		
Audience: Who is the target audience?		
Purpose: What is the message of the text? Why was it written?		
Subject: What is the text about? What is the theme?		
Tone: What is the speaker's attitude toward the reader, subject, and audience?		

Many Voices, Many Selves

SUGGESTED LEARNING STRATEGIES: Sketching, Brainstorming

What are some of the roles you play in life? In the space below, list as many of these roles as you can. Think about your family relationships, your interests and hobbies, your jobs, and groups or subcultures to which you belong.

Your voice changes with each role you play in your life. The groups of which you are a part affect your voice—that is, what you say and how you say it. For example, you probably have one way of speaking to your teammates and another way of speaking to your family. You would use different words and a different tone of voice to talk about different subjects. You might also change how you present your voice non-verbally through your dress, actions, and body language. In the space below, give some examples of your voices and what you say when you use them.

Think about voice, using the metaphor of a house with many rooms, where you would use a different voice in each room of your house. On separate paper, draw a blueprint of a house with many rooms. Leave enough space in each room to write the name of the voice, a description of the voice, the reason for the voice, and some examples of things you would typically say in that voice.

Sharing Your Voice

Look back at the list of roles you created in Activity 1.17. Choose one
of the voices you listed there that you would feel comfortable sharing
with others. Copy the voice, its description, and the examples of things
you would typically say in that voice below. You may add additional
description and examples.

Voice	Description of the Voice	Subjects Typically Discussed in This Voice	Words or Phrases Typically Used in This Voice

Writing Prompt: Now use these notes as you write a paragraph about
the topic of your choice in the voice you have chosen to share with
others. Keep in mind that you are demonstrating the voice, not trying to
describe the voice.

As you write, consider the purpose of the writing, the audience, the
tone, and the occasion. Be sure that your subject matter and word
choice reflect the voice as accurately as possible. Use a separate sheet
of paper for your response.

Reflection: What have you learned about your own voices?

Presenting Two of My Voices

SUGGESTED LEARNING STRATEGIES: **Brainstorming, Drafting**

Assignment

Your assignment is to write two original texts that reflect two distinctive voices you possess. You will share one of the two in an oral presentation. Each text should demonstrate how you present yourself in two different contexts, roles, or subcultures.

Steps

Prewriting

1. Review your notes about your culture and the groups (subcultures) to which you belong. Look back at your brainstorming about voices you possess and the graphic organizer in which you described the ways you speak and the topics you normally discuss.

2. Choose two voices or roles you would be willing to share.

3. Now, begin brainstorming new ideas for your two pieces by considering the people you might address in each role. Are there particular individuals you speak to often using a specific voice? Or might your pieces represent the thoughts in your head (an interior monologue) rather than be directed to a specific individual?

4. Once you have identified two roles or voices, topics, and an audience, consider your purpose and select appropriate genres in which to showcase your ideas.

Drafting

5. In an authentic voice, craft a rough draft of each piece. Consider your diction, tone, imagery and syntax. The two pieces you create should be distinctly different in style, content, context, and voice.

6. Consider which voice would be most appealing as an oral presentation to an audience of your peers, and which voice you might prefer to present in writing.

7. In your oral presentation, you might include a formal introduction, or you might begin by hooking your audience by opening your presentation "in character." In either case, be sure you demonstrate the voice in your draft rather than simply describing it.

Presenting Two of My Voices

Evaluating/Revising

8. Review the ideas and organizational structure sections of the Scoring Guide. Annotate your drafts to ensure that they reflect the expectations for voice, clarity, genre, and organization. Revise your drafts as needed. Consider your purpose and audience as you also revise to improve style, word choice to convey connotation and subtlety of meaning, use of figurative language, sentence structure and variety, and grammatical usage. Refer to the Grammar Handbook, and review the Grammar & Usage features in this unit to help you use correct syntax and varied sentence structures.

9. Share your revised drafts with your peers and your teacher to solicit feedback on how you distinguish your two voices through your syntax, diction, tone, and genre conventions. Revise as needed to incorporate feedback.

Editing

10. Review your drafts for errors in grammar, punctuation, and spelling. Consult appropriate resources to correct mistakes and produce a technically sound document.

Rehearsal

11. Create notes for your oral presentation, highlighting sections you will say loudly or softly, noting what facial expressions you will use, and indicating places where you will pause.

12. Rehearse your piece several times. Get feedback on your facial expressions, pauses, and vocal intonation. Be sure that your delivery is smooth and that your listeners will be able to perceive your verbal and nonverbal cues. Consider use of appropriate props or attire to illuminate your voice.

13. As you prepare for your oral presentation, consider using strategies to manage anxiety (for example, rehearsal, visualizing the delivery, props to illuminate your voice, positive self talk, and so on).

14. Finally, write a reflection that explains the different voices you portrayed in your pieces. In your reflection, explain why using the appropriate voice for a given situation, audience, and purpose could be considered a necessary survival skill in the twenty-first century.

⎯⎯⎯⎯⎯⎯⎯⎯⎯⎯⎯⎯⎯⎯⎯⎯⎯⎯⎯⎯⎯⎯⎯⎯⎯⎯⎯⎯⎯⎯⎯⎯

⏏TECHNOLOGY TIP If you have access to presentation software, you may want to create slides to use as tools during your oral presentation. You might also incorporate graphic elements, such as photos, to help present your role or culture.

SCORING GUIDE

Scoring Criteria	Exemplary	Proficient	Emerging
Ideas	The original texts skillfully demonstrate unique voices reflecting two different subcultures by: • coherently communicating a message about the speaker, the speaker's group, or the speaker's part in a group; • clearly targeting that message to an intended audience; • skillfully employing vivid imagery and language (diction and syntax) to convey specific tones appropriate to the purpose and audience.	The original texts show accurate voices reflecting two different subcultures by: • clearly communicating a message about the speaker, the speaker's group, or the speaker's part in a group; • adequately targeting that message to an intended audience; • using imagery and language (diction and syntax) to convey specific tones appropriate to the purpose and audience.	The original texts fail to sufficiently reveal or differentiate the voices that reflect two different subcultures. They may inadequately do or fail to do one or more of the following: • communicate a message about the speaker, the speaker's group, or the speaker's part in a group; • target that message to an intended audience; • use imagery and language (diction and syntax) to convey specific tones appropriate to the purpose and audience.

SCORING GUIDE

Scoring Criteria	Exemplary	Proficient	Emerging
Organization	Ideas are arranged in a way that perceptively supports a specific voice and communicates the intended message. The texts creatively and accurately relate to specific voices and are appropriately formatted.	Ideas are arranged in a way that adequately supports a specific voice and communicates the intended message. The texts are suitable for specific voices and are appropriately formatted.	Ideas are arranged in a way that detracts from the specific voice and intended message. The texts are not suitable for specific voices and may be inappropriately formatted.
Reflective Text	The reflection insightfully and thoroughly explains the writer's different voices. It justifies using those voices for a given situation, audience, and purpose by thoughtfully analyzing the significance of voice as a necessary life skill and expression of identity.	The reflection explains the writer's different voices. It justifies using those voices for a given situation, audience, and purpose by describing the significance of voice as a necessary life skill and as an aspect of identity.	The reflection may give a minimal response to the writer's different voices. If an attempt is made to justifiy using those voices for a given situation, audience, and purpose, it may do little to describe the significance of voice as a necessary life skill or an expression of identity.
Evidence of the Writing Process and Rehearsal	The texts and oral delivery demonstrate thoughtful planning, significant revision, and careful editing in preparing publishable drafts and the final performance.	The texts and oral delivery demonstrate adequate planning, revision, and editing in preparing publishable drafts and the final performance.	The texts and oral delivery lack evidence of adequate planning, revision, and editing. Drafts may not be ready for publishing and the final performance may not demonstrate adquate rehearsal.
Additional Criteria			

Comments: _____

_____

_____

_____

_____

Portfolio Activity: What Is Good Writing?

SUGGESTED LEARNING STRATEGIES: Marking the Draft, Quickwrite, Think-Pair-Share, Graphic Organizer

"The main thing I try to do is write as clearly as I can. Because I have the greatest respect for the reader, and he's going to the trouble of reading what I've written, the least I can do is make it as easy as possible for him to find out what I'm trying to say, trying to get at. I rewrite a good deal to make it clear." E.B. White

Quickwrite: What are some of the characteristics of good writing?

_____

_____

_____

Throughout this unit you have read several selections that easily qualify as "good writing." Review the list you generated in class that identifies the characteristics of good writing. Then select a piece you studied in this unit that fits the criteria.

Characteristics of Good Writing (Criteria)	Your Selection	This selection meets the criteria because...

Review and critique your independent reading selection. How does it compare with the characteristics of good writing you have identified? Explain.

Reflection

An important aspect of growing as a learner is to reflect on where you have been, what you have accomplished, what helped you to learn, and how you will apply your new knowledge in the future. Use the following questions to guide your thinking and to identify evidence of your learning. Use separate notebook paper.

Thinking about Concepts

1. Using specific examples from this unit, respond to the Essential Questions:

   • How can cultural experiences shape, impact, or influence our perception of the world?

   • How does voice function in and beyond the contexts of writing?

2. Consider the new academic vocabulary from this unit (**Culture, Subculture, Symbol, Perspective, Stereotype**), and select 3–4 terms of which your understanding has grown. For each term, answer the following questions:

   • What was your understanding of the word prior to the unit?

   • How has your understanding of the word evolved throughout the unit?

   • How will you apply your understanding in the future?

Thinking about Connections

3. Review the activities and products (artifacts) you created. Choose those that most reflect your growth or increase in understanding.

4. For each artifact that you choose, record, respond to, and reflect on your thinking and understanding, using the following questions as a guide:

   a. What skill/knowledge does this artifact reflect, and how did you learn this skill/knowledge?

   b. How did your understanding of the power of language expand through your engagement with this artifact?

   c. How will you apply this skill or knowledge in the future?

5. Create this reflection as Portfolio pages—one for each artifact you choose. Use the model in the box for your headings and commentary on questions.

Thinking About Thinking
Portfolio Entry

Concept:

Description of Artifact:

Commentary on Questions:

Cultural
Conversations

Essential Questions

? How do external factors affect one's sense of identity?

? How do we synthesize multiple sources of information into a cohesive argument?

Unit Overview

In Unit 2 you will continue the process of self-discovery by examining one of the basic building blocks of your culture and identity—your family. Everyone has a different experience of family, but the power of a family's influence is universal. In this unit, you will explore the effect your family has had on your life and your perceptions of the world. In addition to thinking about the influence of family, you will consider other potent factors that shape your identity, including ethnicity, race, and gender. No one experiences these factors in exactly the same way; as a result, understanding how those forces shape your own life will help you better understand yourself and how you perceive the world around you. As you complete this unit, you will make connections to the works of multiple writers and use those works to create your own understanding of cultural identity and its effect on individual perceptions.

Cultural Conversations

Contents

Goals

▶ To recognize how we define ourselves as individuals through our interactions with external cultural forces

▶ To understand and apply the basic elements of argument

▶ To recognize the role that culture plays in defining ourselves as individuals

▶ To identify and understand significant cultural conversations within a variety of media sources

▶ To apply the appropriate conventions and elements of a synthesis essay

ACADEMIC VOCABULARY

Persona

Juxtaposition

Cultural Conflict

Satire

Humor

Synthesis

Argument

Theatrical Elements

Texts not included in these materials.

Learning Focus:

Does My Culture Define Me?

Through examining elements of culture, you have learned that culture is a complex web of relationships, influences, values, and identities. One question you may have is "How does my culture affect how I see the world?" When defining ourselves and viewing the world, we often use easily identifiable "sides" such as "me versus you" or "us versus them." When we take actions and make judgments based on such a simplistic view, however, cultures often come into conflict. We see conflicts develop within the family, at school, in national politics, and around the world. In order to deepen our understanding of ourselves, we must examine the biases, prejudices, and misunderstandings that often lead to **cultural conflicts** and explore the way writers use such conflicts to tell a story or present an argument.

In the first part of Unit 2, you will examine your own experiences of family life. You will also apply your analytical skills to examples of art and film that explore family issues. Then you will consider how writers use tone to convey their attitudes toward their subjects and their audience. You will discover how shifts in **tone** can reflect a change in attitude of a character or author. In addition, you will examine **satire** in order to understand how **humor** may affect cultural conversations.

In Level 4, you considered the connection between a director's techniques and his or her purpose and effect. In this unit, you will enlarge your vocabulary to understand that theatrical elements (costumes/make up, props/set, acting choices, cultural conflicts) are a part of the cinematic experience as well. More importantly, you will think about how these theatrical elements help illustrate a cultural conflict.

At the end of the first half of the unit, you will deconstruct a writing prompt. Being able to analyze a writing prompt is a skill you use in test situations when you must respond quickly to prompts on state or other mandated standardized tests. You will then have an opportunity to respond to a prompt by writing an expository essay.

Independent Reading: In this unit, you will read works in a variety of genres that focus on aspects of culture. For independent reading, look for a collection of short stories, essays, satire, or nonfiction works that feature elements of culture as a central theme.

Previewing the Unit

SUGGESTED LEARNING STRATEGIES: Close Reading, Marking the Text,
Summarizing/Paraphrasing, Graphic Organizer, Think-Pair-Share

Essential Questions

- How do external factors affect one's sense of identity?

- How do we synthesize multiple sources of information into a cohesive argument?

Unit Overview and Learning Focus

Predict what you think this unit is about. Use the words or phrases that stood out to you when you read the Unit Overview and the Learning Focus.

Embedded Assessment

What knowledge must you have (what do you need to know)? What skills must you have (what will you need to do to complete the Embedded Assessment successfully)? Write your responses below.

Introduction to Family and Tradition

Quickwrite: Write about an experience that you have had with family (your own or another) that connects to the idea of culture.

How do family and culture connect? Record your ideas in the following Venn diagram:

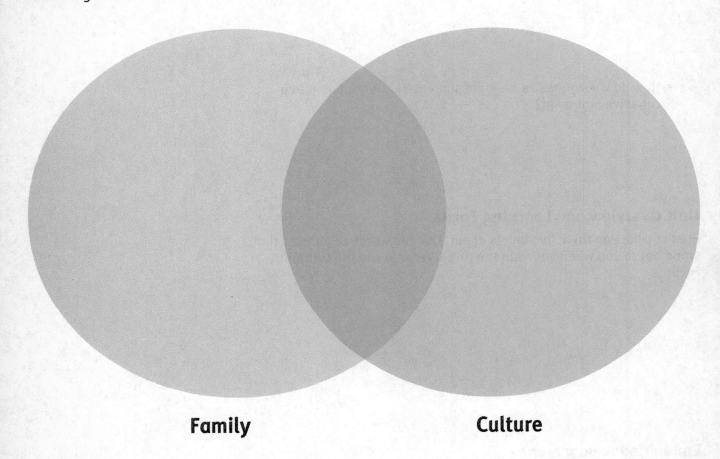

Family   **Culture**

After your class discussion, write a working definition of FAMILY below.

Reading Art: An Artistic Perspective on Family

SUGGESTED LEARNING STRATEGIES: Summarizing, Graphic Organizer, Close Reading, Think-Pair-Share

Like literature, art is a medium that communicates with an audience. As a viewer and reader of art, you must consider the elements of the art before making an interpretation. Use the following 6-step process to begin discovering an artwork's meaning. In the margin, summarize what each stage of "reading art" asks you to do.

First Impressions: Scan the piece for at least 10 seconds. What strikes you first as you look at the piece? What do you like or find interesting, strange, or odd? Do you like it or not? Does it remind you of something? Your initial feelings about the piece are gut-level responses, not a formal interpretation of the work.

A Closer Look: Return to the piece and carefully examine one element that strikes you most. It might be an object in the background, the expression on the subject's face, or an interesting use of color. Describe that detail carefully, noting everything relevant about it.

Questioning: Imagine that you could ask the artist specific interpretive (Level 2) questions about this piece. Write down at least three such questions. You might ask why certain elements were included or excluded from the piece, why a particular color was used, or what the symbols represent. Be sure to base your questions on details in the art.

Artistic Technique: What do you notice about the techniques the artist has used? Examine the colors, the medium, the lighting, and so forth. Why do you think the artist chose these particular techniques?

Subject Matter: What is happening in this piece? How are different elements related? How does the title relate to the picture? Who are the figures, and what is the setting and time period? What historical background does a viewer need to know in order to understand this piece?

Putting It All Together: Choose one of your earlier interpretive questions, or create a new one, and write a paragraph of analysis about a key element of the piece. Be sure to use specific details from the artwork itself.

Reading Art: An Artistic Perspective on Family

Use the graphic organizer below to analyze the art provided by your teacher.

Title of piece: _____ Artist: _____ Type of artwork: _____

First Impressions	
Close Reading	
Ask Questions	
Artistic Techniques	
Subject Matter	

Putting It All Together: Write a topic sentence that answers one of your questions about looking at art. Be sure to identify the artist and title of the work. Then, on separate paper, write a paragraph that supports your statement with evidence from the artwork.

After you have written your paragraph, do a close reading of another painting, using a graphic organizer like the one on the previous page or one of your own choosing.

After completing the close reading of both pieces of artwork, use the Venn diagram below to compare the two works of art.

Title: _____   Title: _____

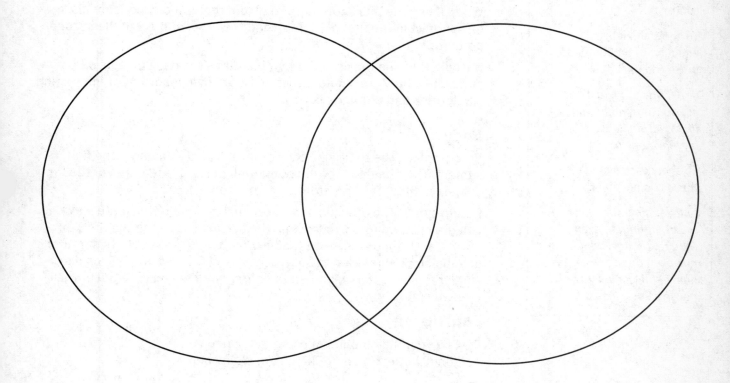

Use the sentence frame below to write a statement of comparison and contrast.

"While both _____ and _____ (titles) are

similar in _____, they are different in

_____."

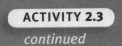
Now, support the statement you wrote on the previous page in a short timed essay that uses examples from the Venn diagram you completed. Your teacher will specify the amount of time you will have to draft your essay. You may use the following organizational format in your compare-and-contrast response. Be sure to include transitions that help convey meaning in your response.

Block Format

When using the block format for a two-paragraph comparison, discuss one subject in the first paragraph and the other subject in the second paragraph.

Introduction The thesis statement identifies the two subjects and states how they are similar or different or have important or interesting similarities and differences.

Body

Paragraph 1: The topic sentence asserts an opinion about the first subject. The remainder of the paragraph describes features of the first subject without referring to the second subject.

Paragraph 2: The opening sentence must contain a transition showing you are comparing or contrasting the second subject to the first; for example, "Unlike subject #1, subject #2 . . . ." Discuss all the features of subject #2 in relation to subject #1, using cue words such as *like, similar to, also, unlike,* and *on the other hand* to compare or contrast the two subjects.

Conclusion

Review your main points of comparison and contrast. End with a personal statement, a prediction, or a clincher.

Thanksgiving: Changes in Perspective

Quickwrite: Describe how Thanksgiving is celebrated either in your home or by characters you have seen in film or on TV. What is the purpose of Thanksgiving?

Perspective

Choose a holiday or celebration and describe how your perspective on or attitude toward the holiday may have changed over time, from childhood to adolescence. Then describe how you think it might change as you get older.

Holiday/Celebration: _____

Childhood Perspective:

Adolescent Perspective:

Future Perspective:

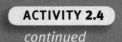

Thanksgiving: Changes in Perspective

Complete the following graphic organizer as you read "Thanksgiving: A Personal History."

Time Period	Tone Toward the Thanksgiving Holiday with Textual Evidence	Words or Phrases Used to Indicate a Transition to This Time Period
Childhood		"When I was a kid..."

Timed Reflection

Write a response to the questions that follow in the time specified by your teacher. Remember to use transitions as you draft your response to the questions. What does the author struggle with as her perspective of Thanksgiving changes? How do the external forces in her life (moving, getting older, influence of others) cause internal conflict? What is the role of reflection in understanding the effect of changing circumstances?

THANKSGIVING:
A Personal History

by Jennifer New

ABOUT THE AUTHOR
Jennifer New lives in Iowa City, Iowa, and writes regularly for online and other publications. She describes herself as a dedicated writer whose "mind is forever on the page, playing with language and new ideas for books or articles."

My Notes

From the mythic Midwest of my childhood to the mesmerizing Chicago of later years, this holiday has always evoked a place.

1   In trying to explain what was missing from her life, how it felt hollow, a friend recently described to me a Thanksgiving she'd once had. It was just two friends and her. They had made dinner and had a wonderful time. "Nothing special happened," she explained, "But we were all funny and vibrant. I thought life would always be like that."

2   This is the holiday mind game: the too-sweet memory of that one shining moment coupled with the painful certainty that the rest of the world must be sitting at a Norman Rockwell table feeling loved. It only gets worse when you begin deconstructing the purpose of such holidays. Pondering the true origins of Thanksgiving, for example, always leaves me feeling more than a bit ashamed and not the least bit festive. Don't even get me started on Christmas.

3   Every year, I think more and more of divorcing myself from these blockbuster holidays. I want to be free from both the material glut[1] and the Pandora's box of emotions that opens every November and doesn't safely close until Jan. 2. Chief among these is the longing for that perfect day that my friend described, the wishful balance of tradition, meaning and belonging. But as an only child in a family that has never been long on tradition, I've usually felt my nose pressed against the glass, never part of the long, lively table and yet not quite able to scrap it all to spend a month in Zanzibar.

4   When I was a kid, of course, there was none of this philosophizing. I was too thrilled by the way the day so perfectly matched the song we'd sung in school. You know the one: "Over the river and through the woods…" Across the gray Midwestern landscape, driving up and down rolling hills, my parents and I would go to my grandmother's house. From

WORD CONNECTIONS
The author uses the term "Pandora's box" as a metaphor for unforeseen troubles. The term comes from a Greek myth about Pandora, a woman whose act of opening a sealed jar released various evils or misfortune into the world. Look at paragraph 3 and use context to determine the denotative and connotative meanings of "Pandora's box" as the author uses it.

---

[1] **glut**: an excessive amount

WORD CONNECTIONS

Philosophizing contains two roots. The root *-soph-* comes from the Greek word *sophos*, meaning "wise." This root also appears in *sophistry, sophisticated,* and *sophomore*. The root *-phil-* comes from the Greek *philos*, which means "love of something." It also appears in *philology, philanthropy, philately,* and *Philharmonic*.

   Empathy contains the root *-path-*, from the Greek word *pathos*, meaning "feeling, suffering, or disease." This root also appears in *pathology, pathetic,* and *sympathy*. The suffix *–y* indicates that the word is a noun. The prefix *em-* means "with."

Notice the words defined in footnotes. Use these definitions (the denotation) and context clues to determine the connotation of the words as the author uses them.

the back seat, I'd peer out at the endless fields of corn, any stray stalks now standing brittle and bleached against the frostbitten black soil. Billboards and gas stations occasionally punctuated the landscape. Everything seemed unusually still, sucked dry of life by winter and the odd quiet of a holiday weekend.

5   In less than an hour, we'd turn off the interstate, entering more familiar territory. My child's mind had created mythic markers for the approach to my grandparents'. First came the sign for a summer campground with its wooden cartoon characters, now caught alone and cold in their faded swimsuits. Farther up the road, a sentry-like² boulder stood atop a hill, the final signpost before we pulled into my grandparents' lane. Suddenly, the sky was obscured by the long, reaching branches of old-growth oak and elm trees. A thick underbrush, a collage of grays and browns, extended from the road and beyond to the 13 acres of Iowa woodland on which their house was situated. A frozen creek bisected the property at the bottom of a large hill. The whole kingdom was enchanted by deer, a long orange fox, battalions of squirrels and birds of every hue.

6   Waiting at the end of the lane was not the house from the song, that home to which the sleigh knew the way. A few years earlier my grandparents had built a new house, all rough-hewn, untreated wood and exposed beams, in lieu of the white clapboard farmhouse where they had raised their children. I vaguely understood that this piece of contemporary architecture, circa 1974, was a twist on that traditional tune, but to me it was better: a magical soaring place full of open spaces, surprises and light.

7   Upon entering the house, I'd stand and look up. Floating above were windows that seemed impossibly high, their curtains controlled by an electric switch. On another wall was an Oriental rug so vast it seemed to have come from a palace. Hidden doors, a glass fireplace that warmed rooms on both sides and faucets sprouting water in high arcs fascinated me during each visit. In the basement, I'd roam through a virtual labyrinth of rooms filled with the possessions of relatives now gone. Butter urns, antique dolls and photo albums of stern-faced people competed fantastically with the intercoms and other gadgetry of the house.

8   I see now that it would have been a great setting for gaggles³ of cousins: having pillow fights, trudging through the snowy woods, dressing up in my grandmother's old gowns and coonskin hat. Instead, I recall holidays as having a museum-like hush. Alone with the friends I'd created in my mind and the belongings of deceased generations, I was content. Upstairs, a football game hummed from the TV, a mixer whirred

---

² **sentry**: a guard
³ **gaggles**: groups or clusters; also, flocks of geese

in the kitchen and the stereo piped one of my grandmother's classical music 8-tracks from room to room. But the house, with its carpeting and wallpaper, absorbed it all. As I'd seen in an illustration from one of my books, I could picture the house as a cross-section, looking into each room where, alone, my family members, read, cooked, watched TV and napped. Pulling the camera farther away, the great house glowed in the violet of early nightfall, as smoke from the chimney wafted through the woodland and then over the endless dark fields, a scattering of tiny, precise stars overhead.

9   The moment that brought us there together—my grandparents, mom and dad, my uncle and his partner, and my great-grandmother—was perhaps the most quiet moment of all. Thanksgiving supper, held in the dim light of late afternoon, was a restrained meal, as though it were a play and we had all lost our scripts. Only the clank of silverware, the passing of dishes and the sharing of small talk seemed to carry us around and through it.

10   If I could go back in time and enter the minds of everyone at that table, I would not be surprised if only my great-grandmother and I were really happy to be there. My grandfather: walking in his fields, calculating numbers from stocks and commodities, fixing a piece of machinery. My parents: with friends in a warmer climate, "The White Album" on the stereo and some unexpected cash in their wallets. My uncle and his partner Bob: willing themselves back home and beyond this annual homage. (Bob himself was a mystery to me, a barrel-chested man who laughed a lot and wore — at least in the one mental snapshot I have of him — a wild patterned smock top and a gold medallion. No one had explained Bob's relationship to our family, so I assigned him a role in my own universe, much like the cartoon characters at the campground or the sentinel rock. I made sense of him and marveled at his ebullience.) And then my grandmother: thinking she should enjoy this, but tired from the cooking and management of the meal, more looking forward to a game later in the evening.

11   That left my great-grandmother and me. Both of us were happy to have this time with family, this mythic meal in which we both believed. And, really, everyone else was there for us: to instill tradition in me, to uphold it for her. Isn't that what most holidays are about? Everyone in the middle gets left holding the bag, squirming in their seats, while the young and old enjoy it. Within a few years, though, by the time I hit adolescence, I'd had my fill of tradition. Not the boulder, the huge house with its secret niches[4] nor even the golden turkey served on an antique platter that my grandmother unearthed every year from the depths of a buffet held any appeal. Gone was my ability to see the world through the almost psychedelic rose-colored glasses of childhood. I also hadn't gained any

---

[4] **niches**: ornamental recesses in a wall for the display of decorative objects

GRAMMAR & USAGE

A writer's diction evokes feelings and images in the reader. Jennifer New chooses vivid verbs and powerful adjectives not only for their meanings but also for their connotations. Notice the verb and adjectives in this sentence:

"From the back seat, I'd **peer** out at the **endless** fields of corn, any **stray** stalks now standing **brittle** and **bleached** against the **frostbitten black** soil."

What tone does the verb *peer* create? What color and feeling do the adjectives *brittle, bleached,* and *frostbitten* suggest?

WORD CONNECTIONS

Jennifer New uses the word "niche" to describe secret places in her house. *Niche* is a French word that may also describe a special market or one's special skills. Try to incorporate this word into your writing.

My Notes

of the empathy that comes with age. Instead, I was stuck with one foot in cynicism and the other in hypersensitivity. The beloved, magical house now looked to me like a looming example of misspent money and greed. My great-grandmother, so tiny and helpless at this point, now struck me as macabre and frightening, her papery white skin on the verge of tearing.

12   Perhaps my parents took my behavior, moody and unkind as it was, as a sign that traditions are sometimes meant to be broken. I'm not sure whether they were using me to save themselves from the repetition of the annual holiday, or if they were saving the rest of the family from me. Either way, we stopped pulling into the wooded lane that fourth Thursday in November. For the next few years, we'd drive instead to Chicago. My mind managed to create similar mythic land markers: the rounded pyramids near Dekalb, Ill., which I've since realized are storage buildings; the office parks of the western suburbs where I imagined myself working as a young, single woman, à la Mary Tyler Moore; the large neon sign of a pair of lips that seemed to be a greeting especially for us, rather than the advertising for a dry cleaner that they actually were. About this point, at the neon lips, the buildings around us grew older and darker, and on the horizon the skyscrapers blinked to life in the cold twilight air. The slow enveloping by these mammoth structures was as heady as the approach down my grandparents' lane had been years earlier.

13   We would stay at a friend's apartment, or better yet, in a downtown hotel. I was mesmerized by the clip of urban life. On the wide boulevard of Michigan Avenue, I'd follow women in their fat fur coats, amazed and appalled. The wisps of hairs from the coat closed tight around their necks, hugging brightly made-up faces. Leather boots tapped along city streets, entering the dance of a revolving door or stepping smartly into the back of a yellow cab. The mezzanines of department stores — Lord & Taylor, Marshall Fields — dazzled me; the glint of light reflected on makeup-counter mirrors, the intoxicating waft of perfume on a cacophony[5] of voices. And my parents, freed of their familiar roles, seemed young and bright. They negotiated maître d's and complex museum maps; they ordered wine from long lists and knew what to tip.

14   Of course, like that adolescent hero, Holden Caulfield, I was that thing we hated most: a hypocrite. I couldn't see the irony in my fascination with the urban splendor vs. my disdain for my grandparents' hard-earned home. Or that my parents possessed the same qualities and talents no matter where we were. I definitely couldn't pan out far enough to see that I was just a teenager yearning for a bigger world, a change of pace.

15   During these city trips, my sense of Thanksgiving shifted. No longer was it a wishbone drying on the kitchen windowsill, or foil-wrapped leftovers in the refrigerator. Instead, late November connoted the

> 📖 **WORD CONNECTIONS**
>
> A *mezzanine* describes a partial story between two floors of a building. The word comes from the French and means "middle." In theaters, the first balcony is often called the mezzanine.

---

[5] **cacophony**: harsh discordant sound; dissonance

moneyed swirl of holiday lights flickering on the Magnificent Mile as an "El" train clamored over the Loop. It was the bellows of drivers and the urbane banter of pedestrians, weighted down with packages. The soft glow of restaurants — the darker the better—cut me so far adrift from my day-to-day world that I might as well have traveled to another continent. Far away from the immense quietude of the house in the woods, the bellhops now served as my uncles, shop clerks and waiters my cousins, and the patrons in theater lobbies and museums became my extended family. Late at night, I'd creep out of my bed to the window and watch with amazement as the city below continued to move to the beat of an all-night rumba. Without having to be invited or born into it, I was suddenly, automatically, part of something bigger and noisier than my small family.

16

In years since, I've cobbled together whatever Thanksgiving is available to me. After college, friends and I, waylaid on the West Coast without family, would whip up green bean casserole and cranberries, reinventing the tastes of childhood with varying success. There were always broken hearts and pining for home at these occasions, but they were full of warmth and camaraderie. Then, for several years, my husband and I battled a sea of crowds in various airports, piecing together flights from one coast to the other in order to share the day with his family.

17

On my first visit, I was startled by the table set for more than 20 people. This was a family in which relatives existed in heaps, all appearing in boldface and underlined with their various eccentricities[6]. Neuroses and guarded secrets, petty jealousies and unpaid debts were all placed on the back burner for this one day while people reacquainted themselves, hugging away any uneasiness. This family — suburban, Jewish, bursting with noise and stories — so unlike my own, made me teeter between a thrilling sense of finally having a place at a long table, and a claustrophobic yearning for a quiet spot in a dark café. Or, better yet, in a dark and quiet woodland.

18

This year for Thanksgiving, I will rent movies, walk with the dog down still streets and have a meal with my parents and husband. Throughout the day, I'll imagine myself moving through the big house in the woods that my grandparents sold years ago. Padding down carpeted hallways, I'll rediscover hidden doorways and unpack that platter from the buffet. A bag of antique marbles will open its contents to me as the grandfather clock chimes. Counting "12," I'll look outside onto the lawn and watch a family of deer make their nightly crossing through the now barren vegetable garden, jumping over the fence that my husband and I put in their path, and into the neighbor's yard. I'll press my nose against the cold glass and wish myself outside and beyond the still of the house.

---

[6] **eccentricity**: a behavioral oddity or peculiarity

My Notes

> ## GRAMMAR & USAGE
> When you want to emphasize parenthetical information, you may use dashes rather than commas (or parentheses). Jennifer New uses this technique in her sentence "This family—suburban, Jewish, bursting with noise and stories—so unlike my own, . . ."

Family Perspectives: Neighbors

ACADEMIC VOCABULARY

Humor is the quality of being amusing.

Satire is a type of writing that pokes fun at or ridicules an individual, a group of people, a behavior or attitude, or a cultural or social institution by pointing out weaknesses in a humorous way.

LITERARY TERMS

Exaggeration represents something as larger, better, or worse than it really is.

Irony is a literary device that exploits reader's expectations; irony occurs when what is expected turns out to be quite different from what actually happens.

Understatement is the representation of something as smaller or less significant than it really is; the opposite of exaggeration.

What Makes Something Funny?

In our daily lives, we hear jokes, watch funny movies, read the comics, and hang out with friends who make us laugh. What exactly makes something funny?

Quickwrite: In the following space, write about what makes you laugh and why those things are funny.

Many times, people use **humor** not only to make us laugh, but to make us think. In literary terms this is called **satire**. We will be working with the following definition in this lesson:

Satire A literary form that is humorous but also contains a critique or criticism of people, ideas, institutions, or society as a whole. A satire exposes its subject's foolishness and uses wit in order to make the reader laugh. Satire often employs the literary elements of **irony, exaggeration**, and **understatement**.

In your own words, satire is . . .

Satire

"Us and Them"

by David Sedaris

> ### ABOUT THE AUTHOR
> Essayist and humorist David Sedaris was born in 1956 in New York. Sedaris gained fame in the 1990s after publishing "The SantaLand Diaries," a story based on diary entries he wrote while working as a Santa's elf at a New York City department store. Sedaris's essays offer sharp-eyed commentary on mundane events and family relationships.

As you read, analyze Sedaris's word choice and tone to determine how they convey satirical comments about his family, neighbors, and life. Consider both denotative and connotative meanings of satirical words and phrases.

GRAMMAR & USAGE

Sedaris uses a number of verbal phrases in his writing. A **verbal** is a form of a verb that is used as some other part of speech —a noun, an adjective, or an adverb. A **verbal phrase** consists of the verbal and all its modifiers and complements.

A **gerund** is a verbal that ends in *-ing* and functions as a noun.

An **infinitive** is a verbal that can function as a noun, an adjective, or an adverb. The word *to* usually appears in front of the verb form.

Examples:

Gerund phrase as subject of a clause: ...**not making friends** was a conscious choice....

Gerund phrase as object of preposition: ...in **walking around after dark**....

Infinitive phrase as subject: **To say that you did not believe in television** was different from ....

When my family first moved to North Carolina, we lived in a rented house three blocks from the school where I would begin the third grade. My mother made friends with one of the neighbors, but one seemed enough for her. Within a year we would move again and, as she explained, there wasn't much point in getting too close to people we would have to say good-bye to. Our next house was less than a mile away, and the short journey would hardly merit tears or even good-byes, for that matter. It was more of a "see you later" situation, but still I adopted my mother's attitude, as it allowed me to pretend that not making friends was a conscious choice. I could if I wanted to. It just wasn't the right time.

Back in New York State, we had lived in the country, with no sidewalks or streetlights; you could leave the house and still be alone. But here, when you looked out the window, you saw other houses, and people inside those houses. I hoped that in walking around after dark I might witness a murder, but for the most part our neighbors just sat in their living rooms, watching TV. The only place that seemed truly different was owned by a man named Mr. Tomkey, who did not believe in television. This was told to us by our mother's friend, who dropped by one afternoon with a basketful of okra. The woman did not editorialize—rather, she just presented her information leaving her listener to make of it what she might. Had my mother said, "That's the craziest thing I've ever heard in my life," I assume that the friend would have agreed, and had she said, "Three cheers for Mr. Tomkey," the friend likely would have agreed as well. It was a kind of test, as was the okra.

To say that you did not believe in television was different from saying that you did not care for it. Belief implied that television has a master plan and that you were against it. It also suggested that you thought too much. When my mother reported that Mr. Tomkey did not believe in television, my father said, "Well, good for him. I don't know that I believe in it, either."

"That's exactly how I feel," my mother said, and then my parents watched the news, and whatever came on after the news.

Word spread that Mr. Tomkey did not own a television, and you began hearing that while this was all very well and good, it was unfair of him to inflict his beliefs upon others, specifically his innocent wife and children. It was speculated that just as the blind man develops a keener sense of hearing, the family must somehow compensate for their loss. "Maybe they read," my mother's friend said. "Maybe they listen to the radio, but you can bet your boots they're doing *something*."

I wanted to know what this something was, and so I began peering through the Tomkeys' windows. During the day I'd stand across the street from their house, acting as though I were waiting for someone, and at night, when the view was better and I had less chance of being discovered, I would creep into their yard and hide in the bushes beside their fence.

Because they had no TV, the Tomkeys were forced to talk during dinner. They had no idea how puny their lives were, and so they were not ashamed that a camera would have found them uninteresting. They did not know what attractive was or what dinner was supposed to look like or even what time people were supposed to eat. Sometimes they wouldn't sit down until eight o'clock, long after everyone else had finished doing the dishes. During the meal, Mr. Tomkey would occasionally pound the table and point at his children with a fork, but the moment he finished, everyone would start laughing. I got the idea that he was imitating someone else, and wondered if he spied on us while we were eating.

When fall arrived and school began, I saw the Tomkey children marching up the hill with paper sacks in their hands. The son was one grade lower than me, and the daughter was one grade higher. We never spoke, but I'd pass them in the halls from time to time and attempt to view the world through their eyes. What must it be like to be so ignorant and alone? Could a normal person even imagine it? Staring at an Elmer Fudd lunch box, I tried to divorce myself from everything I already knew: Elmer's inability to pronounce the letter *r*, his constant pursuit of an intelligent and considerably more famous rabbit. I tried to think of him as just a drawing, but it was impossible to separate him from his celebrity.

One day in class a boy named William began to write the wrong answer on the blackboard, and our teacher flailed her arms, saying, "Warning, Will. Danger, danger." Her voice was synthetic and void of emotion, and we laughed, knowing that she was imitating the robot in a weekly show about a family who lived in outer space. The Tomkeys, though, would have thought she was having a heart attack. It occurred to me that they needed a guide, someone who could accompany them through the course of an average day and point out all the things they were unable to understand. I could have done it on weekends, but friendship would have taken away their mystery and interfered with the good feeling I got from pitying them. So I kept my distance.

In early October the Tomkeys bought a boat, and everyone seemed greatly relieved, especially my mother's friend, who noted that the motor was definitely secondhand. It was reported that Mr. Tomkey's father-in-law owned a house on the lake and had invited the family to use it whenever they liked. This explained why they were gone all weekend, but it did not make their absences any easier to bear. I felt as if my favorite show had been canceled.

Halloween fell on a Saturday that year, and by the time my mother took us to the store, all the good costumes were gone. My sisters dressed as witches and I went as a hobo. I'd looked forward to going in disguise to the Tomkeys' door, but they were off at the lake, and their house was dark. Before leaving, they had left a coffee can full of gumdrops on the front porch, alongside a sign reading DON'T BE GREEDY. In terms of Halloween candy, individual gumdrops were just about as low as you could get. This was evidenced by the large number of them floating in an adjacent dog bowl. It was disgusting to think that this was what a gumdrop might look like in your stomach, and it was insulting to be told not to take too much of something you didn't really want in the first place. "Who do these Tomkeys think they are?" my sister Lisa said.

The night after Halloween, we were sitting around watching TV when the doorbell rang. Visitors were infrequent at our house, so while my father stayed behind, my mother, sisters, and I ran downstairs in a group, opening the door to discover the entire Tomkey family on our front stoop. The parents looked as they always had, but the son and daughter were dressed in costumes—she a ballerina and he as some kind of a rodent with terry-cloth ears and a tail made from what looked to be an extension cord. It seemed they had spent the previous evening isolated at the lake and had missed the opportunity to observe Halloween. "So, well, I guess we're trick-or-treating *now*, if that's okay," Mr. Tomkey said.

I attributed their behavior to the fact that they didn't have a TV, but television didn't teach you everything. Asking for candy on Halloween was called trick-or-treating, but asking for candy on November first was called begging, and it made people uncomfortable. This was one of the things you were supposed to learn simply by being alive, and it angered me that the Tomkeys did not understand it.

"Why of course it's not too late," my mother said. "Kids, why don't you . . . run and get . . . the candy."

"But the candy is gone," my sister Gretchen said. "You gave it away last night."

"Not *that* candy," my mother said. "The other candy. Why don't you run and go get it?"

"You mean *our* candy?" Lisa said. "The candy that we *earned*?"

This was exactly what our mother was talking about, but she didn't want to say this in front of the Tomkeys. In order to spare their feelings, she wanted them to believe that we always kept a bucket of candy lying around the house, just waiting for someone to knock on the door and ask for it. "Go on, now," she said. "Hurry up."

My room was situated right off the foyer, and if the Tomkeys had looked in that direction, they could have seen my bed and the brown paper bag marked MY CANDY. KEEP OUT. I didn't want them to know how much I had, and so I went into my room and shut the door behind me. Then I closed the curtains and emptied my bag onto the bed, searching for whatever was the crummiest. All my life chocolate has made me ill. I don't know if I'm allergic or what, but even the smallest amount leaves me with a blinding headache. Eventually, I learned to stay away from it, but as a child I refused to be left out. The brownies were eaten, and when the pounding began I would blame the grape juice or my mother's cigarette smoke or the tightness of my glasses— anything but the chocolate. My candy bars were poison but they were brand-name, and so I put them in pile no. 1, which definitely would not go to the Tomkeys.

Out in the hallway I could hear my mother straining for something to talk about. "A boat!" she said. "That sounds marvelous. Can you just drive it right into the water?"

"Actually, we have a trailer," Mr. Tomkey said. "So what we do is back it into the lake."

"Oh, a trailer. What kind is it?"

"Well, it's a *boat* trailer," Mr. Tomkey said.

"Right, but is it wooden or, you know . . . I guess what I'm asking is what *style* trailer do you have?"

Behind my mother's words were two messages. The first and most obvious was "Yes, I am talking about boat trailers, but also I am dying." The second, meant only for my sisters and me, was "If you do not immediately step forward with that candy, you will never again experience freedom, happiness, or the possibility of my warm embrace."

I knew that it was just a matter of time before she came into my room and started collecting the candy herself, grabbing indiscriminately, with no regard to my rating systems. Had I been thinking straight, I would have hidden the most valuable items in my dresser drawer, but instead, panicked by the thought of her hand on my doorknob, I tore off the wrappers and began cramming the candy bars into my mouth, desperately, like someone in a contest. Most were miniature, which made them easier to accommodate, but still there was only so much room, and it was hard to chew and fit more in at the same time. The headache began immediately, and I chalked it up to tension.

My mother told the Tomkeys she needed to check on something, and then she opened the door and stuck her head inside my room. "What are you doing?" she whispered, but my mouth was too full to answer. "I'll just be a moment," she called, and as she closed the door behind her and moved toward my bed, I began breaking the wax lips and candy necklaces pulled from pile no. 2. These were the second-best things I had received, and while it hurt to destroy them, it would have hurt even more to give them away. I had just started to mutilate a miniature box of Red Hots when my mother pried them from my hands, accidentally finishing the job for me. BB-size pellets clattered onto the floor, and as I followed them with my eyes, she snatched up a roll of Necco wafers.

"Not those," I pleaded, but rather than words, my mouth expelled chocolate, chewed chocolate, which fell onto the sleeve of her sweater. "Not those. Not those."

She shook her arm, and the mound of chocolate dropped like a horrible turd upon my bedspread. "You should look at yourself," she said. "I mean, *really* look at yourself."

Along with the Necco wafers she took several Tootsie Pops and half a dozen caramels wrapped in cellophane. I heard her apologize to the Tomkeys for her absence, and then I heard my candy hitting the bottom of their bags.

"What do you say?" Mrs. Tomkey asked.

And the children answered, "Thank you."

While I was in trouble for not bringing my candy sooner, my sisters were in more trouble for not bringing theirs at all. We spent the early part of the evening in our rooms, then one by one we eased our way back upstairs, and joined our parents in front of the TV. I was the last to arrive, and took a seat on the floor beside the sofa. The show was a Western, and even if my head had not been throbbing, I doubt I would have had the wherewithal to follow it. A posse of outlaws crested a rocky hilltop, squinting at a flurry of dust advancing from the horizon, and I thought again of the Tomkeys and of how alone and out of place they had looked in their dopey costumes. "What was up with that kid's tail?" I asked.

"Shhhh," my family said.

My Notes

Family Perspectives: Neighbors

For months I had protected and watched over these people, but now, with one stupid act, they had turned my pity into something hard and ugly. The shift wasn't gradual, but immediate, and it provoked an uncomfortable feeling of loss. We hadn't been friends, the Tomkeys and I, but still I had given them the gift of my curiosity. Wondering about the Tomkey family had made me feel generous, but now I would have to shift gears and find pleasure in hating them. The only alternative was to do as my mother had instructed and take a good look at myself. This was an old trick, designed to turn one's hatred inward, and while I was determined not to fall for it, it was hard to shake the mental picture snapped by her suggestion: here is a boy sitting on a bed, his mouth smeared with chocolate. He's a human being, but also he's a pig, surrounded by trash and gorging himself so that others may be denied. Were this the only image in the world, you'd be forced to give it your full attention, but fortunately there were others. This stagecoach, for instance, coming round the bend with a cargo of gold. This shiny new Mustang convertible. This teenage girl, her hair a beautiful mane, sipping Pepsi through a straw, one picture after another, on and on until the news, and whatever came on after the news.

After reading and highlighting "Us and Them," fill out the graphic organizer below. Identify passages that you thought were funny. Then try to explain why they are funny. Consider some of the cultural elements Sedaris treats with humor. Finally, work with a partner to decide what Sedaris is saying—through humor—about himself.

Humorous Passage	What makes it funny?	What is the implied message or critique?

Revisit Sedaris's text to identify examples of figurative language (for example, hyperbole, metaphor, simile, imagery, and irony). How does Sedaris's use of these literary devices add to the satire of this text?

Reflection: How does Sedaris's family influence his perception of others and the world? Why is Halloween important to Sedaris's story?

Theatrical and Cultural Elements in Film

Title of Film: _____

Names of Characters: _____

Costumes/Makeup	Props/Sets	Acting Choices	Cultural Elements

Title of Film: _____   Names of Characters: _____

Costumes/Makeup	Props/Sets	Acting Choices	Cultural Elements

ACADEMIC VOCABULARY

Theatrical elements are the costumes, props, and other things dramatists and directors use to tell a story on stage.

Select one of the film clips that you examined and write a response on a separate paper about the effect that one of the theatrical elements had on you as a viewer.

Be sure to start with a strong, clear thesis statement that indicates the relationship between the theatrical element you chose and the cultural context created. Follow it with evidence that clearly and effectively supports the thesis statement. Research the topic to ensure that the support for your thesis statement is strong and is appropriate to your topic and your position.

Football Versus Family

SUGGESTED LEARNING STRATEGIES: Summarizing, Predicting, Quickwrite, Close Reading, Graphic Organizer, Notetaking, Think-Pair-Share, Word Map

As you watch the film, take notes on the following literary and theatrical elements. Keep track of references to marriage and wedding customs in the segment. Also, make notes about how the theatrical elements underscore or portray the cultural conflict.

ACADEMIC VOCABULARY

A cultural conflict is a struggle that occurs when people with different cultural expectations or attitudes interact.

	Literary Elements		Theatrical Elements
Internal Conflicts		**Costumes/ Makeup**	
External Conflicts		**Props/Sets**	
Cultural Components		**Acting Choices**	

References to marriage and wedding customs in this segment:

How do the theatrical elements underscore or portray the cultural conflict?

Writing Prompt: Identify a conflict from this segment of the film, and explain whether it is an internal or external conflict. Address both sides of the conflict, and describe how the resolution, if any, is reached.

Marriage Is an Arrangement

SUGGESTED LEARNING STRATEGIES: Quickwrite, Graphic Organizer

Before reading the article "Matrimony with a Proper Stranger," what are the first words and phrases that come to mind when you think of arranged marriages?

Quickwrite: Would you accept an arranged marriage? Why or why not?

Before reading the article, what do you think might be the benefits (pros) and drawbacks (cons) of an arranged marriage?

Pros	Cons

As you read the article, keep track of the pros and cons as they are presented in the article.

Pros	Cons

After reading the article, consider the similarities and differences between the dating customs as presented in the article and ones with which you are more familiar.

Indian Culture   **Your Own Culture**

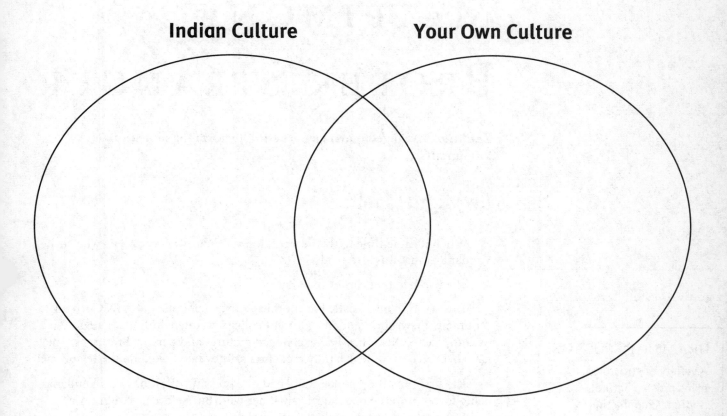

What pressures do you think Jess in *Bend It Like Beckham* may feel about marriage from her family and culture? How do you expect that she will feel?

Article

MATRIMONY *with a* PROPER STRANGER

Tradition: **Arranged marriages are still the norm for some Indian immigrants.**

by Miguel Helft

When it came time to tie the knot, Rajiv Kumar was ready. His wife-to-be, Vandana Sinha, was also ready.

The two had met earlier that day.

This wasn't a blind date. For months Rajiv, an engineer at ASK Corp. in Mountain View, and Vandana, a recent college graduate in India, had gotten to know each other. They had exchanged pictures and personal résumés. They had checked each other's family credentials. They had talked on the telephone.

The first time they spoke, Rajiv had one pressing question: Was Vandana being forced into the marriage against her will? But before he could say a word, she asked him precisely the same question.

"After we talked for one minute," he says, "I was completely comfortable with the whole thing."

Today, almost 11 years later, the couple say their arranged marriage is a truly happy one. They are devoted parents of 8-year-old twins, Vishal and Tushar. Vandana, 32, is events editor at San Jose-based India Currents, a national magazine for the Indian community. Rajiv, 37, is a manager at Altera Corp. in San Jose.

A modern spin on tradition

Arranged marriages in India are as old as the Holy Ganges. But while in the old days parents had complete control over the matchmaking, contemporary arranged marriages are more like what Rajiv and Vandana experienced. Parents may still seek out suitable partners for their children, but the children have much more say in the matter.

As Rajiv puts it, "My parents (did) the legwork, but I was in control."

Arvind Kumar, editor of India Currents, says the prevailing trend among Indian immigrants, some 75,000 strong in the Bay Area, is still the arranged marriage. "Arranged marriage is not always dictatorial," he says. "It used to be. Now, most often it is not."

Kumar said that among immigrant children brought up in the United States, more are choosing what he calls "self-arranged" marriages. But many — even those born and raised here — are still turning to marriages initially proposed by their families.

Other than how they met, Rajiv and Vandana say their marriage is no different from any other. Vandana's brothers and sisters had "love" marriages, as did Rajiv's siblings and cousins.

But when he was 27, Rajiv, who had been in the United States for four years, called his parents in Patna, India, and told them he was ready for marriage. He asked them to find a young woman who had been raised in an Indian city, spoke English and was willing to live in the United States.

His parents dutifully searched the community, asking relatives and friends. They came up with more than 50 candidates, whose pictures and résumés were forwarded to Rajiv. The first packet he liked was Vandana's. He picked a couple more as backup, in case the attraction was not mutual.

Meanwhile, in India, Vandana had finished college with a bachelor's degree in chemistry, and her parents began to get inquiries from parents and relatives of prospective mates. As Vandana was not then in a relationship, she and her parents thought, "Why not?"

She was introduced to several young men, shown numerous pictures, and told about their successful careers and distinguished families. Nothing clicked — until she saw Rajiv's résumé and picture.

He was an engineer. Their families were from the same village. They had attended the same type of school. With similar upbringings and values, they were bound to be compatible.

Reconcilable differences

In Indian culture, says India Currents' Kumar, marriage is the starting point of a relationship. Ideally, love grows out of it. Kumar tells of a conversation his parents had right after their marriage. His father asked his mother if she loved him. "No," his mother said. "I hardly know you." His father replied. "It doesn't matter. I'm going to win your love."

To Americans, whose connubial paths usually follow from passion to love to marriage (with passion often joked about as going downhill after

My Notes

_____

_____

_____

_____

_____

_____

_____

📖 **WORD CONNECTIONS**

The word *résumé* is a brief description of one's work experience and qualifications for a job. The word derives from French. It is commonly written without the accent marks, but that practice may cause confusion of meaning with the verb "resume" so it is more accurate to use the accent marks for clarity of understanding.

Marriage Is an Arrangement

My Notes

the honeymoon), the concept of marrying a virtual stranger seems alien. But as Kumar says, the idea is more acceptable if it is part of your culture. Some children of immigrants born and raised here happily follow the tradition of arranged marriage, considering the practice perfectly normal. Chitra Divakaruni, a writer from India who lives in this area and teaches at Foothill College, explains that arranged marriages "come from a different concept of family. You trust the wisdom of older relatives."

But even those with cultural ties to the practice express some reservations.

"In theory, I'm amazed," says Anjali Aurora, a 21-year-old Indian-born senior at the University of California, Berkeley. "Spending a lifetime with someone you hardly know is astounding."

But she is quick to add that she has seen it work. "In practice, it works in a lot of cases. Comparing love marriages and arranged marriages, I would never say one is better than the other."

Aurora is keeping her options open. "I don't foresee an arranged marriage for myself," she says. "But I wouldn't say 'no' either. If (at the time I want to be married) I found myself lonely, I would ask my parents to introduce me to candidates. I hope that doesn't happen."

Games people play

Loneliness and feeling marginalized from the larger society are reasons some might choose arranged marriages. Kumar said many students and workers who emigrate from India speak of the difficulties they experience in adapting to the American lifestyle.

"How you grow up and how you learn to socialize is very important," he says. "If you haven't learned to date, you can't deal with the dating game. It is difficult in that way to be single in America. You don't have the skills to deal with America, and you don't have the support you get in India. Arranged marriages become more of an option."

Because of the tensions between modern American values and traditional Indian values, arranged marriages in the Indian immigrant community sometimes crumble under the strain. Divakaruni, in her recent anthology of short stories, "Arranged Marriage," writes about the deep forces that tear some couples apart as both women and men come to terms with new identities in a new country.

WORD CONNECTIONS

Graduate contains the root *-grad-*, from the Latin word *gradus*, meaning "step, rank, or degree." This root also appears in *gradual, degrade,* and *grade*. The suffix *-ate* indicates that the word may be a noun or a verb.

Contemporary contains the root *-temp-*, from the Latin word *tempus*, meaning "time." This root also appears in *temporary, tempest,* and *tempo*. The prefix *con-* means "with or together." The suffix *-ary* indicates that the word is either a noun or an adjective.

Inequalities contains the root *-equ-*, from the Latin words *aequalis*, meaning "equal" and *aequus*, meaning "level, even, or flat." This root also appears in *equity, equivalent, equator,* and *equivocate*. The prefix *in-* means "not."

My Notes

"In India, the needs of the individual are taken care of by the family and society at large, so you can let go of your own needs," says Divakaruni of the acculturation process. "Here, there is no such support — you have to take care of yourself. It makes you pull into yourself and find your own inner strength."

Divakaruni was instrumental in opening Maitri, the first social services agency for South Asian women in the Bay Area. Some of the women Maitri serves, she says, are in arranged marriages with abusive husbands. "(These) women are afraid to rock the boat because it is seen as a disgrace in Indian society," says Divakaruni.

The problem, she says, is not arranged marriages, but the inequalities between men and women in Indian society. "In Indian culture, the man has greater freedom. Society supports what the man wants."

But today, many Indian women are highly educated and participate in greater numbers in the workforce.

"Women definitely have more freedom and power and more control over their own destinies," says Sheela Jhaveri, 29, an Indian student at UC Berkeley who has lived in the U.S. for four years. Those destinies, of course, include marriage — arranged or not.

In their San Jose home, Vandana and Rajiv Kumar are sitting on their couch, thumbing through a wedding photo album. "I look back at it and say, 'Oh my god! How could I have done it?' " Vandana says, laughing. "I don't know if I'd do it again," says Rajiv.

Although both say they expect their boys will want to choose their own mates, if either asks them to arrange a marriage, they'll be happy to help.

"Marriage is something you have to work at all the time," Rajiv says. "Once you are married, it doesn't matter how you got together. You have to work to make it work."

Reflection: Compare the ideas in this article with the film *Bend It Like Beckham*. How does the article expand ideas and concepts from the film?

Conflicting Expectations

As you watch the film clip provided by your teacher, take notes that relate to the literary and theatrical elements. In addition, note specific words and phrases that indicate conflicts between mothers and daughters.

	Literary Elements		Theatrical Elements
Internal Conflicts		**Costumes/ Makeup**	
External Conflicts		**Props/Sets**	
Components of Culture		**Acting Choices**	

Words or phrases describing relationship of mothers and daughters:

How do the theatrical elements underscore or portray the cultural conflict?

Writing Prompt: Identify a conflict from this segment of the film, and explain whether it is an internal or external conflict. In your analysis, be sure to address both sides of the conflict and the resolution, if any is reached.

SUGGESTED LEARNING STRATEGIES: Graphic Organizer, TP-CASTT, Marking the Text, Drafting

1. Think about what you know about conflicts between family members. Based on your own experiences, those of your friends, or those you have seen on television or in books and movies, describe the types of conflicts that occur between the family members shown in the graphic organizer below. Then answer the question.

Relationship	Types of Conflicts
Mothers and daughters	
Fathers and daughters	
Mothers and sons	
Fathers and sons	
What are some of the reasons for the conflicts you listed above?	

2. Read the poem "Father and Son" by Tomasz Jastrun on the following page. Then, on separate paper, describe the conflict between the son and his father. What is the cause of the conflict? How is the conflict resolved?

3. Look back at the words and phrases you recorded in Activity 2.9. Share them with a partner or a small group. Now, copy the words and phrases into the space below. On a separate sheet of paper, arrange the words and phrases into a "found poem" with the title "Mother and Daughter." Your poem can be specific to the film or to your own experiences, or it can deal with mother-daughter relationships in general.

My Notes

Poetry

> **ABOUT THE AUTHOR**
> Tomasz Jastrun is a Polish poet, essayist, and reporter. Born in Warsaw in 1950, at the beginning of the Cold War, Jastrun has spent his professional life engaged in and reporting on political activities. The subjects of his poems, however, range from the political to the personal.

FATHER and SON

Written by Tomasz Jastrun
Translated by Daniel Bourne

Here is not good enough
And he looks at me with reproach
But what can I do
I'm not about to offer excuses
5   So I let my silence speak
Finally he hugs me
As if he suddenly realizes
We have to get along
To come to an agreement
10 There is no one else
To deal with

And after a while
We both get to work
He collects
15 Old bus tickets
I fuss with words
Out of which I can whittle
My crutches and cane

Soccer Culture

SUGGESTED LEARNING STRATEGIES: Graphic Organizer,
Close Reading, Brainstorming, Notetaking, Think-Pair-Share

As you watch the film clip provided by your teacher, take notes that
relate to the literary and theatrical elements. In addition, take notes on
any references to the subculture of soccer.

	Literary Elements		Theatrical Elements
Internal Conflicts		**Costumes/ Makeup**	
External Conflicts		**Props/Sets**	
Components of Culture		**Acting Choices**	

References to the subculture of the soccer team:

How do the theatrical elements underscore or portray the cultural conflict?

Writing Prompt: Identify a conflict from this segment of the film, and
explain whether it is an internal or external conflict. In your analysis, be
sure to address both sides of the conflict and the resolution, if any is
reached.

Soccer Culture

A *subculture* is smaller part of a cultural group and may be defined by common interests, gender, ethnicity, or other factors that group members have in common. Your own school could be considered a culture, and within your school are probably many subcultures. In the space below, brainstorm the subcultures in your school's culture.

Choose any two groups and describe them in the graphic organizer below.

	Interests/ Language	Where they spend their time	Mode of Dress (Clothing/Hairstyles)
Subculture 1: _____			
Subculture 2: _____			

Why do you think subcultures exist in a high school? What types of conflicts can arise among subcultures?

What are some subcultures that exist in society? Do the subcultures exist for the same reasons as they do in a high school? Explain.

Stereotypes and Conflict

SUGGESTED LEARNING STRATEGIES: Graphic Organizer, Close Reading,
Notetaking, Think-Pair-Share

As you watch the film clip provided by your teacher, take notes that
relate to the following literary and theatrical elements. In addition, take
notes on any stereotypes you see.

	Literary Elements		Theatrical Elements
Internal Conflicts		**Costumes / Makeup**	
External Conflicts		**Props/Sets**	
Components of Culture		**Acting Choices**	

References to stereotypes in this segment:

How do the theatrical elements underscore or portray the cultural conflict?

Writing Prompt: Identify a conflict from this segment of the film, and
explain whether it is an internal or external conflict. In your analysis,
be sure to address both sides of the conflict and the resolution, if any
is reached. Consider the significance of the conflict you identified, and
discuss how this conflict sheds light on the meaning of the film as a
whole.

Deconstructing a Prompt

Writing prompts often contain many details but little direction. It is easy to get caught up in the details and forget the main task. You may write an excellent response with flawless syntax, but if you do not respond to the prompt, you will not receive a high score. This activity offers guidance in deconstructing—or reading, analyzing, and understanding—writing prompts.

When considering any prompt, look for five basic parts. Most if not all of the parts will be present. Finding as many as you can will help you figure out what you need to do and how to respond to the prompt correctly.

Five Parts to Look for in a Writing Prompt

1. **Subject:** What is the subject you need to write about? A well-written prompt will identify the subject, but it may be vague. For example, a prompt might tell you to think of a childhood experience. What common themes or ideas (either implicit or explicit) are associated with the subject?

2. **Speaker:** Who is writing the answer? (You are, but are you writing it as a student, a citizen, an authority?) The prompt should tell you who you are as the writer.

3. **Type of Essay:** What kind of response are you writing—expository, persuasive, synthesis, personal narrative? An effective prompt must tell you the type of writing you need to do. It may give you a choice. Choose wisely.

4. **Task:** What is the prompt asking you to do? For example, your task may be to take a stand on an issue and write a five-paragraph persuasive essay. Read the details carefully to identify exactly what you need to do.

5. **Hints:** Does the prompt give you suggestions to get started? The prompt may suggest ideas to think about or literary devices to identify and analyze.

> **ACADEMIC VOCABULARY**
>
> **Synthesis** is the act of combining ideas from different sources to create, express, or support a new idea.

Identify all the parts in the four prompts below. You may use different colored markers to highlight different parts in each prompt. The first prompt may be done together as a class. Afterward, complete the remaining prompts.

Prompt 1: Think of something at your school that you would like to change in order to create a more positive learning environment. The change could affect anything from a policy or procedure to an attitude or tradition. In a well-organized persuasive letter, write to an adult at your school presenting the problem, your solution to that problem, and why the environment would change.

Subject:

Speaker:

Type of Essay:

Task:

Hints:

Prompt 2: Contemporary life is marked by controversy. Choose a controversial local, national, or global issue with which you are familiar. Then, using appropriate evidence, write an essay that carefully considers opposing positions on this issue and proposes a solution or compromise.

Prompt 3: The following is a mock press release from *The Onion*, a publication devoted to humor and satire. Read the article carefully. Then write an essay in which you analyze the strategies used in the article to satirize how products are marketed to consumers.

Prompt 4: Choose a character from a text you have read (not necessarily the **protagonist**) whose mind is pulled in conflicting directions by two compelling desires, ambitions, obligations, or influences. Then, in a well-organized essay, identify each side of the conflict and examine the reasons for the conflict, the conflict's resolution, and how this conflict illuminates the meaning of the work as a whole.

WORD CONNECTIONS

Synthesis contains the root *-thes-*, from the Greek word *thesis* meaning "put, place, or set." This root also appears in *hypothesis, photosynthesis,* and *antithesis. Syn-* is a prefix meaning "with or together."

LITERARY TERM

A **protagonist** is the main character of a fictional story.

Writing About a Cultural Conflict

SUGGESTED LEARNING STRATEGIES: **Brainstorming, Drafting, Peer Editing**

Assignment

Your assignment is to analyze the conflict of a character (not necessarily the protagonist) from one of the texts (including the film clips) you encountered in Unit 1 or the first part of this unit. Choose a character whose mind is pulled in conflicting directions by two compelling desires, ambitions, obligations or influences. Using an organizing structure appropriate for your audience, identify each side of the conflict and examine the reasons for the conflict, the conflict's resolution, and how this conflict illuminates the meaning of the work as a whole.

Steps

Prewriting/Planning

1. Deconstruct the prompt and list all the essential features of the response. (You should have done this in Activity 2.13.)

2. Next, brainstorm your topic—a conflict from one of the texts you read or films you viewed in Units 1 and 2. If you are writing about the film *Bend It Like Beckham*, you might choose from among these conflicts: reality versus family expectations, parents versus children, or mothers versus daughters. Choose a conflict that you want to talk about because an authentic voice is always more powerful than something that sounds forced.

3. Once you have chosen a topic, plan your organizational structure. For example, you might use one body paragraph to explain one side of the conflict and another for the other side. You might reserve another paragraph to discuss the conflict's resolution.

Drafting

4. Draft a response to the prompt to include an introduction and a conclusion as well as body paragraphs that describe the conflict, examine its causes, and explain how it is resolved. Use specific examples from the text, the film, or the artwork to support your statements. Be sure to correctly cite your sources within the body of the text.

Evaluating/Revising

5. Share your draft and ask for peer response to the clarity of the thesis, coherence of the organization, clarity of ideas, smooth transitions between paragraphs, and how well you have addressed questions of purpose, audience, and genre. Use comments to revise your draft. Also revise your draft to improve style, word choice, figurative language, sentence variety, and subtlety of meaning.

Editing/Publishing

6. Identify errors and consult appropriate resources (dictionary, thesaurus, spell-check, grammar handbook, etc.) to ensure grammatically correct sentences, appropriate punctuation, and correct spelling.

7. Generate a legible and technically sound final draft.

SCORING GUIDE

Scoring Criteria	Exemplary	Proficient	Emerging
Ideas	Analysis focuses on an appropriate character and explains with clarity and precision the nature and resolution of the character's internal conflict and its implications for the meaning of the work as a whole. Use of specific and well-chosen examples yields solid support for the position. Thorough and perceptive literary analysis creates a clearly convincing text.	Analysis focuses on an appropriate character and adequately explains the nature and resolution of the character's internal conflict while attempting to make a connection to the meaning of the work as a whole. Use of appropriate examples supports the position. Solid literary analysis creates a convincing text.	Analysis may focus on an appropriate character yet inadequately explain the nature and resolution of the character's internal conflict and also fail to make a connection to the meaning of the work as a whole. Evidence to support the position is lacking. Too few examples are used. Analysis may be oversimplified or replaced by summary.
Organization	Organization is exceptional. Ideas move smoothly and comfortably with effective use of transitions enhancing the essay's coherence.	Organization is clear and easy to follow. Transitions make connections clear.	Organization is poor, making the essay difficult to follow. It lacks transitions between ideas.
Use of Language	Diction and syntax are purposeful and appropriate for an academic audience.	Diction and syntax are appropriate for an academic audience but may demonstrate incorrect or awkward word choice or sentence structure.	Diction and syntax may be simplistic or inappropriate for an academic audience. Slang, informal word choice, or awkward sentence structure may be present.
Conventions	The writing demonstrates strong control and mastery of standard conventions. Either no errors appear, or they are so slight that they do not interfere with the meaning.	The writing demonstrates control of standard writing conventions. Though some errors may appear, they do not seriously impede readability.	The writing demonstrates a lack of control of standard writing conventions. As a result, frequent errors seriously interfere with the meaning.

Writing About a Cultural Conflict

SCORING GUIDE

Scoring Criteria	Exemplary	Proficient	Emerging
Evidence of Writing Process	The writing demonstrates thoughtful planning, significant revision, and careful editing in preparing a publishable draft.	The writing demonstrates adequate planning, revision, and editing in preparing a publishable draft.	The writing lacks evidence of planning, revision, or editing. The draft is not ready for publication.
Additional Criteria			

Comments: _____

_____

_____

_____

_____

_____

Learning Focus:

Synthesizing Many Parts into a Whole

You are already masters of synthesis, even if you don't realize it. Throughout your studies in this book, you have combined new and various pieces of information with your existing ideas. You were synthesizing the pieces.

A **synthesis prompt** asks you to write a composition that develops a position on an issue and then synthesize, or incorporate, information from multiple sources, including your own experiences.

In order to synthesize information, you need a focusing idea or question for which you gather ideas from multiple texts or sources of information. In this part of the unit, your focusing question is, "To what extent does one's culture inform the way one views others and the world?"

The first two texts you will read focus on an individual's attitudes and perspectives when faced with colliding cultures. Both pieces ask you to use your knowledge of *diction*, *syntax*, *allusion*, and *persona* to analyze the texts.

The next section focuses on the structure of an **argument** (the hook, claim, concession/refutation, support, and call to action). You will examine these elements in a text, consider their effectiveness, and then later apply these concepts to an argument of your own.

In addition, you will read three texts—two humorous texts and a short story. The activities will build on your prior work with satire and short stories.

In Embedded Assessment 2, you will prepare a synthesis essay. To help you prepare, the activities at the end of the unit explain the process of reviewing the prompt, brainstorming possible responses, reaching consensus, and choosing specific textual and real-life examples that support your argument. You will see that synthesis asks you to do three important tasks:

▶ Perform a thoughtful analysis of the texts you read.

▶ Understand and apply the elements of argument.

▶ Define and support a position that incorporates all of these parts in the whole.

Colliding Worlds

ACADEMIC VOCABULARY

Writers use **juxtaposition** when they look at two or more things side-by-side for the purpose of comparison.

Your teacher will begin this activity by reading aloud from Pico Iyer's essay "Where Worlds Collide." In this piece, Iyer describes what people experience as they arrive at Los Angeles International Airport (LAX). While your teacher is reading, listen carefully and mark the text by highlighting or underlining images that create a picture of the scene. Think about how Iyer uses **juxtaposition** in his description of unlike images. You may want to record these words and/or phrases in the margins of the pages.

Theme

A text may contain more than one theme. There may be a primary theme and one or more underlying themes. Or, the writer may use several parallel themes. In many texts, theme is understood through the writer's diction, language construction, and use of literary devices. In these situations the theme is **implied** because the writer does not make a specific statement telling readers the theme of the text. In contrast, a theme may be **explicit** because the writer clearly states the message of the text.

As you listen to your teacher reading Iyer's essay, read along in your book and highlight words that indicate both explicit and implicit themes.

You will also read the essay "The Hunger of Memory," by Richard Rodriguez. Note the explicit theme in the last line of the essay. As you read, look for implied themes relating to "education has changed my life."

After the reading of Iyer's essay, review the images that you noticed in the text. In the space below, draw or sketch a few significant images from the text. When you are finished, find specific words, phrases, or sentences that correspond to your pictures. Write them below each drawing. Then, in small groups, share your drawings and respond to the questions your teacher poses.

Where Worlds Collide

by Pico Iyer

ABOUT THE AUTHOR
Pico Iyer is a British-born journalist, novelist, and travel
writer of Indian descent who grew up in Britain and
California. Unlike typical travel writing, Iyer's works explore
unusual or unexpected aspects of the places he visits. His
book *Video Night in Kathmandu: And Other Reports from
the Not-So-Far East* (1988) focuses on the West's influence
on Asian culture and daily life. Critics describe his writing
style as both ironic and culturally sensitive.

My Notes

Read carefully the following passage from "Where Worlds Collide," Pico
Iyer's 1995 essay about what travelers experience when they arrive at
Los Angeles International Airport.

They come out, blinking, into the bleached, forgetful sunshine, in Dodgers
caps and Rodeo Drive T-shirts, with the maps their cousins have drawn for
them and the images they've brought over from *Cops* and *Terminator 2*; they
come out, dazed, disoriented, heads still partly in the clouds, bodies still
several time zones – or centuries—away, and they step into the Promised Land.

In front of them is a Van Stop, a Bus Stop, a Courtesy Tram Stop, and
a Shuttle Bus Stop (the shuttles themselves tracing circuits A, B, and C). At
the Shuttle Bus Stop, they see the All American Shuttle, the Apollo Shuttle,
Celebrity Airport Livery, The Great American Stageline, the Movie Shuttle,
the Transport, Ride-4-You, and forty-two other magic buses waiting to whisk
them everywhere from Bakersfield to Disneyland. They see Koreans piling
into the Taeguk Airport Shuttle and the Seoul Shuttle, which will take them to
Koreatown without their ever feeling they've left home; they see newcomers
from the Middle East disappearing under the Arabic script of the Sahara
Shuttle. They see fast-talking, finger-snapping, palm-slapping jive artists
straight from their TV screens shouting incomprehensible slogans about
deals, destinations, and drugs. Over there is a block-long white limo, a Lincoln
Continental, and, over there, a black Chevy Blazer with Mexican stickers all
over its windows, being towed. They have arrived in the Land of Opportunity,
and the opportunities are swirling dizzily, promiscuously[1], around them.

**WORD
CONNECTIONS**
An **allusion** is a reference
to a well-known person,
event, or place from
history, music, art, or
another literary work. Note
the allusions the author
uses in this work, such
as "Promised Land" and
"Land of Opportunity."
Find other allusions in this
text.

As you read the text, notice
the glossed words in the
footnotes. Consider the
denotation of each word, and
underline or highlight the
context clues that help you
understand the connotation
of the word. How does the
author's diction add meaning
to the ideas he presents?

---

[1] **promiscuously:** in an indiscriminate or loose manner

My Notes

INTERSTATE
10 Fwy

Los Angeles

WORD CONNECTIONS

Terminal is a word that can have different meanings. Among its meanings are a building at an airport, an end, or a fatal outcome. Context clues help you determine which meaning the writer intends.

They have already braved the ranks of Asian officials, the criminal-looking security men in jackets that say "Elsinore Airport Services," the men shaking tins that say "Helping America's Hopeless." They have already seen the tilting mugs that say "California: a new slant on life" and the portable fruit machines in the gift shop.

They have already, perhaps, visited the rest room where someone has written, "Yes on Proposition 187. Mexicans go home," the snack bar where a slice of pizza costs $3.19 (18 quetzals, they think in horror, or 35,000 dong), and the sign that urges them to try the Cockatoo Inn Grand Hotel. The latest arrivals at Los Angeles International Airport are ready now to claim their new lives.

Above them in the terminal, voices are repeating, over and over, in Japanese, Spanish, and unintelligible[2] English, "Maintain visual contact with your personal property at all times." Out on the sidewalk, a man's voice and a woman's voice are alternating an unending refrain: "The white zone is for loading and unloading of passengers only. No parking." There are "Do Not Cross" yellow lines cordoning off parts of the sidewalk and "Wells Fargo Alarm Services" stickers on the windows; there are "Aviation Safeguard" signs on the baggage carts and "Beware of Solicitors" signs on the columns; there are even special phones "To Report Trouble." More male and female voices are intoning[3] continuously, "Do not leave your car unattended" and "Unattended cars are subject to immediate tow-away." There are no military planes on the tarmac here, the newcomers notice, no khaki soldiers in fatigues, no instructions not to take photographs, as at home; but there are civilian restrictions every bit as strict as in many a police state.

"This Terminal Is in a Medfly Quarantine Area," says the sign between the terminals. "Stop the Spread of Medfly!" If, by chance, the new Americans have to enter a parking lot on their way out, they will be faced with "Cars left over 30 days may be impounded at Owner's Expense" and "Do not enter without a ticket." It will cost them $16 if they lose their parking ticket, they read, and $56 if they park in the wrong zone. Around them is an unending cacophony of antitheft devices, sirens, beepers, and car-door openers; lights are flashing everywhere, and the man who fines them $16 for losing their parking ticket has the tribal scars of Tigre across his forehead.

The blue skies and palm trees they saw on TV are scarcely visible from here: just an undifferentiated smoggy haze, billboards advertising Nissan and Panasonic and Canon, and beyond those an endlessly receding mess of gray streets. Overhead, they can see the all-too-familiar signs of Hilton and Hyatt and Holiday Inn; in the distance, a sea of tract houses, mini-malls, and high rises. The City of Angels awaits them.

---

[2] **unintelligible**: difficult to understand, incomprehensible
[3] **intoning**: speaking or reciting in a singing voice; chanting or singing in monotone

Struggling with Identity: Rethinking Persona

Memoir

> **ABOUT THE AUTHOR**
> Richard Rodriguez has written extensively about his own life and his struggles to reconcile his origins as the son of Mexican immigrants and his rise through American academia. In his memoir, *The Hunger of Memory*, written in English, his second language, Rodriguez examines how his assimilation into American culture affected his relationship to his Mexican roots.

As you read the following selection by Richard Rodriguez, highlight or underline any words or allusions with which you are unfamiliar. Then follow your teacher's directions.

Excerpt from

The HUNGER of MEMORY

by Richard Rodriguez

I have taken Caliban's advice. I have stolen their books. I will have some run of this isle.

Once upon a time, I was a "socially disadvantaged" child. An enchantedly happy child. Mine was a childhood of intense family closeness. And extreme public alienation.

Thirty years later I write this book as a middle-class American man. Assimilated.

WORD CONNECTIONS

In the first line, Rodriguez refers to "Caliban's advice." This term is a literary allusion to the character of Caliban in Shakespeare's *The Tempest*. Caliban wants to steal the books and magic of another character to gain power. Rodriguez uses the allusion to refer to education, which can confer power. How do literary and other allusions help you to understand text?

Struggling with Identity: Rethinking Persona

My Notes

Dark-skinned. To be seen at a Belgravia dinner party. Or in New York. Exotic in a tuxedo. My face is drawn to severe Indian features which would pass notice on the page of a *National Geographic*, but at a cocktail party in Bel Air somebody wonders: "Have you ever thought of doing any high-fashion modeling? Take this card." (In Beverly Hills will this monster make a man.)

A lady in a green dress asks, "Didn't we meet at the Thompsons' party last month in Malibu?"

And, "What do you do, Mr. Rodriguez?"

I write: I am a writer.

A part-time writer. When I began this book, five years ago, a fellowship bought me a year of continuous silence in my San Francisco apartment. But the words wouldn't come. The money ran out. So I was forced to take temporary jobs. (I have friends who, with a phone call, can find me well-paying work.) In past months I have found myself in New York. In Los Angeles. Working. With money. Among people with money. And as leisure – a weekend guest in Connecticut; at a cocktail party in Bel Air.

Perhaps because I have always, accidentally, been a classmate to children of rich parents, I long ago came to assume my association with their world; came to assume that I could have money, if it was money I wanted. But money, big money, has never been the goal of my life. My story is not a version of Sammy Glick's. I work to support my habit of writing. The great luxury of my life is the freedom to sit at this desk.

"Mr?..."

Rodriguez. The name on the door. The name on my passport. The name I carry from my parents – who are no longer my parents, in a cultural sense. This is how I pronounce it: Rich-heard Road-re-guess. This is how I hear it most often.

The voice through the microphone says, "Ladies and gentlemen, it is with pleasure that I introduce Mr. Richard Rodriguez."

I am invited very often these days to speak about modern education in college auditoriums and in Holiday Inn ballrooms. I go, still feel a calling to act the teacher, though not licensed by the degree. One time my audience is a convention of university administrators; another time high school teachers of English; another time a women's alumnae group.

"Mr. Rodriguez has written extensively about contemporary education."

Several essays. I have argued particularly against two government programs – affirmative action and bilingual education.

"He is a provocative speaker."

I have become notorious among certain leaders of America's Ethnic Left. I am considered a dupe, an ass, the fool – Tom Brown, the brown Uncle Tom, interpreting the writing on the wall to a bunch of cigar-smoking pharaohs.

A dainty white lady at the women's club luncheon approaches the podium after my speech to say, after all, wasn't it a shame that I wasn't able to 'use' my Spanish in school. What a shame. But how dare her lady-fingered pieties extend to my life!

There are those in White America who would anoint me to play out for them some drama of ancestral reconciliation. Perhaps because I am marked by indelible color they easily suppose that I am unchanged by social mobility, that I can claim unbroken ties with my past. The possibility! At a time when many middle-class children and parents grow distant, apart, no longer speak, romantic solutions appeal.

But I reject the role. (Caliban won't ferry a TV crew back to his island, there to recover his roots.)

Aztec ruins hold no special interest for me. I do not search Mexican graveyards for ties to unnamable ancestors. I assume I retain certain features of gesture and mood derived from buried lives. I also speak Spanish today. And read Garcia Lorca and García Márquez at my leisure. But what consolation can that fact bring against the knowledge that my mother and father have never heard of Garcia Lorca or García Márquez?

GRAMMAR & USAGE
Writers may place quotation marks around a word to suggest irony or sarcasm. Rodriguez does this when he ironically reports a listener's comment to him: "...wasn't it a shame that I wasn't able to 'use' my Spanish in school."

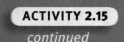
Struggling with Identity: Rethinking Persona

My Notes

What preoccupies me is immediate; the separation I endure with my parents is loss. This is what matters to me; the story of the scholarship boy who returns home one summer from college to discover bewildering silence, facing his parents. This is my story. An American story. Consider me if you choose, a comic victim of two cultures. This is my situation; writing these pages, surrounded in the room I am in by volumes of Montaigne and Shakespeare and Lawrence. They are mine now.

A Mexican woman passes in a black dress. She wears a white apron; she carries a tray of hors d'oeuvres. She must only be asking if there are any I want as she proffers the tray like a wheel of good fortune. I shake my head. No. Does she wonder how I am here? In Bel Air.

It is education that has altered my life. Carried me far.

Directions: During a second reading of the text, use the guiding questions below to deepen your understanding of Rodriquez's purpose. In groups of four, divide the questions among yourselves. Jot down answers to the questions, and then share your notes with each other.

1. **Allusions**: What allusions are made? Who are Caliban, Uncle Tom, and García Márquez?

2. **Conflicts**: What forces (either internal or external) are pulling Rodriguez in different directions?

3. **Diction**: What words have strong connotations and which images paint a vivid picture?

4. **Syntax**: Note the use of abrupt, choppy sentence fragments. What effect do they have on your reading?

5. What universal ideas about life and society does Rodriguez convey in this text?

Your teacher will lead you in a Socratic Seminar in which you discuss this piece more fully.

LITERARY TERMS

An **allusion** is a reference to another piece of literature or to a culturally or historically important figure or event.

A **conflict** is a struggle between opposing forces or characters.

Diction is a writer's choice of words.

Syntax is the order in which a writer places words in a sentence.

Theme is a writer's central idea or main message about life.

A Father's Plea: Evaluating a Cultural Argument

SUGGESTED LEARNING STRATEGIES: **Marking the Text, Quickwrite, Graphic Organizer, Close Reading**

ACADEMIC VOCABULARY

An argument is a set of statements, each supporting the others, that presents a position or viewpoint. An argument contains the following elements:

- hook
- claim
- concession and refutation
- support
- call to action.

The Structure of an Argument

Arguments come in many shapes and sizes. Although arguments are varied in their structure, content, and context, five key elements are almost always found in an effective argument.

The Hook

- The hook grabs the reader's attention.
- It often establishes a connection between reader and writer and provides background information.
- It can be, but is not limited to, an anecdote, an image, a definition, or a quotation.

The Claim

- The claim comes in the opening section of your paper.
- It states your belief and what you wish to argue.
- It can be straightforward and clear, for example, "I believe that... ."

Support

- Your support is the reasoning behind your argument.
- You provide supporting evidence for your claim (data, quotes, anecdotes, and so on).
- You use support to blend together logical and emotional appeals.

Concessions and Refutations

- With a concession, you recognize the arguments made by the other side.
- A concession builds your credibility. It shows that you can discuss the other side with objectivity.
- A concession grants that the other side has some validity.
- Following the concession, a refutation argues at length against the opposing viewpoint by proving your side has MORE validity.

Call to Action

- It draws your argument to a close, restates your claim, and makes a final appeal to values.
- It voices a final plea.
- It does not repeat information, but sums up the argument with a few final facts and appeals.

An Indian Father's Plea

by Robert Lake

> **ABOUT THE AUTHOR**
> Robert Lake, also known as Bobby Lake-Thom and Medicine Grizzly Bear, is a descendent of three Native American tribes. He has written numerous articles and two books on Native American culture and spirituality.

Wind-Wolf knows the names and migration patterns of more than 40 birds. He knows there are 13 tail feathers on a perfectly balanced eagle. What he needs is a teacher who knows his full measure.

Dear teacher, I would like to introduce you to my son, Wind-Wolf. He is probably what you would consider a typical Indian kid. He was born and raised on the reservation. He has black hair, dark brown eyes, and an olive complexion. And like so many Indian children his age, he is shy and quiet in the classroom. He is 5 years old, in kindergarten, and I can't understand why you have already labeled him a "slow learner."

At the age of 5, he has already been through quite an education compared with his peers in Western society. As his first introduction into this world, he was bonded to his mother and to the Mother Earth in a traditional native childbirth ceremony. And he has been continuously cared for by his mother, father, sisters, cousins, aunts, uncles, grandparents, and extended tribal family since this ceremony.

From his mother's warm and loving arms, Wind-Wolf was placed in a secure and specially designed Indian baby basket. His father and the medicine elders conducted another ceremony with him that served to bond him with the essence of his genetic father, the Great Spirit, the Grandfather Sun, and the Grandmother Moon. This was all done in order to introduce him properly into the new and natural world, not the world of artificiality, and to protect his sensitive and delicate soul. It is our people's way of showing the newborn respect, ensuring that he starts his life on the path of spirituality.

The traditional Indian baby basket became his "turtle's shell" and served as the first seat for his classroom. He was strapped in for safety, protected from injury by the willow roots and hazel wood construction. The basket was made by a tribal elder who had gathered her materials with prayer and in a ceremonial way. It is the same kind of basket that our people have used for thousands of years. It is specially designed to provide the child with the kind of knowledge and experience he will need in order to survive in his culture and environment.

GRAMMAR & USAGE

Verbs do important work in sentences. They show time (**tense**), voice (**active or passive**), and action or being (action and linking verbs). Therefore, a writer's choice of verbs is very important.

Notice the tense and voice of the verbs (action verbs) in this sentence:

The basket **was made** (past tense, passive voice) by a tribal elder who **had gathered** (past perfect tense, active voice) her materials with prayer....

The passive voice gives attention to the subject, *basket*. The past perfect tense indicates that the action was completed in the past before another past action (making the basket).

A Father's Plea: Evaluating a Cultural Argument

My Notes

Wind-Wolf was strapped in snugly with a deliberate restriction upon his arms and legs. Although you in Western society may argue that such a method serves to hinder motor-skill development and abstract reasoning, we believe it forces the child to first develop his intuitive faculties, rational intellect, symbolic thinking, and five senses. Wind-Wolf was with his mother constantly, closely bonded physically, as she carried him on her back or held him in front while breast-feeding. She carried him everywhere she went, and every night he slept with both parents. Because of this, Wind-Wolf's educational setting was not only a "secure" environment, but it was also very colorful, complicated, sensitive, and diverse. He has been with his mother at the ocean at daybreak when she made her prayers and gathered fresh seaweed from the rocks, he has sat with his uncles in a rowboat on the river while they fished with gill nets, and he has watched and listened to elders as they told creation stories and animal legends and sang songs around the campfires.

He has attended the sacred and ancient White Deerskin Dance of his people and is well-acquainted with the cultures and languages of other tribes. He has been with his mother when she gathered herbs for healing and watched his tribal aunts and grandmothers gather and prepare traditional foods such as acorn, smoked salmon, eel, and deer meat. He has played with abalone shells, pine nuts, iris grass string, and leather while watching the women make beaded jewelry and traditional native regalia. He has had many opportunities to watch his father, uncles, and ceremonial leaders use different kinds of colorful feathers and sing different kinds of songs while preparing for the sacred dances and rituals.

As he grew older, Wind-Wolf began to crawl out of the baby basket, develop his motor skills, and explore the world around him. When frightened or sleepy, he could always return to the basket, as a turtle withdraws into its shell. Such an inward journey allows one to reflect in privacy on what he has learned and to carry the new knowledge deeply into the unconscious and the soul. Shapes, sizes, colors, texture, sound, smell, feeling, taste, and the learning process are therefore functionally integrated—the physical and spiritual, matter and energy, conscious and unconscious, individual and social.

This kind of learning goes beyond the basics of distinguishing the difference between rough and smooth, square and round, hard and soft, black and white, similarities and extremes.

For example, Wind-Wolf was with his mother in South Dakota while she danced for seven days straight in the hot sun, fasting, and piercing herself in the sacred Sun Dance Ceremony of a distant tribe. He has been doctored in a number of different healing ceremonies by medicine men and women from diverse places ranging from Alaska and Arizona to New York and California. He has been in more than 20 different sacred sweat-lodge rituals—used by native tribes to purify mind, body, and soul—since he was 3 years old, and he has already been exposed to many different religions of his racial brothers: Protestant, Catholic, Asian Buddhist, and Tibetan Lamaist.

It takes a long time to absorb and reflect on these kinds of experiences, so maybe that is why you think my Indian child is a slow learner. His aunts and grandmothers taught him to count and know his numbers while they sorted out the complex materials used to make the abstract designs in the native baskets. He listened to his mother count each and every bead and sort out numerically according to color while she painstakingly made complex beaded belts and necklaces. He learned his basic numbers by helping his father count and sort the rocks to be used in the sweat lodge—seven rocks for a medicine sweat, say, or 13 for the summer solstice ceremony. (The rocks are later heated and doused with water to create purifying steam.) And he was taught to learn mathematics by counting the sticks we use in our traditional native hand game. So I realize he may be slow in grasping the methods and tools that you are now using in your classroom, ones quite familiar to his white peers, but I hope you will be patient with him. It takes time to adjust to a new cultural system and learn new things.

He is not culturally "disadvantaged," but he is culturally "different." If you ask him how many months there are in a year, he will probably tell you 13. He will respond this way not because he doesn't know how to count properly, but because he has been taught by our traditional people that there are 13 full moons in a year according to the native tribal calendar and that there are really 13 planets in our solar system and 13 tail feathers on a perfectly balanced eagle, the most powerful kind of bird to use in ceremony and healing.

But he also knows that some eagles may only have 12 tail feathers, or seven, that they do not all have the same number. He knows that the flicker has exactly 10 tail feathers; that they are red and black, representing the directions of east and west, life and death; and that this bird is considered a "fire" bird, a power used in native doctoring and healing. He can probably count more than 40 different kinds of birds, tell you and his peers what kind of bird each is and where it lives, the seasons in which it appears, and how it is used in a sacred ceremony. He may have trouble writing his name on a piece of paper, but he knows how to say it and many other things in several different Indian languages. He is not fluent yet because he is only 5 years old and required by law to attend your educational system, learn your language, your values, your ways of thinking, and your methods of teaching and learning.

So you see, all of these influences together make him somewhat shy and quiet—and perhaps "slow" according to your standards. But if Wind-Wolf was not prepared for his first tentative foray into your world, neither were you appreciative of his culture. On the first day of class, you had difficulty with his name. You wanted to call him Wind, insisting that Wolf somehow must be his middle name. The students in the class laughed at him, causing further embarrassment.

My Notes

A Father's Plea: Evaluating a Cultural Argument

While you are trying to teach him your new methods, helping him learn new tools for self- discovery and adapt to his new learning environment, he may be looking out the window as if daydreaming. Why? Because he has been taught to watch and study the changes in nature. It is hard for him to make the appropriate psychic switch from the right to the left hemisphere of the brain when he sees the leaves turning bright colors, the geese heading south, and the squirrels scurrying around for nuts to get ready for a harsh winter. In his heart, in his young mind, and almost by instinct, he knows that this is the time of year he is supposed to be with his people gathering and preparing fish, deer meat, and native plants and herbs, and learning his assigned tasks in this role. He is caught between two worlds, torn by two distinct cultural systems.

Yesterday, for the third time in two weeks, he came home crying and said he wanted to have his hair cut. He said he doesn't have any friends at school because they make fun of his long hair. I tried to explain to him that in our culture, long hair is a sign of masculinity and balance and is a source of power. But he remained adamant in his position.

To make matters worse, he recently encountered his first harsh case of racism. Wind-Wolf had managed to adopt at least one good school friend. On the way home from school one day, he asked his new pal if he wanted to come home to play with him until supper. That was OK with Wind-Wolf's mother, who was walking with them. When they all got to the little friend's house, the two boys ran inside to ask permission while Wind-Wolf's mother waited. But the other boy's mother lashed out: "It is OK if you have to play with him at school, but we don't allow those kind of people in our house!" When my wife asked why not, the other boy's mother answered, "Because you are Indians and we are white, and I don't want my kids growing up with your kind of people."

So now my young Indian child does not want to go to school anymore (even though we cut his hair). He feels that he does not belong. He is the only Indian child in your class, and he is well-aware of this fact. Instead of being proud of his race, heritage, and culture, he feels ashamed. When he watches television, he asks why the white people hate us so much and always kill our people in the movies and why they take everything away from us. He asks why the other kids in school are not taught about the power, beauty, and essence of nature or provided with an opportunity to experience the world around them firsthand. He says he hates living in the city and that he misses his Indian cousins and friends. He asks why one young white girl at school who is his friend always tells him, "I like you, Wind-Wolf, because you are a good Indian."

Now he refuses to sing his native songs, play with his Indian artifacts, learn his language, or participate in his sacred ceremonies. When I ask him to go to an urban powwow or help me with a sacred sweat-lodge ritual, he says no because "that's weird" and he doesn't want his friends at school to think he doesn't believe in God.

So, dear teacher, I want to introduce you to my son, Wind-Wolf, who is not really a "typical" little Indian kid after all. He stems from a long line of hereditary chiefs, medicine men and women, and ceremonial leaders whose accomplishments and unique forms of knowledge are still being studied and recorded in contemporary books. He has seven different tribal systems flowing through his blood; he is even part white. I want my child to succeed in school and in life. I don't want him to be a dropout or juvenile delinquent or to end up on drugs and alcohol because he is made to feel inferior or because of discrimination. I want him to be proud of his rich heritage and culture, and I would like him to develop the necessary capabilities to adapt to, and succeed in, both cultures. But I need your help.

What you say and what you do in the classroom, what you teach and how you teach it, and what you don't say and don't teach will have a significant effect on the potential success or failure of my child. Please remember that this is the primary year of his education and development. All I ask is that you work with me, not against me, to help educate my child in the best way. If you don't have the knowledge, preparation, experience, or training to effectively deal with culturally different children, I am willing to help you with the few resources I have available or direct you to such resources.

Millions of dollars have been appropriated by Congress and are being spent each year for "Indian Education." All you have to do is take advantage of it and encourage your school to make an effort to use it in the name of "equal education." My Indian child has a constitutional right to learn, retain, and maintain his heritage and culture. By the same token, I strongly believe that non-Indian children also have a constitutional right to learn about our Native American heritage and culture, because Indians play a significant part in the history of Western society. Until this reality is equally understood and applied in education as a whole, there will be a lot more schoolchildren in grade K-2 identified as "slow learners."

My son, Wind-Wolf, is not an empty glass coming into your class to be filled. He is a full basket coming into a different environment and society with something special to share. Please let him share his knowledge, heritage, and culture with you and his peers.

My Notes

GRAMMAR & USAGE

A **contrasting expression** emphasizes the point with which it contrasts, as in this sentence:

All I ask is that you work with me, **not against me,** to help educate my child...

Notice that commas set off a contrasting expression.

A Father's Plea: Evaluating a Cultural Argument

In the graphic organizer below, identify examples of the five elements of argument that appear in "An Indian Father's Plea."

Element of Argument	Example from the Text
Hook	
Claim	
Support	
Concessions / Refutations	
Call to Action	

As a class, discuss the effectiveness of the writer's organization of ideas. Does the organization help or hinder the argument? Why?

Quickwrite: Write your responses on a separate sheet of paper.

Who is the author's audience? Is there more than one possibility? Is he effective in speaking to each of these audiences?

What is the author's persona? How does he come across to his audience? Is he believable? Thoughtful? Informed? Honest?

Why Choose Humor?

SUGGESTED LEARNING STRATEGIES: Discussion Group, SOAPSTone, Graphic Organizer

You have each been assigned to a group to complete this task. Each group member has one of the following responsibilities:

Reader(s): Read aloud the reading selection to the group, stopping after each numbered section.

Group Leader: After each section is completed, lead a group discussion using the question.

Recorder: Summarize and record the main talking points of the group for each question answered.

Timekeeper: Keep the group on task and on time. You may also share in the reading responsibilities.

Once you have your assigned tasks, as a group read the excerpt from *Dave Barry Does Japan*. After reading each chunk of text, answer each question below for that chunk. Write notes in the My Notes space on pages 116–121.

Chunk 1: Who is the speaker? What do you know about him? What is the problem?

Chunk 2: Share a time when you have been outside your cultural element and had difficulty communicating.

Chunk 3: Explain how what Barry says often leads to misunderstandings among cultures. Provide some examples.

Chunk 4: What ideas does Barry convey about Japanese culture or his own culture?

Chunk 5: How does this conversation lead Barry to his concluding statement?

Satire

> **ABOUT THE AUTHOR**
> Dave Barry is a humor writer and syndicated columnist known for his goofy observations of American life. The author of thirty books, the winner of the 1988 Pulitzer Prize, and lead guitarist of the literary rock band the Rock Bottom Remainders, Barry lives and writes in Miami, Florida.

From DAVE BARRY

DOES JAPAN ⬤

by Dave Barry

Chunk 1

Before I fell asleep I was able to devote nearly an hour to the study of the Japanese language. My ultimate goal was to learn how to say "I do not speak Japanese" in fluent Japanese, but I decided to start with "Thank you." According to *Japanese at a Glance*, the way you say this is: **DOH-moh ah-REE-gah-toh** For some reason—again, it could have been the wine—I found this almost impossible to remember. I tried practicing on the cabin attendants, who continued to come around every few minutes with complimentary items.

"DI-moh ah-bli-GA-toh," I would say.

Or: "DE-mi AL-le-GRET-oh."

Or: "DA-moh o-RE-ga-noh."

All of these seemed to work pretty well, but I think the cabin attendants were just being polite. I was worried about how I'd do with regular Japanese civilians, especially in light of the following stern warning from *Japanese at a Glance:* Take long vowels seriously; pronouncing a long vowel incorrectly can result in a different word, or even an unintelligible one.

So I tried hard to take my long vowels seriously. The last thing I wanted was to try to thank a bellhop and instead, because of a vowel problem, ask for his hand in marriage. After a solid hour I was still not at all confident in my "Thank you," and most of the other phrases in

Japanese at a Glance were even worse. It was as if they had been cranked out by the Random Syllable Generator. The harder I tried to concentrate, the more confusing the phrases became, until they all looked like this:

HELLO (formal): Wa-SO-hah-na-GO-ma-na-SO-la-ti-DOH

HELLO (informal): Hah-to-RAH-ma-ka-NYAH-nyah-nyah

HELLO (during rain): KO-rah-na-mah-NAY-ah-MOO-baaaaa

I fell asleep babbling politely and dreamed about the Russians.

The result of this language-training program was that I arrived in Tokyo speaking Japanese at essentially the same fluency level as cement. I never did get much better while we were there. The only word I became really good at saying was "beer," which is pronounced "bee-roo," unless you want a big beer, in which case it is pronounced "BIG bee-roo." I semimastered a few other Japanese words, but I tended to use them randomly. To give you a true example: One evening a hotel waiter brought me a beer; I thanked him in Japanese, and he bowed politely and went away, at which point my son observed that what I had actually said to the waiter was "Very much good morning, sir."

Fortunately, my inability to learn Japanese was not much of a problem, thanks to a little pocket-sized reference card that came with *Japanese at a Glance*, entitled THE 32 MOST USEFUL JAPANESE PHRASES. I carried this card everywhere. On the left-hand side it listed 32 English phrases, such as "Do you speak English?"; "I'm lost"; "Where's the rest room?"; etc. On the right-hand side, the card told you how to pronounce these phrases in Japanese. Here, for example, with no exaggeration, is how you're supposed to pronounce "I'm lost": Mee-chee nee, mah-YOHT-the shee-mah-ee-mah-shtah

Even reading from this card, it would probably take me fifteen minutes to pronounce this successfully, and I'm not sure how much good it would do me. Let's say I actually managed to say to a Japanese person, "Mee-chee nee, mah-YOHT-the shee-mah-ee-mah-shtah." The Japanese person would probably respond with something like, "na-go-wah-ME-yoh-nah-mah-TSOY-yah-ska-wo-mah," meaning "I see." And then I'd need *another* phrase, requiring another fifteen minutes to pronounce. In terms of time management, it seemed more efficient simply to remain lost, which is pretty much what we did for the whole three weeks.

This is not to say that THE 32 MOST USEFUL JAPANESE PHRASES was not helpful. *Au contraire.*[1] I found the card to be invaluable, once I grasped how to use it. The trick was to *ignore the right-hand, or Japanese, side.* Very few Japanese persons understood me when I attempted to pronounce useful phrases in Japanese. But I did pretty well when I read the *left* side of the card very slowly. I'd say:

Chunk 2

WORD CONNECTIONS

Au contraire is a French term meaning "on the contrary."

---

[1] Or, as the Japanese say, "Ee-gah-wo-nah-TKSKA-ka-do-ma-oo-mau-mau."

My Notes

Where-is-the-REST-room?

And almost always somebody would understand well enough to point me in the right direction. (This was not always a good thing, because the Japanese concept of "toilet" is basically the same as our concept of "a hole in the floor that somebody forgot to put a toilet on top of.")

My point is that many Japanese people know a little English. But it's often *very* little. Japan is not like, for example, Germany, where everybody seems to speak English better than the average U.S. congressperson. In Japan, you will often find yourself in situations where nobody speaks any English. And the weird thing is, English pops up *everywhere* in Japan. You constantly see signs and advertisements with English words in them, and you constantly hear American rock music being played in stores and restaurants. But to the Japanese, the English doesn't seem to *mean* anything. It's there purely for decorative purposes, like a hood ornament, or a SPEED LIMIT 55 sign.

This can be frustrating. I remember being in a Kentucky Fried Chicken restaurant[2] in a small town called Beppu, trying to communicate the concept of "ketchup" to the young man behind the counter, who, like virtually every other Japanese person we met, was extremely polite and diligent. He was trying hard to understand me, frowning with intense concentration as I used the Official United Nations International Gesture for "ketchup," which is to pound the bottom of an upside-down imaginary ketchup bottle while saying

Ketchup? Ketchup? Ketchup?

like a person with a hiccups-related nerve disorder. But I wasn't getting through so the young man called two young women over, and all three of them solemnly watched me repeat

Ketchup? Ketchup? Ketchup?

for a while longer, none of them saying a word, and all the while the store's music system was playing:

There she was, just a-walkin' down the street

Singin' do-wah diddy diddy dum diddy-do

Chunk 3

And I wanted to scream, HOW CAN YOU NOT UNDERSTAND ENGLISH WHEN ALL DAY LONG YOU LISTEN TO "DO-WAH DIDDY DIDDY DUM DIDDY DO"??

The answer is that they don't really care what the words say; they just like the sound. It's the same with printed English words. The Japanese don't care what they mean; they just like the way they look. They especially like clothes imprinted with English words, words that often seem to be chosen at random. This results in a phenomenon that has vastly amused thousands of English-speaking visitors: the unintentionally

---

[2] Of *course* they have Kentucky Fried Chicken restaurants. Don't be an idiot.

hilarious T-shirt. Anybody who has spent any time in Japan can give you examples. Tom Reid, of the *Washington Post,* told me that he once covered a ceremony where a Japanese high-school student received a very prestigious science award; the student accepted the award wearing a T-shirt that said SNOT HOUSE. I once saw an attractive, stroller-pushing young mother wearing heels, a nice skirt, and a blouse imprinted with CIRCUIT BEAVER.

Here are just a few of the other fascinating statements we saw on T-shirts, and as I am fond of saying when reporting facts, I am not making this up:

I AM PLUMP MARY.

WE'RE BONE NOB. WE'RE HAPPY OUR ORIGINAL DANCE.

NURSE MENTALITY

WE HOPE TO ALWAYS HAVE AN OPEN

A SOUVENIR GOODS MAKE US HAPPY ANYTIME,
DON'T YOU THINK SO?

BONERACTIVE WEAR

We also saw signs that told us where we could find:

VENOM FOOD AND BAR[3]

LIQUOR BY THE GRASS OR IN COOKTAIL

JIVE COFFEE

FASHION VS. HAIR

On a cigarette-vending machine in Kyoto, we found the following quotations, with no further explanation:

"It is common practice over there to offer each other a cigarette as daily greetings."

"So I heard. Cigarettes are offered to the other to express friendliness and affection."

The important lesson for the English-speaking visitor to learn from all this is that, again, in Japan, English words do not necessarily mean anything. Adding to the confusion is the fact that, even when English words DO mean something, it may not be what you think. The Japanese are not big on saying things directly. Another way of putting this: Compared with the Japanese, the average American displays in communication all the subtlety of Harpo hitting Zeppo with a dead chicken. The Japanese tend to communicate via nuance and euphemism, often leaving important things unsaid; whereas Americans tend to think

---

[3] This establishment was in a section of Tokyo called Roppogi, whose motto is: "A High Touch Town."

WORD CONNECTIONS

Ultimate contains the root *-ult-*, from the Latin word *ultimus*, meaning "last or beyond." This root also appears in *ultimatum*, *penultimate*, and *ulterior*.

Attendant contains the root *-tend-*, from the Latin word *tendere*, meaning "to stretch or wait for." This root also appears in *distend*, *tendency*, *tension*, *pretend*, and *extend*.

they're being subtle when they refrain from grabbing the listener by the shirt.

This difference in approach often leads to misunderstandings between the two cultures. One of the biggest problems — all the guidebooks warn you about this — is that the Japanese are extremely reluctant to come right out and say no, a word they generally regard as impolite. My wife, Beth, learned this before we even got to Japan, when she was making airplane and hotel arrangements through a Japanese travel agent. Beth, who is an extremely straight-ahead type of communicator, was having a hell of a time, because she kept having conversations like this:

Chunk 4

BETH: …and then we want to take a plane from Point A to Point B.

TRAVEL AGENT: I see. You want to take a plane?

BETH: Yes.

TRAVEL AGENT: From Point A?

BETH: Yes.

TRAVEL AGENT: To Point B?

BETH: Yes.

TRAVEL AGENT: Ah.

BETH: Can we do that?

TRAVEL AGENT: Perhaps you would prefer to take a train.

BETH: No, we would prefer to take a plane.

TRAVEL AGENT: Ah-hah. You would prefer to take a plane?

BETH: Yes. A plane.

TRAVEL AGENT: I see. From Point A?

And so it would go, with arrangement after arrangement. Inevitably, by the time Beth got off the phone, she was a raving madwoman.

"What is the PROBLEM??" she would shout, causing the dogs to crawl around on their stomachs (in case they had done something wrong). "Why can't these people COMMUNICATE???"

The answer, of course, is that the travel agent was communicating. A person familiar with the Japanese culture would recognize instantly that the agent was virtually screaming, "THERE IS NO PLANE, YOU ZITBRAIN!"

To the best of my knowledge, in all the time we traveled around Japan, nobody ever told us we couldn't do anything, although it turned out that there were numerous things we couldn't do. Life became easier for us once we learned to interpret certain key phrases, which I'll summarize in this convenient table:

ENGLISH STATEMENT MADE BY JAPANESE PERSON	ACTUAL MEANING IN AMERICAN
I see.	No.
Ah.	No.
Ah-hah.	No.
Yes.	No.
That is difficult.	That is completely impossible.
That is very interesting.	That is the stupidest thing I ever heard.
We will study your proposal.	We will feed your proposal to a goat.

Before we left for Japan, I had several phone conversations with Hiroshi Ishikawa of the Foreign Press Center in Tokyo, who was of great help in arranging interviews and interpreters, and whom I now consider a friend. In our first conversation, we had this exchange:

HIROSHI: You are going to be here three weeks?

ME: Yes.

HIROSHI: I see. And you are going to write a book?

ME: Yes.

HIROSHI: I see. And you expect to gather enough material in three weeks to write a book?

ME: Well, it's not going to be a *good* book. (*Pause for laughter.*)

HIROSHI: I see.

After we got to Japan, I realized that Hiroshi had been expressing vast skepticism about the whole idea, but fortunately I was oblivious to this at the time. I'm sure I was oblivious to the true meaning of almost everything everybody said to me over there. I frankly wonder how Americans and Japanese ever communicate with each other about *anything*.

Chunk 5

My Notes

_____

Essay

> **ABOUT THE AUTHOR**
> Barbara Kingsolver is a novelist and essayist who began her career in the sciences. She worked as an archaeologist and scientific researcher before turning her hand to writing articles and fiction. Her novels include *The Bean Trees* (1988), *Animal Dreams* (1990), and *The Poisonwood Bible* (1998). All have won awards. Kingsolver's nonfiction has focused on the environment and human rights.

"Going to Japan"

from Small Wonder

by Barbara Kingsolver

My great-aunt Zelda went to Japan and took an abacus, a bathysphere, a conundrum, a diatribe, an eggplant. That was a game we used to play. All you had to do was remember everything in alphabetical order. Right up to Aunt Zelda.

Then I grew up and was actually invited to go to Japan, not with the fantastic Aunt Zelda but as myself. As such, I had no idea what to take. I knew what I planned to be doing: researching a story about the memorial at Hiroshima; visiting friends; trying not to get lost in a place where I couldn't even read the street signs. Times being what they were—any times—I intended to do my very best to respect cultural differences, avoid sensitive topics I might not comprehend, and, in short, be anything but an Ugly American. When I travel, I like to try to blend in. I've generally found it helps to be prepared. So I asked around, and was warned to expect a surprisingly modern place.

My great-aunt Zelda went to Japan and took Appliances, Battery packs, Cellular technology. . . . That seemed to be the idea.

And so it came to pass that I arrived in Kyoto an utter foreigner, unprepared. It's true that there are electric streetcars there, and space-age gas stations with uniformed attendants who rush to help you from all directions at once. There are also golden pagodas on shimmering lakes, and Shinto shrines in the forests. There are bamboo groves and nightingales. And finally

My Notes

there are more invisible guidelines for politeness than I could fathom. When I stepped on a streetcar, a full head taller than all the other passengers, I became an awkward giant. I took up too much space. I blended in like Igor would blend in with the corps de ballet in *Swan Lake*. I bumped into people. I crossed my arms when I listened, which turns out to be, in Japanese body language, the sign for indicating brazenly that one is bored.

But I wasn't! I was struggling through my days and nights in the grip of boredom's opposite—i.e., panic. I didn't know how to eat noodle soup with chopsticks, and I did it most picturesquely *wrong*. I didn't know how to order, so I politely deferred to my hosts and more than once was served a cuisine with heads, including eyeballs. I managed to wrestle these creatures to my lips with chopsticks, but it was already too late by the time I got the message that *one does not spit out anything*.

I undertook this trip in high summer, when it is surprisingly humid and warm in southern Japan. I never imagined that in such sweltering heat women would be expected to wear stockings, but every woman in Kyoto wore nylon stockings. Coeds in shorts *on the tennis court* wore nylon stockings. I had packed only skirts and sandals; people averted their eyes.

When I went to Japan I took my Altitude, my Bare-naked legs, my Callous foreign ways. I was mortified.

My hosts explained to me that the Japanese language does not accommodate insults, only infinite degrees of apology. I quickly memorized an urgent one, "*Sumimasen*," and another for especially extreme cases, "*Moshi wake gozaimasen*." This translates approximately to mean, "If you please, my transgression is so inexcusable that I wish I were dead."

I needed these words. When I touched the outside surface of a palace wall, curious to know what it was made of, I set off screeching alarms and a police car came scooting up the lawn's discreet gravel path. "*Moshi wake gozaimasen*, Officer! Wish I were dead!" And in the public bath, try as I might, I couldn't get the hang of showering with a hand-held nozzle while sitting fourteen inches from a stranger. I sprayed my elderly neighbor with cold water. In the face.

"*Moshi wake gozaimasen*," I declared, with feeling.

She merely stared, dismayed by the foreign menace.

I visited a Japanese friend, and in her small, perfect house I spewed out my misery. "Everything I do is wrong!" I wailed like a child. "I'm a blight on your country."

"Oh, no," she said calmly. "To forgive, for us, is the highest satisfaction. To forgive a foreigner, ah! Even better." She smiled. "You have probably made many people happy here."

> ## GRAMMAR & USAGE
>
> Formal diction often requires the use of the **subjunctive** form, or mood, of a verb to express doubts, wishes, or possibilities. Kingsolver uses the subjunctive (*were*) to express a wish in this sentence:
>
> ...I wish I **were** dead.

Why Choose Humor?

To stomp about the world ignoring cultural differences is arrogant, to be sure, but perhaps there is another kind of arrogance in the presumption that we may ever really build a faultless bridge from one shore to another, or even know where the mist has ceded to landfall. When I finally arrived at Ground Zero in Hiroshima, I stood speechless. What I found there was a vast and exquisitely silent monument to forgiveness. I was moved beyond words, even beyond tears, to think of all that can be lost or gained in the gulf between any act of will and its consequences. In the course of every failure of understanding, we have so much to learn.

I remembered my Japanese friend's insistence on forgiveness as the highest satisfaction, and I understood it really for the first time: What a rich wisdom it would be, and how much more bountiful a harvest, to gain pleasure not from achieving personal perfection but from understanding the inevitability of imperfection and pardoning those who also fall short of it.

I have walked among men and made mistakes without number. When I went to Japan I took my Abject goodwill, my Baleful excuses, my Cringing remorse. I couldn't remember everything, could not even recite the proper alphabet. So I gave myself away instead, evidently as a kind of public service. I prepared to return home feeling empty-handed.

At the Osaka Airport I sat in my plane on the runway, waiting to leave for terra cognita, as the aircraft's steel walls were buffeted by the sleet and winds of a typhoon. We waited for an hour, then longer, with no official word from the cockpit, and then suddenly our flight was canceled. Air traffic control in Tokyo had been struck by lightning; no flights possible until the following day.

"We are so sorry," the pilot told us. "You will be taken to a hotel, fed, and brought back here for your flight tomorrow."

As we passengers rose slowly and disembarked, we were met by an airline official who had been posted in the exit port for the sole purpose of saying to each and every one of us, "Terrible, terrible. *Sumimasen*." Other travelers nodded indifferently, but not me. I took the startled gentleman by the hands and practically kissed him.

"You have no idea," I told him, "how thoroughly I forgive you."

S	
Subject	
O	
Occasion	
A	
Audience	
P	
Purpose	
S	
Speaker	
Tone	

Why Choose Humor?

Use the following Venn diagram to indicate how the Dave Barry and Barbara Kingsolver essays are similar and different. Before you fill in the diagram below, ask yourself the following questions:

- How did the authors relate their experiences?
- What universal truths about life and society does each text convey?
- What tone did the authors use in relating their experiences?
- What kinds of reactions did each author elicit from readers?
- Compare and contrast the forms of narration (for example, first-person narrative, varying personas) the writers use to convey perspective about a cultural encounter.

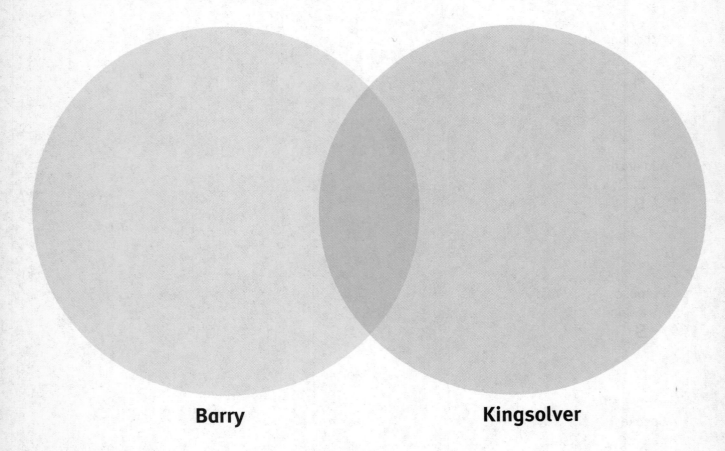

Barry　　　　　　　　**Kingsolver**

Writing Prompt: Imagine that you are interviewing each author. Write two to three questions in the subjunctive form to elicit responses on doubts about their preparations for or experiences in a foreign country.

SUGGESTED LEARNING STRATEGIES: SIFT, Graphic Organizer

Short Story

ABOUT THE AUTHOR

Alice Walker (1944–) is a novelist, poet, and essayist who established her reputation with the publication of *The Color Purple* (1982), which won the Pulitzer Prize and the American Book Award and tells of a young woman's efforts to overcome the obstacles posed by racism, sexism, and poverty. Critics have praised Walker's sensitivity to the points of view and problems of characters from different walks of life.

'EverydayUSE'

by Alice Walker

I will wait for her in the yard that Maggie and I made so clean and wavy yesterday afternoon. A yard like this is more comfortable than most people know. It is not just a yard. It is like an extended living room. When the hard clay is swept clean as a floor and the fine sand around the edges lined with tiny, irregular grooves, anyone can come and sit and look up into the elm tree and wait for the breezes that never come inside the house.

Maggie will be nervous until after her sister goes: She will stand hopelessly in corners, homely and ashamed of the burn scars down her arms and legs, eyeing her sister with a mixture of envy and awe. She thinks her sister had held life always in the palm of one hand, that "no" is a word the world never learned to say to her.

You've no doubt seen those TV shows where the child who has "made it" is confronted, as a surprise, by her own mother and father, tottering in weakly from backstage. (A pleasant surprise, of course: What would they do if parent and child came on the show only to curse out and insult each other?) On TV mother and child embrace and smile into each other's faces. Sometimes the mother and father weep; the child wraps them in her arms and leans across the table to tell how she would not have made it without their help. I have seen these programs.

My Notes

Sometimes I dream a dream in which Dee and I are suddenly brought together on a TV program of this sort. Out of a dark and softseated limousine I am ushered into a bright room filled with many people. There I meet a smiling, gray, sporty man like Johnny Carson and he shakes my hand and tells me what a fine girl I have. Then we are on the stage, and Dee is embracing me with tears in her eyes. She pins on my dress a large orchid, even though she had told me once that she thinks orchids are tacky flowers.

In real life I am a large, big-boned woman with rough, man-working hands. In the winter I wear flannel nightgowns to bed and overalls during the day. I can kill and clean a hog as mercilessly as a man. My fat keeps me hot in zero weather. I can work outside all day, breaking ice to get water for washing; I can eat pork liver cooked over the open fire minutes after it comes steaming from the hog. One winter I knocked a bull calf straight in the brain between the eyes with a sledgehammer and had the meat hung up to chill before nightfall. But of course all this does not show on television. I am the way my daughter would want me to be: a hundred pounds lighter, my skin like an uncooked barley pancake. My hair glistens in the hot bright lights. Johnny Carson has much to do to keep up with my quick and witty tongue.

But that is a mistake. I know even before I wake up. Who ever knew a Johnson with a quick tongue? Who can even imagine me looking a strange white man in the eye? It seems to me I have talked to them always with one foot raised in flight, with my head turned in whichever way is farthest from them. Dee, though. She would always look anyone in the eye. Hesitation was no part of her nature.

"How do I look, Mama?" Maggie says, showing just enough of her thin body enveloped in pink skirt and red blouse for me to know she's there, almost hidden by the door.

"Come out into the yard," I say.

Have you ever seen a lame animal, perhaps a dog run over by some careless person rich enough to own a car, sidle up to someone who is ignorant enough to be kind to him? That is the way my Maggie walks. She has been like this, chin on chest, eyes on ground, feet in shuffle, ever since the fire that burned the other house to the ground.

Dee is lighter than Maggie, with nicer hair and a fuller figure. She's a woman now, though sometimes I forget. How long ago was it that the other house burned? Ten, twelve years? Sometimes I can still hear the flames and feel Maggie's arms sticking to me, her hair smoking and her dress falling off her in little black papery flakes. Her eyes seemed stretched open, blazed open by the flames reflected in them. And Dee. I see her standing off under the sweet gum tree she used to dig gum out of, a look of concentration on her face as she watched the last dingy gray board of the house fall in toward the red-hot brick chimney. Why don't you do a dance around the ashes? I'd wanted to ask her. She had hated the house that much.

My Notes

I used to think she hated Maggie, too. But that was before we raised the money, the church and me, to send her to Augusta to school. She used to read to us without pity, forcing words, lies, other folks' habits, whole lives upon us two, sitting trapped and ignorant underneath her voice. She washed us in a river of make-believe, burned us with a lot of knowledge we didn't necessarily need to know. Pressed us to her with the serious ways she read, to shove us away at just the moment, like dimwits, we seemed about to understand.

Dee wanted nice things. A yellow organdy dress to wear to her graduation from high school; black pumps to match a green suit she'd made from an old suit somebody gave me. She was determined to stare down any disaster in her efforts. Her eyelids would not flicker for minutes at a time. Often I fought off the temptation to shake her. At sixteen she had a style of her own: and knew what style was.

I never had an education myself. After second grade the school closed down. Don't ask me why: In 1927 colored asked fewer questions than they do now. Sometimes Maggie reads to me. She stumbles along good-naturedly but can't see well. She knows she is not bright. Like good looks and money, quickness passed her by. She will marry John Thomas (who has mossy teeth in an earnest face), and then I'll be free to sit here and I guess just sing church songs to myself. Although I never was a good singer. Never could carry a tune. I was always better at a man's job. I used to love to milk till I was hooked in the side in '49. Cows are soothing and slow and don't bother you, unless you try to milk them the wrong way.

I have deliberately turned my back on the house. It is three rooms, just like the one that burned, except the roof is tin; they don't make shingle roofs anymore. There are no real windows, just some holes cut in the sides, like the portholes in a ship, but not round and not square, with rawhide holding the shutters up on the outside. This house is in a pasture, too, like the other one. No doubt when Dee sees it she will want to tear it down. She wrote me once that no matter where we "choose" to live, she will manage to come see us. But she will never bring her friends. Maggie and I thought about this and Maggie asked me, "Mama, when did Dee ever have any friends?"

She had a few. Furtive boys in pink shirts hanging about on washday after school. Nervous girls who never laughed. Impressed with her, they worshiped the well-turned phrase, the cute shape, the scalding humor that erupted like bubbles in lye. She read to them.

When she was courting Jimmy T, she didn't have much time to pay to us but turned all her faultfinding power on him. He *flew* to marry a cheap city girl from a family of ignorant, flashy people. She hardly had time to recompose herself.

When she comes, I will meet—but there they are!

A Family Perspective on Heritage

My Notes

GRAMMAR & USAGE

Commas (or lack of them) can establish or clarify subtlety of meaning in a sentence.

Phrases that are not essential to the meaning of a sentence are set off with commas. These are **nonrestrictive** phrases. Others are essential (**restrictive**) to the meaning; therefore, no commas are used. Examples:

Nonrestrictive participial phrase: She turns, **showing white heels through her sandals,**... (This phrase is not essential; it is set off with commas.)

Restrictive participial phrases: ...picture after picture of me **sitting there in front of the house** with Maggie **cowering behind me.** (Both of these phrases are essential, so no commas are used.)

Maggie attempts to make a dash for the house, in her shuffling way, but I stay her with my hand. "Come back here," I say. And she stops and tries to dig a well in the sand with her toe.

It is hard to see them clearly through the strong sun. But even the first glimpse of leg out of the car tells me it is Dee. Her feet were always neat looking, as if God himself shaped them with a certain style. From the other side of the car comes a short, stocky man. Hair is all over his head a foot long and hanging from his chin like a kinky mule tail. I hear Maggie suck in her breath. "Uhnnnh" is what it sounds like. Like when you see the wriggling end of a snake just in front of your foot on the road. "Uhnnnh."

Dee next. A dress down to the ground, in this hot weather. A dress so loud it hurts my eyes. There are yellows and oranges enough to throw back the light of the sun. I feel my whole face warming from the heat waves it throws out. Earrings gold, too, and hanging down to her shoulders. Bracelets dangling and making noises when she moves her arm up to shake the folds of the dress out of her armpits. The dress is loose and flows, and as she walks closer, I like it. I hear Maggie go "Uhnnnh" again. It is her sister's hair. It stands straight up like the wool on a sheep. It is black as night and around the edges are two long pigtails that rope about like small lizards disappearing behind her ears.

"Wa-su-zo-Tean-o!" she says, coming on in that gliding way the dress makes her move. The short, stocky fellow with the hair to his navel is all grinning, and he follows up with "Asalamalakim, my mother and sister!" He moves to hug Maggie but she falls back, right up against the back of my chair. I feel her trembling there, and when I look up I see the perspiration falling off her chin.

"Don't get up," says Dee. Since I am stout, it takes something of a push. You can see me trying to move a second or two before I make it. She turns, showing white heels through her sandals, and goes back to the car. Out she peeks next with a Polaroid. She stoops down quickly and lines up picture after picture of me sitting there in front of the house with Maggie cowering behind me. She never takes a shot without making sure the house is included. When a cow comes nibbling around in the edge of the yard, she snaps it and me and Maggie *and* the house. Then she puts the Polaroid in the back seat of the car and comes up and kisses me on the forehead.

Meanwhile, Asalamalakim is going through motions with Maggie's hand. Maggie's hand is as limp as a fish, and probably as cold, despite the sweat, and she keeps trying to pull it back. It looks like Asalamalakim wants to shake hands but wants to do it fancy. Or maybe he don't know how people shake hands. Anyhow, he soon gives up on Maggie.

"Well," I say. "Dee."

"No, Mama," she says. "Not 'Dee,' Wangero Leewanika Kemanjo!"

"What happened to Dee'?" I wanted to know.

"She's dead," Wangero said. "I couldn't bear it any longer, being named after the people who oppress me."

"You know as well as me you was named after your aunt Dicie," I said. Dicie is my sister. She named Dee. We called her "Big Dee" after Dee was born.

"But who was *she* named after?" asked Wangero.

"I guess after Grandma Dee," I said.

"And who was she named after?" asked Wangero.

"Her mother," I said, and saw Wangero was getting tired. "That's about as far back as I can trace it," I said. Though, in fact, I probably could have carried it back beyond the Civil War through the branches.

"Well," said Asalamalakim, "there you are."

"Uhnnnh," I heard Maggie say.

"There I was not," I said, "before 'Dicie' cropped up in our family, so why should I try to trace it that far back?"

He just stood there grinning, looking down on me like somebody inspecting a Model A car. Every once in a while he and Wangero sent eye signals over my head.

"How do you pronounce this name?" I asked.

"You don't have to call me by it if you don't want to," said Wangero.

"Why shouldn't I?" I asked. "If that's what you want us to call you, we'll call you."

"I know it might sound awkward at first," said Wangero.

"I'll get used to it," I said. "Ream it out again."

Well, soon we got the name out of the way. Asalamalakim had a name twice as long and three times as hard. After I tripped over it two or three times, he told me to just call him Hakim-a-barber. I wanted to ask him was he a barber, but I didn't really think he was, so I didn't ask.

"You must belong to those beef-cattle peoples down the road," I said. They said "Asalamalakim" when they met you, too, but they didn't shake hands. Always too busy: feeding the cattle, fixing the fences, putting up salt-lick shelters, throwing down hay. When the white folks poisoned some of the herd, the men stayed up all night with rifles in their hands. I walked a mile and a half just to see the sight.

My Notes

A Family Perspective on Heritage

Hakim-a-barber said, "I accept some of their doctrines, but farming and raising cattle is not my style." (They didn't tell me, and I didn't ask, whether Wangero—Dee—had really gone and married him.)

We sat down to eat and right away he said he didn't eat collards, and pork was unclean. Wangero, though, went on through the chitlins and corn bread, the greens, and everything else. She talked a blue streak over the sweet potatoes. Everything delighted her. Even the fact that we still used the benches her daddy made for the table when we couldn't afford to buy chairs.

"Oh, Mama!" she cried. Then turned to Hakim-a-barber. "I never knew how lovely these benches are. You can feel the rump prints," she said, running her hands underneath her and along the bench. Then she gave a sigh, and her hand closed over Grandma Dee's butter dish. "That's it!" she said. "I knew there was something I wanted to ask you if I could have." She jumped up from the table and went over in the corner where the churn stood, the milk in it clabber by now. She looked at the churn and looked at it.

"This churn top is what I need," she said. "Didn't Uncle Buddy whittle it out of a tree you all used to have?"

"Yes," I said.

"Uh huh," she said happily. "And I want the dasher, too."

"Uncle Buddy whittle that, too?" asked the barber.

Dee (Wangero) looked up at me.

"Aunt Dee's first husband whittled the dash," said Maggie so low you almost couldn't hear her. "His name was Henry, but they called him Stash."

"Maggie's brain is like an elephant's," Wangero said, laughing. "I can use the churn top as a centerpiece for the alcove table," she said, sliding a plate over the churn, "and I'll think of something artistic to do with the dasher."

When she finished wrapping the dasher, the handle stuck out. I took it for a moment in my hands. You didn't even have to look close to see where hands pushing the dasher up and down to make butter had left a kind of sink in the wood. In fact, there were a lot of small sinks; you could see where thumbs and fingers had sunk into the wood. It was beautiful light-yellow wood, from a tree that grew in the yard where Big Dee and Stash had lived.

After dinner Dee (Wangero) went to the trunk at the foot of my bed and started rifling through it. Maggie hung back in the kitchen over the dishpan. Out came Wangero with two quilts. They had been pieced by Grandma Dee, and then Big Dee and me had hung them on the quilt frames on the front porch and quilted them. One was in the Lone Star pattern. The other was Walk Around the Mountain. In both of them were scraps of dresses Grandma Dee had worn fifty and more years ago. Bits and pieces of Grandpa Jarrell's paisley shirts. And one teeny faded blue piece, about the size of a penny matchbox, that was from Great Grandpa Ezra's uniform that he wore in the Civil War.

"Mama," Wangero said sweet as a bird. "Can I have these old quilts?"

I heard something fall in the kitchen, and a minute later the kitchen door slammed.

"Why don't you take one or two of the others?" I asked. "These old things was just done by me and Big Dee from some tops your grandma pieced before she died."

"No," said Wangero. "I don't want those. They are stitched around the borders by machine."

"That'll make them last better," I said.

"That's not the point," said Wangero. "These are all pieces of dresses Grandma used to wear. She did all this stitching by hand. Imagine!" She held the quilts securely in her arms, stroking them.

"Some of the pieces, like those lavender ones, come from old clothes her mother handed down to her," I said, moving up to touch the quilts. Dee (Wangero) moved back just enough so that I couldn't reach the quilts. They already belonged to her.

"Imagine!" she breathed again, clutching them closely to her bosom.

"The truth is," I said, "I promised to give them quilts to Maggie, for when she marries John Thomas."

She gasped like a bee had stung her.

"Maggie can't appreciate these quilts!" she said. "She'd probably be backward enough to put them to everyday use."

"I reckon she would," I said. "God knows I been saving 'em for long enough with nobody using 'em. I hope she will!" I didn't want to bring up how I had offered Dee (Wangero) a quilt when she went away to college. Then she had told me they were old-fashioned, out of style.

"But they're *priceless*!" she was saying now, furiously; for she has a temper. "Maggie would put them on the bed and in five years they'd be in rags. Less than that!"

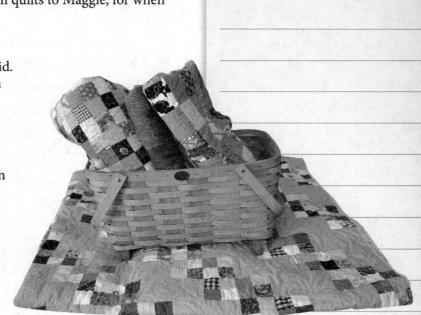

"She can always make some more," I said. "Maggie knows how to quilt."

Dee (Wangero) looked at me with hatred. "You just will not understand. The point is *these* quilts, these quilts!"

"Well," I said, stumped. "What would you do with them?"

"Hang them," she said. As if that was the only thing you *could* do with quilts.

Maggie by now was standing in the door. I could almost hear the sound her feet made as they scraped over each other.

"She can have them, Mama," she said, like somebody used to never winning anything or having anything reserved for her. "I can 'member Grandma Dee without the quilts."

I looked at her hard. She had filled her bottom lip with checkerberry snuff, and it gave her face a kind of dopey, hangdog look. It was Grandma Dee and Big Dee who taught her how to quilt herself. She stood there with her scarred hands hidden in the folds of her skirt. She looked at her sister with something like fear, but she wasn't mad at her. This was Maggie's portion. This was the way she knew God to work.

When I looked at her like that, something hit me in the top of my head and ran down to the soles of my feet. Just like when I'm in church and the spirit of God touches me and I get happy and shout. I did something I never had done before: hugged Maggie to me, then dragged her on into the room, snatched the quilts out of Miss Wangero's hands, and dumped them into Maggie's lap. Maggie just sat there on my bed with her mouth open.

"Take one or two of the others," I said to Dee. But she turned without a word and went out to Hakim-a-barber.

"You just don't understand," she said, as Maggie and I came out to the car.

"What don't I understand?" I wanted to know.

"Your heritage," she said. And then she turned to Maggie, kissed her, and said, "You ought to try to make something of yourself, too, Maggie. It's really a new day for us. But from the way you and Mama still live, you'd never know it."

She put on some sunglasses that hid everything above the tip of her nose and her chin.

Maggie smiled, maybe at the sunglasses. But a real smile, not scared. After we watched the car dust settle, I asked Maggie to bring me a dip of snuff. And then the two of us sat there just enjoying, until it was time to go in the house and go to bed.

Symbols

Images

Figures of Speech

Tone/Theme

Synthesis: Drafting Your Position

Remember that a synthesis essay expects you to present a position on an issue and then synthesize and incorporate perspectives from multiple sources, including your own experiences, in support of that position. For this activity, you will work in a group to create a group synthesis essay. Begin by reading and discussing the prompt below and then brainstorming three different ways one could respond to this type of prompt—by defending, challenging, or qualifying it.

Prompt: To what extent does a person's culture inform the way he or she views others and the world?

Response #1 (Defend):

Response #2 (Challenge):

Response #3 (Qualify):

Group Brainstorm: Review texts you read in Units 1 and 2. Determine how you could use several of those texts to defend, challenge, or qualify the prompt.

Individual Brainstorm: On a separate piece of paper, consider the texts you have read as well as your own personal experiences. Then quickwrite a response to the prompt.

Group Consensus: After sharing and discussing your individual quickwrites, work together as a group to reach a consensus on the position you will adopt in your group essay.

Synthesis: Presenting Your Position

SUGGESTED LEARNING STRATEGIES: Rereading, Drafting, Graphic Organizer, Role Playing

Each member of your group should select an author of a text from the unit that is relevant to the conversation about how culture informs perspective. Your task is to reread the text and fill in the graphic organizer below. When you have finished, be prepared to report your findings to your group.

What is your group's position?	
Which author is relevant to the conversation? Why?	
Would he/she agree, disagree, or qualify your position?	
What specific examples could you use to support/refute the claim? (Include at least three.)	

After reporting your findings to your group and discussing your answers, write your revised thesis on separate paper.

Writing a Synthesis Paper

SUGGESTED LEARNING STRATEGIES: **Drafting, Sharing and Responding, Peer Editing**

Assignment

Your assignment is to write an essay in which you analyze how cultural identity influences an individual's perspective. You will work in groups to compose a group essay that responds to the following synthesis prompt:

To what extent does one's culture inform the way one views others and the world?

Support your claim with evidence from at least three different texts you have read, viewed, or listened to this year, as well as personal experience and insights.

Steps

Prewriting

1. In previous activities, your group should have defined a preliminary thesis for your argument about how a person's culture shapes his or her individual perspective. In addition, you should have reviewed texts and compiled a list of ways in which the attitudes and actions of the authors were influenced by their cultural backgrounds.

2. Now that you have identified your thesis and identified supporting evidence, choose an organizational framework for your essay. Consider the following questions, which address the structural elements of an argument—hook, claim, support, concessions/refutations, and call to action.

   a. What makes your hook interesting enough to grab readers' attention?

   b. What are your best supporting examples of types of influence?

   c. What is the most effective way to present or organize your supporting evidence?

   d. What are your concessions and refutations?

   e. What makes your call to action effective?

3. When your organizational framework is clear to all members of your group, assign each individual (or partner group) a chunk to compose. Consider writing the body paragraphs separately and then composing your opening and conclusion as a group. This strategy can help you synthesize your information.

Drafting

4. Draft your essay with each group member contributing a section. Be sure to build your essay around your thesis, supporting it with claims identifying cultural influences on attitudes and actions and textual evidence from your readings.

5. Synthesize evidence from your sources into your paragraphs, using correct punctuation for quotations and the format your teacher provides for in-text parenthetical citations.

Evaluating/Revising

6. After you have written your rough draft, engage in peer response (sharing and responding) with members of your writing group. Members of the writing group should specifically address the following revision questions:

   - Is the thesis clear and well developed?

   - How can we add or revise transitions between the paragraphs to make the essay flow easily from one idea to the next?

   - Have we included textual evidence in the form of paraphrases and quotations, with commentary about each piece of evidence? Can we clearly identify the evidence and commentary?

   - Can we revise quotations, using phrases rather than complete sentences from the original?

   - Evaluate the degree to which you have included a variety of texts and experiences as evidence.

7. Listen to the feedback of group members and revise your essay to address their comments. In addition, consider your purpose, audience, and the essay genre and revise your draft to address questions relating to each. Also revise to improve style, word choice, figurative language, sentence variety, and subtlety of meaning.

Editing

8. Each member of your group should read the draft silently, marking corrections in grammar, punctuation, and spelling. Use available resources (dictionary, grammar handbooks, spell-check, etc.) to complete your peer editing and produce a technically sound draft.

9. Read your draft to generate a list of possible titles. Discuss the titles and choose an appropriate one for the group essay.

10. Submit your final draft in legible handwriting, or use a word processing program to create a typed draft. Be sure to include a works cited page.

....

↗**TECHNOLOGY TIP** If you are using a word processing program to create your essay, take advantage of its spell-check features to help avoid errors. You may also want to use the grammar-check feature, but do not automatically accept all changes. For example, most grammar-checking software recognizes direct sentences (those that start with a verb, such as "Get off the sofa.") as sentence fragments. Many also do not distinguish contractions or possessives correctly, so be sure the change is one you want to make before accepting it.

SCORING GUIDE

Scoring Criteria	Exemplary	Proficient	Emerging
Ideas	The essay takes a definite position on culture's impact on individual perspectives. The argument is extraordinarily developed and convincing throughout the essay and is based on the integration of illustrative examples from a variety of texts and personal insight.	The essay takes a clear position on culture's impact on individual perspectives, but the thesis may not be clearly developed or supported throughout. The argument is plausible and draws on the integration of evidence from relevant sources.	The essay takes a position that is difficult to distinguish; the development of culture's impact on individual perspective is lacking. The argument may be less convincing, using inadequate evidence from minimal sources as support.
Organization	Organization is exceptional. Ideas are presented and connected with sophisticated transitions in an order most conducive to a coherent argument.	Organization is clear and easy to follow. Ideas are logically arranged to support the argument with transitions that promote connection and flow.	Organization does not fully support the argument, demonstrating a weak arrangement of ideas and limited or awkward transitions throughout.
Use of Language	Diction and syntax reflect an authentic, confident, authoritative voice.	Diction and syntax reflect a convincing and appropriate voice.	Diction and syntax do not reflect a convincing or confident voice.
Conventions	The writing demonstrates strong control and mastery of standard conventions. Either no errors appear, or they are so slight that they do not interfere with the meaning. Evidence from sources is accurately embedded into the text with correct punctuation and parenthetical citation.	The writing demonstrates control of standard writing conventions. Though some errors may appear, they do not seriously impede readability. Evidence from sources is embedded into the text with general correctness in punctuation and parenthetical citation.	There are frequent errors in standard conventions that seriously interfere with the meaning. Evidence from sources embedded into the text is incorrectly punctuated and/or cited.

SCORING GUIDE

Scoring Criteria	Exemplary	Proficient	Emerging
Evidence of the Writing Process	The writing demonstrates thoughtful planning, significant revision, and careful editing in preparing a publishable draft.	The writing demonstrates planning, revision, and editing in preparing a publishable draft.	The writing lacks evidence of planning, revision, and / or editing. The draft is not ready for publication.
Additional Criteria			

Comments: _____

_____

_____

_____

_____

Reflection

An important aspect of growing as a learner is to reflect on where you have been, what you have accomplished, what helped you to learn, and how you will apply your new knowledge in the future. Use the following questions to guide your thinking and to identify evidence of your learning. Use separate notebook paper.

Thinking about Concepts

1. Using specific examples from this unit, respond to the Essential Questions:

   • How do external factors affect one's sense of identity?

   • How do we synthesize multiple sources of information into a cohesive argument?

2. Consider the new academic vocabulary from this unit (**Persona, Juxtaposition, Cultural Conflict, Satire, Humor, Synthesis, Argument, Theatrical Elements**) as well as academic vocabulary from previous units, and select 3-4 terms of which your understanding has grown. For each term, answer the following questions:

   • What was your understanding of the word prior to the unit?

   • How has your understanding of the word evolved throughout the unit?

   • How will you apply your understanding in the future?

Thinking about Connections

3. Review the activities and products (artifacts) you created. Choose those that most reflect your growth or increase in understanding.

4. For each artifact that you choose, record, respond to, and reflect on your thinking and understanding, using the following questions as a guide:

   a. What skill/knowledge does this artifact reflect, and how did you learn this skill/knowledge?

   b. How did your understanding of the power of language expand through your engagement with this artifact?

   c. How will you apply this skill or knowledge in the future?

5. Create this reflection as Portfolio pages—one for each artifact you choose. Use the model in the box for your headings and commentary on questions.

Thinking About Thinking
Portfolio Entry

Concept:

Description of Artifact:

Commentary on Questions:

Community

Essential Questions

? How can an author use a work of fiction to make a statement about culture?

? How might the cultural fabric of a community be stretched or altered when it encounters new ideas and members?

Unit Overview

"Until the lion has a voice, stories of safaris will always glorify the hunter." To illustrate this African proverb, Chinua Achebe wrote the acclaimed novel *Things Fall Apart*, in which he provides a powerful voice for the Ibo, a community nearly silenced by European colonialism. In this unit, you will continue your exploration of culture by reading and studying Achebe's novel. By immersing yourself in the culture and community of the Ibo people, you will analyze a complex community, the institutions that enable it to function, the conflicting roles of its members, and the way in which it is affected by political and social change. Your opinions of the Ibo community's response to change may be positive, negative, or mixed; however, like millions of others who have read the novel, you may find that the characters and community of *Things Fall Apart* remain with you long after your study is complete.

Unit 3 Community

Goals

▶ To analyze character relationships and motives in a literary work

▶ To apply academic writing skills to a literary analysis

▶ To research and make connections between one's culture and the culture of another time and place

Contents

Texts not included in these materials.

Learning Focus:

Connecting to an Unfamiliar Community

You should now have a pretty good idea of what a culture is and what it means to people. As you explored the ideas of culture, you reviewed the concept of **voice** and learned to write an effective **argument** and a **synthesis paper**. Unlike simply reading a novel, studying a novel requires careful reading, skillful annotation, and deliberate effort to make connections between the novel and your own life, other texts, and the real world. This is especially true of a text that presents a cultural world foreign to the culture in which you live. As you have begun to realize, though, certain aspects of culture remain constant: family, community, food, religion, social organization, and government. All cultures are organized around these and other essential elements.

Things Fall Apart tells the story of an African community and its response to outsiders and their cultural influences. In the first part of the unit, you will read the novel and familiarize yourself with the culture of an imaginary African village, Umuofia. In order to help you and your classmates make connections between your community and Umuofia, you will research aspects of Ibo culture described in the novel. You will hone your research skills by learning to find, evaluate, and cite sources, take meaningful notes, write without plagiarizing, and synthesize your findings. Finally, you will work with your classmates to plan and present an oral presentation—complete with visuals—of your research. As you view your classmates' presentations, you will practice effective listening skills and look for meaningful connections between the Ibo culture and your own.

Independent Reading: In this unit, you will read a novel as well as companion pieces to expand your knowledge of culture and how a community's culture can be affected by outside influences. For independent reading, look for texts that explore the thematic concept of culture and community.

Previewing the Unit

SUGGESTED LEARNING STRATEGIES: Quickwrite, Close Reading, Previewing, Marking the Text, Summarizing/Paraphrasing, Graphic Organizer, Think-Pair-Share

Essential Questions

1. How can an author use a work of fiction to make a statement about culture?

2. How might the cultural fabric of a community be stretched or altered when it encounters new ideas and members?

Unit Overview and Learning Focus

Predict what you think this unit is about. Use the words or phrases that stood out when you read the Unit Overview and the Learning Focus.

Embedded Assessment

What knowledge must you have (what do you need to know)? What skills must you have (what will you need to do to complete the Embedded Assessment successfully)? Write your responses below.

Palatable Proverbs and Fascinating Folk Tales

LITERARY TERMS

A **folk tale** is a story without a known author that has been preserved through oral retellings.

An **oral tradition** is the passing down of stories, tales, proverbs, and other culturally important stories and ideas through oral retellings.

In your study of culture in earlier units, you have learned about the traditions and beliefs of groups of people. Traditions and beliefs are often passed from one generation to the next orally, usually through storytelling. Proverbs and **folk tales** are one part of a culture's **oral tradition**. People share proverbs and folk tales in order to express important stories, ideas, and beliefs about their culture. Proverbs and folk tales are short but also entertaining and memorable.

As you read the novel *Things Fall Apart*, you will encounter many proverbs and folk tales that illustrate the beliefs of the Ibo people. One memorable Ibo proverb is "Proverbs are the palm oil with which words are eaten." Discuss the proverb with your classmates and your teacher. What do you think it means?

Listed below are additional proverbs from *Things Fall Apart*. Work with your group to discuss and explain each of them.

Proverb	Explanation
If a child washes his hands, he could eat with kings.	
When the moon is shining, the cripple becomes hungry for a walk.	
Since men have learned to shoot without missing, [the bird] has learned to fly without perching.	
A chick that will grow into a cock can be spotted the very day it hatches.	
The clan was like a lizard. If it lost its tail it soon grew another.	
I cannot live on the bank of a river and wash my hands with spittle.	
A man who pays respect to the great paves the way for his own greatness.	

In addition to proverbs, you will also encounter a number of folk tales in the novel. Use the organizer below to record details about the folk tales discussed in class. Then, either copy this organizer or create your own organizer to record details about the folk tales you find in *Things Fall Apart*, especially in Chapters 7, 9, 11, and 15.

> ## LITERARY TERMS
>
> A **symbol** is a person, place, thing, or event that stands for itself and also for a larger idea.
>
> An **archetype** is a pattern, symbol, image, or idea that recurs in literature.

Fascinating Folk tales

Characters:

Setting:

Plot Summary:

Symbols and Archetypes:

Meaning of the Folk Tale:

Significance (reason for its retelling across generations and its inclusion in the novel):

Introducing the Novel: Predictions and Pronunciations

SUGGESTED LEARNING STRATEGIES: **Think Aloud, Predicting, Quickwrite**

WORD CONNECTIONS

Predictions contains the root *-dict-*, from the Latin word *dicere*, meaning "to tell or say." This root also appears in *contradict, dictate,* and *dictionary.* The prefix *pre-* means "before." The suffix *-ion* indicates that the word is a noun.

As you examine the cover and epigraph of *Things Fall Apart*, what predictions can you make about the novel? Consider the title. To what "things" might Achebe be referring?

Copy the following names and pronunciations onto a blank bookmark supplied by your teacher.

Achebe	(Ah-chay-bay)	Nwoye	(Nuh-woh-yeh)
Chinua	(Chin-oo-ah)	Ojiubo	(Oh-jee-ooh-boh)
Ekwefi	(Eh-kweh-fee)	Okonkwo	(Oh-kawn-kwoh)
Ezinma	(Eh-zeen-mah)	Umuofia	(Oo-moo-oh-fee-ah)
Ikemefuna	(Ee-keh-meh-foo-nah)	Unoka	(Ooh-no-kah)
Obierika	(Oh-bee-air-ee-kah)		

Things Fall Apart focuses on a culture that may be unfamiliar to you. Even though the novel is written in English, the author uses words and phrases from his native Ibo language. Review the glossary at the back of the novel. Add additional words and definitions to your bookmark as you read. Consider including: *chi, ilo, nza,* and *obi.*

ABOUT THE AUTHOR

Chinua Achebe is one of Nigeria's most celebrated novelists. Born an Ibo in Ogidi, Nigeria in 1930, Achebe was educated in English. Since the 1960s, Achebe has taught English at the university level at colleges in Africa and the United States. His first and best-known novel, *Things Fall Apart*, was published in 1958. Since then, Achebe has written several novels, short story collections, and books of essays.

Relevant Research: Putting Text in Context

SUGGESTED LEARNING STRATEGIES: **KWHL Chart, Graphic Organizer, Notetaking, Paraphrasing, Word Map**

With group members, brainstorm a list of possible questions about your assigned topic. Use your questions to guide your group's research on one topic. Use note cards to gather information about your topic. After you listen to your classmates' presentations, fill in the organizer with information about their topics, or write information on separate paper.

Topic	Facts and Ideas
Chinua Achebe	
Nigeria: History	
Nigeria: Geography and Agriculture	
British Colonialism and Nigeria	
Missionary Involvement in Africa	
Tribal Life	

Locate a world map, and examine the geographical context of the novel. Write a research question and conduct research to deepen your knowledge of the Nigerian culture, Africa, British colonialism, and so on. Use this knowledge to help you understand the cultural, social, and historical contexts of *Things Fall Apart*.

Relevant Research: Putting Text in Context

The Internet provides access to a multitude of information. As with any other source, it is important to evaluate the **validity** and **reliability** of the information you find on the Internet. It is also important to determine who wrote the information to avoid **plagiarism**. Internet sites may not always give credit to original authors, so it is important to use sites that do give credit. As you research, keep good notes about your sources and direct quotations so you can cite them accurately. Note the URL as you may also want to revisit as needed to collect further information.

Use this chart to help you evaluate Internet sources. Look especially at the *authority* of the source (i.e., is the source's information written by experts in the field) and its *objectivity* (i.e., does the author demonstrate bias or an even-handed presentation of verifiable facts from which readers may draw conclusions).

Topics and Questions	Responses
The URL: (Check reliability/validity) • What is the Web site's domain? (.com = for-profit organization; .gov, .mil, .us (or other country code) = a government site; .edu = an educational institution; .org = a nonprofit organization) • Is this URL a professional or personal page? • Why might using information from a personal page be a problem?	List Web site (title and URL). What can you tell from the URL?
Sponsor: (Check objectivity/subjectivity) • What organization or group sponsors the Web page? • If it has a link (often called "About Us") that leads you to that information, what can you learn about the sponsor?	What can you learn about the page's sponsor?
Timeliness: (Check reliability and relevance) • When was the page last updated (usually posted at the top or bottom of the page)? A current date usually means the information is up-to-date.	What can you learn about the page's timeliness?
Purpose: (Check validity) • What is the purpose of the page? • Who is the target audience? • Does the page present information or opinion? Is the information objective or subjective? How do you know?	What can you tell about the page's purpose?
Author/Publisher: (Check authority) • Who publishes this page? If you don't know, try to find out whether the publisher is an expert on the topic. • What credentials does the author have? • Is this person or group considered an authority on the topic? How do you know?	What else can you learn about the author?
Links: (Check validity, reliability, authority, objectivity) • Does the page provide links that work? • Do the links go to authoritative sources? • Are they objective or subjective?	What can you tell from the links provided?

Culture Wheel

First, work with your group members to review the Ibo words and their definitions below. Then, place the words into the appropriate section of the Culture Wheel organizer on the following page. Finally, use art supplies to draw an artistic rendering of your Culture Wheel.

Glossary of Selected Ibo Words and Phrases*

agbala	woman; also used for a man who has taken no title
ani	earth goddess
chi	personal god
efulefu	worthless man
egwugwu	masquerader who impersonates one of the ancestral spirits of the village
ekwe	type of drum made from wood
foo foo	food made from yams that serves a chief role in the annual Feast of the New Yam
ilo	the village green where assemblies for sports, discussions, and so on take place
iyi-uwa	a special kind of stone that forms the link between an ogbanje and the spirit world (Only if the iyi-uwa were discovered and destroyed would the child not die.)
jigida	string of waist beads worn by women
kola nut	food used to greet visitors and guests
kwenu	shout of approval and greeting
ndichie	elders
obi	large living quarters of the head of the family
ochu	murder or manslaughter
ogbanje	changeling; a child who repeatedly dies and returns to its mother to be reborn
ogene	musical instrument; a kind of gong
osu	outcast (Having been dedicated to a god, the osu was taboo and not allowed to mix with the freeborn in any way.)
oye	one of the four market days
palm wine	fermented palm sap used for celebration and ceremony
udu	musical instrument; a type of drum made from pottery
yam	edible root; most valuable cash crop grown in the village

*Source: *Things Fall Apart*, Chinua Achebe (London: William Heinemann Ltd., 1958).

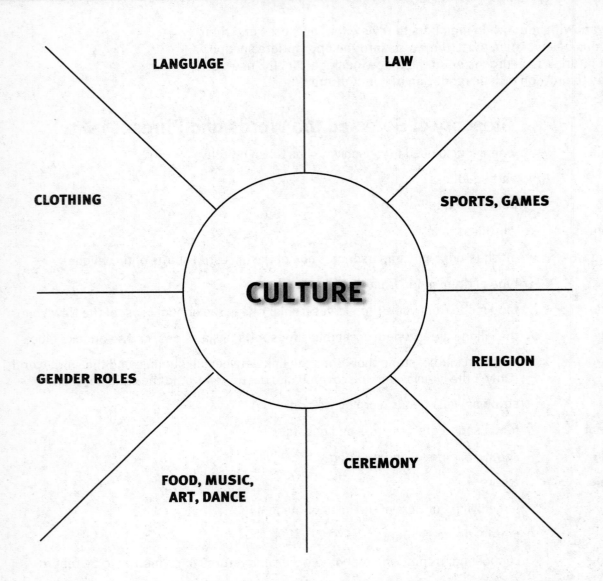

LANGUAGE

LAW

CLOTHING

SPORTS, GAMES

CULTURE

RELIGION

GENDER ROLES

CEREMONY

FOOD, MUSIC,
ART, DANCE

**WORD
CONNECTIONS**

Gender contains the root
-gen-, from the Greek
word *genos*, meaning
"race or class." This root
also appears in *engender*,
generate, and *genealogy*.

Embedded Assessment 1 is a group research and presentation project.
After you have selected a topic to research, work in your groups to
complete a project plan for your research. Your project plan should
include the following:

- Names of group members and contact information
- Meeting schedule
- Topic or research question
- Plan for collecting information
- Plan for critiquing the research process at each step to identify
  changes and revise or implement new steps as needed
- Rules and responsibilities of each group member

In the Beginning

Refer to your highlighted text to find facts and details that describe Okonkwo and his father. Compare the two men by writing facts and details about each in the Venn diagram below. What can you learn about Okonkwo by comparing him to his father?

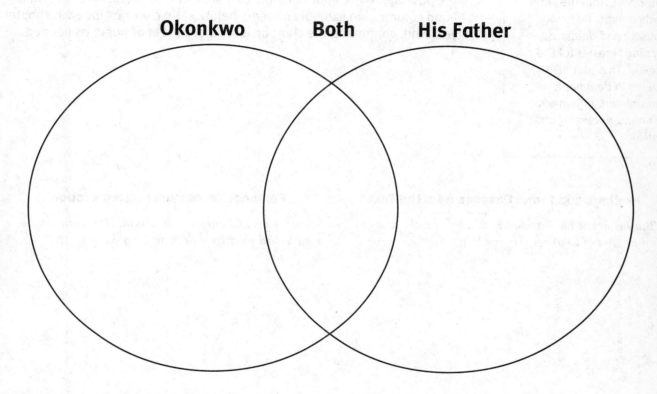

Okonkwo   **Both**   **His Father**

After reading and rereading the first chapter of the novel and completing the Venn diagram, compose a thesis statement for a paragraph that connects Okonkwo's character traits to his father's influence. Share your statement with a partner to make sure that the connection you make between the characters is clear.

Using specific details from the novel, write a paragraph. Include one or more direct quotations from the novel as textual support, but be careful not to simply restate what is written in the text. Your goal is to *synthesize* the information in one paragraph.

Find a picture of your vision of Okonkwo. Your picture can be either realistic or symbolic, and you may either draw it or find one.

Charting Fears and Feelings

WORD CONNECTIONS

Dominated contains the root *-dom-*, from the Latin words *domus*, meaning "house," and *dominus*, meaning "master (of the house)." This root also appears in *dominant*, *predominant*, *domineer*, *dominion*, *domestic*, and *domicile*.

As you read, look for examples of Okonkwo's dominant feelings and fears, the stated or implied reasons for those fears, and the effect of these fears on his actions. Write appropriate examples or passages in the left-hand column in the chart below. Be sure to list the page number of the passage. Write your personal response or interpretation in the right-hand column. (An example appears below.) Make entries for each chapter you read, continuing the chart on a separate sheet of paper as needed.

Feelings and Fears: Passage from the Text	Personal Response or Interpretation
"But his whole life was dominated by fear, the fear of failure and of weakness." (page 13)	I wonder why Okonkwo is so afraid. How could he be a successful wrestler if he is dominated by fear?

A Man of Prestige

In the first four chapters of *Things Fall Apart*, writer Achebe presents Okonkwo as a man of high status in his village. Fill in the chart below with details from those chapters, and compare Okonkwo's achievements and status to the traits and actions that sometimes contradict his nobility.

Okonkwo's Achievements and Status	Traits and Actions That Contradict His Nobility

Once your teacher has assigned you to a group, work with your group to draw Okonkwo's compound on a separate sheet of paper (using information from Chapter 2). Be sure to label any features of your drawing that are not clearly identified. Try to attach some three-dimensional objects to enhance your drawing. Ensure that each group member has contributed. Be prepared to display your group's drawing and explain it to the class.

A Man of Prestige

As you read about the Week of Peace, what were your thoughts? Does the idea of such a week sound appealing? If you could create a Week of Peace for your home, school, workplace, or community, what would it be like? Does your culture, like that of Umuofia, require a Week of Peace? Use the organizer below to plan your Peace Week. Then, create a poster or brochure inviting others to participate.

Planning a Week of Peace	
Time of Year	
Invited Guests	
Purpose of Feast	
Rules	
Punishment for Opposing the Plan	
Social Activities	
Predicted Outcomes	

Okonkwo's Family

After you have read Chapters 4, 5, and 6, work with a small group to note the names and relationships of the characters. Pay special attention to Okonkwo's family. Include quotes from the novel to support your ideas. Share your responses with a partner or group.

Character	Relationship to Okonkwo and others in the family	What do you learn about the character?	What is your reaction to the character?

Okonkwo's Family

Using the information you have learned about Nigerian culture, the notes you have taken in your journal, and the chapters you have read, complete the graphic organizer below to create Okonkwo's family tree. Write in each relative's name. Under each character's name, list two facts about him or her. Add additional boxes and connecting lines as needed.

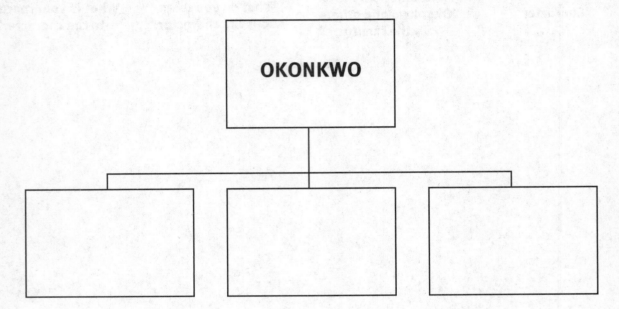

Writing Prompt: After you have completed the family tree, draft an analytical essay that answers the following question: How does Achebe's portrayal of Okonkwo's family relationships make Okonkwo a sympathetic and unsympathetic character?

Be sure to create a thesis statement that addresses the question, and include supporting details and appropriate quotations from the novel. Choose an organizing structure appropriate to the context of the question and the compare-contrast essay format. Remember to use transitional words and phrases that signal comparison and contrast, and use effective transitions between paragraphs. After you draft your essay, share your work with a partner to get feedback on the effectiveness of your transitional words and phrases.

An Ibo Tableau

SUGGESTED LEARNING STRATEGIES: **Role Playing**

Your teacher will assign you to a group. Work with your group members and follow the instructions below to create a tableau (a freeze-frame snapshot) of characters from *Things Fall Apart*.

Characters:

Okonkwo, first wife, Ojiubo, Chielo, Nwoye, Ikemefuna, Ezinma, Obierika, Ekwefi, Unoka

STEP ONE: Begin by writing the name of each character on its own index card. Give each group member a character card. Each group member will display the card of his or her character while standing in the tableau.

STEP TWO: If you are portraying a character, review the basic facts about your character. Then write a short statement that your character will deliver. The statement should begin with "I am..."; then state your character's name, and reveal an interesting fact about that character. Just as the characters' positions in the tableau will explain their relationships with one another, let the lines you write and the way you deliver them reveal your character's attitude and personality.

STEP THREE: With your group, decide where each character should stand, how he or she should pose, and where he or she should be positioned in relation to others. Be prepared to present your tableau to the class. You and fellow characters should strike the pose and then step out of the freeze-frame one at a time to deliver the lines you wrote in Step Two.

WORD CONNECTIONS

Tableau is a French word meaning a graphic description or representation. Unlike English words that usually form a plural by adding an "s" or "es," the plural of tableau is *tableaux*.

GRAMMAR & USAGE

Note the reciprocal pronoun "one another" in the next to last line of Step Two. This pronoun indicates that more than two characters' relationships are being described. Check your own writing to ensure that you are using the reciprocal pronouns "one another" and "each other" correctly.

Understanding a Pivotal Chapter

As you read Chapter 7, look for answers to the questions in the organizer below. Take notes on details in the text that support your answers to these questions. Write the page numbers next to each answer. On a separate sheet of paper, write two Level 2 and two Level 3 questions about your assigned question to use as part of a Socratic Seminar.

Question	Answer and Support	Page Number
How has Nwoye changed and what has caused the changes?		
Describe the arrival of the locusts. What is the reaction of the people of Umuofia?		
Do you think that Ikemefuna suspects that he is going to be killed? Why or why not?		
How does Okonkwo feel about Ikemefuna's death? How does Nwoye feel?		
Genesis 22:1–19 of The Bible presents the story of Abraham and Isaac. What similarities and differences are there in the sacrifices of Isaac and Ikemefuna? How does this incident illustrate the novel's father/son motif?		
How do you think the death of Ikemefuna will affect the relationship between Okonkwo and Nwoye?		
Okonkwo does not heed the advice of the old man, Ogbuefi Ezeudu. What consequences do you think there may be for his part in the death of Ikemefuna?		

You have examined several questions related to Chapter 7, shared information with your classmates, and participated in a class Socratic Seminar. Select one of the questions as the basis for an analytical paragraph. Before you draft your paragraph, look at your notes, which are probably written in an informal voice. As you draft your paragraph, use a formal voice to lend credibility to this academic writing.

What are some differences between formal (academic) and informal voice?

Characteristics of Academic Voice	Characteristics of Informal Voice
Typically uses objective third-person point of view	

When drafting, choose language carefully to provide balanced and thoughtful representation of others.

Keep the characteristics of academic voice in mind as you write your draft. As you revise your paragraph, check that you have included a clear thesis, details and quotations from the text, and appropriate commentary. Then, share and respond with a peer or peers to ensure your paragraph uses an academic voice. Make sure you maintained an objective third-person point of view, correct sentence structure, and formal diction. Consider feedback as you revise and edit your paragraph.

GRAMMAR & USAGE

Achebe maintains an *academic voice*, which avoids the use of slang and contractions. Consider the formal diction in this passage from *Things Fall Apart*: "As soon as his father walked in that night, Nwoye knew that Ikemefuna had been killed. . . . He **did not** cry. He just hung limp. He **had had** the same feeling not long ago . . . ." The formal diction helps set a tone of dignity and sorrow.

Character Responses

Consider the character of Ikemefuna. Use the space below to create a graphic organizer in which you list details about him. Your organizer may be a chart, a web, or another graphic. Be sure to list details about Ikemefuna's appearance and actions as well as the attitudes other people have toward him.

Writing Prompt: Consider the impact of Ikemefuna's time in Umuofia. On a separate sheet of paper, write a short narrative from the point of view of either Okonkwo or Nwoye that reveals Ikemefuna's influence on the community (his arrival, presence, death). Employ the voice of the character and include specific details from the novel. Use the subjunctive mood to express a wish in the voice of the character you choose.

Researching and Reflecting on Community

SUGGESTED LEARNING STRATEGIES: **Generating Questions, Drafting**

Assignment

Your assignment is to work with a group to examine one aspect of tribal culture presented in *Things Fall Apart*, research its significance to the Ibo community, and create a multimedia presentation (with graphics, images, and sound) that reflects your research and makes connections between your own culture and that of the Ibo. Your presentation should present a distinctive point of view and should explain what the novel reveals about Ibo beliefs, values, and practices. Choose an audience for your presentation, and develop your appeal for that audience. Finally, write a reflective essay in which you evaluate the effectiveness of your presentation in terms of encouraging cultural connections within your own classroom or community.

Steps

Prewriting/Planning

1. Examine the Scoring Guide and be sure you understand the requirements of the assessment.

2. Consider several different aspects of Ibo culture from the list provided on the following page, and choose a topic for your presentation.

3. Review the first nine chapters of *Things Fall Apart* and highlight or list details about the topic you wish to discuss. Make note of the page numbers where you find your details.

4. Review the notes you have taken in this unit, including Activity 3.4, where you listed information about Ibo culture. Examine your charts and notes for any information about your topic.

5. Research African culture in general and Ibo culture specifically. Modify the major research question as necessary to refocus the research plan. As you did in Activity 3.4, select and evaluate a variety of appropriate sources to develop the main idea for your presentation. Use note cards to capture and synthesize information, noting any discrepancies among sources. Include citations for each source.

6. Connect the details from the novel to the information you researched. Using both, define key principles of Ibo culture and formulate your ideas into general statements that you can explore in your presentation.

Creating Your Presentation

7. Organize your presentation by transforming your general statements into specific questions. As you formulate questions, consider similarities and differences between the Ibo culture and your own culture.

8. Prepare your presentation, considering the needs of your audience and a logical progression of ideas with a clear perspective on the topic. Where appropriate, include informative visuals such as audio or video clips, charts, maps, or other illustrations to help present concepts clearly.

9. Develop several Level 3 questions that ask your classmates to draw comparisons between Ibo cultural attitudes and their own. Remember to be sensitive to language that offends, stereotypes, or excludes. Conclude your presentation by posing these questions.

10. Using the format suggested by your teacher, consult an appropriate style manual (such as that published by MLA) to find guidelines for your bibliography. MLA also has guidelines for presentations that may help you develop and format your presentation.

Presenting and Reflecting

11. Once your presentation is ready, present it to the class. You and your classmates will use listening and viewing skills to respond to each group's presentation in writing.

12. As you take on the role of viewer and listener, complete a viewing guide (provided by your teacher) for each presentation. Take notes. After each presentation, write a paragraph that responds to the presenter's Level 3 questions and explores connections between Ibo cultural attitudes and your own.

13. Be prepared to participate in a discussion of cultural connections.

14. After viewing all presentations, write a reflection in which you identify the elements of the most successful presentations. Rate your own presentation in relation to those elements. Support your evaluations with peers' comments. In particular, consider the reactions your classmates had to your presentation as reflected in their answers to your questions. Finally, critique your research process and presentation plan, and identify any changes you would make if you were to revise this project.

Aspects of Culture from Which to Formulate Research Questions:

Music	Food	Family
Weddings	Funeral rites	Sports
War	Status	Housing
Festivals/Holidays	Justice	Medicine
Farming	Gender roles	View of Nature
Language	Clothing	Religion
Hospitality	Business dealings	

⌐TECHNOLOGY TIP Consider using software to create slides for your presentation. You may also want to incorporate photos representing artifacts from your culture and the Ibo culture. Review your slides before your presentation to ensure that the organization of information flows smoothly.

SCORING GUIDE

Scoring Criteria	Exemplary	Proficient	Emerging
Ideas of Presentation	The presentation thoroughly and creatively portrays the significance of a cultural aspect, provides considerable, detailed examples of the similarities and differences, and makes connections between cultures. The bibliography is properly documented and contains a wide variety of sources that are formatted correctly.	The presentation clearly explains the significance of a cultural aspect, provides adequate examples of similarities and differences, and makes connections between cultures. Sources are adequate, reliable, and well documented in the bibliography.	The presentation does not provide enough information to explain the significance of a cultural aspect. The examples and connections between cultures are weak. The bibliography is limited and not formatted correctly.
Delivery of Presentation	Visual and/or audiovisual elements are exceptionally creative and provide a thorough description of the cultural aspect. The overall organization of the presentation demonstrates an impressive commitment to encouraging audience engagement.	Visual and/or audiovisual elements are useful and relevant and enable the audience to gain a deeper understanding of the cultural aspect. The overall organization of the presentation shows a thoughtful attempt to encourage audience engagement.	Visual and/or audiovisual elements are not present or are present to a limited degree and do not assist the audience's understanding of the cultural aspect. The presentation is disorganized and shows little attempt to encourage audience engagement.
Audience Participation	The viewing guide demonstrates a genuine exploration between the two cultures by thoughtfully and explicitly answering the presenters' questions.	The viewing guide demonstrates an exploration between the two cultures by completely answering the presenters' questions.	The viewing guide is incomplete. It demonstrates little exploration between the two cultures by insufficiently answering the presenters' questions.

SCORING GUIDE

Scoring Criteria	Exemplary	Proficient	Emerging
Reflective Text	The reflection perceptively evaluates the presentation by comparing it to other presentations. Specific and well-chosen examples are cited to support the evaluation, including references to viewers' responses. Future revisions are clearly identified and carefully explained.	The reflection evaluates the presentation by comparing it to other presentations. Relevant examples are cited to support the evaluation, including references to viewers' responses. Future revisions are clearly identified.	The reflection does not adequately evaluate the presentation by comparing it to other presentations Too few or no examples are cited to support evaluation. Future revisions, if present, are weakly explained.
Additional Criteria			

Comments: _____

_____

_____

_____

_____

Learning Focus:

Analyzing a Literary Work

Now that you have read the first nine chapters of *Things Fall Apart,* you are familiar with the novel's characters, setting, and style. It is fitting, then, for you to apply your analytical skills to the rest of the novel. In the past, you have been introduced to and applied the archetype of the hero's journey to a literary work. Another archetypal image or concept is that of the tragic hero. Aristotle's influential work *The Poetics* focuses on defining and characterizing tragedy and the **tragic hero**. Aritstotle's definitions have become the basis for analyzing literary heroes. According to Aristotle:

▶ A tragic hero is often of noble birth or status, or rises to greatness.

▶ The hero has a **tragic flaw** or *hamartia*, which is the cause of her or his downfall.

▶ The suffering of the hero is meaningful.

▶ The hero sees and understands his or her doom and recognizes that personal actions brought about that fate.

▶ The hero learns something from his or her decision or action.

In developing a literary analysis essay, you will write with an academic voice. Your diction, syntax, and tone will take a more formal turn as you revise your writing to ensure it is appropriate for an academic audience. By the end of the unit, you will know much more about another culture, as presented in the novel *Things Fall Apart*, as well as your own abilities as a reader, writer, and communicator.

A Matter of Civility

In the space below, write your definition of a civilized society:

Writing Prompt: On separate paper, write a paragraph in which you argue the degree to which the Ibo culture depicted in *Things Fall Apart* represents a civilized society. In your paragraph, include a clear topic sentence that states your view and details from the novel to support your view. Remember to include direct quotations from the text and to use academic voice in your writing.

Next, use your notes and paragraph to compose several Level 3 questions on the topic of what makes a society civilized. Write the questions below. Use them as you participate in a Socratic Seminar.

At the conclusion of the seminar, refer back to your paragraph and write a short reflection about how the Socratic Seminar either strengthened or challenged your position. If your position remained unchanged, explain how your peers' comments reinforced your ideas. If you now question your position, explain how your peers' positions changed your thinking.

Multiple Roles and Responses

After reading Chapter 11, spend a few moments reflecting on what has happened and how Okonkwo, Ekwefi, and Ezinma reacted to the events. Write your notes in the space provided below:

RAFT (Role-Audience-Format-Topic) ACTIVITY

In your group, assign each person the **role** of a different character. While in that role, each group member should write what his or her character is thinking, using the pronoun *I*, from the time Chielo, as Priestess of Agbala, comes for Ezinma until the end of the chapter. (The character's thoughts serve as your **topic**.) Try to capture the character's voice, diction, and syntax by imitating the character's speech or thought patterns.

Select your **audience** and **format**. Consider writing a monologue, a letter addressed to another character, a diary entry, or a prayer in the voice of the character. When you are finished, share your work with the group and listen attentively as your group members share their writing with you.

Acts of Violence

Consider: While at public gatherings, observances of rites, or festivals, Okonkwo often commits acts of violence that ruin the occasion and generate public disapproval. Review the chapters you have read so far and identify the violent acts Okonkwo has committed and their consequences. Do you see a pattern? Write your ideas below.

Discuss: If you were to draft an essay that explored Okonkwo's violent behavior and the resulting public disapproval, what details would you include? What would your thesis statement be? Write them below. Discuss your thoughts with a writing partner.

GRAMMAR & USAGE

Note the use of the verb *were* in the clause "If you were to draft an essay...." A verb written in the **subjunctive mood** indicates possibilities or wishes rather than actual facts. In this case, you are being asked to think about what you would write in an essay rather than to write the essay. Writers use the subjunctive mood to express a hoped-for condition or a supposition. Think about how you would use the subjunctive mood in your own writing.

Plan: Select a prewriting strategy and use it to formulate thoughts about the topic of Okonkwo's violent tendencies and their consequences. Then, on a separate sheet of paper, create an outline that shows how you would organize your essay. Include a thesis statement and supporting details, textual references, as well as effective opening and concluding sentences.

Gender Views in the Novel

SUGGESTED LEARNING STRATEGIES: Graphic Organizer, Skimming/
Scanning, Quickwrite

In your reading of *Things Fall Apart*, you may have noticed that the characters have clear ideas about how men and women should act or be. For example, in Chapter 2, Okonkwo expresses a fear of appearing to be feminine, a characteristic he equates with weakness and ineffectualness. Use the chart below to record additional examples of characters' ideas about what it means to be a man or a woman. In the second column, respond to the examples you find. Use additional paper as needed.

WORD CONNECTIONS

Resented contains the root *-sent-*, from the Latin word *sentire*, meaning "to feel." This root also appears in *sentimental, consent,* and *dissent*. The prefix *re-* means "back or again."

Ideas About Gender in *Things Fall Apart*

Quote	Your Comments
"Even as a little boy he [Okonkwo] had resented his father's failure and weakness, and even now he still remembered how he had suffered when a playmate had told him that his father was agbala. That was how Okonkwo first came to know that agbala was not only another name for a woman, it could also mean a man who had taken no title."(Chapter 2, p.13)	

Quickwrite: How do you feel about the attitudes toward gender that the novel expresses? Do you think those attitudes are specific to the Ibo culture? Do they exist in your own culture? Do you agree or disagree with them?

Is Okonkwo a Tragic Hero?

Quickwrite: In your opinion, what makes someone a hero? Write your response below.

Keep in mind that a hero is not always a **tragic hero**. Read Aristotle's classical definition of a tragic hero in the chart below. Now think about Okonkwo. Is he a hero? Is he a tragic hero? Complete the chart by providing examples from Okonkwo's life as well as from the lives of other characters from literature or film.

Aristotle's Definition of a Tragic Hero	Examples of Okonkwo's Heroic Behavior	Examples of Heroic Behavior from Books and Film
A person of noble or high status who has a mixture of good and bad in his personality.		
He has a fatal flaw, or *hamartia*, which leads to his downfall.		
He has a large capacity for suffering.		
His downfall is often preceded by self-realization.		

Consider what you have discussed regarding a tragic hero. In the space provided below, write a brief essay that responds to the prompt. Be sure to include a clear thesis statement and textual support from the novel.

Writing Prompt: To what degree does Okonkwo fit Aristotle's definition of a tragic hero? What flaw leads to his downfall?

ACADEMIC VOCABULARY

A **tragic hero** is a central or main character who is usually of high or noble birth and demonstrates a "fatal flaw"—a characteristic that prompts him or her to take an action or make a decision that ultimately leads to his or her downfall or death.

LITERARY TERMS

Hamartia is a tragic hero's fatal flaw; an ingrained character trait that causes the hero to make decisions leading to death or downfall.

Colliding Cultures

Chapters 15–19 span six years in the life of Okonkwo and his village. As you read the chapters, mark your text to indicate significant events and characters' reactions to them.

With a partner, share and discuss your notes and then complete the left-hand column of the graphic organizer below by listing key events from each chapter. In the right-hand column, include your interpretations of how the events support the theme or themes of the novel.

Key Events of Chapter	Why They Are Important
Chapter 15 – 2nd year of exile	
Chapter 16 – 4th year of exile	
Chapter 17	
Chapter 18 – last year of exile	
Chapter 19	

Missionaries and Misunderstandings

Read the excerpt below from Chapter 20 of *Things Fall Apart*. Underline or highlight the points of misunderstanding between the Ibo and the missionaries.

Does the white man understand our customs about land?

How can he when he does not even speak our tongue? But he says that our customs are bad; and our own brothers who have taken up his religion also say that our customs are bad. How do you think we can fight when our own brothers have turned against us? The white man is very clever. He came quietly and peaceably with his religion. We were amused at his foolishness and allowed him to stay. Now he has won our brothers, and our clan can no longer act like one. He has put a knife on the things that held us together and we have fallen apart.

Is the speaker justified in his remarks? What actions by the missionaries and the speaker's kinsmen prompt his statements? Write your answers on a separate sheet of paper.

Next, compare the two missionaries, Mr. Brown and Mr. Smith. Record what each of them says and does, along with their attitudes and beliefs.

GRAMMAR & USAGE

In making syntactical choices, a writer can use clauses in a variety of ways. Notice Achebe's use of clauses in these two **complex sentences**:

He knew **that he had lost his place** (noun clause as direct object) among the nine masked spirits **who administered justice in the clan** (adjective clause modifying *spirits*).

How do you think **we can fight** (noun clause as direct object) **when our own brothers have turned against us** (adverb clause modifying *can fight*)?

Mr. Brown	Mr. Smith

Writing Prompt: Consider your own thoughts about the excerpt from Chapter 20 as well as the missionaries' actions and attitudes in Chapters 21 and 22. Draft a one-page written response to the excerpt from Chapter 20, **or** draft a one-page essay comparing the two missionaries.

Culture Clash

Work with group members to read the practices or beliefs listed in the left-hand column of the organizer below. Then, in the right-hand column, suggest why someone from another culture might think the practices or beliefs are strange. After you respond to the cultural practices or beliefs listed here, add at least two more to the organizer along with your responses.

Cultural Practice or Belief	Why Someone from Another Culture Might Find the Practice or Belief Strange
In the novel *The Poisonwood Bible*, an African man, Anatole, comes to America with his American wife. He is shocked to find out that Americans use the bathroom *in* their house and not outside away from the home.	
Many Americans adorn their bodies with different types of tattoos and piercing.	
Many people idolize sports figures, even to the point of wearing clothing with someone else's name on it.	

Look back through *Things Fall Apart* and identify some Ibo beliefs and practices that differ from those of modern American culture. Contrast them below. One example is provided.

Ibo Belief or Practice	Modern American Belief or Practice
Twins are considered evil and abandoned in the Evil Forest.	Twins are usually welcomed and cared for by their families.

Use the subjunctive mood to describe the possibilities of how you might fit into Ibo society. Would you be an outcast? A ruler? Dead?

Can one culture be "right" and another culture "wrong"? Explain your answer.

Use the two charts and your answers to the above questions to formulate questions to bring to your Socratic Seminar. Be sure to bring your notes so that you can provide textual references for your responses.

Poetic Connections

WORD CONNECTIONS

Anarchy contains the root *-arch-*, from the Greek word *archos*, meaning "leader." This root also appears in *architect*, *patriarch*, *archangel*, and *monarchy*. The prefix *an-* means "not or without."

Group One: Use SIFT to conduct a close reading of the excerpt from Chapter 22 in *Things Fall Apart* on the following page. Then answer the following questions:

1. What do the masks represent to the people of Umuofia? What power do they have for people?

2. Who are the egwugwu and why do Enoch's actions so horrify the people of Umuofia?

Group Two: Use TP-CASTT to conduct a close reading of the poem "Prayer to the Masks" on page 182. Then answer the question below:

What similarities do you see between the poem and *Things Fall Apart*?

Group Three: Use TP-CASTT to conduct a close reading of the poem "The Second Coming" on page 183. Then answer the following questions:

1. What kind of "anarchy is loosed upon the world"?

2. How does the line "The best lack all conviction, while the worst / Are full of passionate intensity" relate to the characters in *Things Fall Apart*?

All Groups: Consider the title of the novel, *Things Fall Apart*. Discuss what you think it means. Use evidence from the text and the poems. Share your ideas with your group members and classmates. Work with your group to design your own masks. Be prepared to share your masks and explain your creative choices and symbolic representations.

Excerpt from Chapter 22

Things Fall Apart

[In Chapter 22, Enoch tears the mask from an *egwugwu*.]

The other *egwugwu* immediately surrounded their desecrated[1] companion to shield him from the profane gaze of women and children, and led him away. Enoch had killed an ancestral spirit, and Umuofia was thrown into confusion.

That night the Mother of the Spirits walked the length and breadth of the clan, weeping for her murdered son. It was a terrible night. Not even the oldest man in Umuofia had ever heard such a strange and fearful sound, and it was never to be heard again. It seemed as if the very soul of the tribe wept for a great evil that was coming—its own death.

WORD CONNECTIONS

Desecrated contains the root *-sacr-*, from the Latin word *sacer*, meaning "holy or sacred." This root also appears in *consecrate*, *sacred*, *sacrament*, and *sacrifice*. The prefix *de-* means "from or away."

---

[1] **desecrated**: acted to deprive something of its sacred character; treated with contempt

Poetry

ABOUT THE AUTHOR

Léopold Senghor was an influential poet, teacher, and politician. Educated in Senegal, a French colony at the time of his birth, and France, Senghor became one of the first black teachers in the French educational system. He co-founded the literary movement Negritude, which validated the artistic expressions of black Africans. He served for more than twenty years as Senegal's first freely elected president.

PRAYER to the MASKS

by Léopold Sédar Senghor

Masks! Masks!
Black mask red mask, you white-and-black masks
Masks of the four points from which the spirit blows
In silence I salute you!
5   Nor you the least, the Lion-headed Ancestor
You guard this place forbidden to all laughter of women, to all smiles that
    fade
You distill this air of eternity in which I breathe the air of my Fathers.
Masks of unmasked faces, stripped of the marks of illness and the lines of
    age
You who have fashioned this portrait, this my face bent over the altar of
    white paper
10 In your own image, hear me!
The Africa of the empires is dying, see, the agony of a pitiful princess
And Europe too where we are joined by the navel.
Fix your unchanging eyes upon your children, who are given orders
Who give away their lives like the poor their last clothes.
15 Let us report present at the rebirth of the World
Like the yeast which white flour needs.
For who would teach rhythm to a dead world of machines and guns?
Who would give the cry of joy to wake the dead and the bereaved at dawn?
Say, who would give back the memory of life to the man whose hopes are
    smashed?
20 They call us men of coffee cotton oil
They call us men of death.
We are the men of the dance, whose feet draw new strength pounding the
hardened earth.

The Second Coming
(1921)

by William Butler Yeats

ABOUT THE AUTHOR
Winner of the 1923 Nobel Prize for Literature, William Butler Yeats produced some of the most enduring poems written in English in the twentieth century. Despite living in Ireland during decades of great political and religious upheaval, Yeats's poems are marked by a deep mysticism, specific symbolism, and universal emotions.

My Notes

Turning and turning in the widening gyre

The falcon cannot hear the falconer;

Things fall apart; the center cannot hold;

Mere anarchy is loosed upon the world,

The blood-dimmed tide is loosed, and everywhere   5

The ceremony of innocence is drowned;

The best lack all conviction, while the worst

Are full of passionate intensity.

Surely some revelation is at hand;

Surely the Second Coming is at hand;   10

The Second Coming! Hardly are those words out

When a vast image out of *Spiritus Mundi*

Troubles my sight: somewhere in sands of the desert

A shape with lion body and the head of a man,

A gaze blank and pitiless as the sun,   15

Is moving its slow thighs, while all about it

Reel shadows of the indignant desert birds.

The darkness drops again; but now I know

That twenty centuries of stony sleep

Were vexed to nightmare by a rocking cradle,   20

And what rough beast, its hour come round at last,

Slouches towards Bethlehem to be born?

A Letter to the District Commissioner

LITERARY TERMS

Dramatic irony occurs when the reader or audience knows more about the circumstances or future events in a story than the characters within it; as a result, the audience can see a discrepancy between characters' perceptions and the reality they face.

Read the two excerpts below. Then discuss the District Commissioner's attitude toward the Ibo.

Excerpt from Chapter 23

"We shall not do you any harm," said the District Commissioner to them later, "if only you agree to cooperate with us. We have brought a peaceful administration to you and your people so that you may be happy. If any man ill-treats you, we shall come to your rescue. But we will not allow you to ill-treat others. We have a court of law where we judge cases and administer justice just as it is done in my own country under a great queen. I have brought you here because you joined together to molest others, to burn people's houses and their place of worship. That must not happen in the dominion of our queen, the most powerful ruler in the world. I have decided that you will pay a fine of two hundred bags of cowries. You will be released as soon as you agree to this and undertake to collect that fine from your people. What do you say to that?"

Excerpt from Chapter 25

In the many years in which he had toiled to bring civilization to different parts of Africa he had learned a number of things. One of them was that a District Commissioner must never attend to such undignified details as cutting a hanged man from the tree. Such attention would give the natives a poor opinion of him. In the book which he planned to write he would stress that point. As he walked back to the court he thought about that book. Every day brought him some new material. The story of this man who had killed a messenger and hanged himself would make interesting reading. One could almost write a whole chapter on him. Perhaps not a whole chapter but a reasonable paragraph, at any rate. There was so much else to include, and one must be firm in cutting out details. He had already chosen the title of the book, after much thought: *The Pacification of the Primitive Tribes of the Lower Niger.*

Quickwrite: How is the excerpt from Chapter 25 an example of **dramatic irony**? Explain.

Writing Prompt: Think about the attitude of the District Commissioner toward the Ibo people. Then, write a letter to the District Commissioner expressing your opinion about his attitude and suggesting ways that he might change how he deals with the Ibo.

SUGGESTED LEARNING STRATEGIES: Discussion Groups, Notetaking

Interview

Chinua Achebe, the author of one of the enduring works of modern African literature, sees postcolonial cultures taking shape story by story.

An AFRICAN Voice

by Katie Bacon

Chinua Achebe's emergence as "the founding father of African literature . . . in the English language," in the words of the Harvard University philosopher K. Anthony Appiah, could very well be traced to his encounter in the early fifties with Joyce Cary's novel *Mister Johnson*, set in Achebe's native Nigeria. Achebe read it while studying at the University College in Idaban during the last years of British colonial rule, and in a curriculum full of Shakespeare, Coleridge, and Wordsworth, *Mister Johnson* stood out as one of the few books about Africa. *Time* magazine had recently declared *Mister Johnson* the "best book ever written about Africa," but Achebe and his classmates had quite a different reaction. The students saw the Nigerian hero as an "embarrassing nitwit." *Mister Johnson*, Achebe writes, "open[ed] my eyes to the fact that my home was under attack and that my home was not merely a house or a town but, more importantly, an awakening story."

In 1958, Achebe responded with his own novel about Nigeria, *Things Fall Apart*, which was one of the first books to tell the story of European colonization from an African perspective. (It has since become a classic, published in fifty languages around the world.) *Things Fall Apart* marked a turning point for African authors, who in the fifties and sixties began to take back the narrative of the so-called "dark continent."

Achebe depicts his gradual realization that *Mister Johnson* was just one in a long line of books written by Westerners that presented Africans to the world in a way that Africans didn't agree with or recognize, and he examines the "process of 're-storying' peoples who had been knocked silent by all kinds of dispossession." He ends with a hope for the twenty-first century—that this "re-storying" will continue and will eventually result in a "balance of stories among the world's peoples."

Achebe encourages writers from the Third World to stay where they are and write about their own countries, as a way to help achieve this balance. Yet he himself has lived in the United States for the past ten years—a reluctant exile. In 1990, Achebe was in a car accident in Nigeria, and was paralyzed from the waist down. While recuperating in a London hospital, he received a call from Leon Botstein, the president

Chunk 1

My Notes

GRAMMAR & USAGE

Writers use a **dash** to indicate a break in their thoughts. The dash may mean "in other words" or "that is to say," or it may set off parenthetical information or thoughts. A dash fits between two words without spaces between the dash and the words.

My Notes

of Bard College, offering him a teaching job and a house built for his needs. Achebe thought he would be at Bard, a small school in a quiet corner of the Hudson River Valley, for only a year or two, but the political situation in Nigeria kept worsening. During the military dictatorship of General Sani Abacha, who ruled from 1993 to 1998, much of Nigeria's wealth—the country has extensive oil fields—went into the pocket of its leader, and public infrastructure that had been quite good, like hospitals and roads, withered. In 1999, Olusegan Obasanjo became Nigeria's first democratically elected President since 1983, and the situation in Nigeria is improving, albeit slowly and shakily. Achebe is watching from afar, waiting for his country to rebuild itself enough for him to return.

Achebe, who is sixty-nine, has written five novels, including *Arrow of God* (1964) and *Anthills of the Savannah* (1987), five books of nonfiction, and several collections of short stories and poems. Achebe spoke recently with *Atlantic Unbound's* Katie Bacon at his home in Annandale-on-Hudson, in New York.

QUESTION 1

Chunk 2
You have been called the progenitor of the modern African novel, and *Things Fall Apart* has maintained its resonance in the decades since it was written. Have you been surprised by the effect the book has had?

Was I surprised? Yes, at the beginning. There was no African literature as we know it today. And so I had no idea when I was writing *Things Fall Apart* whether it would even be accepted or published. All of this was new—there was nothing by which I could gauge how it was going to be received.

But, of course, something doesn't continue to surprise you every day. After a while I began to understand why the book had resonance. I began to understand my history even better. It wasn't as if when I wrote it I was an expert in the history of the world. I was a very young man. I knew I had a story, but how it fit into the story of the world—I really had no sense of that. Its meaning for my Igbo people was clear to me, but I didn't know how other people elsewhere would respond to it. Did it have any meaning or resonance for them? I realized that it did when, to give you just one example, the whole class of a girls' college in South Korea wrote to me, and each one expressed an opinion about the book. And then I learned something, which was that they had a history that was similar to the story of *Things Fall Apart*—the history of colonization. This I didn't know before. Their colonizer was Japan. So these people across the waters were able to relate to the story of dispossession in Africa. People from different parts of the world can respond to the same story, if it says something to them about their own history and their own experience.

QUESTION 2

It seems that people from places that haven't experienced colonization in the same way have also responded to the story.

There are different forms of dispossession, many, many ways in which people are deprived or subjected to all kinds of victimization—it doesn't have to be colonization. Once you allow yourself to identify with the people in a story, then you might begin to see yourself in that story even if on the surface it's far removed from your situation. This is what I try to tell my students: this is one great thing that literature can do—it can make us identify with situations and people far away. If it does that, it's a miracle. I tell my students, it's not difficult to identify with somebody like yourself, somebody next door who looks like you. What's more difficult is to identify with someone you don't see, who's very far away, who's a different color, who eats a different kind of food. When you begin to do that then literature is really performing its wonders.

QUESTION 3

A character in *Things Fall Apart* remarks that the white man "has put a knife on the things that held us together, and we have fallen apart." Are those things still severed, or have the wounds begun to heal?

Chunk 3

What I was referring to there, or what the speaker in the novel was thinking about, was the upsetting of a society, the disturbing of a social order. The society of Umuofia, the village in *Things Fall Apart*, was totally disrupted by the coming of the European government, missionary Christianity, and so on. That was not a temporary disturbance; it was a once and for all alteration of their society. To give you the example of Nigeria, where the novel is set, the Igbo people had organized themselves in small units, in small towns and villages, each self-governed. With the coming of the British, Igbo land as a whole was incorporated into a totally different polity, to be called Nigeria, with a whole lot of other people with whom the Igbo people had not had direct contact before. The result of that was not something from which you could recover, really. You had to learn a totally new reality, and accommodate yourself to the demands of this new reality, which is the state called Nigeria. Various nationalities, each of which had its own independent life, were forced by the British to live with people of different customs and habits and priorities and religions. And then at independence, fifty years later, they were suddenly on their own again. They began all over again to learn the rules of independence. The problems that Nigeria is having today could be seen as resulting from this effort that was initiated by colonial rule to create a new nation. There's nothing to indicate whether it will fail or succeed. It all depends.

My Notes

The Author's Perspective

One might hear someone say, How long will it take these people to get their act together? It's going to take a very, very long time, because it's really been a whole series of interruptions and disturbances, one step forward and two or three back. It has not been easy. One always wishes it had been easier. We've compounded things by our own mistakes, but it doesn't really help to pretend that we've had an easy task.

QUESTION 4

Chunk 4

In *Home and Exile*, you talk about the negative ways in which British authors such as Joseph Conrad and Joyce Cary portrayed Africans over the centuries. What purpose did that portrayal serve?

It was really a straightforward case of setting us up, as it were. The last four or five hundred years of European contact with Africa produced a body of literature that presented Africa in a very bad light and Africans in very lurid terms. The reason for this had to do with the need to justify the slave trade and slavery. The cruelties of this trade gradually began to trouble many people in Europe. Some people began to question it. But it was a profitable business, and so those who were engaged in it began to defend it—a lobby of people supporting it, justifying it, and excusing it. It was difficult to excuse and justify, and so the steps that were taken to justify it were rather extreme. You had people saying, for instance, that these people weren't really human, they're not like us. Or, that the slave trade was in fact a good thing for them, because the alternative to it was more brutal by far.

And therefore, describing this fate that the Africans would have had back home became the motive for the literature that was created about Africa. Even after the slave trade was abolished, in the nineteenth century, something like this literature continued, to serve the new imperialistic needs of Europe in relation to Africa. This continued until the Africans themselves, in the middle of the twentieth century, took into their own hands the telling of their story.

My Notes

QUESTION 5

And that's what started with *Things Fall Apart* and other books written by Africans around the 1950s.

Yes, that's what it turned out to be. It was not actually clear to us at the time what we were doing. We were simply writing our story. But the bigger story of how these various accounts tie in, one with the other, is only now becoming clear. We realize and recognize that it's not just colonized people whose stories have been suppressed, but a whole range of people across the globe who have not spoken. It's not because they don't have something to say, it simply has to do with the division of power, because storytelling has to do with power. Those who win tell the story; those who are defeated are not heard. But that has to change. It's in the interest of everybody, including the winners, to know that there's another story. If you only hear one side of the story, you have no understanding at all.

QUESTION 6

Do you see this balance of stories as likely to emerge in this era of globalization and the exporting of American culture?

Chunk
5

That's a real problem. The mindless absorption of American ideas, culture, and behavior around the world is not going to help this balance of stories, and it's not going to help the world, either. People are limiting themselves to one view of the world that comes from somewhere else. That's something that we have to battle with as we go along, both as writers and as citizens, because it's not just in the literary or artistic arena that this is going to show itself. I think one can say this limiting isn't going to be very healthy for the societies that abandon themselves.

QUESTION 7

In an *Atlantic Unbound* interview this past winter Nadine Gordimer said, "English is used by my fellow writers, blacks, who have been the most extreme victims of colonialism. They use it even though they have African languages to choose from. I think that once you've mastered a language it's your own. It can be used against you, but you can free yourself and use it as black writers do—you can claim it and use it." Do you agree with her?

Yes, I definitely do. English is something you spend your lifetime acquiring, so it would be foolish not to use it. Also, in the logic of colonization and decolonization it is actually a very powerful weapon in the fight to regain what was yours. English was the language of colonization itself. It is not simply something you use because you have it anyway; it is something which you can actively claim to use as an effective weapon, as a counterargument to colonization.

QUESTION 8

Chunk 6

There are those who say that media coverage of Africa is one-sided— that it focuses on the famines, social unrest, and political violence, and leaves out coverage of the organizations and countries that are working. Do you agree? If so, what effect does this skewed coverage have? Is it a continuation of the anti-Africa British literature you talk about in *Home and Exile*?

Yes, I do agree. I think the result has been to create a fatigue, whether it's charity fatigue or fatigue toward being good to people who are less fortunate. I think that's a pity. The reason for this concentration on the failings of Africans is the same as what we've been talking about—this tradition of bad news, or portraying Africa as a place that is different from the rest of the world, a place where humanity is really not recognizable. When people hear the word *Africa*, they have come to expect certain images to follow. If you see a good house in Lagos, Nigeria, it doesn't quite fit the picture you have in your head, because you are looking for the slum—that is what the world expects journalists covering a city in Africa to come back with.

Now, if you are covering America, you are not focusing on slums every day of your life. You see a slum once in a while, maybe you talk about it, but the rest of the time you are talking about other things. It is that ability to see the complexity of a place that the world doesn't seem to be able to take to Africa, because of this baggage of centuries of reporting about Africa. The result is the world doesn't really know Africa. If you are an African or you live in Africa, this stands out very clearly to you, you are constantly being bombarded with bad news, and you know that there

My Notes

is good news in many places. This doesn't mean that the bad news doesn't exist, that's not what I'm saying. But it exists alongside other things. Africa is not simple—people want to simplify it. Africa is very complex. Very bad things go on—they should be covered—but there are also some good things.

This is something that comes with this imbalance of power that we've been talking about. The people who consume the news that comes back from the rest of the world are probably not really interested in hearing about something that is working. Those who have the ability to send crews out to bring back the news are in a position to determine what the image of the various places should be, because they have the resources to do it. Now, an African country doesn't have a television crew coming to America, for instance, and picking up the disastrous news. So America sends out wonderful images of its success, power, energy, and politics, and the world is bombarded in a very partial way by good news about the powerful and bad news about the less powerful.

QUESTION 9

You mentioned that literature was used to justify slavery and imperialism. What is this negative coverage of Africa being used to justify now?

Chunk 7

It's going to be used to justify inaction, which is what this fatigue is all about. Why bother about Africa? Nothing works there, or nothing ever will work. There is a small minority of people who think that way, and they may be pushing this attitude. But even if nobody was pushing it, it would simply happen by itself. This is a case of sheer inertia, something that has been happening for a long time just goes on happening, unless something stops it. It becomes a habit of mind.

QUESTION 10

Has living here changed the way you think about Nigeria?

It must have, but this is not something you can weigh and measure. I've been struck, for instance, by the impressive way that political transition is managed in America. Nobody living here can miss that if you come from a place like Nigeria which is unable so far to manage political transitions in peace. I wish Nigeria would learn to do this. There are other things, of course, where you wish Americans would learn from Nigerians: the value of people as people, the almost complete absence of race as a factor in thought, in government. That's something that I really wish for America, because no day passes here without some racial factor coming up somewhere, which is a major burden on this country.

The Author's Perspective

My Notes

QUESTION 11

Could you talk about your dream, expressed in *Home and Exile*, of a "universal civilization"—a civilization that some believe we've achieved and others think we haven't?

What the universal civilization I dream about would be, I really don't know, but I know what it is not. It is not what is being presented today, which is clearly just European and American. A universal civilization is something that we will create. If we accept the thesis that it is desirable to do, then we will go and work on it and talk about it. We have not really talked about it. All those who are saying it's there are really suggesting that it's there by default—they are saying to us, let's stop at this point and call what we have a universal civilization. I don't think we want to swindle ourselves in that way; I think if we want a universal civilization, we should work to bring it about. And when it appears, I think we will know, because it will be different from anything we have now.

There may be cultures that may sadly have to go, because no one is rooting for them, but we should make the effort to prevent this. We have to hold this conversation, which is a conversation of stories, a conversation of languages, and see what happens.

Writing a Literary Analysis Essay

SUGGESTED LEARNING STRATEGIES: Drafting, Self-Editing,
Peer Editing

Assignment

Your assignment is to write an analytical essay about *Things Fall Apart* in
which you examine a character's response to the cultural collision caused by
the introduction of Western ideas into Ibo culture. In your essay, analyze how
the collision challenges the character's sense of identity and explain how his
response shapes the meaning of the work as a whole.

Steps

Prewriting/Planning

1. Examine the Scoring Guide and ensure you understand the requirements.

2. Choose a character and analyze that character's sense of identity prior to
   encountering Western influences.

3. Examine the character's response to the new culture. Consider the
   following questions: What does the character do? How do others react to
   his actions? What are the repercussions of his actions? How does his role
   in the community change? Does his perspective change? What are the
   consequences of the character's willingness or refusal to change?

4. Consider the character's responses and the consequences of those
   responses. What does the author seem to say about the outcomes when
   different cultures meet? Craft a thesis that reflects your interpretation of
   the novel's theme.

5. Locate textual support for your assertion. In light of the textual support
   you have selected, revisit your thesis and refine it as needed.

Drafting

6. Draft the essay, using a variety of methods to integrate your textual
   support, including direct quotations, paraphrased text, and examples
   from the text.

7. Experiment with syntax by varying sentence length, type and
   complexity. Keep in mind that your diction also lends credibility
   to your academic voice.

Revising, Editing and Publishing

8. Consider the genre of a literary analysis essay, and revise your draft to ensure
   that you have addressed all elements of the genre. In addition, look for other
   areas that need revision (such as word choice, syntax, variation in sentences,
   rhetorical devices, and grammatical usage). Mark your text and solicit
   feedback from your peers and your teacher to aid you in the revision process.

9. Have your peers help you determine the credibility of your academic
   voice, effectiveness of stylistic choices, and coherence.

10. Edit your essay, using all the tools and resources available to you to
    create a technically sound document.

11. Use word processing software to create a final draft, or write your essay
    in legible handwriting.

Writing a Literary Analysis Essay

SCORING GUIDE

Scoring Criteria	Exemplary	Proficient	Emerging
Ideas	Analysis focuses on an appropriate character and examines with clarity and precision the character's response to the cultural collision, the challenge to the character's identity, and how the character's actions impact the meaning of the work. Use of specific and well-chosen examples yields solid support for the thesis. Thorough and perceptive literary analysis creates a convincing text.	Analysis focuses on an appropriate character and adequately examines the character's response to the cultural collision, the challenge to the character's identity, and how the character's actions impact the meaning of the work. Use of appropriate examples supports the thesis. Solid literary analysis creates a convincing text.	Analysis may focus on an appropriate character yet inadequately examine the character's response to the cultural collision and the challenge to the character's identity, and fail to show how the character's actions impact the meaning of the work. Evidence to support the thesis is lacking. Too few examples are used. Analysis may be over-simplified or replaced by summary.
Organization	Organization is exceptional. Effective use of transitions enhances the essay's coherence.	Organization is clear and easy to follow. Transitions are used to move between ideas.	The essay is difficult to follow. It may jump too rapidly between ideas and lack transitions.
Use of Language	Diction and syntax is purposeful and appropriate for an academic audience.	Diction and syntax is appropriate for an academic audience but may include some unsophisticated or incorrect word choice or sentence structure.	Diction and syntax may be coherent yet simplistic or inappropriate for an academic audience. Slang, informal word choice, or awkward sentence structure may be present.
Conventions	The writing demonstrates strong control and mastery of standard conventions. Either no errors appear, or they are so slight that they do not interfere with the meaning.	The writing demonstrates control of standard writing conventions. Though some errors may appear, they do not seriously impede readability.	There are frequent errors in standard conventions that seriously interfere with the meaning.

SCORING GUIDE

Scoring Criteria	Exemplary	Proficient	Emerging
Evidence of the Writing Process	The writing demonstrates thoughtful planning, significant revision, and careful editing in preparing a publishable draft.	The writing demonstrates adequate planning, revision, and editing in preparing a publishable draft.	The writing lacks evidence of planning, revision, and / or editing. The draft is not ready for publication.
Additional Criteria			

Comments: _____

_____

_____

_____

_____

_____

Reflection

An important aspect of growing as a learner is to reflect on where you have been, what you have accomplished, what helped you to learn, and how you will apply your new knowledge in the future. Use the following questions to guide your thinking and to identify evidence of your learning. Use separate notebook paper.

Thinking about Concepts

1. Using specific examples from this unit, respond to the Essential Questions:

   - How can an author use a work of fiction to make a statement about culture?

   - How might the cultural fabric of a community be stretched or altered when it encounters new ideas and members?

2. Consider the new academic vocabulary from this unit (**Validity, Reliability, Plagiarism, Tragic Hero**) as well as academic vocabulary from previous units, and select 3-4 terms of which your understanding has grown. For each term, answer the following questions:

   - What was your understanding of the word prior to the unit?

   - How has your understanding of the word evolved throughout the unit?

   - How will you apply your understanding in the future?

Thinking about Connections

3. Review the activities and products (artifacts) you created. Choose those that most reflect your growth or increase in understanding.

4. For each artifact that you choose, record, respond to, and reflect on your thinking and understanding, using the following questions as a guide:

   a. What skill/knowledge does this artifact reflect, and how did you learn this skill/knowledge?

   b. How did your understanding of the power of language expand through your engagement with this artifact?

   c. How will you apply this skill or knowledge in the future?

5. Create this reflection as Portfolio pages—one for each artifact you choose. Use the model in the box for your headings and commentary on questions.

Thinking About Thinking
Portfolio Entry

Concept:

Description of Artifact:

Commentary on Questions:

Justice

Essential Questions

? What is the nature of justice?

? How does one construct a persuasive argument?

Unit Overview

Everyone must deal with issues of justice. What is a fair consequence for breaking a rule in class? Do students have freedom of speech in school? Should the principal be allowed to search lockers randomly? You have examined culture through many lenses. You can define a culture by its beliefs about what is right and wrong—its sense of justice. Different cultures may have different standards and methods for arriving at justice, but every society has to ask the questions about what is right and fair. Unit 4 presents nonfiction, drama, and art from around the world and across time that ask the key question: What is justice?

Unit 4 Justice

Goals

▶ To examine perspectives of justice across cultures and over time

▶ To recognize effective elements of persuasion

▶ To create a persuasive piece

▶ To rehearse and present a dramatic interpretation

ACADEMIC VOCABULARY

Justice

Chorus

Contents

Learning Focus:

What Can You Do?

Every day you encounter issues involving justice and injustice, fairness, and equal treatment. You may experience these issues in your own life, or through others that you know, or you may read about them in newspapers or hear about them on the news. Literature often deals with issues of justice and injustice. *To Kill a Mockingbird* and *Things Fall Apart* are just two examples of texts that examine issues of justice on a societal level.

Societies create systems of justice to maintain order by establishing rules and laws that reasonable people understand and abide by. Even in well-organized systems, though, there are differences of opinion about what is just, what is fair, and what is right. Instances of injustice often provoke strong emotional reactions that give rise to conflicts. Examining important social issues relating to justice demands that you examine multiple perspectives and evaluate arguments for all sides of an issue.

When presenting their support for a particular point of view, writers use persuasive language to make their cases about unjust treatment or situations. A powerful argument is crafted using emotional, logical, and ethical appeals to those who have the power to take action on an issue. To take a stand against an injustice and provide a passionate and persuasive argument that convinces others of your point of view is the responsibility and right of every effective communicator.

The leap from making your point on a personal issue of fairness to delivering a convincing argument on an issue of injustice to a broader, more demanding audience is part of expanding your personal influence into a wider arena.

Independent Reading: In this unit, you will read both print and nonprint texts that explore issues of justice and injustice in various cultures. For independent reading, look for a play, novel, nonfiction book, informational text, or a collection of essays or artwork that presents an aspect of justice or injustice.

Previewing the Unit

SUGGESTED LEARNING STRATEGIES: Skimming and Scanning, Marking the Text, KWL, Close Reading, Summarizing/Paraphrasing, Graphic Organizer, Think-Pair-Share

Essential Questions

1. What is the nature of justice?

   fairness, equal treatment,

2. How does one construct a persuasive argument?

   ethical appeal, logical, emotional.

Unit Overview and Learning Focus

Predict what you think this unit is about. Use the words or phrases that stood out to you when you read the Unit Overview and the Learning Focus.

Justice

Embedded Assessment

What knowledge must you have (what do you need to know)? What skills must you have (what will you need to do to complete the Embedded Assessment successfully)? Write your responses below.

All point of views. Need to be a good writer.

My Notes

Drama

> **ABOUT THE AUTHOR**
> William Shakespeare (1564–1616) is considered one of the most perceptive writers in the English language.
> He pursued a career in London as an actor but found more success as a playwright and poet, producing more than three dozen plays and many sonnets that are still performed and read today. His strength as a writer was in his ability to portray basic human emotions and situations in memorable, often heart-breaking, verse.

Excerpt from Romeo and Juliet

by William Shakespeare

Summary: Two families—the Montagues and the Capulets—are enemies. Romeo, a Montague, has killed Tybalt, a Capulet, after Tybalt killed Romeo's friend, Mercutio. Both sides appeal to the Prince for justice. Benvolio pleads for the Montagues, while Lady Capulet speaks for her family. As you read, mark the text by underlining words and phrases related to justice.

ACT III, SCENE 1:

PRINCE

Where are the vile beginners of this fray?

BENVOLIO

O noble prince, I can discover[1] all
The unlucky manage of this fatal brawl:
There lies the man, slain by young Romeo,
5 That slew thy kinsman, brave Mercutio.

WORD CONNECTIONS

Shakespeare uses the word "fair" in line 13 of Benvolio's speech. Among the many meanings of *fair* are attractive in appearance, impartial, and a public show. The word may be used as an adjective, a noun, a verb, or an adverb. Research other meanings and use context clues to determine Shakespeare's meaning for the word *fair*.

---

[1] **discover**: to explain

LADY CAPULET

    Tybalt, my cousin! O my brother's child!
    O prince! O cousin! husband! O, the blood is spilt
    Of my dear kinsman! Prince, as thou art true,
    For blood of ours, shed blood of Montague.
    O cousin, cousin!   10

PRINCE

    Benvolio, who began this bloody fray?

BENVOLIO

    Tybalt, here slain, whom Romeo's did slay;
    Romeo that spoke him fair, bade him bethink
    How nice[2] the quarrel was, and urged withal
    Your high displeasure: all this uttered   15
    With gentle breath, calm look, knees humbly bow'd,
    Could not take truce with the unruly spleen
    Of Tybalt deaf to peace, but that he tilts
    With piercing steel at bold Mercutio's breast,
    Who all as hot, turns deadly point to point,   20
    And, with a martial scorn, with one hand beats
    Cold death aside, and with the other sends
    It back to Tybalt, whose dexterity,
    Retorts it: Romeo he cries aloud,
    'Hold, friends! friends, part!' and, swifter than   25
    his tongue,
    His agile arm beats down their fatal points,
    And 'twixt them rushes; underneath whose arm
    An envious thrust from Tybalt hit the life
    Of stout Mercutio, and then Tybalt fled;   30
    But by and by comes back to Romeo,
    Who had but newly entertain'd revenge,
    And to 't they go like lightning, for, ere I
    Could draw to part them, was stout Tybalt slain.
    And, as he fell, did Romeo turn and fly.   35
    This is the truth, or let Benvolio die.

My Notes

---

[2] **nice**: trivial

Justice in *Romeo and Juliet*

LADY CAPULET

He is a kinsman to the Montague;
Affection makes him false; he speaks not true:
Some twenty of them fought in this black strife,

40 And all those twenty could but kill one life.
I beg for justice, which thou, prince, must give;
Romeo slew Tybalt, Romeo must not live.

PRINCE

Romeo slew him, he slew Mercutio;
Who now the price of his dear blood doth owe?

MONTAGUE

45 Not Romeo, prince, he was Mercutio's friend;
His fault concludes but what the law should end,
The life of Tybalt.

PRINCE

And for that offence
Immediately we do exile him hence:

50 I have an interest in your hate's proceeding,
My blood for your rude brawls doth lie a-bleeding;
But I'll amerce you with so strong a fine
That you shall all repent the loss of mine:
I will be deaf to pleading and excuses:

55 Nor tears nor prayers shall purchase out abuses:
Therefore use none: let Romeo hence in haste,
Else, when he's found, that hour is his last.
Bear hence this body and attend our will:
Mercy but murders, pardoning those that kill.
Exeunt

WORD CONNECTIONS

Conclude contains the root *-clud-*, from the Latin word *claudere*, meaning "to shut or close." This root also appears in *include*, *preclude*, and *recluse*. The prefix *con-* means "with or together."

1. This scene seems as though it could be played in a TV courtroom drama.

   a. Who is being accused of a crime? *Romeo*

   b. What is the crime? *Murder of Tybalt*

   c. Who is the judge? *Prince*

   d. Who provides eyewitness testimony? Is this testimony impartial? Why do you think this? *Benvolio.   yes because*

   e. What is the sentence? *exile*

2. Both the Capulets and the Montagues ask the Prince for justice.

   a. What do the Capulets ask for, and why do they think that would be a just decision?

   Death for Romeo because of the murder of Tybalt

   b. What do the Montagues want, and why do they believe that justice has already been served?

   Tybalt was supposes to be killed for killing Mercutio

   c. Why is neither family satisfied with the verdict?

   Cupulet want him dead, Montague thinks he doesn't deserve to die.

   d. Is the Prince an impartial judge of the case?

   yes.

   WORD CONNECTIONS

   Satisfied contains the root -sat-, from the Latin word *satis*, meaning "enough." This root also appears in *sated*, *satiate*, and *dissatisfy*.

3. Is the Prince's decision just? Explain.

   yes because the montague weren't the ones who started it.

4. If this case were being decided in a real courtroom today, what do you expect Romeo's punishment would be? Explain.

   Life in jail or death sentesve. You let the law handle it.

5. What does this scene reveal to you about the nature of justice? Be sure to provide support for your thoughts from the text.

   you don't decide someone's fate.

   You don't have the authority to kill someone who killed another person.

What Is Justice?

Think about the following terms and, in the chart, write associations you have about them.

Term	What words come to mind when you see or hear these terms?	What has influenced your opinion of these terms?
Justice, justice system	fair, punishments, rulings, courts, money	The government. money
Laws, rules, codes, constitution	Courts, ethics	The government
Judge, jury, lawyers, witnesses, prosecutor, defendant, victim	Justice, courtroom, stories.	The news
Ethics, morality	Teachers, right, wrong.	Internet
Punishment, rehabilitation	years, jail, timeout	Internet.

After you have shared your thoughts as a class, go back to your work with forms of the word *just* and add terms that help you understand justice. Explain how the terms relate to the concept of justice.

The punishment of wrongdoers.

Now, using the ideas you have recorded, write a personal definition of the word *justice*. What does justice mean to you? Share your definition with a partner.

Quickwrite: Now complete the quickwrite below about a time in which justice was served and a time it was not. You may write about a personal experience or something you learned from the news. Share your quickwrite with a partner when you have finished.

Justice—A time it was served:

A time Justice was served was when Hernandez was sentence to life in prison for killing a lady.

Justice—A time it was not served:

A time justice wasn't served was when X didn't get locked up longer for beating his ex.

Discussion: After you have heard from others in the class, discuss why it is important to have a justice system in society.

Justice and Culture

1. **Quickwrite:** Imagine that you, an American teenager, went out one night with some friends and vandalized a car and street signs. Imagine then that you were arrested by the police. What do you expect your punishment would be? Would it involve jail time, repairing the damage, or some other penalty? How do you think justice would be best served?

I expect the punishment of repairing the damage and 1 month of community service.

2. **Quickwrite:** What is the attitude toward vandalism of this nature in your family? In your school? In your community?

My family hates when I do bad things.

My school would think twice about thing

My community will not trust me.

3. **Quickwrite:** In Unit 3, when you read the novel *Things Fall Apart*, you may have thought about what happens when cultures have different perspectives on issues of justice. What do you think might be the response to this kind of vandalism in another country?

Michael Fay Controversy

Background Information

Michael Fay, an American teenager living in Singapore, was arrested in 1994 for possession of stolen street signs and for vandalism of automobiles. The criminal justice system in Singapore sentenced Fay to a series of "canings," in which the accused is struck several times on the buttocks with a long, rattan cane. Amnesty International has declared this punishment "torture."

Before the punishment was carried out, Fay's father publicized his case all over America, hoping that people would be so horrified by the act that they would protest. What the case touched off instead was a huge debate over the effectiveness of such punishments on criminals. Proponents of caning pointed out that Singapore has very little crime, while America provides its criminals with cable TV. The case dominated much of talk radio in the months leading up to the scheduled caning.

The Clinton Administration did intervene somewhat and was able to get the number of strokes reduced. In the end, Fay was struck four times with the cane, and the case—and Fay—slipped out of the public's mind.

The Michael Fay case generated a lot of publicity. Newspaper reporters and editorial writers expressed different points of view on whether the punishment was justified.

- If a reporter thought that the punishment was *unjustified*, what kinds of words and phrases would you expect him or her to use to describe the caning and Fay himself? *corrupt, horific, cruel, Just a child*
- If a reporter thought that the punishment was *justified*, what kinds of words and phrases might you expect him or her to use to describe the caning and Michael Fay? *lesson learn, Irresponsible action, suspect, tolerate, criminal*

Forms of Evidence

When presenting an argument, writers use evidence to support their positions. For example:

- **Empirical evidence** is based on experiences and direct observation through research.
- **Logical evidence** is based on facts and a clear rationale.
- **Anecdotal evidence** is based on personal accounts of incidents.

Anecdotal evidence is the least reliable because it may have been passed from one person to another to another. As you read pages 210-214, look for the evidence presented to support the arguments. Mark the text to identify each type of evidence, and discuss with peers the effect of that persuasive technique on the text as a whole as well as its impact on the reader.

WORD CONNECTIONS

Proponent contains the root *-pon-*, from the Latin word *ponere*, meaning "to set forth or put." This root also appears in *component, opponent,* and *exponent.*

Punishment contains *-puni-*, a version of the root *-pen-*, from the Latin word *poena*, meaning "punishment or penalty." This root also appears in *penalty, penal, punitive,* and *penance.* The suffix *-ment* indicates that the word is a noun.

Justice and Culture

Directions: Skim the following two articles from the *New York Times* and determine whether each writer is a proponent of Fay's punishment or is opposed to the punishment. Mark the text, indicating words and phrases that indicate the writer's stance. Take notes in the My Notes section about any biases you detect. At the top of the page, write *For* or *Against*.

Editorial

Time to Assert AMERICAN VALUES

from The New York Times

Singapore's founding leader, Lee Kuan Yew, returned to a favorite theme yesterday in defending the threatened caning of Michael Fay, an 18-year-old American found guilty of vandalism. Western countries value the individual above society; in Asia, he said, the good of society is deemed more important than individual liberties. This comfortable bit of sophistry[1] helps governments from China to Indonesia rationalize abuses and marginalize courageous people who campaign for causes like due process and freedom from torture. Western nations, it is asserted, have no right to impose their values on countries that govern themselves successfully according to their own values.

So, the argument goes, when Americans express outrage over a punishment that causes permanent scarring—in this case, caning—they are committing an act of cultural arrogance, assuming that American values are intrinsically superior to those of another culture.

There is a clear problem with this argument. It assumes that dissidents, democrats and reformers in these countries are somehow less authentic representatives of their cultures than the members of the political elite who enforce oppressive punishments and suppress individual rights.

At times like this, Americans need to remember that this country was also founded by dissidents—by people who were misfits in their own society because they believed, among other things, that it was wrong to punish pilferage with hanging or crimes of any sort with torture.

---

[1] **Sophistry:** false or misleading argument

These are values worth asserting around the world. Americans concerned with the propagation[2] of traditional values at home should be equally energetic in asserting constitutional principles in the international contest of ideas. There are millions of acts of brutality that cannot be exposed and combated. A case like Michael Fay's is important because it provides a chance to challenge an inhumane practice that ought not to exist anywhere.

While this country cannot dictate to the Government of Singapore, no one should fail to exhort it to behave mercifully. President Clinton provided a sound example when he called for a pardon. Principled private citizens ought now to call for American companies doing business in Singapore to bring their influence to bear.

Our colleague William Safire is right to call upon American corporations with subsidiaries in Singapore to press President Ong Teng Cheong to cancel Mr. Fay's punishment. According to Dun & Bradstreet and the U.S.-Asean Council, some C.E.O.'s and companies in this category are: Riley P. Bechtel of the Bechtel Group Inc.; John S. Reed of Citicorp; Roberto C. Goizueta of the Coca-Cola Company Inc.; Edgar S. Woolard Jr. of E. I. du Pont de Nemours & Company; Lee R. Raymond of Exxon Corporation; John F. Welch Jr. of the General Electric Company; Michael R. Bonsignore of Honeywell Inc.; Louis V. Gerstner Jr. of the International Business Machines Corporation, and Ralph S. Larsen of Johnson & Johnson Inc.

Singapore needs such people as friends. Now is the time for them to make their voices heard. The Fay case provides a legitimate opening for American citizens and companies to bring political and economic pressure to bear in the propagation of freedom and basic rights. Former President Bush can lead the effort by using his speech at a Citibank seminar in Singapore Thursday to call for clemency for Michael Fay.

---

[2] **propagation**: dissemination; spread

My Notes

Veiwpoint:
They are against
the beating.

My Notes

Article

ROUGH Justice

A Caning in Singapore Stirs Up a Fierce Debate About Crime and Punishment

by Alejandro Reyes

The Vandalism Act of 1966 was originally conceived as a legal weapon to combat the spread of mainly political graffiti common during the heady days of Singapore's struggle for independence. Enacted a year after the republic left the Malaysian Federation, the law explicitly mandates between three and eight strokes of the cane for each count, though a provision allows first offenders to escape caning "if the writing, drawing, mark or inscription is done with pencil, crayon, chalk or other delible substances and not with paint, tar or other indelible substances…."

Responding to reporters' questions, U.S. chargé d'affaires Ralph Boyce said: "We see a large discrepancy between the offense and the punishment. The cars were not permanently damaged; the paint was removed with thinner. Caning leaves permanent scars. In addition, the accused is a teenager and this is his first offense."

By evening, the Singapore government had its reply: "Unlike some other societies which may tolerate acts of vandalism, Singapore has its own standards of social order as reflected in our laws. It is because of our tough laws against anti-social crimes that we are able to keep Singapore orderly and relatively crime-free." The statement noted that in the past five years, fourteen young men aged 18 to 21, twelve of whom were Singaporean, had been sentenced to caning for vandalism. Fay's arrest and sentencing shook the American community in Singapore. Schools advised parents to warn their children not to get into trouble. The American Chamber of Commerce said "We simply do not understand how the government can condone the permanent scarring of any 18-year-old boy—American or Singaporean—by caning for such an offense." Two dozen American senators signed a letter to Ong on Fay's behalf.

But according to a string of polls, Fay's caning sentence struck a chord in the U.S. Many Americans fed up with rising crime in their cities actually supported the tough punishment. Singapore's embassy in Washington said that the mail it had received was overwhelmingly approving of the tough sentence. And a radio call-in survey in Fay's hometown of Dayton, Ohio, was strongly pro-caning.

It wasn't long before Singapore patriarch Lee Kuan Yew weighed in. He reckoned the whole affair revealed America's moral decay. "The U.S. government, the U.S. Senate and the U.S. media took the opportunity to ridicule us, saying the sentence was too severe," he said in a television interview. "[The U.S.] does not restrain or punish individuals, forgiving them for whatever they have done. That's why the whole country is in chaos: drugs, violence, unemployment and homelessness. The American society is the richest and most prosperous in the world but it is hardly safe and peaceful."

The debate over caning put a spotlight on Singapore's legal system. Lee and the city-state's other leaders are committed to harsh punishments. Preventive detention laws allow authorities to lock up suspected criminals without trial. While caning is mandatory in cases of vandalism, rape and weapons offenses, it is also prescribed for immigration violations such as overstaying visas and hiring of illegal workers. The death penalty is automatic for drug trafficking and firing a weapon while committing a crime. At dawn on May 13, six Malaysians were hanged for drug trafficking, bringing to seventeen the number executed for such offenses so far this year, ten more than the total number of prisoners executed in all of 1993.

Most Singaporeans accept their brand of rough justice. Older folk readily speak of the way things were in the 1950s and 1960s when secret societies and gangs operated freely. Singapore has succeeded in keeping crime low. Since 1988, government statistics show there has been a steady decline in the crime rate from 223 per 10,000 residents to 175 per 10,000 last year. Authorities are quick to credit their tough laws and harsh penalties for much of that….

"If there is a single fundamental difference between the Western and Asian world view, it is the dichotomy between individual freedom and collective welfare," said Singapore businessman and former journalist Ho Kwon Ping in an address to lawyers on May 5, the day Fay was caned. "The Western cliché that it would be better for a guilty person to go free than to convict an innocent person is testimony to the importance of the individual. But an Asian perspective may well be that it is better that an innocent person be convicted if the common welfare is protected than for a guilty person to be free to inflict further harm on the community."

There is a basic difference too in the way the law treats a suspect. "In Britain and in America, they keep very strongly to the presumption of innocence," says Walter Woon, associate professor of law at the National University of Singapore and a nominated MP. "The prosecution must prove that you are guilty. And even if the judge may feel that you are guilty, he

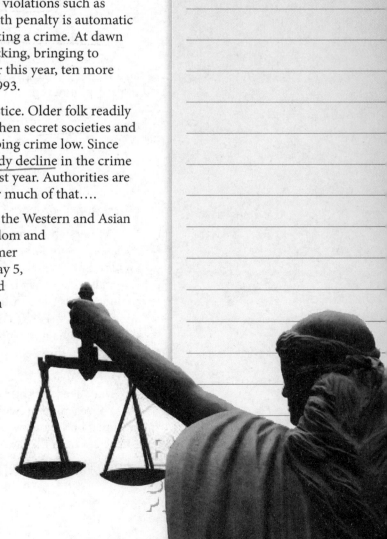

My Notes
For Rough
Justice

cannot convict you unless the prosecution has proven it. So in some cases it becomes a game between the defense and the prosecuting counsel. We would rather convict even if it doesn't accord with the purist's traditions of the presumption of innocence."

Singapore's legal system may be based on English common law, but it has developed its own legal traditions and philosophy since independence. The recent severance of all appeals to the Privy Council in London is part of that process. In fundamental ways, Singapore has departed from its British legal roots. The city-state eliminated jury trials years ago—the authorities regard them as error-prone. Acquittals can be appealed and are sometimes overturned. And judges have increased sentences on review. Recently an acquittal was overturned and a bus driver was sentenced to death for murder based only on circumstantial evidence. "Toughness is considered a virtue here," says Woon. "The system is stacked against criminals. The theory is that a person shouldn't get off on fancy argument."

Woon opposes caning to punish non-violent offenses. But he is not an admirer of the American system. Last year, Woon and his family were robbed at gunpoint at a bus stop near Disneyworld in Orlando, Florida. The experience shook him. America's legal system, he argues, "has gone completely berserk. They're so mesmerized by the rights of the individual that they forget that other people have rights too. There's all this focus on the perpetrator and his rights, and they forget the fellow is a criminal." Fay is no more than that, Woon says. "His mother and father have no sense of shame. Do they not feel any shame for not having brought him up properly to respect other people's property? Instead they consider themselves victims."

Yet harsh punishments alone are clearly not the salvation of Singapore society. The predominantly Chinese city-state also has a cohesive value system that emphasizes such Confucian virtues as respect for authority, "No matter how harsh your punishments, you're not going to get an orderly society unless the culture is in favor of order," says Woon. "In Britain and America, they seem to have lost the feeling that people are responsible for their own behavior. Here, there is still a sense of personal responsibility. If you do something against the law, you bring shame not only to yourself but to your family."

That "sense of shame," Woon reckons, is more powerful than draconian laws. "Loosening up won't mean there will be chaos," he says. "But the law must be seen to work. The punishment is not the main thing. It's the enforcement of the law. The law has to be enforced effectively and fairly."

International Justice

SUGGESTED LEARNING STRATEGIES: **Brainstorming, Paraphrasing, Previewing, Think-Pair-Share, Skimming, Sketching, Notetaking, Discussion Groups, Marking the Text**

Anticipation Guide

Mark whether you agree or disagree with each of the statements below. You will have an opportunity to revisit these statements later in the unit to see if you still hold the same opinion.

Now		Statement	Later	
Agree	**Disagree**		**Agree**	**Disagree**
		1. Different cultures cannot agree on what is just.		
		2. Children and teenagers are given special protection.		
		3. The physical needs of children and teenagers are a high priority.		
		4. The emotional needs of children and teenagers are a high priority.		
		5. Children and teenagers should be required to attend school.		
		6. Children and teenagers are protected against all forms of neglect, cruelty, and exploitation.		
		7. Children and teenagers face discrimination.		

To which of the statements above do you respond most strongly? List your reasons below.

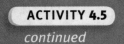
Before Reading

Imagine a country whose culture has always had a deep-seated fear of red hair, has passed a law that says that all red-haired children are to be banished when they turn 10. Is this a just law? How do you determine a law's justness? Can you remove it from culture, time, and place and still have it be relevant? How are laws established in a state? In a country? How would you go about changing our country's laws?

The United Nations is an organization that tries to determine issues of justice that transcend individual cultures and societal rules. What do you know about the United Nations? Are there any laws to which all nations on the planet would agree?

Think about children (defined as any person under the age of 18, unless an earlier age of majority is recognized by a country's law) around the world. If all nations could agree on a set of laws that concern the treatment of children, what kinds of laws do you think would appear on the list of laws?

During Reading

Read the Declaration of the Rights of the Child. Next to each Principle, sketch an illustration or symbolic representation of that Principle.

Next, read President Nelson Mandela's Statement on International Children's Day. In this statement, Mandela recaps programs put in place by the South African government. Next to each, note what kinds of similar programs you have heard about in your community or state.

Mandela also mentions issues under "urgent consideration." What is the situation regarding these issues in your community? Make notes in the margin.

After Reading

After reading the declaration and Mandela's proclamation, form discussion groups and answer this question: Do you believe that the principles are being met in the United States? In the rest of the world?

When you attempt to convince others to agree with you about a statement, remember to adhere to the discussion norms of your class. One way to show respect to your classmates is to acknowledge and even paraphrase what the person just said before you respond. For example:

- "I understand when you say . . . (paraphrase). To that idea, I would like to add . . . "

- "When you said . . . (paraphrase), did you also think about . . . ?"

- "You made a good point when you said . . . (paraphrase). I'd also like to suggest . . . "

WORD CONNECTIONS

Adhere contains the root *-her-*, from the Latin word *haerere*, meaning "to stick." This root also appears in *cohere, hereditary,* and *inherit*. The prefix *ad-* means "to."

Proclamation

DECLARATION *of the* RIGHTS *of the* CHILD

PROCLAIMED BY GENERAL ASSEMBLY RESOLUTION 1386(XIV) OF 20 NOVEMBER 1959

Whereas the peoples of the United Nations have, in the Charter, reaffirmed their faith in fundamental human rights and in the dignity and worth of the human person, and have determined to promote social progress and better standards of life in larger freedom,

Whereas the United Nations has, in the Universal Declaration of Human Rights, proclaimed that everyone is entitled to all the rights and freedoms set forth therein, without distinction of any kind, such as race, colour, sex, language, religion, political or other opinion, national or social origin, property, birth or other status,

Whereas the child, by reason of his physical and mental immaturity, needs special safeguards and care, including appropriate legal protection, before as well as after birth,

Whereas the need for such special safeguards has been stated in the Geneva Declaration of the Rights of the Child of 1924, and recognized in the Universal Declaration of Human Rights and in the statutes of specialized agencies and international organizations concerned with the welfare of children,

Whereas mankind owes to the child the best it has to give,

Now therefore,

The General Assembly

Proclaims this Declaration of the Rights of the Child to the end that he may have a happy childhood and enjoy for his own good and for the good of society the rights and freedoms herein set forth, and calls upon parents, upon men and women as individuals, and upon voluntary organizations, local authorities and national Governments to recognize these rights and strive for their observance by legislative and other measures progressively taken in accordance with the following principles:

Principle 1

The child shall enjoy all the rights set forth in this Declaration. Every child, without any exception whatsoever, shall be entitled to these rights, without distinction or discrimination on account of race, color, sex, language, religion, political or other opinion, national or social origin, property, birth or other status, whether of himself or of his family.

Principle 2

The child shall enjoy special protection, and shall be given opportunities and facilities, by law and by other means, to enable him to develop physically, mentally, morally, spiritually and socially in a healthy and normal manner and in conditions of freedom and dignity. In the enactment of laws for this purpose, the best interests of the child shall be the paramount consideration.

Principle 3

The child shall be entitled from his birth to a name and a nationality.

Principle 4

The child shall enjoy the benefits of social security. He shall be entitled to grow and develop in health; to this end, special care and protection shall be provided both to him and to his mother, including adequate pre-natal and post-natal care. The child shall have the right to adequate nutrition, housing, recreation and medical services.

Principle 5

The child who is physically, mentally or socially handicapped shall be given the special treatment, education and care required by his particular condition.

Principle 6

The child, for the full and harmonious development of his personality, needs love and understanding. He shall, wherever possible, grow up in the care and under the responsibility of his parents, and, in any case, in an atmosphere of affection and of moral and material security; a child of tender years shall not, save in exceptional circumstances, be separated from his mother. Society and the public authorities shall have the duty to extend particular care to children without a family and to those without adequate means of support. Payment of State and other assistance towards the maintenance of children of large families is desirable.

Principle 7

The child is entitled to receive education, which shall be free and compulsory, at least in the elementary stages. He shall be given an education which will promote his general culture and enable him, on a basis of equal opportunity, to develop his abilities, his individual judgement, and his sense of moral and social responsibility, and to become a useful member of society.

The best interests of the child shall be the guiding principle of those responsible for his education and guidance; that responsibility lies in the first place with his parents.

GRAMMAR & USAGE

Verbs have **active and passive voice** in all six **tenses**. A passive-voice verb always contains a form of *be* followed by the past participle of the verb.

The voice of a verb (active or passive) indicates whether the subject performs (active) or receives (passive) the action.

Active voice, future tense: The child **shall enjoy** all the rights....

Passive voice, future tense: Every child **shall be entitled**....

Generally, it is preferable to use the active voice in your writing. The active voice is more direct and concise. However, sometimes the passive voice is more appropriate when the doer of the action is unknown or doesn't matter. This formal document effectively uses the passive voice to emphasize that the recipient of actions (the child) is more important than those who do the actions (parents, government, voluntary organizations, etc.).

My Notes

The child shall have full opportunity for play and recreation, which should be directed to the same purposes as education; society and the public authorities shall endeavour to promote the enjoyment of this right.

Principle 8
The child shall in all circumstances be among the first to receive protection and relief.

Principle 9
The child shall be protected against all forms of neglect, cruelty and exploitation. He shall not be the subject of traffic, in any form.

The child shall not be admitted to employment before an appropriate minimum age; he shall in no case be caused or permitted to engage in any occupation or employment which would prejudice his health or education, or interfere with his physical, mental or moral development.

Principle 10
The child shall be protected from practices which may foster racial, religious and any other form of discrimination. He shall be brought up in a spirit of understanding, tolerance, friendship among peoples, peace and universal brotherhood, and in full consciousness that his energy and talents should be devoted to the service of his fellow men.

Speech

> **ABOUT THE AUTHOR**
>
> Nelson Mandela (1918–) spent nearly three decades in South African prisons and, as a result, became an international symbol of the injustice of South African apartheid, a system of political, economic, and social segregation. After his release in 1990, Mandela helped dismantle apartheid. He and President F.W. de Klerk won the 1993 Nobel Prize for Peace for their efforts. A year later, Mandela ran for president in the first all-race elections held in South Africa and won. He served as South Africa's president until 1999.

PRESIDENT NELSON MANDELA'S STATEMENT ON INTERNATIONAL CHILDREN'S DAY

1 June 1994

Today, 1 June, is International Children's Day.

I wish to take this opportunity to reiterate the commitment of the South African Government to a comprehensive programme to ensure that children of our country grow up secure in family life, enjoying all the rights and privileges they deserve. We recommit ourselves to the UN Declaration on the Rights of the Child.

In order to realise these objectives, the Government has already set in motion mechanisms to implement various programmes that we announced at the Opening of the last Parliamentary Session. These include:

- Free medical care in state hospitals and clinics for children under six years of age: A decision has been taken that this should come into effect immediately where mechanisms have been put in place, and it will apply to all cases where such a need exists.

- A nutritional feeding scheme in primary schools: The relevant ministry is already identifying the areas most in need for the urgent implementation of this measure.

- The Departments of Justice and Welfare will soon announce a detailed programme to empty our jails of children and to provide alternative care centres.

- Legislation to introduce free and quality education for all children will be introduced at the next parliamentary session.

My Notes

Among the measures that are also under urgent consideration are the conditions of street children, and ways in which the Government can contribute to alleviate and finally eradicate their plight. Further, legislation on the eradication of child abuse and child labour will be processed with deliberate speed.

On this day, we also extend our solidarity with children throughout the world whose lives are ravaged by the scourges of hunger, war and ignorance. We commit ourselves to contribute, to the best of our ability, to the international efforts aimed at resolving these problems.

The South African Government's approach to the question of children's social and political rights derives from the basic principle that to value our children is to value our future.

SCHOOL'S OUT for Summer

by Anna Quindlen

ABOUT THE AUTHOR
Anna Quindlen is a novelist and an award-winning and popular newspaper columnist who has written for some of the nation's most prestigious newspapers, including *The New York Times*, where she was a reporter, editor, and contributor for many years. Critics suggest that her appeal as a columnist lies in her personal approach and her insights into problems experienced by ordinary readers. She won the Pulitzer Prize for commentary in 1992.

My Notes

WHEN THE AD COUNCIL CONVENED focus groups not long ago to help prepare a series of public service announcements on child hunger, there was a fairly unanimous response from the participants about the subject. Not here. Not in America. If there was, we would know about it. We would read about it in the paper, we would see it on the news. And of course we would stop it. In America.

Is it any wonder that the slogan the advertising people came up with was "The Sooner You Believe It, the Sooner We Can End It"?

It's the beginning of summer in America's cement cities, in the deep hidden valleys of the country and the loop-de-loop sidewalkless streets of the suburbs. For many adults who are really closet kids, this means that their blood hums with a hint of freedom, the old beloved promise of long aimless days of dirt and sweat and sunshine, T-shirts stained with Kool-Aid and flip-flops gray with street grit or backyard dust.

But that sort of summer has given way to something more difficult, even darker, that makes you wonder whether year-round school is not a notion whose time has come. With so many households in which both parents are working, summer is often a scramble of scheduling: day camps, school programs, the Y, the community center. Some parents who can't afford or find those kinds of services park their vacationing children in front of the television, lock the door, and go to work hoping for the best, calling home on the hour. Some kids just wander in a wilder world than the one that existed when their parents had summers free.

And some kids don't get enough to eat, no matter what people want to tell themselves. Do the math: During the rest of the year fifteen million students get free or cut-rate lunches at school, and many of them get breakfast, too. But only three million children are getting lunches through the federal

My Notes

summer lunch program. And hunger in the United States, particularly since the institution of so-called welfare reform, is epidemic. The numbers are astonishing in the land of the all-you-can-eat buffet. The Agriculture Department estimated in 1999 that twelve million children were hungry or at risk of going hungry. A group of big-city mayors released a study showing that in 2000, requests for food assistance from families increased almost 20 percent, more than at any time in the last decade. And last Thanksgiving a food bank in Connecticut gave away four thousand more turkeys than the year before—and still ran out of birds.

But while the Christmas holidays make for heartrending copy, summer is really ground zero in the battle to keep kids fed. The school lunch program, begun in the 1970s as a result of bipartisan[1] federal legislation, has been by most measures an enormous success. For lots of poor families it's become a way to count on getting at least one decent meal into their children, and when it disappears it's catastrophic. Those who work at America's Second Harvest, the biggest nonprofit supply source for food banks, talk of parents who go hungry themselves so their kids can eat, who put off paying utility and phone bills, who insist their children attend remedial summer school programs simply so they can get a meal. The parents themselves are loath to talk: Of all the humiliations attached to being poor in a prosperous nation, not being able to feed your kids is at the top of the list.

In most cases these are not parents who are homeless or out of work. The people who run food banks report that most of their clients are minimum-wage workers who can't afford enough to eat on their salaries. "Families are struggling in a way they haven't done for a long time," says Brian Loring, the executive director of Neighborhood Centers of Johnson County, Iowa, which provides lunches to more than two hundred kids at five locations during the summer months. For a significant number of Americans, the cost of an additional meal for two school-age children for the eight weeks of summer vacation seems like a small fortune. Some don't want or seek government help because of the perceived stigma[2]; some are denied food stamps because of new welfare policies. Others don't know they're eligible, and none could be blamed if they despaired of the exercise. The average length of a food stamp application is twelve often impenetrable pages; a permit to sell weapons is just two.

The success of the school lunch program has been, of course, that the food goes where the children are. That's the key to success for summer programs, too. Washington, D.C., has done better than any other city in the country in feeding hungry kids, sending fire trucks into housing projects to distribute leaflets about lunch locations, running a referral hotline and radio announcements. One food bank in Nevada decided to send trucks to the parks for tailgate lunches. "That's where the kids are," its director told the people at Second Harvest.

---

[1] **bipartisan:** supported by both major political parties
[2] **stigma:** sign of shame or disgrace

We Americans like need that takes place far from home, so we can feel simultaneously self-congratulatory and safe from the possibility that hard times could be lurking around the corner. Maybe that's why our mothers told us to think of the children in Africa when we wouldn't clean our plates. I stopped believing in that when I found myself in a bodega[3] with a distraught woman after New York City had declared a snow day; she had three kids who ate breakfast and lunch at school, her food stamps had been held up because of some bureaucratic snafu[4], and she was considering whether to pilfer food from the senior center where she worked as an aide. Surely there should be ways for a civilized society to see that such a thing would never happen, from providing a simpler application for food stamps to setting a decent minimum wage. But wishing don't make it so, as they say in policy meetings, and proposals aren't peanut butter and jelly. Find a food bank and then go grocery shopping by proxy[5]. Somewhere nearby there is a mother who covets a couple of boxes of spaghetti, and you could make her dream come true. That's right. In America.

In her essay "School's Out for Summer," Anna Quindlen makes an argument about the implementation of one of the principles in America. As you read the first six paragraphs, identify her **hook** and her **thesis** by marking the text. What solutions does Quindlen present? What solutions can you and your classmates add?

My Notes

> ### LITERARY TERMS
>
> A **hook** is an interesting quotation, anecdote, or example that grabs readers' attention.
>
> A **thesis** is the main idea or argument.

---

[3] **bodega:** small grocery shop
[4] **snafu:** a confusing situation
[5] **proxy:** to act in the place of someone else

International Justice

Take a few minutes to assess your skills in the areas of speaking and listening in group discussions.

My Strengths as a Listener	My Weaknesses as a Listener	Goals for Improvement

My Strengths as a Speaker	My Weaknesses as a Speaker	Goals for Improvement

Reflect on how well you and your group adhered to the norms of discussion during this activity. Include in your reflection how the discussion norms connect to speaking and listening skills.

Arguing for Justice

SUGGESTED LEARNING STRATEGIES: **SMELL, Sketching, Marking the Text, Previewing, Graphic Organizer, Think-Pair-Share, Rereading**

> **Writing Prompt: Scenario A**—You arrive home 20 minutes after your curfew and your parent or guardian has decided to ground you for a week as punishment. On separate paper, try to persuade your parent or guardian to change his or her mind by using one of three types of arguments explained below.

Argument 1: Appeal to your parent or guardian by showing that you are trustworthy and that you care deeply about the situation and its effect on him or her. You should use "I."

Argument 2: Appeal to your parent or guardian by telling a story with lots of details to create pity for yourself and your situation. You can use "I," though you may refer to other people as well.

Argument 3: Appeal to your parent or guardian by being rational and by giving statistics and commonly held beliefs. Refer to experts and facts that can be supported and explained. You should use "I" sparingly.

Types of Appeals

Sketch a symbol to represent each of these types of persuasive appeals.

Logos (Logical): This type of appeal uses inductive or deductive reasoning by citing statistics, facts, experts, and evidence. When using this type of argument, you offer your audience examples that are similar to this subject and convince them to draw the conclusion you want. How did you use logos in Argument 3 above?

Ethos (Ethical): This type of argument requires that you establish yourself as trustworthy and respectful of the audience. You do this by demonstrating that you have taken the time to research your topic, which establishes your credibility on the subject. How did you use ethos in Argument 1 above?

Pathos (Emotional): This is when you appeal to the emotions of your audience by describing in detail the effect of a particular situation. You should try to arouse a sense of pity, anger, fear, or other emotion in your audience. How did you use pathos in Argument 2 above?

> **Writing Prompt: Scenario B**—Your community recreation center could sponsor free lunches for children and teenagers during the summer but does not currently do so. Using the appeals of logos, ethos, and pathos, write an essay in which you convince the director to sponsor free lunches. As you write the essay, think of the context and the audience (the director) and how best to organize the essay and present your argument to achieve your desired result.

Arguing for Justice

As you read this scene from *Julius Caesar*, notice how Antony is able to persuade his audience. After you read the scene, use the SMELL reading strategy to help you understand how Antony persuades the crowd.

Sender-receiver relationship

What is the relationship between Antony, the sender of the message, and the crowd?

How does Antony respond to the crowd?

Message

Summarize Antony's argument.

Emotional strategies

What does he want the crowd to think, feel, and do?

Logical strategies

What logic is Antony using?

How does this logic affect his message?

Language

What kinds of words and images does Antony use?

How does Antony's word choice affect the speech?

by William Shakespeare

ACT III, SCENE 2

Antony
Friends, Romans, countrymen, lend me your ears.
I come to bury Caesar, not to praise him.
The evil that men do lives after them;
The good is oft interrèd with their bones.
So let it be with Caesar. The noble Brutus   5
Hath told you Caesar was ambitious.
If it were so, it was a grievous fault,
And grievously hath Caesar answered it.
Here, under leave of Brutus and the rest—
For Brutus is an honorable man   10
So are they all, all honorable men—
Come I to speak in Caesar's funeral.
He was my friend, faithful and just to me;
But Brutus says he was ambitious,
And Brutus is an honorable man.   15
He hath brought many captives home to Rome,
Whose ransoms did the general coffers[1] fill.
Did this in Caesar seem ambitious?
When that the poor have cried, Caesar hath wept;
Ambition should be made of sterner stuff.   20
Yet Brutus says he was ambitious,
And Brutus is an honorable man.
You all did see that on the Lupercal
I thrice presented him a kingly crown,
Which he did thrice refuse. Was this ambition?   25
Yet Brutus says he was ambitious,
And sure he is an honorable man.
I speak not to disprove what Brutus spoke,
But here I am to speak what I do know.
You all did love him once, not without cause   30
What cause withholds you, then, to mourn for him?
O judgment! Thou art fled to brutish beasts,
And men have lost their reason. Bear with me;
My heart is in the coffin there with Caesar,
And I must pause till it come back to me. *[He weeps.]*   35

---

[1] **coffers:** treasury

My Notes

First Plebeian
Methinks there is much reason in his sayings.

Second Plebeian
If thou consider rightly of the matter,
Caesar has had great wrong.

Third Plebeian
Has he, masters?
40   I fear there will a worse come in his place.

Fourth Plebeian
Marked you his words? He would not take the crown;
Therefore 'tis certain he was not ambitious.

First Plebeian
If it be found so, some will dear abide it.

Second Plebeian
Poor soul, his eyes are red as fire with weeping.

Third Plebeian
45   There's not a nobler man in Rome than Antony.

Fourth Plebeian
Now mark him, he begins again to speak.

Antony
But yesterday the word of Caesar might
Have stood against the world. Now lies he there,
And none so poor to do him reverence.
50   O masters, if I were disposed to stir
Your hearts and minds to mutiny and rage,
I should do Brutus wrong, and Cassius wrong,
Who, you all know, are honorable men.
I will not do them wrong; I rather choose
55   To wrong the dead, to wrong myself and you,
Than I will wrong such honorable men.
But here's a parchment with the seal of Caesar.
I found it in his closet; 'tis his will.
Let but the commons hear this testament—
60   Which, pardon me, I do not mean to read—
And they would go and kiss dead Caesar's wounds
And dip their napkins in his sacred blood,

WORD CONNECTIONS

Testament contains the root *-test-*, from the Latin word *testis*, meaning "a witness." This root also appears in *testimony*, *attest*, *detest*, and *intestate*. The suffix *-ment* indicates that the word is a noun.

Yea, beg a hair of him for memory,
And, dying, mention it within their wills,
Bequeathing it as a rich legacy   65
Unto their issue².

Fourth Plebeian
We'll hear the will! Read it, Mark Antony.

All
The will, the will! We will hear Caesar's will.

Antony
Have patience, gentle friends; I must not read it.
It is not meet you know how Caesar loved you.   70
You are not wood, you are not stones, but men;
And, being men, hearing the will of Caesar,
It will inflame you, it will make you mad. '
Tis good you know not that you are his heirs,
For if you should, O, what would come of it?   75

Fourth Plebeian
Read the will! We'll hear it, Antony.
You shall read us the will, Caesar's will

Antony
Will you be patient? Will you stay awhile?
I have o'ershot myself to tell you of it.
I fear I wrong the honorable men   80
Whose daggers have stabbed Caesar. I do fear it.

Fourth Plebeian
They were traitors. "Honorable men!"

All
The will! The testament!

Second Plebeian
They were villains, murderers. The will! Read the will!

Antony
You will compel me, then, to read the will?   85
Then make a ring about the corpse of Caesar,
And let me show you him that made the will.
Shall I descend? And will you give me leave?

---

² **issue:** offspring

Several Plebeians
Come down.

Second Plebeian
90   Descend.

Third Plebeian
You shall have leave.

[*Antony descends.*]

Fourth Plebeian
A ring; stand round.

First Plebeian
Stand from the hearse. Stand from the body.

Second Plebeian
Room for Antony, most noble Antony.

Antony
95   Nay, press not so upon me. Stand far off.

Several Plebeians
Stand back! Room! Bear back!

Antony
If you have tears, prepare to shed them now.
You all do know this mantle. I remember
The first time ever Caesar put it on;
100   'Twas on a summer's evening, in his tent,
That day he overcame the Nervii.
Look, in this place ran Cassius' dagger through.
See what a rent the envious Casca made.
Through this the well-beloved Brutus stabbed,
105   And as he plucked his cursed steel away,
Mark how the blood of Caesar followed it,
As rushing out of doors to be resolved
If Brutus so unkindly knocked or no;
For Brutus, as you know, was Caesar's angel.
110   Judge, O you gods, how dearly Caesar loved him!
This was the most unkindest cut of all.
For when the noble Caesar saw him stab,
Ingratitude, more strong than traitors' arms,
Quite vanquished him. Then burst his mighty heart,

> **WORD CONNECTIONS**
>
> ***Ingratitude*** contains the root *-grat-*, from the Latin word *gratus*, meaning "pleasing." This root also appears in *grateful*, *ingrate*, *gratify*, and *congratulate*. The prefix *in-* means "not."

And in his mantle muffling up his face, 115
Even at the base of Pompey's statue,
Which all the while ran blood, great Caesar fell.
O, what a fall was there, my countrymen!
Then I, and you, and all of us fell down,
Whilst bloody treason flourished over us. 120
O, now you weep, and I perceive you feel
The dint of pity. These are gracious drops.
Kind souls, what weep you when you but behold
Our Caesar's vesture³ wounded? Look you here,
Here is himself, marr'd, as you see, with traitors. 125

[*Antony lifts Caesar's cloak.*]

First Plebeian
O piteous spectacle!

³ **vesture:** clothing

Arguing for Justice

Reread the text to find Antony's reasons that the murder of Caesar was unjust. Then, identify and explain the persuasive techniques or appeals Antony uses with each reason. An example is provided below.

Reasons that Murder was Unjust	Identify as Logos, Pathos, or Ethos and Explain Your Choice
"He hath brought many captives home to Rome, Whose ransoms did the general coffers fill." This example tries to prove that Caesar could not have been too ambitious if he brought all this wealth to Rome, not to himself.	This technique is an example of logos because it is offering logical supporting examples. It is one of three or four pieces of evidence that Antony provides to prove that Caesar was not ambitious.

LITERARY TERMS

An **argument** presents a particular opinion or idea and supports it with evidence.

Which of the **arguments** above seems the most persuasive for the audience? Which do you think is the strongest? Was ethos, pathos, or logos the most effective here? Why?

Generate or revise a response to this essential question: "How does one construct a persuasive argument?"

Legal Justice

SUGGESTED LEARNING STRATEGIES: Quickwrite, Graphic Organizer, Brainstorming, Previewing, Discussion Groups, Marking the Text, Summarizing, Rereading

As you read the articles on the next few pages, take notes about the issues related to clothing.

	"Comment" by Pat Lancaster	"Germany Divided Over Hijab" by Andreas Tzortzis
Thesis		
Summary of Support		
Persuasive Appeals		
Genre Features		
Culture and Justice		

Legal Justice

In "An Immodest Idea," Jamin Raskin says that an issue like banning religious garb would never happen in U.S. schools. Which Principle of the Declaration of the Rights of the Child (Activity 4.5) protects students from religious discrimination? How does Nashala Hearn's situation fit in with these ideas?

Brainstorm issues related to dress that are relevant in your school and/ or your community. At this point, it does not matter whether you are in favor of or are opposed to the issue.

Draft a working thesis regarding an issue related to dress.

Reflection Reflect on your progress toward your goals of improving speaking and listening in small group situations. Refine your goals as needed.

An **Immodest** Idea

by Anna Mulrine, *U.S. News & World Report*

Across this country last month, from Boston to Honolulu, newspaper editorials came to the defense of head scarves for Muslim women in France. The outcry was prompted by French President Jacques Chirac's call for a ban on the hijab worn by Muslim girls attending public schools. While that might be controversial enough, the measure also would prohibit other "ostentatious" displays of religious allegiance at schools, including yarmulkes[1] and large crosses. "Boy," the *Honolulu Advertiser* noted, "could this head-scarf ban backfire."

The issue has historical roots, but reflects the very contemporary tensions between protecting religious freedom and concern in France that extremism may be growing among the nation's estimated 5 million Muslims. At the heart of the French debate is the country's struggle a century ago to break free of the strong hold of the Roman Catholic Church. Chirac portrays the Muslim practice of wearing a head scarf as challenging the politically sacred separation of church and state. Former French Education Minister Bernard Stasi is more emphatic, asserting the ban is intended to counter "forces that are trying to destabilize the country."

By choice or by pressure. Muslims now make up nearly 8 percent of France's population, the largest Muslim community in Western Europe. Only about 2,000 French girls, by government estimate, wear head scarves to school, many out of religious conviction. But family pressure and gang rapes of women considered "immodest" in the housing projects of Paris where many recent Muslim immigrants live play a role, as well, concluded the commission that recommended the ban.

Elsewhere in Europe, too, the hijab debate is in the news. The German supreme court in September ruled that the 1998 dismissal of a teacher who refused to remove her head scarf was illegal and would remain so—unless Germany's 16 states created their own laws against head scarves. Seven of these states have announced plans to do just that.

This clothing conundrum[2] wouldn't happen in American public schools, says American University constitutional law scholar Jamin Raskin, author of *We the Students: Supreme Court Cases for and About Students*. "If your veil or yarmulke isn't preventing anyone from learning, then of course you have the right to wear it," he says. John Hanford, the U.S. ambassador at large for religious freedom, has come out against the ban, prompting mutterings among French politicos that they wouldn't dream of weighing in on an American domestic issue, such as whether the Pledge of Allegiance should include the phrase "under God"—a topic that the U.S. Supreme Court is slated to tackle this year.

---

[1] **yarmulke**: skullcap worn by Jewish men and boys
[2] **conundrum**: dilemma, problem

My Notes

Editorial

Comment

by **Pat Lancaster,** *Middle East*

French government threats to impose a ban on the wearing of the Islamic headscarf, or hijab, in schools has created fury in sections of the country's Muslim community. Demonstrations on the streets of several French cities in January served to confirm that the ban on "overt displays of religious paraphernalia," will extend to the wearing of Jewish skullcaps and large Christian crosses, will only serve to exacerbate racial tension in the country.

The demonstrations were largest in Paris, where thousands took to the streets in protest. Meanwhile, Muslims in London, Berlin and Baghdad came out in solidarity.

The centre-right government of France has taken a hard line against those opposing the proposed legislation, insisting the country must uphold the republican values enshrined in the 1789 revolution and preserve its secular identity. In a speech recommending the ban should become law, President Jacques Chirac warned that if France chooses to capitulate to the will of its religious communities "it would lose its soul."

However, this is by no means a one sided debate, while some who profess to have no religious beliefs are outraged at what they see as a serious threat to the infringement of civil liberty, others, including Dalil Boubaker, head of the leading Paris mosque and president of the officially sanctioned umbrella organisation of Muslim groups in France, supports the ban and has attempted to discourage Muslims from participating. 'We absolutely do not want confrontation," he said.

Many French feminists, including prominent Muslim women, also support the ban, arguing that the hijab is a patriarchal symbol, imposed on Muslim women by male family members. In any event, the Koranic verse which discusses veiling is, they argue, open to interpretation.

For some the feminist argument is a persuasive one. Historically, female emancipation[1] has been closely linked with dress, fashion, and the casting off of restrictive garments such as long skirts, hats, gloves and shape altering undergarments. However, we should not be seduced into believing that a law

---

[1] **emancipation:** freedom from control of another

which forces Muslim women into removing the hijab is a feminist law. Let them discard it if they choose to do so but let that choice be a personal one.

Many French people genuinely believe the hijab issue is one of liberal principle, namely that of preserving the secular nature of the state education system. In reality the proposed ban plays right into the hands of extremist national parties that have found favour in the Republic in recent years. Jews and Muslims have been the chief targets of these racial attacks; synagogues have been burned and mosques attacked and defaced.

A further escalation of anti-Muslim violence was assumed the day after the hijab street demonstrations when a bomb destroyed the car belonging to a recently appointed government official born in Algeria. Aissa Dermouche, aged 57, had been named as prefect — or top state representative — of the Jura region in early January. Dermouche is the first Muslim for decades to reach the elite ranks of the prefects and his appointment attracted much discussion. The veteran leader of the xenophobic[2] National Front, Jean-Marie Le Pen, described it as a step towards "positive discrimination" towards immigrants. François Fillon, the Minister of Social Affairs condemned the car bomb, in which mercifully no one was hurt, as "the odious act" of someone wishing to "impede" racial and religious integration in France.

So is this about headscarves? Yes, and much more; it is also about the need to uphold personal freedoms, the necessity for dialogue, compromise and the nurturing of mutual respect between France's white, Christian majority, its five million strong Muslim population and all the other ethnic groups that contribute to its development and success as a leading European power. It is also about liberty, egality[3] and fraternity, for without those three vital principles where would France be today?

---

[2] **xenophobic**: fearful of foreigners
[3] **egality**: equality

My Notes

GRAMMAR & USAGE

A rhetorical question is a device writers use to engage audiences and to focus on an idea they plan to explore or explain. Writers often pose rhetorical questions because they think the answers are obvious; for example, when the young German woman in "Germany Divided Over Hijab" asks, "'How can I lay my identity at the door of the classroom?'" she—like the writer—expects people to respond, "You can't!" Writers also raise rhetorical questions in order to answer or dispute them with evidence.

Article

Germany Divided Over Hijab

Controversy surrounds a recent court decision in favor of a school teacher wearing a headscarf.

by Andreas Tzortzis, *Christian Science Monitor*

BERLIN – Having spent the last 15 years of her life wearing the Muslim *hijab*, or head scarf, teacher Emine Öztürk can't imagine taking it off in public, even for just one minute.

But that's exactly what Ms. Öztürk might have to do if she ever wants to get a teaching job in a Berlin public school.

"It's part of my identity," says this young German of Turkish descent. "How can I lay my identity at the door of the classroom?"

It is a question on the minds of many here following a decision by Germany's highest court, allowing teacher Fereshta Ludin to wear her head scarf in class as long as there are no state laws against it. Since the decision came down two weeks ago, a majority of German states, including Berlin, have announced plans to pass such laws.

In the debate that has ensued, politicians and Muslim leaders have begun to ask some serious questions about the place their religion and identity holds in a Europe rooted in Christianity and Judaism, but with a growing Muslim population.

"You have a new generation of Muslims . . . reasonably educated, fluent in cultures of languages they live in . . . demanding a sort of legitimization; they want it without having to become assimilated," says Shireen Hunter, the head of the Center for Strategic Studies Islam Program, and editor of "Islam, Europe's Second Religion."

In France, the ban on head scarves in everything from schools to ID cards has provoked an outcry in recent years by that country's increasingly strong Muslim population. In the United Kingdom and Sweden, a more open attitude prevails. Teachers and even female Muslim police officers are allowed to wear their head scarves.

Germany's relationship to its 3.2 million Muslims is decidedly more fragile.

Touchy issues of integration such as Muslim dress and the ritual slaughter of sheep in accordance with Islamic law have been brought before courts to decide in recent years. Earlier this summer, the constitutional court ruled that a department store could not fire a Muslim woman because she wanted to wear her head scarf during work.

The legal conflicts are symptoms of the German government and Turkish community neglecting to address the issue of integration, say historians. By the time integration became a topic, the sons and grandsons of the Turkish guest workers who had arrived in the 1960s had already carved out little Ankaras and Istanbuls in Germany's major cities.

They built up parallel societies that made the Turkish grocer, corner doener[1] stand, and mosque part of the everyday urban landscape in Germany. Many Muslim leaders are puzzled why a *hijab*-wearing woman wanting to teach in a public school is such a big deal nowadays.

"We live in a free, modern society, where everyone has their own self-awareness," says Ali Kizilkaya, head of the powerful and controversial Islamrat, Germany's largest Muslim group. "Are we so weak that a square foot of cloth can make us feel threatened?"

Opponents argue that it is not the head scarf, but the fact that Ludin wants to wear it in a public school classroom. Germany has no official religion, and the state is constitutionally bound to maintain a position of neutrality in religious matters.

Eight years ago, the constitutional court ruled that crucifixes would have to be removed from classrooms in Bavaria if just one student objected.

Some observers see the push to wear the Muslim head scarf in a school setting as incompatible with this principle of state neutrality. The fact that Muslims want what many see as more freedom to express their religion than German Christians makes parliamentarian Wolfgang Bosbach angry.

"The debate is absurd," says the domestic affairs expert for the conservative Christian Democrats in the German parliament. "This is not an Islamic country, it's a Christian country, and we should not be forced to accommodate Islam."

Other Germans perceive the scarf as a threat not so much to a Judeo-Christian heritage, but to Western secularism[2] and women's rights.

---

[1] **doener**: a Turkish dish sold by street vendors
[2] **secularism**: separation of church and civil concerns

My Notes

GRAMMAR & USAGE

To achieve **variety** in sentence structure, length, and rhythm, writers may begin sentences in different ways:

- With an adverb or adverbial phrase: **In France,** the ban on head scarves....

  Earlier this summer, the constitutional court....

- With an adverbial clause: **By the time integration became a topic,** the sons and grandsons....

- With a participial phrase: **Referring to Germany's integration problems,** Professor Spielhaus says....

Use similar structural elements to vary your sentence beginnings when you write.

"There are very few women who wear the head scarf voluntarily, and their number is so small they are not worth talking about," says Seyran Ates, a women's right activist and lawyer in Berlin.

Since running away from her parents' traditional Turkish household in Berlin at 18, Ms. Ates has spent her life fighting for the rights of women yearning to break free of the traditional and religious mold their parents foresee for them.

In the two weeks since the decision came down, she has been a favorite of TV news producers looking for the choice sound bite. The 40-year-old, who wrote a book about leaving her strict home, says she is astounded at the legitimacy with which some German politicians give the head scarf.

"We need to never forget that what we're talking about here is fundamentalism[3]," she says.

Rather than decide what place a piece of cloth that represents religious freedom to some, fundamentalism to others, has in a state-run school, Germany's constitutional court referred the question to the state parliaments and the public domain—where many believe it belongs.

"We're not ready for such a decision," says Riem Spielhaus, an Islamic Studies professor at Berlin's Humboldt University. Referring to Germany's integration problems, Professor Spielhaus says, "We need an atmosphere of openness where we can admit that other religions might also change our values."

The direction the debate is going worries both Muslims and Germans. Misconceptions that the head scarf is an umbilical cord to a fundamentalist Islam could have the opposite effect. Pockets of devout Muslims, facing limited job prospects because of their religious dress, could withdraw into parallel societies harboring the type of terror nests that produced the Sept. 11 attackers.

"There's not a fundamentalist under every head scarf, and thinking that would be fatal," says Spielhaus. "Ms. Ludin's head scarf, which she willingly puts on, is good for the Western society. Banning head scarves would be a victory for fundamentalists."

Öztürk makes a similar argument, adding that her head scarf could even begin dismantling prejudices before they arise in her young students.

"I think it's very sad that this society continues to look at the head scarf as something of a threat," said Öztürk. "I find it shocking that so many things are projected onto the head scarf without anyone ever asking the women who wear them."

---

[3] **fundamentalism**: a point of view characterized by a rigid adherence to fundamental principles; often intolerant of other views

AN UNFAIR Dress Code?

On March 30, the U.S. Justice Department filed a complaint against the Muskogee Public School District in Muskogee, Oklahoma. The trouble: The Justice Department says the way the district uses its dress-code policy violates the U.S. Constitution.

Last fall, school officials twice suspended sixth-grader Nashala Hearn. They said her head scarf violated the dress code, which prohibits hats and other head coverings.

Nashala, 11, wears the head scarf, called a hijab, as part of her Muslim religious beliefs. Nashala's family is suing the school district, saying that its dress code discriminates unfairly against religious clothing. The Justice Department agrees and wants the school to change its policy.

"No student should be forced to choose between following her faith and enjoying the benefits of a public education," says Assistant Attorney General R. Alexander Acosta.

 WORD CONNECTIONS

Articles of clothing can be used to describe relationships. Complete this analogy.

hijab : female ::
yarmulke : _____

Testimony

Religious

EXPRESSION

by Nashala Hearn

Transcript of Testimony
United States Senate Committee on the Judiciary

Testimony of Nashala Hearn

The Subcommittee on the Constitution, Civil Rights and Property Rights
U.S. Senator John Cornyn, Chairman

"Beyond the Pledge of Allegiance:
Hostility to Religious Expression in the Public Square"

Tuesday, June 8, 2004
Washington, D.C.

Transcript:
Thank you Senator Cornyn. It is an honor to be here. And thank you
Senator Feingold, too.

My name is Nashala Hearn. I am 12 years old and I live in Muskogee,
Oklahoma with my father—who is here with me today—and my mother, and
my brother and my sister. I attend the Benjamin Franklin Science Academy,
which is a public middle school in my home town.

My Notes

On October 1st, 2003 I was suspended for 3 days from the Muskogee Public Schools for wearing my hijab – which is a headscarf required by religion—Islam.

I didn't know it was going to be a problem because on August 18, 2003 – my first day of school last year—I explained to my homeroom teacher that I am Muslim and I wear a hijab—and that I also pray between 1:00 and 1:30. She said that was fine and that she had a room for me to pray in.

From that day forward—I received compliments from other kids as well as school officials.

But my problems started on September 11, 2003. I was in the breakfast line when my teacher came up to me and said that after I was done eating to call my parents because my hijab looks like a bandanna or a handkerchief and that I was not allowed to wear it.

So after I was finished, I went to the office.

Mrs. Walker had already called my parents. When my parents got there they were very upset. The principal said it was a bandana and I had to change it or go home.

And this is how the battle of being obedient to God by wearing my hijab to be modest in Islam versus the school dress code policy began.

I continued to wear my hijab—because it would be against my religion not to.

So—like I said before, I was suspended from school on October 1st for 3 days. When I came back to school on October 7th—I was suspended again. This time it was for 5 days.

I was not able to go back to school after that until the problem was fixed.

This experience has been very stressful, very depressing and humiliating.

But thanks to the Department of Justice, the Rutherford Institute and my lawyer, Mrs. Leah Farish, the problem no longer exists in the Muskogee Public Schools. The school agreed to let me and other kids wear our religious clothing.

Thank you for listening and thank you very much for having me here today!

Civil Disobedience

SUGGESTED LEARNING STRATEGIES: KWL, Discussion Groups, Think-Pair-Share, Marking the Text

Fill in the KWL chart below with ideas about civil disobedience.

What I Know	What I Want to Know	What I Learned

Timed Writing Prompt: Draft a response to the following question: What is the effect of civil disobedience on changing social attitudes? Your teacher will specify the amount of time you will have to write your response. In your response, write an effective thesis, support your thesis with evidence, use appropriate rhetorical devices (such as rhetorical questions; appeals to ethos, pathos, or logos; metaphors; irony; etc.), and include effective transitions to develop your opinion and provide a logical flow of ideas.

My Notes

Speech

> **ABOUT THE AUTHOR**
> Born in 1869, Mohandas Karamchand Gandhi was a great believer in the power of using civil disobedience against governments that oppressed the poor and the disenfranchised. He spent seven years in South Africa leading and defending Indians born and living there without legal rights. It was there that he began practicing *satyagraha*, or passive resistance. Later, he returned to his homeland of India where he helped the country gain its independence from the British in 1947. He became known there as Mahatma, or "Great Soul." India, though free from Britain, suffered from internal turmoil as religious factions fought for power. Gandhi was assassinated by a fanatic in 1948.

As you read "On Civil Disobedience," consider how Gandhi might advise you to respond to an unjust law.

Excerpt from

"ON CIVIL DISOBEDIENCE"

by Mohandas K. Gandhi

JULY 27, 1916

There are two ways of countering injustice. One way is to smash the head of the man who perpetrates injustice and to get your own head smashed in the process. All strong people in the world adopt this course. Everywhere wars are fought and millions of people are killed. The consequence is not the progress of a nation but its decline. . . . No country has ever become, or will ever become, happy through victory in war. A nation does not rise that way;

it only falls further. In fact, what comes to it is defeat, not victory. And if, perchance, either our act or our purpose was ill-conceived, it brings disaster to both belligerents[1].

But through the other method of combating injustice, we alone suffer the consequences of our mistakes, and the other side is wholly spared. This other method is *satyagraha*[2]. One who resorts to it does not have to break another's head; he may merely have his own head broken. He has to be prepared to die himself suffering all the pain. In opposing the atrocious laws of the Government of South Africa, it was this method that we adopted. We made it clear to the said Government that we would never bow to its outrageous laws. No clapping is possible without two hands to do it, and no quarrel without two persons to make it. Similarly, no State is possible without two entities, the rulers and the ruled. You are our sovereign, our Government, only so long as we consider ourselves your subjects. When we are not subjects, you are not the sovereign either. So long as it is your endeavour to control us with justice and love, we will let you to do so. But if you wish to strike at us from behind, we cannot permit it. Whatever you do in other matters, you will have to ask our opinion about the laws that concern us. If you make laws to keep us suppressed in a wrongful manner and without taking us into confidence, these laws will merely adorn the statute books[3]. We will never obey them. Award us for it what punishment you like; we will put up with it. Send us to prison and we will live there as in a paradise. Ask us to mount the scaffold[4] and we will do so laughing. Shower what sufferings you like upon us; we will calmly endure all and not hurt a hair of your body. We will gladly die and will not so much as touch you. But so long as there is yet life in these our bones, we will never comply with your arbitrary[5] laws.

Discussion Group:

On separate paper, create a graphic organizer that illustrates Gandhi's argument.

Who is Gandhi's audience? What in the text tells you this?

WORD CONNECTIONS

Belligerents contains the root *-belli-*, from the Latin word *bellum*, meaning "war." This root also appears in *bellicose*, *antebellum*, and *rebellion*.

Suppressed contains the root *-press-*, from the Latin word *premere*, meaning "to press." This root also appears in *repress*, *impress*, *impression*, and *pressure*.

LITERARY TERMS

An **audience** is the reader, listener, or viewer of a particular piece of writing, speaking, or visual.

---

[1] **belligerents**: participants in a war
[2] **satyagraha**: (Sanskrit) insistence on truth—a term used by Gandhi to describe his policy of seeking reform by means of nonviolent resistance
[3] **statute books**: books of law
[4] **scaffold**: a platform on which people are executed by hanging
[5] **arbitrary**: illogical, unreasonable

Speech

ABOUT THE AUTHOR

Martin Luther King, Jr. (1929–1968) is considered the most important voice of the Civil Rights Movement in the United States. Under King's leadership, African Americans gathered forces to overcome the legalized racism of segregation in the South. King enjoined communities to participate in nonviolent acts of resistance. In 1963, King and many others were sent to jail for peacefully demonstrating in Birmingham, Alabama. While in jail, King wrote a letter in which he articulated his ideas about civil disobedience and nonviolent resistance. Soon after, King and a crowd of 200,000 participated in the historic March on Washington, D.C., where King gave perhaps his most famous speech, "I Have a Dream." King was assassinated at age 39.

Dr. King also advocated civil disobedience. Annotate "Letter from Birmingham Jail" as your teacher directs a guided reading.

Excerpt from

Letter from Birmingham Jail

Dr. Martin Luther King, Jr.

APRIL 17, 1963

Chunk 1

My Dear Fellow Clergymen:

While confined here in the Birmingham city jail, I came across your recent statement calling my present activities "unwise and untimely." Seldom do I pause to answer criticisms of my work and ideas. If I sought to answer all the criticism that cross my desk, my secretaries would have little time for anything other than such correspondence in the course of the day, and I would have no time for constructive work. But since I feel that you are men of genuine goodwill and that your criticisms are sincerely set forth, I want to try to answer your statement in what I hope will be patient and reasonable terms.

I think I should indicate why I am here in Birmingham, since you have been influenced by the view which argues against "outsiders coming in." I have the honor of serving as president of the Southern Christian Leadership Conference, an organization operating in every Southern state, with headquarters in Atlanta, Georgia. We have some eighty-five affiliated organizations across the South, and one of them is the Alabama Christian Movement for Human Rights. Frequently we share staff, educational, and financial resources with our affiliates. Several months ago the affiliate here in Birmingham asked us to be on call to engage in a nonviolent direct-action program if such were deemed necessary. We readily consented, and when the hour came, we lived up to our promise. So I, along with several members of my staff, am here because I was invited here. I am here because I have organizational ties here.

But more basically, I am in Birmingham because injustice is here. Just as the prophets of the eighth century B.C. left their villages and carried their "thus saith the Lord" far beyond the boundaries of their hometowns, and just as the Apostle Paul left his village of Tarsus and carried the gospel of Jesus Christ to the far corners of the Greco-Roman world, so am I compelled to carry the gospel of freedom beyond my own hometown. Like Paul, I must constantly respond to the Macedonian call for aid.

Moreover, I am cognizant of the interrelatedness of all communities and states. I cannot sit idly by in Atlanta and not be concerned about what happens in Birmingham. Injustice anywhere is a threat to justice everywhere. We are caught in an inescapable network of mutuality, tied in a single garment of destiny. Whatever affects one directly, affects all indirectly. Never again can we afford to live with the narrow, provincial "outside agitator" idea. Anyone who lives inside the United States can never be considered an outsider anywhere within its bounds.

You deplore the demonstrations taking place in Birmingham. But your statement, I am sorry to say, fails to express a similar concern for the conditions that brought about the demonstrations. I am sure that none of you would want to rest content with the superficial kind of social analysis that deals merely with effects and does not grapple with underlying causes. It is unfortunate that demonstrations are taking place in Birmingham, but it is even more unfortunate that the city's white power structure left the Negro community with no alternative. . . .

You may well ask: "Why direct action? Why sit-ins, marches, and so forth? Isn't negotiation a better path?" You are quite right in calling for negotiation. Indeed, this is the very purpose of direct action. Nonviolent direct action seeks to create such a crisis and foster such a tension that a community which has constantly refused to negotiate is forced to confront the issue. It seeks so to dramatize the issue that it can no longer be ignored. My citing the creation of tension as part of the work of the nonviolent-resister may sound rather shocking. But I must confess that I am not afraid of the word "tension." I have earnestly opposed violent tension, but there is a type of constructive, nonviolent tension which is necessary for growth. Just as Socrates felt that it was necessary to create a tension in the mind so that individuals could rise from the bondage of myths and halftruths to the unfettered realm of creative analysis and objective appraisal, so must we see the need for nonviolent gadflies[1] to create the kind of tension in society that will help men rise from the dark depths of prejudice and racism to the majestic heights of understanding and brotherhood.

Chunk 2

---

[1] **gadflies**: pests

The purpose of our direct-action program is to create a situation so crisis-packed that it will inevitably open the door to negotiation. I therefore concur with you in your call for negotiation. Too long has our beloved Southland been bogged down in a tragic effort to live in monologue rather than dialogue. . . .

Chunk 3

You express a great deal of anxiety over our willingness to break laws. This is certainly a legitimate concern. Since we so diligently urge people to obey the Supreme Court's decision of 1954[2] outlawing segregation in the public schools, at first glance it may seem rather paradoxical[3] for us consciously to break laws. One may ask: "How can you advocate breaking some laws and obeying others?" The answer lies in the fact that there are two types of laws: just and unjust. I would be the first to advocate obeying just laws. One has not only a legal but a moral responsibility to obey just laws. Conversely, one has a moral responsibility to disobey unjust laws. I would agree with St. Augustine[4] that "an unjust law is no law at all."

Now, what is the difference between the two? How does one determine whether a law is just or unjust? A just law is a man-made code that squares with the moral law or the law of God. An unjust law is a code that is out of harmony with the moral law. To put it in the terms of St. Thomas Aquinas: An unjust law is a human law that is not rooted in eternal law and natural law. Any law that uplifts human personality is just. Any law that degrades human personality is unjust. All segregation statutes are unjust because segregation distorts the soul and damages the personality. It gives the segregator a false sense of superiority and the segregated a false sense of inferiority. Segregation, to use the terminology of the Jewish philosopher Martin Buber, substitutes an "I-it" relationship for an "I-thou" relationship and ends up relegating persons to the status of things. Hence segregation is not only politically, economically and sociologically unsound, it is morally wrong and sinful. Paul Tillich has said that sin is separation. Is not segregation an existential expression of man's tragic separation, his awful estrangement, his terrible sinfulness? Thus is it that I can urge men to obey the 1954 decision of the Supreme Court, for it is morally right; and I can urge them to disobey segregation ordinances, for they are morally wrong.

Chunk 4

Let us consider a more concrete example of just and unjust laws. An unjust law is a code that a numerical or power majority group compels a minority group to obey but does not make binding on itself. This is difference made legal. By the same token, a just law is a code that a majority compels a minority to follow and that it is willing to follow itself. This is sameness made legal.

Let me give another explanation. A law is unjust if it is inflicted on a minority that, as a result of being denied the right to vote, had no part in

---

[2] **1954 decision of the Supreme Court**: *Brown v. Board of Education of Topeka*, which stated that racially separated schools were unequal and violated the 14th Amendment of the U.S. Constitution

[3] **paradoxical**: self-contradictory

[4] **St. Augustine, St. Thomas Aquinas, Martin Buber, Paul Tillich**: theologians

My Notes

enacting or devising the law. Who can say that the legislature of Alabama which set up that state's segregation laws was democratically elected? Throughout Alabama all sorts of devious methods are used to prevent Negroes from becoming registered voters, and there are some counties in which, even though Negroes constitute a majority of the population, not a single Negro is registered. Can any law enacted under such circumstances be considered democratically structured?

Sometimes a law is just on its face and unjust in its application. For instance, I have been arrested on a charge of parading without a permit. Now, there is nothing wrong in having an ordinance which requires a permit for a parade. But such an ordinance becomes unjust when it is used to maintain segregation and to deny citizens the First-Amendment privilege of peaceful assembly and protest.

I hope you are able to see the distinction I am trying to point out. In no sense do I advocate evading or defying the law, as would the rabid segregationist. That would lead to anarchy. One who breaks an unjust law must do so openly, lovingly, and with a willingness to accept the penalty. I submit that an individual who breaks a law that conscience tells him is unjust, and who willingly accepts the penalty of imprisonment in order to arouse the conscience of the community over its injustice, is in reality expressing the highest respect for law.

Of course, there is nothing new about this kind of civil disobedience. It was evidenced sublimely in the refusal of Shadrach, Meshach, and Abednego[5] to obey the laws of Nebuchadnezzar, on the ground that a higher moral law was at stake. It was practiced superbly by the early Christians, who were willing to face hungry lions and the excruciating pain of chopping blocks rather than submit to certain unjust laws of the Roman Empire. To a degree, academic freedom is a reality today because Socrates practiced civil disobedience. In our own nation, the Boston Tea Party represented a massive act of civil disobedience.

Chunk 5

We should never forget that everything Adolf Hitler did in Germany was "legal" and everything the Hungarian[6] freedom fighters did in Hungary was "illegal." It was "illegal" to aid and comfort a Jew in Hitler's Germany. Even so, I am sure that, had I lived in Germany at the time, I would have aided and comforted my Jewish brothers. If today I lived in a Communist country where certain principles dear to the Christian faith are suppressed, I would openly advocate disobeying that country's anti-religious laws. . . .

Oppressed people cannot remain oppressed forever. The yearning for freedom eventually manifests itself, and that is what has happened to the American Negro. Something within has reminded him of his birthright of

Chunk 6

---

[5] **Shadrach, Meshach, and Abednego; Nebuchadnezzar**: In the Bible (Daniel), King Nebuchadnezzar of Babylon required citizens to worship an idol. Shadrach, Meshach, and Abednego refused, accepting the punishment of a fiery furnace. They were miraculously saved, unharmed by the fire.

[6] Hungarian freedom fighters demanded democracy for Hungary but were defeated in a Soviet attack in 1956.

Civil Disobedience

WORD CONNECTIONS

Dr. King relates the word "Zeitgeist" to the momentum of the Civil Rights Movement. The word derives from German, meaning "spirit of the times." Its parts provide a literal meaning: *zeit* meaning time and *geist* meaning spirit.

My Notes

LITERARY TERMS

An **allusion** is a reference to a well-known person, event, or place from literature, history, music, or art.

freedom, and something without has reminded him that it can be gained. Consciously or unconsciously, he has been caught up by the Zeitgeist[7], and with his black brothers of Africa and his brown and yellow brothers of Asia, South America, and the Caribbean, the United States Negro is moving with a sense of great urgency toward the promised land of racial justice. If one recognizes this vital urge that has engulfed the Negro community, one should readily understand why public demonstrations are taking place. The Negro has many pent-up resentments and latent frustrations, and he must release them. So let him march; let him make prayer pilgrimages to the city hall; let him go on freedom rides — and try to understand why he must do so. If his repressed emotions are not released in nonviolent ways, they will seek expression through violence; this is not a threat but a fact of history. So I have not said to my people, "Get rid of your discontent." Rather, I have tried to say that this normal and healthy discontent can be channeled into the creative outlet of nonviolent direct action. And now this approach is being termed extremist.

Chunk 7

But though I was initially disappointed at being categorized as an extremist, as I continued to think about the matter I gradually gained a measure of satisfaction from the label. Was not Jesus an extremist for love: "Love your enemies, bless them that curse you, do good to them that hate you, and pray for them which despitefully use you, and persecute you." Was not Amos[8] an extremist for justice: "Let justice roll down like waters and righteousness like an ever-flowing stream." Was not Paul an extremist for the Christian gospel: "I bear in my body the marks of the Lord Jesus." Was not Martin Luther an extremist: "Here I stand; I cannot do otherwise, so help me God." And John Bunyan: "I will stay in jail to the end of my days before I make a butchery of my conscience." And Abraham Lincoln: "This nation cannot survive half slave and half free." And Thomas Jefferson: "We hold these truths to be self-evident, that all men are created equal . . . ." So the question is not whether we will be extremists, but what kind of extremists we will be. Will we be extremists for hate or for love? Will we be extremists for the preservation of injustice or for the extension of justice? In that dramatic scene on Cavalry's hill three men were crucified. We must never forget that all three were crucified for the same crime — the crime of extremism. Two were extremists for immorality, and thus fell below their environment. The other, Jesus Christ, was an extremist for love, truth, and goodness, and thereby rose above his environment. Perhaps the South, the nation, and the world are in dire need of creative extremists. . . . I wish you had commended the Negro sit-inners and demonstrators of Birmingham for their sublime courage, their willingness to suffer, and their amazing discipline in the midst of great provocation. One day the South will recognize its real heroes. They will be the James Merediths, with the noble sense of purpose that enables them to face jeering and hostile mobs, and with the agonizing loneliness

---

[7] **Zeitgeist**: German for "the spirit of the times"

[8] **Amos, Martin Luther, John Bunyan, James Meredith**: all known for courageous opposition to injustice

that characterizes the life of the pioneer. They will be old, oppressed, battered Negro women, symbolized in a seventy-two-year-old woman in Montgomery, Alabama, who rose up with a sense of dignity and when her people decided not to ride segregated buses, and who responded with ungrammatical profundity to one who inquired about her weariness: "My feets is tired, but my soul is at rest." They will be the young high school and college students, the young ministers of the gospel and a host of their elders, courageously and nonviolently sitting in at lunch counters and willingly going to jail for conscience' sake. One day the South will know that when these disinherited children of God sat down at lunch counters, they were in reality standing up for what is best in the American dream and for the most sacred values in our Judaeo-Christian heritage, thereby bringing our nation back to those great wells of democracy which were dug deep by the founding fathers in their formulation of the Constitution and the Declaration of Independence.

Never before have I written so long a letter. I'm afraid it is much too long to take your precious time. I can assure you that it would have been much shorter if I had been writing from a comfortable desk, but what else can one do when he is alone in a narrow jail cell, other than write long letters, think long thoughts, and pray long prayers?

Chunk 8

If I have said anything in this letter that overstates the truth and indicates an unreasonable impatience, I beg you to forgive me. If I have said anything that understates the truth and indicates my having a patience that allows me to settle for anything less than brotherhood, I beg God to forgive me.

I hope this letter finds you strong in the faith. I also hope that circumstances will soon make it possible for me to meet each of you, not as an integrationist or a civil-rights leader but as a fellow clergyman and a Christian brother. Let us all hope that the dark clouds of racial prejudice will soon pass away and the deep fog of misunderstanding will be lifted from our fear-drenched communities, and in some not too distant tomorrow the radiant stars of love and brotherhood will shine over our great nation with all their scintillating beauty.

Yours for the cause of Peace and Brotherhood, Martin Luther King, Jr.

After reading the letter, analyze how Dr. King uses his knowledge of his audience to shape a persuasive argument.

Taking into consideration the reading, writing, thinking, and discussing that you have done in the unit so far, reflect on your growing understanding of the essential questions in this unit:

- What is the nature of justice?
- How does one construct a persuasive argument?

My Notes

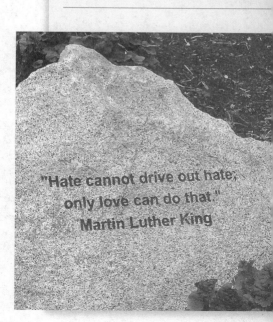

"Hate cannot drive out hate; only love can do that."
Martin Luther King

Justice and Moral Reasoning

Survey: How Just Are You?

Circle only *one* choice in each of the following:

1. I should not exceed the speed limit on the highway because

   a. I will get a ticket that will cost me a lot of money and time at court.

   b. it is the law, and laws need to be followed.

   c. I am concerned about everyone else on the highway and their right to be safe and free from danger.

2. I should not cheat on my geometry test because

   a. I will get an "F" if I get caught.

   b. my teacher and my parents will think I'm a bad person if I get caught.

   c. I will hurt others through my actions by lowering the standards of student behavior whether I am caught or not.

3. I should not smoke in the school bathroom because

   a. there's not enough ventilation and I might make myself sick.

   b. the principal said it is against school rules.

   c. others might come in after me, breathe in the smoke, and become ill.

4. I should pay all my taxes because

   a. I could go to jail if I do not.

   b. people will think of me as a good citizen.

   c. my taxes, along with those of others, will help to pay for services used by all.

Total #a _____   Total # b _____   Total # c _____

If you have mainly "a" responses, you are at the **preconventional level**. What might people who make decisions at the preconventional level be like?

If you have mainly "b" responses, you are at the **conventional level**. What might people who make decisions at the conventional level be like?

If you have mainly "c" responses, you are at the **post-conventional level**. What might people who make decisions at the post-conventional level be like?

Which level are you? Do you think that the description fits you? Explain.

Kohlberg's Six Stages of MORAL REASONING

Lawrence Kohlberg (1927–1987) was a teacher of education and social psychology at two American universities, the University of Chicago and Harvard University. In 1981, he published *The Philosophy of Moral Development*, a definitive study on how a child's conscience and moral awareness develops. The text that follows explains Kohlberg's studies and the theories he developed to describe the stages people go through as they develop moral reasoning.

In the late 1950s, Lawrence Kohlberg began to collect data related to moral questions. Kohlberg had studied Jean Piaget's earlier work in cognitive and moral development and used this as a foundation for a 15-year study of moral reasoning. Piaget's work focused primarily on uncovering cognitive stages.[1] Kohlberg's study also focused on a developmental sequence of stages and revealed that individuals restructure their thinking about social and moral questions just as they develop their cognitive structure from the very concrete toward the more abstract.

Specifically, Kohlberg introduced a developmental theory for moral reasoning. The theory presents six stages of moral reasoning:[2]

I. PRECONVENTIONAL LEVEL

At this level the child is responsive to cultural rules and labels of good and bad, right and wrong, but interprets these labels in terms of either the physical or the hedonistic consequences of action (punishment, reward, exchange of favors) or in terms of the physical power of those who enunciate the rules and labels. The level is divided into two stages:

---

[1] As most clearly reflected in thinking, cognition means putting things together, relating events. In cognitive theories, such relating is assumed to be an active connecting process, not a passive connection of events through external association and repetition (Kohlberg, "The Concepts of Developmental Psychology as the Central Guide to Education," Proceedings of the Conference on Psychology and the Process of Schooling in the Next Decade [Washington: U.S.O.E., 1973], p. 4.)

[2] Kohlberg, Lawrence, "From Is to Ought: How to Commit the Naturalistic Fallacy and Get Away with It in the Study of Moral Development," in *Cognitive Development and Epistemology*, edited by T. Mischel. (New York: 1971), p. 164.

Justice and Moral Reasoning

Stage 1: The punishment and obedience orientation. The physical consequences of action determine its goodness or badness regardless of the human meaning or value of these consequences. Avoidance of punishment and unquestioning deference to power are valued in their own right, not in terms of respect for an underlying moral order supported by punishment and authority (the latter being Stage 4).

Stage 2: The instrumental relativist orientation. Right action consists of that which instrumentally satisfies one's own needs and occasionally the needs of others. Human relations are viewed in terms like those of the market place. Elements of fairness, reciprocity, and equal sharing are present, but they are always interpreted in a physical or pragmatic way.

Reciprocity is a matter of "you scratch my back and I'll scratch yours," not of loyalty, gratitude, or justice.

II. CONVENTIONAL LEVEL

At this level, maintaining the expectations of the individual's family, group, or nation is perceived as valuable in its own right, regardless of immediate and obvious consequences. The attitude is not only one of conformity to personal expectations and social order, but of loyalty to it, of actively maintaining, supporting, and justifying the order and of identifying with the persons or group involved in it. At this level, there are two stages:

Stage 3: The interpersonal concordance of "good boy–nice girl" orientation. Good behavior is that which pleases or helps and is approved by others. There is much conformity to stereotypical images of what is majority or natural behavior. Behavior is frequently judged by intention. "He means well" becomes important for the first time. One earns approval by being nice.

Stage 4: The law and order orientation. This is orientation toward authority, fixed rules, and the maintenance of the social order. Right behavior consists of doing one's duty, showing respect for authority, and maintaining the given social order for its own sake.

III. POST-CONVENTIONAL, AUTONOMOUS, OR PRINCIPLED LEVEL

At this level, there is a clear effort to define moral values and principles which have validity and application apart from the authority of the groups or persons holding these principles and apart from the individual's own identification with these groups. This level has two stages:

Stage 5: The social-contract legalistic orientation, generally with utilitarian overtones. Right action tends to be defined in terms of general individual rights and in terms of standards which have been critically examined and agreed upon by the whole society. There is a clear awareness of the relativism of personal values and opinions and a corresponding emphasis upon procedural rules for reaching consensus. Aside from what is constitutionally and democratically agreed upon, the right is a matter of personal values

My Notes

and opinion. The result is an emphasis upon the legal point of view, but with an emphasis upon the possibility of changing law in terms of rational considerations of social utility (rather than rigidly maintaining it in terms of Stage 4 law and order). Outside the legal realm, free agreement and contract are the binding elements of obligation. This is the official morality of the American government and Constitution.

Stage 6: The universal ethical principle orientation. Right is defined by the decision of conscience in accord with self-chosen ethical principles appealing to logical comprehensiveness, universality, and consistency. These principles are abstract and ethical (the Golden Rule, the categorical imperative) and are not concrete moral rules like the Ten Commandments. At heart, these are universal principles of justice, of the reciprocity and equality of human rights, and of respect for dignity of human beings as individual persons.

The six stages represent a pattern of thinking which integrates each person's experience and perspective on specific moral issues.

Justice and Moral Reasoning

After reading about Kohlberg's three levels of moral development, examine the following fictional scenario.

> A man named Heinz had a wife dying from a rare disease. A drug that might save her was available from a druggist in town, but he was charging $200,000, a sum that Heinz could never pay and was ten times what the druggist paid for the drug himself. Heinz borrowed all the money he could and went to the druggist with half the amount needed and asked him to sell the drug cheaper, but the druggist refused.
>
> Heinz became desperate and broke into the druggist's store one night and stole the drug.
>
> Should Heinz have done that?

How might a person at each level of development respond to Heinz's situation? Provide a reason for your decisions.

Level	Would he have stolen?	Why or why not? (Use a quote from the text to support)
Preconventional		
Conventional		
Post-conventional		

What would *you* have done in this situation? Why? Which level does this represent?

What light do Kohlberg's levels shed on your understanding of the nature of justice?

Conflicts in Justice

SUGGESTED LEARNING STRATEGIES: **Paraphrasing, Quickwrite**

Preparation for Socratic Seminar

Would Heinz go to jail if he were caught? Should he? Is he willing to go to jail for his crime?

Martin Luther King, Jr., Mahatma Gandhi, Susan B. Anthony, and many others have gone to jail when they broke laws with which they did not agree. What do you know about their actions or those of others who made similar choices? What types of laws were these individuals willing to break despite the penalty?

Issue to Discuss

When is it acceptable to break a law?

Generating Questions

Thought-provoking questions keep a Socratic Seminar interesting. Brainstorm some questions that you might bring into the discussion:

Reflection on Seminar

Reflect on two aspects of this seminar. On separate paper, write thoughtfully about what you learned about the nature of justice from this discussion. Next, describe how successful you feel the discussion was. What might you change the next time your class holds a Socratic Seminar?

Depicting Injustice

Protesting Injustice through an Essay

Based on what you have learned about this writer, why do you think injustice would be of particular concern to him?

Your teacher will guide your reading of an essay by Alexandr Solzhenitsyn. Afterwards, visualize and create an artistic depiction of the power of literature over the power of lies.

One Word of TRUTH Outweighs the World

by Alexandr Solzhenitsyn

ABOUT THE AUTHOR
Aleksandr Isayevich Solzhenitsyn (1918–2008) became a worldwide figure when he was exiled from the Soviet Union in 1974 for publishing a historical account of the wretched system of Soviet prison camps known as gulags. Solzhenitsyn had been imprisoned as a young soldier during World War II for writing a letter critical of Stalin, the Soviet dictator. His experiences in a Siberian prison became the basis for one of his best-known works, *One Day in the Life of Ivan Denisovitch*. For years afterward, Solzhenitsyn was forced to publish his works secretly and often abroad because of the threat of further incarceration. Solzhenitsyn lived in the United States for twenty years, but when he regained his Soviet citizenship in 1994, he returned home and continued writing.

My Notes

I THINK THAT WORLD LITERATURE has the power in these frightening times to help mankind see itself accurately despite what is advocated by partisans and by parties. It has the power to transmit the condensed experience of one region to another, so that different scales of values are combined, and so that one people accurately and concisely knows the true history of another with a power of recognition and acute awareness as if it had lived through that history itself–and could thus be spared repeating old mistakes. At the same time, perhaps we ourselves may succeed in developing our own WORLD-WIDE VIEW, like any man, with the center of the eye seeing what is nearby but the periphery of vision taking in what is happening in the rest of the world. We will make correlations and maintain world-wide standards.

Who, if not writers, are to condemn their own unsuccessful governments (in some states this is the easiest way to make a living; everyone who is not too lazy does it) as well as society itself, whether for its cowardly humiliation or for its self-satisfied weakness, or the lightheaded escapades of the young, or the youthful pirates brandishing knives?

We will be told: What can literature do against the pitiless onslaught of naked violence? Let us not forget that violence does not and cannot flourish by itself; it is inevitably intertwined with LYING. Between them there is the closest, the most profound and natural bond: nothing screens violence

WORD CONNECTIONS
The title of this essay has its origins in a Russian proverb. The two key words here are "truth" and "outweighs." What are the denotative and connotative meanings of the words, and what do they convey as the meaning of this title?

My Notes

except lies, and the only way lies can hold out is by violence. Whoever has once announced violence as his METHOD must inexorably choose lying as his PRINCIPLE. At birth, violence behaves openly and even proudly. But as soon as it becomes stronger and firmly established, it senses the thinning of the air around it and cannot go on without befogging itself in lies, coating itself with lying's sugary oratory. It does not always or necessarily go straight for the gullet; usually it demands of its victims only allegiance to the lie, only complicity in the lie.

The simple act of an ordinary courageous man is not to take part, not to support lies! Let *that* come into the world and even reign over it, but not through me. Writers and artists can do more: they can VANQUISH LIES! In the struggle against lies, art has always won and always will.

Conspicuously, incontestably for everyone. Lies can stand up against much in the world, but not against art.

Once lies have been dispelled, the repulsive nakedness of violence will be exposed—and hollow violence will collapse.

That, my friend, is why I think we can help the world in its red-hot hour: not by the nay-saying of having no armaments, not by abandoning oneself to the carefree life, but by going into battle!

In Russian, proverbs about TRUTH are favorites. They persistently express the considerable, bitter, grim experience of the people, often astonishingly:

ONE WORD OF TRUTH OUTWEIGHS THE WORLD.

On such a seemingly fantastic violation of the law of the conservation of mass and energy are based both my own activities and my appeal to the writers of the whole world.

GRAMMAR & USAGE

The stylistic device of parallel structure gives sentences balance and emphasis. Sentences with parallel structure include words, phrases, or clauses with the same grammatical form. The purpose is to show that ideas or images have an equal weight or importance. In this example from "One Word of Truth Outweighs the World," Solzhenitsyn uses two infinitive phrases to emphasize his point: "The simple act of an ordinary courageous man is *not to take part, not to support lies!*"

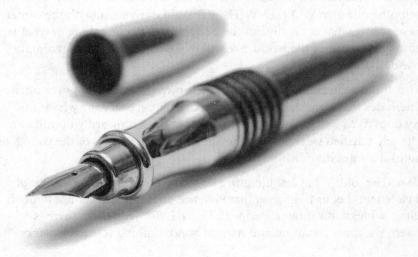

Protesting Injustice through a Painting

Your teacher will show you a copy of *Guernica*, a famous painting by Pablo Picasso. As you study Picasso's *Guernica*, use the OPTIC strategy to help you analyze it.

Overview Take a first look at the artwork, noticing the subject. Brainstorm some questions about it.	
Parts Look closely at the artwork, making note of important elements and details.	
Title Pay attention to the title and any captions.	
Interrelationships Look for connections between and among the title, caption, and the parts of the art.	
Conclusion Form a conclusion about the meaning of the artwork. Remember the questions you asked when you first examined it. Be prepared to support your conclusion with evidence.	

Depicting Injustice

Protesting Injustice through a Photo Essay

Use the OPTIC strategy to analyze other visual art forms, such as a photo essay.

Overview

Take a first look at the photo essay, noticing the main subjects.

Brainstorm some questions about the photo essay.

Parts

Look closely at the photo essay, making note of important elements and details.

Notice the audio track, if the photo essay is a multi-media presentation.

Title

Pay attention to the title and any captions.

Interrelationships

Look for connections between and among the title, captions, and the parts of the graphic.

Notice the order of the images; what meaning is created by sequencing the images in this way?

How are images juxtaposed for effect?

Conclusion

Form a conclusion about the meaning of the photo essay. Remember the questions you asked when you first examined the visual.

What is the photographer's thesis?

What is his support?

What persuasive appeals does he use?

Be prepared to support your idea with evidence from the text.

GUERNICA:
Testimony of War

It is modern art's most powerful antiwar statement... created by the twentieth century's most well-known and least understood artist. But the mural called *Guernica* is not at all what Pablo Picasso has in mind when he agrees to paint the centerpiece for the Spanish Pavilion of the 1937 World's Fair.

For three months, Picasso has been searching for inspiration for the mural, but the artist is in a sullen mood, frustrated by a decade of turmoil in his personal life and dissatisfaction with his work. The politics of his native homeland are also troubling him, as a brutal civil war ravages Spain. Republican forces, loyal to the newly elected government, are under attack from a fascist coup led by Generalissimo Francisco Franco. Franco promises prosperity and stability to the people of Spain. Yet he delivers only death and destruction.

Hoping for a bold visual protest to Franco's treachery from Spain's most eminent artist, colleagues and representatives of the democratic government have come to Picasso's home in Paris to ask him to paint the mural. Though his sympathies clearly lie with the new Republic, Picasso generally avoids politics - and disdains overtly political art.

The official theme of the Paris Exposition is a celebration of modern technology. Organizers hope this vision of a bright future will jolt the nations out of the economic depression and social unrest of the thirties.

As plans unfold, much excitement is generated by the Aeronautics Pavilion, featuring the latest advances in aircraft design and engineering. Who would suspect that this dramatic progress would bring about such dire consequences?

On April 27th, 1937, unprecedented atrocities are perpetrated on behalf of Franco against the civilian population of a little Basque village in northern Spain. Chosen for bombing practice by Hitler's burgeoning war machine, the hamlet is pounded with high-explosive and incendiary bombs for over three hours. Townspeople are cut down as they run from the crumbling buildings. Guernica burns for three days. Sixteen hundred civilians are killed or wounded.

By May 1st, news of the massacre at Guernica reaches Paris, where more than a million protesters flood the streets to voice their outrage in the largest May Day demonstration the city has ever seen. Eyewitness reports fill the front pages of Paris papers. Picasso is stunned by the stark black and white photographs. Appalled and enraged, Picasso rushes through the crowded streets to his studio, where he quickly sketches the first images for the mural he will call *Guernica*. His search for inspiration is over.

From the beginning, Picasso chooses not to represent the horror of Guernica in realist or romantic terms. Key figures - a woman with outstretched arms, a bull, an agonized horse - are refined in sketch after sketch, then transferred to the capacious canvas, which he also reworks several times. "A painting is not thought out and settled in advance," said Picasso. "While it is being done, it changes as one's thoughts change. And when it's finished, it goes on changing, according to the state of mind of whoever is looking at it."

Depicting Injustice

Three months later, *Guernica* is delivered to the Spanish Pavilion, where the Paris Exposition is already in progress. Located out of the way, and grouped with the pavilions of smaller countries some distance from the Eiffel Tower, the Spanish Pavilion stood in the shadow of Albert Speer's monolith to Nazi Germany. The Spanish Pavilion's main attraction, Picasso's *Guernica*, is a sober reminder of the tragic events in Spain.

Initial reaction to the painting is overwhelmingly critical. The German fair guide calls *Guernica* "a hodgepodge of body parts that any four-year-old could have painted." It dismisses the mural as the dream of a madman. Even the Soviets, who had sided with the Spanish government against Franco, react coolly. They favor more overt imagery, believing that only more realistic art can have political or social consequence. Yet Picasso's tour de force would become one of this century's most unsettling indictments of war.

After the Fair, *Guernica* tours Europe and Northern America to raise consciousness about the threat of fascism. From the beginning of World War II until 1981, *Guernica* is housed in its temporary home at the Museum of Modern Art in New York, though it makes frequent trips abroad to such places as Munich, Cologne, Stockholm, and even São Paulo in Brazil. The one place it does not go is Spain. Although Picasso had always intended for the mural to be owned by the Spanish people, he refuses to allow it to travel to Spain until the country enjoys "public liberties and democratic institutions."

Speculations as to the exact meaning of the jumble of tortured images are as numerous and varied as the people who have viewed the painting. There is no doubt that *Guernica* challenges our notions of warfare as heroic and exposes it as a brutal act of self-destruction. But it is a hallmark of Picasso's art that any symbol can hold many, often contradictory meanings, and the precise significance of the imagery in *Guernica* remains ambiguous. When asked to explain his symbolism, Picasso remarked, "It isn't up to the painter to define the symbols. Otherwise it would be better if he wrote them out in so many words! The public who look at the picture must interpret the symbols as they understand them."

In 1973, Pablo Picasso, the most influential artist of the twentieth century, dies at the age of ninety-two. And when Franco dies in 1975, Spain moves closer to its dream of democracy. On the centenary of Picasso's birth, October 25th, 1981, Spain's new Republic carries out the best commemoration possible: the return of *Guernica* to Picasso's native soil in a testimony of national reconciliation. In its final journey, Picasso's apocalyptic vision has served as a banner for a nation on its path toward freedom and democracy.

Now showcased at the Reina Sofía, Spain's national museum of modern art, *Guernica* is acclaimed as an artistic masterpiece, taking its rightful place among the great Spanish treasures of El Greco, Goya and Velazquez. "A lot of people recognize the painting," says art historian Patricia Failing. "They may not even know that it's a Picasso, but they recognize the image. It's a kind of icon."

Consider the genres you studied in this activity. What are their similarities and differences? What can one **genre** do that another cannot?

> **LITERARY TERMS**
>
> A **genre** is a kind or style of literature or art. For example, poetry, short story, and memoir are literary genres. Painting and sculpture are artistic genres. Each genre has specific characteristics.

Brainstorm other art forms that can be used in protest of injustice.

Choose the art form represented in this activity that you believe is most persuasive, and write a reflection on what elements of the text most move you. Be sure to address the essential question, "How does one construct a persuasive argument?"

"Get Up, Stand Up": Protest Music

1. Music has a long tradition as a vehicle for protesting injustice. What do you know about protest songs? Brainstorm a list of protest songs, artists, and issues.

2. Listen to a protest song and read the lyrics. Who do you think was the target audience for this song? Support your answer with evidence from the lyrics.

3. Describe the language used in the song. Is this language appropriate for the target audience? Why or why not?

4. **Timed Writing Prompt:** How could someone use music to raise awareness and raise funds to fight another important concern? Draft a plan and write an appeal to your audience. In your draft, use appropriate rhetorical devices such as metaphors, hyperbole, rhetorical questions, or appeals to logos, ethos, or pathos. Consider how you can use parallel structure of sentences or phrases to convey meaning and enhance the impact of your appeal. Include appropriate transitions to convey meaning. Your teacher will specify the amount of time you have to write your plan and your appeal.

5. Examine the features of *genres* you have studied in this unit. Space is provided for you to include additional features and genres on the graphic organizer. Be prepared to explain your thinking.

	Use powerful words	Use powerful images	Use music	Appeal to logos	Appeal to ethos	Appeal to pathos	Take audience into account	Use facts for support		
Editorial										
Essay										
Print Ad										
Film										
Drama										
News Article										
Speech										
Letter										
Painting										
Photo Essay										
Song										

6. Revisit the anticipation guide you completed for the International Justice activity (Activity 4.5). Have you changed your mind about any of the statements? Explain.

Composing a Persuasive Text

SUGGESTED LEARNING STRATEGIES: Drafting, Sharing and
Responding

Assignment

Your assignment is to compose a persuasive text about an issue of justice
that is important to you. You will choose an appropriate *audience* and *genre*
for your *argument*. Conduct research as needed to help you clarify your issue
and to support your argument. Consider the whole range of views on your
topic and what information you might include to address these views.

Steps

Prewriting

1. You and your classmates have brainstormed several issues related to
justice. Choose an issue that matters to you personally. If you need
to learn more about the issue, conduct research to help you make a
convincing argument. Formulate goals and a working *thesis* and begin to
think of support.

2. Identify potential audiences for your persuasive piece. For each, analyze
their interest in and power of influence on the issue. Based on your
analysis, narrow your list. Once you decide on an audience, you will
want to further analyze the background knowledge of the audience; in
addition, consider which persuasive appeals might be most effective with
this audience.

3. Consider genres that would be appropriate for persuading this audience
about your issue. Review the features of the genre you think would work
best. You might want to discuss your plan with a classmate to clarify and
refine your thinking about this issue, audience, and genre.

Drafting/Revising

4. Use ideas from your prewriting to generate a draft. Be sure to adhere
to essential features of the genre you selected. As you compose your
persuasive piece, you will probably want to refine your thesis, always
striving to match your language to the intended audience.

5. Review your piece carefully from the perspective of your purpose and
your intended audience and revise accordingly. Then share your piece
to get response from at least one other person. Your reviewer(s) should
be able to find or infer your thesis and should provide feedback on the
support you have provided. He or she should also provide feedback on
your use of genre and on the connection between the issue, audience,
and genre.

Editing/Publishing

6. Use all available resources to prepare a polished piece, including
consulting an appropriate style manual (such as MLA) for formatting
guidelines. Share the piece with your intended audience.

7. Reflect on the product you have created and what you have learned about
constructing a persuasive argument. If you receive a response from your
intended audience, evaluate your work in terms of that response, as well.

SCORING GUIDE

Scoring Criteria	Exemplary	Proficient	Emerging
Ideas	The text presents a significant and compelling thesis on an issue of justice that is clearly developed and supported. The argument is convincing and adeptly utilizes a variety of persuasive appeals.	The text presents a clear thesis on an issue of justice that is sufficiently developed and supported. The argument is plausible and effectively uses persuasive appeals.	The text takes on a position that is difficult to distinguish on an issue of justice. The position is insufficiently developed and supported. An attempt has been made to make an argument, but it is not plausible and uses persuasive appeals ineffectively.
Organization	The text is organized aptly for the genre. Ideas are presented in the order most conducive to a coherent argument.	The text is organized appropriately for the genre. Ideas are logically arranged to support the argument.	The organization of the text does not match the genre. A weak arrangement of ideas detracts from the argument at times.
Genre-Specific Features	Genre-specific features such as diction, syntax, factual support, and so on create a specific tone for a particular audience and purpose. These features reflect an authentic, confident, authoritative voice.	Genre-specific features such as diction, syntax, factual support, and so on are chosen to create a clear tone for a particular audience and purpose. These features reflect a convincing and appropriate voice.	Genre-specific features such as diction, syntax, factual support, and so on convey an ambiguous tone inconsistent for a particular audience and purpose. These features do not reflect a convincing voice.
Conventions	A strong control and mastery of standard conventions is demonstrated. Either no errors appear, or they are so slight that they do not interfere with the meaning.	Control of standard writing conventions is demonstrated. Though some errors may appear, they do not seriously interfere with the meaning.	There are frequent errors in standard conventions that seriously interfere with the meaning.
Writing Process	The final product demonstrates thoughtful planning, significant revision, and careful editing in preparing for publication.	The final product demonstrates planning, revision, and editing in preparing for publication.	The final product lacks evidence of planning, revision, and/or editing. It is not ready for publication.

SCORING GUIDE

Scoring Criteria	Exemplary	Proficient	Emerging
Reflection	The reflection perceptively analyzes what the author has learned about constructing a persuasive argument. Specific and well-chosen examples support the analysis, including reference to the audience's response if given.	The reflection analyzes what the author has learned about constructing a persuasive argument. Relevant examples are cited to support the analysis, including reference to the audience's response if given.	The reflection does not thoroughly analyze what the author has learned about constructing a persuasive argument. Too few or no examples are cited to support analysis.
Additional Criteria			

Comments: _____

_____

_____

_____

_____

_____

Learning Focus:

From Ancient Beliefs to Our Own

You have studied texts, ancient and contemporary, that address issues of justice. You have learned that the need to determine what is right is timeless; all cultures in all times have dealt with issues of justice in their own ways. Great literature, beginning with the literature of ancient Greece, gives us insight into the universality of the human struggle with issues of justice and injustice. Sophocles, one of the great Greek tragic dramatists, dramatizes the story of *Antigone* as a struggle for what is right, fair, and just, capturing the timeless truth that the quest for meaning is just as much a personal and political quest as it is a metaphysical one. A *metaphysical* search is, in essence, a search for the meaning of existence.

In your previous performances, you used **theatrical elements** to express your group's interpretation of the text. In this unit, you will have the opportunity to spotlight an issue of justice from the play through your own writing and performance. You and your group will collaborate to create a stylized expression of social and metaphysical truths about one of the most basic of human impulses – the quest for justice in a world that is not always just.

How Do You Feel?

LITERARY TERMS

A **tragedy** is a play in which the hero dies or experiences a downfall, usually because of his or her fatal flaw and poor decisions.

Read the brief character situations from the plot of the tragedy *Antigone*. Next, work with a small group to adopt the point of view of three of the characters. Fill out the chart below with your group. Then, join with another group to describe the remaining characters.

Creon

Your nephews have killed each other in a battle over who should be king. You are now king and decree that one brother can be buried according to the customs of your land but the other cannot. You find out that someone has defied your rule.

Three adjectives that describe how you feel	Why do you feel this way?	What will you do?	Why do you think this is a *just* response?

Antigone

Your brother has been killed in battle. The king has decreed that no one should bury him. You break the law and bury your brother.

Three adjectives that describe how you feel	Why do you feel this way?	What will you do?	Why do you think this is a *just* response?

Ismene

Your sister has committed a serious offense against the law of the land, something you would never do. One of your brothers has been buried lawfully; the other has not.

Three adjectives that describe how you feel	Why do you feel this way?	What will you do?	Why do you think this is a *just* response?

Haemon

Your fiancée has buried her brother, which she has been forbidden to do by your father, the king.

Three adjectives that describe how you feel	Why do you feel this way?	What will you do?	Why do you think this is a *just* response?

How Do You Feel?

The Chorus

The king has made a law. Someone you respect has broken that law for reasons you think are justifiable.

Three adjectives that describe how you feel	Why do you feel this way?	What will you do?	Why do you think this is a *just* response?

The Guard

Your job is to guard a corpse to make sure no one buries it. During a dust storm, someone buries the body. Later you catch someone burying the body again. You take the person to the king.

Three adjectives that describe how you feel	Why do you feel this way?	What will you do?	Why do you think this is a *just* response?

Meet the Cadmus Family

SUGGESTED LEARNING STRATEGIES: Discussion Groups, Notetaking, Graphic Organizer

About the Author	It's a Tragedy	Greek Theater	Antigone and Her Family
$200 He was the author of *Oedipus Rex, Oedipus at Colonus* and *Antigone*.	**$200** This civilization made tragedy into an art.	**$200** This city was where tragedies were produced as part of a religious festival.	**$200** The other two plays in the series with *Antigone*
$400 This is the number of Sophocles' plays that exist today out of a total of more than 100.	**$400** Downfall, usually ending with destruction or death	**$400** The part of a Greek play usually chanted (or sung) in unison	**$400** The King and Queen of Thebes
$600 It was the "Golden Age" in ancient Greece.	**$600** Pity and fear, wonder and awe	**$600** Platform shoes and masks with built-in megaphones	**$600** "Your son will kill his father and marry his own mother."
$800 This was Sophocles' age when he won his first drama competition.	**$800** A single flaw in character, or hamartia	**$800** A group of actors that moved and sang together, acting as one character	**$800** Both mother and wife of Oedipus
$1,000 This was the number of actors Sophocles had in the cast of his plays.	**$1,000** Horrible truth that leads to release	**$1,000** The Greek word for actor	**$1,000** The decree of Creon that begins the action of the play

Tragedy

- The legend of the phoenix stems from Greek mythology—strength and life arise from destruction.
- A difficult and rewarding form of drama—made into an art by the Greeks.
- Involves the downfall of a hero, usually ending with his or her destruction or death.

Meet the Cadmus Family

- Involves intense emotion; horrible truth that leads to release or *catharsis*.
- Aristotle's *Poetics* states that:
  ▶ Tragedy arouses the emotions of pity and fear, wonder and awe.
  ▶ A tragic hero must be a man or woman capable of great suffering.
  ▶ Tragedy explores the interactions of gods and mortals.
  ▶ Tragedy purifies the emotions.
  ▶ Tragedy shows how the hero is brought to disaster by *hamartia*, or a single flaw in character.

Greek Theater

- Tragedies were produced as part of a religious festival every year in Athens.
- Awards were given to the playwright who presented the best series of three dramas.
- Plays were performed in vast outdoor amphitheaters that could seat 40,000.
- All actors were men. They wore masks with built-in megaphones so they could be heard; they also wore platform shoes for added height.
- The stage was a slightly raised platform.
- Actors' movements were bold and definite.
- The Chorus—a group of actors who moved and sang together— acted as one character and spoke in unison during the Choral Odes, which separated the scenes of the drama.
- The Chorus set the mood, summarized the action, represented a point of view, sided with various characters, or warned of disaster.
- Greek theater incorporated unities of time, place, and action, which meant that there were no scene changes, and no complicated subplots; the plays took place in one day and in one place and focused on one event.
- Violent action took place offstage; messengers told the audience what happened.
- The audience knew the story ahead of time. The emotion of the characters is what they came to see.

Author Information: Sophocles

- Was one of three great Greek tragic playwrights (with Aeschylus and Euripides); wrote during the "Golden Age" of ancient Greece
- Born in 496 BC—lived for 90 years
- Wrote over 100 plays—only seven remain
- Served his city of Colonus, near Athens, in various capacities
- Entered his plays in contests—won his first at age 28
- Defeated Aeschylus in that competition
- Awarded first prize about 20 times and second place prizes all other times
- Added the third actor to the cast of his plays—before this, all dramas were played with only two characters other than the Chorus

Antigone and Her Family Background

- *Antigone* is a complete play, but it is part of a cycle of three plays, including *Oedipus Rex* and *Oedipus at Colonus*, written by Sophocles about the generations of the Cadmus family.
- The plays deal with the curse placed upon the family for a crime committed against the gods. The curse begins with a prophecy to King Laius and Queen Jocasta of Thebes that their son, Oedipus, will kill his father and marry his own mother.
- To avoid fulfillment of the prophecy, the baby Oedipus was left in the mountains to die of exposure, but was found and raised by the king and queen of Corinth, not knowing his birth parents.
- Later Oedipus unknowingly kills his father and wins the hand of Jocasta, the widowed queen, thus fulfilling the prophecy. They have four children, Antigone, Ismene, Eteocles, and Polyneices.
- When Jocasta discovers the truth, she hangs herself. When Oedipus discovers the truth, he blinds and exiles himself. He leaves his brother-in-law, Creon, to look after his children.
- Before he dies, Oedipus leaves orders that his two sons share the kingship; however, Eteocles, the first to reign, refuses to step down. Polyneices, his brother, attacks the city and his brother. They kill each other in battle.
- Creon becomes king and orders Eteocles buried with religious rites and honors. He orders that Polyneices be left unburied and uncovered for birds and animals to feed on his body. According to Greek beliefs, his soul could thus never rest. Antigone buries her brother against the order of her uncle. Thus begins the play's action.

> **GRAMMAR & USAGE**
>
> When the Chorus Leader says that Antigone's brothers "...set their conquering spears against each other" (line 172), he uses a reciprocal pronoun: *each other*. Reciprocal pronouns include *each other* and *one another*. When you write, use *each other* to refer to two people and *one another* to refer to three or more.

Meet the Cadmus Family

Drama Games

You are going to be either an actor or an audience member in a drama game. Whichever you are, you should be actively engaged. The rules of the game are as follows:

- Only four words can be spoken: "Hi Honey, I'm Home." Actors will receive cards with these words and a brief scenario. Each will make an entrance saying only the four words and using appropriate gestures and movements to convey the situation.

- Actors will make a mask that reflects the emotion of the scenario on the card and wear it during the entrance.

- You will watch this enactment and try to guess what the scenario is by observing the actor's movements and listening to his or her voice. After you take notes on the performance, share them verbally with the class, discussing elements that were effective.

Text: "Hi Honey, I'm Home"

Visual Delivery (gestures, posture, movement, eye contact)	Facial Expression on Mask	Vocal Delivery (pitch, volume, pace, rate, pauses, vocal variety, pronunciation/ articulation)	Scenario

Reflection: You have worked toward goals for improving your speaking and listening skills in small groups. In the remainder of the unit, you will have opportunities to speak before a larger group and to listen to presentations. Think about your strengths and weaknesses in presentation situations.

My Strengths as a Listener	My Weaknesses as a Listener	Goals for Improvement

My Strengths as a Speaker	My Weaknesses as a Speaker	Goals for Improvement

Charting the Action

ACADEMIC VOCABULARY

In traditional or classic drama, the **chorus** is a group of performers who speak as one and comment on the action of the play.

The word **chorus** has multiple meanings. Add details to the graphic organizer to show how chorus functions in the texts listed in the circles.

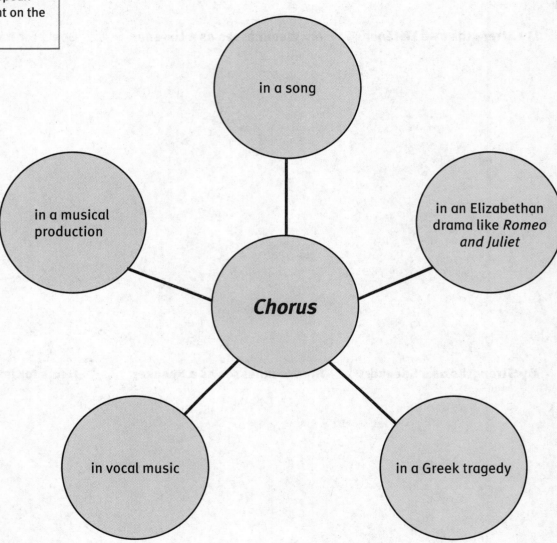

in a song

in an Elizabethan drama like *Romeo and Juliet*

in a musical production

Chorus

in vocal music

in a Greek tragedy

Read the opening scene from *Antigone* through the Second Ode, which ends at line 423.

As you read, focus on the dramatic, emotional nature of the dialogue. Take notes on different aspects of the play, keeping in mind the elements of Greek tragedy as well as character intent and emotion, which you will incorporate in your performance later in this unit.

For this scene, your teacher will assign parts. Read aloud with appropriate vocal inflection. Antigone and Ismene in the opening scene, and then Creon and the Guard in the second scene, use a convention called *stichomythia*—fast-paced alternating dialogue. If you are playing one of those characters, practice this convention as you read and incorporate appropriate gestures with your lines.

If you are assigned to the Chorus, practice moving and chanting as you read. While reading Strophe 1, the Chorus should chant and "dance" across to the right, and while chanting Antistrophe 2, dance back to the left. The point is to practice with multiple voices to understand the choral nature of the speeches.

Character	Adjectives to Describe the Character	Quotes that Show Character Intent or Emotion	Is the character involved in an issue of justice? Explain.
Antigone			
Ismene			
Chorus			
Creon			
Guard			

Drama

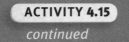

> **ABOUT THE AUTHOR**
> Few records exist that can tell the story of the life of Sophocles (c. 496 B.C.–406 B.C.), one of the great playwrights of the golden age of ancient Greece. He spent his life in the historically and politically important city-state of Athens, where he benefited from family wealth, good social connections, an excellent education, a winning personality, and a talent for writing plays that perfectly captured the spirit of his time and place. Sophocles is credited with several innovations to the dramatic form. Increasing the number of characters in a play, for example, allowed him to make the plots more complex and interesting to audiences. By focusing on characters' fatal flaws, poor decisions, and moral dilemmas, he created suspenseful plays that also evoked audiences' sympathies.

Antigone

by Sophocles

ANTIGONE: daughter of Oedipus.

ISMENE: daughter of Oedipus, sister of Antigone

CREON: king of Thebes

EURYDICE: wife of Creon

HAEMON: son of Creon and Eurydice, engaged to Antigone

TEIRESIAS: an old blind prophet

BOY: a young lad guiding Teiresias

GUARD: a soldier serving Creon

MESSENGER

CHORUS: Theban Elders

ATTENDANTS

[Thebes[1], in front of the palace, which stands in the background, its main doors facing the audience. Enter Antigone leading Ismene away from the palace]

ANTIGONE   Now, dear Ismene, my own blood sister,
do you have any sense of all the troubles
Zeus keeps bringing on the two of us,
as long as we're alive? All that misery
which stems from Oedipus? There's no suffering,
no shame, no ruin—not one dishonour—
which I have not seen in all the troubles
you and I go through. What's this they're saying now,
something our general has had proclaimed
throughout the city? Do you know of it?   10
Have you heard? Or have you just missed the news?
Dishonours which better fit our enemies
are now being piled up on the ones we love.   [10]

ISMENE   I've had no word at all, Antigone,
nothing good or bad about our family,
not since we two lost both our brothers,
killed on the same day by a double blow.
And since the Argive[2] army, just last night,
has gone away, I don't know any more
if I've been lucky or face total ruin.   20

ANTIGONE   I know that. That's why I brought you here,
outside the gates, so only you can hear.

ISMENE   What is it? The way you look makes it seem   [20]
you're thinking of some dark and gloomy news.

ANTIGONE   Look—what's Creon doing with our two brothers?
He's honouring one with a full funeral
and treating the other one disgracefully!
Eteocles, they say, has had his burial
according to our customary rites,
to win him honour with the dead below.   30
But as for Polyneices, who perished
so miserably, an order has gone out
throughout the city—that's what people say.
He's to have no funeral or lament,
but to be left unburied and unwept,
a sweet treasure[3] for the birds to look at,
for them to feed on to their heart's content.   [30]
That's what people say the noble Creon
has announced to you and me—I mean to me—

---

[1] **Thebes**: capital city of ancient Egypt
[2] **Argive army**: refers to the city of Argos, where Polyneices raised an army to fight his brother Eteocles for the throne
[3] **sweet treasure**: refers to Polyneices' body left unburied, which birds and other creatures will gorge on

40		and now he's coming to proclaim the fact,
		to state it clearly to those who have not heard.
		For Creon this matter's really serious.
		Anyone who acts against the order
		will be stoned to death before the city.
		Now you know, and you'll quickly demonstrate
		whether you are nobly born, or else
		a girl unworthy of her splendid ancestors.
	ISMENE	Oh my poor sister, if that's what's happening,
		what can I say that would be any help
50 [40]		to ease the situation or resolve it?
	ANTIGONE	Think whether you will work with me in this
		and act together.
	ISMENE	In what kind of work?
		What do you mean?
	ANTIGONE	Will you help these hands
		take up Polyneices' corpse and bury it?
	ISMENE	What? You're going to bury Polyneices,
		when that's been made a crime for all in Thebes?
	ANTIGONE	Yes. I'll do my duty to my brother—
		and yours as well, if you're not prepared to.
		I won't be caught betraying him.
	ISMENE	You're too rash.
60		Has Creon not expressly banned that act?
	ANTIGONE	Yes. But he's no right to keep me from what's mine.
	ISMENE	O dear. Think, Antigone. Consider
[50]		how our father died, hated and disgraced,
		when those mistakes which his own search revealed
		forced him to turn his hand against himself
		and stab out both his eyes. Then that woman,
		his mother and his wife—her double role—
		destroyed her own life in a twisted noose.
		Then there's our own two brothers, both butchered
70		in a single day—that ill-fated pair
		with their own hands slaughtered one another
		and brought about their common doom.
		Now, the two of us are left here quite alone.
		Think how we'll die far worse than all the rest,
[60]		if we defy the law and move against
		the king's decree[4], against his royal power.
		We must remember that by birth we're women,

---

[4] **king's decree**: a rule or edict issued by the king

	and, as such, we shouldn't fight with men.		
	Since those who rule are much more powerful,		
	we must obey in this and in events	80	
	which bring us even harsher agonies.		
	So I'll ask those underground for pardon—		
	since I'm being compelled, I will obey		
	those in control. That's what I'm forced to do.		
	It makes no sense to try to do too much.		

ANTIGONE
I wouldn't urge you to. No. Not even
if you were keen to act. Doing this with you
would bring me no joy. So be what you want.   [70]
I'll still bury him. It would be fine to die
while doing that. I'll lie there with him,   90
with a man I love, pure and innocent,
for all my crime. My honours for the dead
must last much longer than for those up here.
I'll lie down there forever. As for you,
well, if you wish, you can show contempt
for those laws the gods all hold in honour.

ISMENE
I'm not disrespecting them. But I can't act
against the state. That's not in my nature.

ANTIGONE
Let that be your excuse. I'm going now   [80]
to make a burial mound for my dear brother.   100

ISMENE
Oh poor Antigone, I'm so afraid for you.

ANTIGONE
Don't fear for me. Set your own fate in order.

ISMENE
Make sure you don't reveal to anyone
what you intend. Keep it closely hidden.
I'll do the same.

ANTIGONE
No, no. Announce the fact—if you don't let everybody know,
I'll despise your silence even more.

ISMENE
Your heart is hot to do cold deeds.

ANTIGONE
But I know, I'll please the ones I'm duty bound to please.

ISMENE
Yes, if you can. But you're after something   110   [90]
which you're incapable of carrying out.

ANTIGONE
Well, when my strength is gone, then I'll give up.

ISMENE
A vain attempt should not be made at all.

ANTIGONE
I'll hate you if you're going to talk that way.
And you'll rightly earn the loathing of the dead.
So leave me and my foolishness alone—
we'll get through this fearful thing. I won't suffer
anything as bad as a disgraceful death.

	ISMENE	All right then, go, if that's what you think right.
120		But remember this—even though your mission
		makes no sense, your friends do truly love you.

[Exit Antigone and Ismene. Enter the Chorus of Theban elders]

FIRST ODE[5]

CHORUS – **Strophe 1**[6]

[100]
> O ray of sunlight,
> most beautiful that ever shone
> on Thebes, city of the seven gates,
> you've appeared at last,
> you glowing eye of golden day,
> moving above the streams of Dirce[7],
> driving into headlong flight
> the white-shield warrior from Argos,

130
> who marched here fully armed,
> now forced back by your sharper power.

[110] CHORUS LEADER
> Against our land he marched,
> sent here by the warring claims
> of Polyneices, with piercing screams,
> an eagle flying above our land,
> covered wings as white as snow,
> and hordes of warriors in arms,
> helmets topped with horsehair crests.

CHORUS – **Antistrophe 1**[8]

140
> Standing above our homes,
> he ranged around our seven gates,
> with threats to swallow us
> and spears thirsting to kill.

[120]
> Before his jaws had had their fill
> and gorged themselves on Theban blood,
> before Hephaistos'[9] pine-torch flames
> had seized our towers, our fortress crown,
> he went back, driven in retreat.
> Behind him rings the din of war—
> his enemy, the Theban dragon-snake,

150
> too difficult for him to overcome.

CHORUS LEADER
> Zeus hates an arrogant boasting tongue.
> Seeing them march here in a mighty stream,

---

[5] **First Ode**: odes are choral songs chanted by the Chorus in a Greek tragedy
[6] **Strophe 1**: part of the ode the Chorus chants while moving right to left across the stage
[7] **streams of Dirce**: stream near Thebes
[8] **Antistrophe 1**: part of the ode the Chorus chants while moving back across the stage from left to right
[9] **Hephaistos**: blacksmith of the gods; he hammered out lightning bolts for Zeus

in all their clanging golden pride,   [130]
he hurled his fire and struck the man,
up there, on our battlements, as he began
to scream aloud his victory.

CHORUS – **Strophe 2**

The man swung down, torch still in hand,
and smashed into unyielding earth—
the one who not so long ago attacked,
who launched his furious, enraged assault,   160
to blast us, breathing raging storms.
But things turned out not as he'd hoped.
Great war god Ares[10] assisted us—
he smashed them down and doomed them all   [140]
to a very different fate.

CHORUS LEADER   Seven captains at seven gates
matched against seven equal warriors
paid Zeus[11] their full bronze tribute,
the god who turns the battle tide,
all but that pair of wretched men,   170
born of one father and one mother, too—
who set their conquering spears against each other
and then both shared a common death.

CHORUS – **Antistrophe 2**

Now victory with her glorious name
has come, bringing joy to well-armed Thebes.
The battle's done—let's strive now to forget
with songs and dancing all night long,   [150]
with Bacchus[12] leading us to make Thebes shake.

[The palace doors are thrown open and guards appear at the doors]

CHORUS LEADER   But here comes Creon, new king of our land,
son of Menoikeos. Thanks to the gods,
who've brought about our new good fortune.   180
What plan of action does he have in mind?
What's made him hold this special meeting,   [160]
with elders summoned by a general call?

[Enter Creon from the palace]

CREON   Men, after much tossing of our ship of state,
the gods have safely set things right again.
Of all the citizens I've summoned you,

---

[10] **Ares:** god of war
[11] **Zeus:** supreme ruler of all the gods on Mount Olympus; also known as the weather god who controlled thunder, lightning, and rain
[12] **Bacchus:** Roman god of wine; equated to Dionysius, the Greek god of wine

because I know how well you showed respect
for the eternal power of the throne,
190   first with Laius and again with Oedipus,
once he restored our city. When he died,
you stood by his children, firm in loyalty.
Now his sons have perished in a single day,
killing each other with their own two hands,
[170]   a double slaughter, stained with brother's blood.
And so I have the throne, all royal power,
for I'm the one most closely linked by blood
to those who have been killed. It's impossible
to really know a man, to know his soul,
200   his mind and will, before one witnesses
his skill in governing and making laws.
For me, a man who rules the entire state
and does not take the best advice there is,
[180]   but through fear keeps his mouth forever shut,
such a man is the very worst of men—
and always will be. And a man who thinks
more highly of a friend than of his country,
well, he means nothing to me. Let Zeus know,
the god who always watches everything,
210   I would not stay silent if I saw disaster
moving here against the citizens,
a threat to their security. For anyone
who acts against the state, its enemy,
I'd never make my friend. For I know well
our country is a ship which keeps us safe,
[190]   and only when it sails its proper course
do we make friends. These are the principles
I'll use in order to protect our state.
That's why I've announced to all citizens
220   my orders for the sons of Oedipus—
Eteocles, who perished in the fight
to save our city, the best and bravest
of our spearmen, will have his burial,
with all those purifying rituals
which accompany the noblest corpses,
as they move below. As for his brother—
that Polyneices, who returned from exile,
[200]   eager to wipe out in all-consuming fire
his ancestral city and its native gods,
230   keen to seize upon his family's blood
and lead men into slavery—for him,
the proclamation in the state declares
he'll have no burial mound, no funeral rites,

and no lament. He'll be left unburied,
his body there for birds and dogs to eat,
a clear reminder of his shameful fate.
That's my decision. For I'll never act
to respect an evil man with honours
in preference to a man who's acted well.
Anyone who's well disposed towards our state,   240
alive or dead, that man I will respect.   [210]

CHORUS LEADER Son of Menoikeos, if that's your will
for this city's friends and enemies,
it seems to me you now control all laws
concerning those who've died and us as well—
the ones who are still living.

CREON See to it then, and act as guardians of what's been proclaimed.

CHORUS Give that task to younger men to deal with.

CREON There are men assigned to oversee the corpse.

CHORUS LEADER Then what remains that you would have us do?   250

CREON Don't yield to those who contravene[13] my orders.

CHORUS LEADER No one is such a fool that he loves death.   [220]

CREON Yes, that will be his full reward, indeed.
And yet men have often been destroyed
because they hoped to profit in some way.

[Enter a guard, coming towards the palace]

GUARD My lord, I can't say I've come out of breath
by running here, making my feet move fast.
Many times I stopped to think things over—
and then I'd turn around, retrace my steps.
My mind was saying many things to me,   260
"You fool, why go to where you know for sure
your punishment awaits?"—"And now, poor man,
why are you hesitating yet again?
If Creon finds this out from someone else,   [230]
how will you escape being hurt?" Such matters
kept my mind preoccupied. And so I went,
slowly and reluctantly, and thus made
a short road turn into a lengthy one.
But then the view that I should come to you
won out. If what I have to say is nothing,   270
I'll say it nonetheless. For I've come here
clinging to the hope that I'll not suffer
anything that's not part of my destiny.

---

[13] **contravene**: oppose, or act contrary to

	CREON	What's happening that's made you so upset?
	GUARD	I want to tell you first about myself.
		I did not do it. And I didn't see
		the one who did. So it would be unjust
[240]		if I should come to grief.
	CREON	You hedge[14] so much. Clearly you have news of something ominous.
280	GUARD	Yes. Strange things that make me pause a lot.
	CREON	Why not say it and then go—just leave.
	GUARD	All right, I'll tell you. It's about the corpse.
		Someone has buried it and disappeared,
		after spreading thirsty dust onto the flesh
		and undertaking all appropriate rites.
	CREON	What are you saying? What man would dare this?
	GUARD	I don't know. There was no sign of digging,
[250]		no marks of any pick axe or a mattock.
		The ground was dry and hard and very smooth,
290		without a wheel track. Whoever did it
		left no trace. When the first man on day watch
		revealed it to us, we were all amazed.
		The corpse was hidden, but not in a tomb.
		It was lightly covered up with dirt,
		as if someone wanted to avert a curse.
		There was no trace of a wild animal
		or dogs who'd come to rip the corpse apart.
		Then the words flew round among us all,
[260]		with every guard accusing someone else.
300		We were about to fight, to come to blows—
		no one was there to put a stop to it.
		Every one of us was responsible,
		but none of us was clearly in the wrong.
		In our defence we pleaded ignorance.
		Then we each stated we were quite prepared
		to pick up red-hot iron, walk through flames,
		or swear by all the gods that we'd not done it,
		we'd no idea how the act was planned,
		or how it had been carried out. At last,
310		when all our searching had proved useless,
		one man spoke up, and his words forced us all
[270]		to drop our faces to the ground in fear.
		We couldn't see things working out for us,
		whether we agreed or disagreed with him.
		He said we must report this act to you—

---

[14] **hedge**: avoid giving a clear response

we must not hide it. And his view prevailed.
I was the unlucky man who won the prize,
the luck of the draw. That's why I'm now here,
not of my own free will or by your choice.
I know that—for no one likes a messenger   320
who comes bearing unwelcome news with him.

CHORUS LEADER   My lord, I've been wondering for some time now—
could this act not be something from the gods?

CREON   Stop now—before what you're about to say   [280]
enrages me completely and reveals
that you're not only old but stupid, too.
No one can tolerate what you've just said,
when you claim gods might care about this corpse.
Would they pay extraordinary honours
and bury as a man who'd served them well,   330
someone who came to burn their offerings,
their pillared temples, to torch their lands
and scatter all its laws? Or do you see
gods paying respect to evil men? No, no.
For quite a while some people in the town
have secretly been muttering against me.   [290]
They don't agree with what I have decreed.
They shake their heads and have not kept their necks
under my yoke, as they are duty bound to do
if they were men who are content with me.
I well know that these guards were led astray—   340
such men urged them to carry out this act
for money. To foster evil actions,
to make them commonplace among all men,
nothing is as powerful as money.
It destroys cities, driving men from home.
Money trains and twists the minds in worthy men,
so they then undertake disgraceful acts.
Money teaches men to live as scoundrels,   [300]
familiar with every profane¹⁵ enterprise.   350
But those who carry out such acts for cash
sooner or later see how for their crimes
they pay the penalty. For if great Zeus
still has my respect, then understand this—
I swear to you on oath—unless you find
the one whose hands really buried him,
unless you bring him here before my eyes,
then death for you will never be enough.
No, not before you're hung up still alive

---

¹⁵ **profane**: vulgar or improper

360		and you confess to this gross, violent act.
[310]		That way you'll understand in future days,
		when there's a profit to be gained from theft,
		you'll learn that it's not good to be in love
		with every kind of monetary gain.
		You'll know more men are ruined than are saved
		when they earn profits from dishonest schemes.

GUARD   Do I have your permission to speak now,
or do I just turn around and go away?

CREON   But I find your voice so irritating—
don't you realize that?

370   GUARD   Where does it hurt? Is it in your ears or in your mind?

CREON   Why try to question where I feel my pain?

GUARD   The man who did it—he upsets your mind.
I offend your ears.

CREON   My, my, it's clear to see
[320]   it's natural for you to chatter on.

GUARD   Perhaps. But I never did this.

CREON   This and more—you sold your life for silver.

GUARD   How strange and sad when the one who sorts this out gets it all wrong.

CREON   Well, enjoy your sophisticated views.
380   But if you don't reveal to me who did this,
you'll just confirm how much your treasonous gains
have made you suffer.

[Exit Creon back into the palace. The doors close behind him]

GUARD   Well, I hope he's found.
That would be best. But whether caught or not—
and that's something sheer chance will bring about—
you won't see me coming here again.
[330]   This time, against all hope and expectation,
I'm still unhurt. I owe the gods great thanks.

[Exit the Guard away from the palace]

SECOND ODE

CHORUS – **Strophe 1**

There are many strange and wonderful things,
but nothing more strangely wonderful than man.
390   He moves across the white-capped ocean seas
blasted by winter storms, carving his way
under the surging waves engulfing him.
With his teams of horses he wears down

	the unwearied and immortal earth, the oldest of the gods, harassing her, as year by year his ploughs move back and forth.	[340]

Antistrophe 1

He snares the light-winged flocks of birds,
herds of wild beasts, creatures from deep seas,
trapped in the fine mesh of his hunting nets.
O resourceful man, whose skill can overcome   400
ferocious beasts roaming mountain heights.   [350]
He curbs the rough-haired horses with his bit
and tames the inexhaustible mountain bulls,
setting their savage necks beneath his yoke.

Strophe 2

He's taught himself speech and wind-swift thought,
trained his feelings for communal civic life,
learning to escape the icy shafts of frost,
volleys of pelting rain in winter storms,
the harsh life lived under the open sky.
That's man—so resourceful in all he does.   410   [360]
There's no event his skill cannot confront—
other than death—that alone he cannot shun,
although for many baffling sicknesses
he has discovered his own remedies.

Antistrophe 1

The qualities of his inventive skills
bring arts beyond his dreams and lead him on,
sometimes to evil and sometimes to good.
If he treats his country's laws with due respect
and honours justice by swearing on the gods,
he wins high honours in his city.   420
But when he grows bold and turns to evil,   [370]
then he has no city. A man like that—
let him not share my home or know my mind.

[Enter the Guard, with Antigone.]

CHORUS LEADER   What's this? I fear some omen from the gods.
I can't deny what I see here so clearly—
that young girl there—it's Antigone.
Oh you poor girl, daughter of Oedipus,
child of a such a father, so unfortunate,
what's going on? Surely they've not brought you here
because you've disobeyed the royal laws,   430
because they've caught you acting foolishly?   [380]

GUARD   This here's the one who carried out the act.
We caught her as she was burying the corpse.
Where's Creon?

[The palace doors open. Enter Creon with attendants]

		CHORUS LEADER	He's coming from the house—and just in time.
		CREON	Why have I come "just in time"? What's happening? What is it?
		GUARD	My lord, human beings should never take an oath there's something they'll not do—for later thoughts
[390]			contradict what they first meant. I'd have sworn
440			I'd not soon venture here again. Back then, the threats you made brought me a lot of grief. But there's no joy as great as what we pray for against all hope. And so I have come back, breaking that oath I swore. I bring this girl, captured while she was honouring the grave. This time we did not draw lots. No. This time I was the lucky man, not someone else. And now, my lord, take her for questioning. Convict her. Do as you wish. As for me,
450	[400]		by rights I'm free and clear of all this trouble.
		CREON	This girl here—how did you catch her? And where?
		GUARD	She was burying that man. Now you know all there is to know.
		CREON	Do you understand just what you're saying? Are your words the truth?
		GUARD	We saw this girl giving that dead man's corpse full burial rites—an act you'd made illegal. Is what I say simple and clear enough?
		CREON	How did you see her, catch her in the act?
		GUARD	It happened this way. When we got there,
460			after hearing those awful threats from you, we swept off all the dust covering the corpse,
	[410]		so the damp body was completely bare. Then we sat down on rising ground up wind, to escape the body's putrid rotting stench. We traded insults just to stay awake, in case someone was careless on the job. That's how we spent the time right up 'til noon, when the sun's bright circle in the sky had moved half way and it was burning hot.
470			Then suddenly a swirling windstorm came, whipping clouds of dust up from the ground, filling the plain—some heaven-sent trouble. In that level place the dirt storm damaged
	[420]		all the forest growth, and the air around was filled with dust for miles. We shut our mouths

and just endured this scourge sent from the gods.
A long time passed. The storm came to an end.
That's when we saw the girl. She was shrieking—
a distressing painful cry, just like a bird
who's seen an empty nest, its fledglings gone. 480
That's how she was when she saw the naked corpse.
She screamed out a lament, and then she swore,
calling evil curses down upon the ones
who'd done this. Then right away her hands
threw on the thirsty dust. She lifted up
a finely made bronze jug and then three times [430]
poured out her tributes to the dead.
When we saw that, we rushed up right away
and grabbed her. She was not afraid at all.
We charged her with her previous offence 490
as well as this one. She just kept standing there,
denying nothing. That made me happy—
though it was painful, too. For it's a joy
escaping troubles which affect oneself,
but painful to bring evil on one's friends.
But all that is of less concern to me
than my own safety. [440]

CREON   You there—you with your face
bent down towards the ground, what do you say?
Do you deny you did this or admit it?

ANTIGONE   I admit I did it. I won't deny that. 500

CREON [to the Guard]
You're dismissed—go where you want. You're free—
no serious charges made against you.

[Exit the Guard. Creon turns to interrogate Antigone]

Tell me briefly—not in some lengthy speech—
were you aware there was a proclamation
forbidding what you did?

ANTIGONE   I'd heard of it. How could I not? It was public knowledge.

CREON   And yet you dared to break those very laws?

ANTIGONE   Yes. Zeus did not announce those laws to me. [450]
And Justice living with the gods below
sent no such laws for men. I did not think 510
anything which you proclaimed strong enough
to let a mortal override the gods
and their unwritten and unchanging laws.
They're not just for today or yesterday,
but exist forever, and no one knows

[460]
520

where they first appeared. So I did not mean
to let a fear of any human will
lead to my punishment among the gods.
I know all too well I'm going to die—
how could I not?—it makes no difference
what you decree. And if I have to die
before my time, well, I count that a gain.
When someone has to live the way I do,
surrounded by so many evil things,
how can she fail to find a benefit
in death? And so for me meeting this fate
won't bring any pain. But if I'd allowed
my own mother's dead son to just lie there,
an unburied corpse, then I'd feel distress.

530

What's going on here does not hurt me at all.
If you think what I'm doing now is stupid,

[470]

perhaps I'm being charged with foolishness
by someone who's a fool.

CHORUS LEADER   It's clear enough
the spirit in this girl is passionate—
her father was the same. She has no sense
of compromise in times of trouble.

CREON *[to the Chorus Leader]*
But you should know the most obdurate[16] wills
are those most prone to break. The strongest iron
tempered in the fire to make it really hard—

540

that's the kind you see most often shatter.
I'm well aware the most tempestuous horses
are tamed by one small bit. Pride has no place
in anyone who is his neighbour's slave.

[480]

This girl here was already very insolent
in contravening laws we had proclaimed.
Here she again displays her proud contempt—
having done the act, she now boasts of it.
She laughs at what she's done. Well, in this case,
if she gets her way and goes unpunished,

550

then she's the man here, not me. No. She may be
my sister's child, closer to me by blood
than anyone belonging to my house
who worships Zeus Herkeios[17] in my home,
but she'll not escape my harshest punishment—
her sister, too, whom I accuse as well.

---

[16] **obdurate**: hardhearted or inflexible

[17] **Zeus Herkeios**: refers to an altar where sacrifices and libations were offered to Zeus ; Zeus was the Divine
protector of the house and the fence surrounding it; *herkos* means fence in Greek

	She had an equal part in all their plans	[490]
	to do this burial. Go summon her here.	
	I saw her just now inside the palace,	
	her mind out of control, some kind of fit.	

[Exit attendants into the palace to fetch Ismene]

	When people hatch their mischief in the dark	560
	their minds often convict them in advance,	
	betraying their treachery. How I despise	
	a person caught committing evil acts	
	who then desires to glorify the crime.	
ANTIGONE	Take me and kill me—what more do you want?	
CREON	Me? Nothing. With that I have everything.	
ANTIGONE	Then why delay? There's nothing in your words	
	that I enjoy—may that always be the case!	[500]
	And what I say displeases you as much.	
	But where could I gain greater glory	570
	than setting my own brother in his grave?	
	All those here would confirm this pleases them	
	if their lips weren't sealed by fear—being king,	
	which offers all sorts of various benefits,	
	means you can talk and act just as you wish.	
CREON	In all of Thebes, you're the only one	
	who looks at things that way.	
ANTIGONE	They share my views, but they keep their mouths shut just for you.	
CREON	These views of yours—so different from the rest—	
	don't they bring you any sense of shame?	580 [510]
ANTIGONE	No—there's nothing shameful in honouring	
	my mother's children.	
CREON	You had a brother killed fighting for the other side.	
ANTIGONE	Yes—from the same mother and father, too.	
CREON	Why then give tributes which insult his name?	
ANTIGONE	But his dead corpse won't back up what you say.	
CREON	Yes, he will, if you give equal honours	
	to a wicked man.	
ANTIGONE	But the one who died was not some slave—it was his own brother.	
CREON	Who was destroying this country—the other one	590
	went to his death defending it.	
ANTIGONE	That may be, but Hades[18] still desires equal rites for both.	

---

[18] **Hades**: King of the Underworld and god of the dead

CREON	A good man does not wish what we give him to be the same an evil man receives.
ANTIGONE	Who knows? In the world below perhaps such actions are no crime.
CREON	An enemy can never be a friend, not even in death.
ANTIGONE	But my nature is to love. I cannot hate.
CREON	Then go down to the dead. If you must love, love them. No woman's going to govern me— no, no—not while I'm still alive.

600

[Enter two attendants from the house bringing Ismene to Creon]

| CHORUS LEADER | Ismene's coming. There—right by the door. She's crying. How she must love her sister! From her forehead a cloud casts its shadow down across her darkly flushing face— and drops its rain onto her lovely cheeks. |

[530]

| CREON | You there—you snake lurking in my house, sucking out my life's blood so secretly. I'd no idea I was nurturing two pests, who aimed to rise against my throne. Come here. Tell me this—do you admit you played your part in this burial, or will you swear an oath you had no knowledge of it? |

610

ISMENE	I did it—I admit it, and she'll back me up. So I bear the guilt as well.
ANTIGONE	No, no—justice will not allow you to say that. You didn't want to. I didn't work with you.
ISMENE	But now you're in trouble, I'm not ashamed of suffering, too, as your companion.

[540]

| ANTIGONE | Hades and the dead can say who did it— I don't love a friend whose love is only words. |

620

ISMENE	You're my sister. Don't dishonour me. Let me respect the dead and die with you.
ANTIGONE	Don't try to share my death or make a claim to actions which you did not do. I'll die— and that will be enough.
ISMENE	But if you're gone, what is there in life for me to love?
ANTIGONE	Ask Creon. He's the one you care about.
ISMENE	Why hurt me like this? It doesn't help you.

[550]

| ANTIGONE | If I am mocking you, it pains me, too. |

630

| ISMENE | Even now is there some way I can help? |

ANTIGONE	Save yourself. I won't envy your escape.	
ISMENE	I feel so wretched leaving you to die.	
ANTIGONE	But you chose life—it was my choice to die.	
ISMENE	But not before I'd said those words just now.	
ANTIGONE	Some people may approve of how you think— others will believe my judgment's good.	
ISMENE	But the mistake's the same for both of us.	

ANTIGONE   Be brave. You're alive. But my spirit died
            some time ago so I might help the dead.   640   [560]

CREON   I'd say one of these girls has just revealed
            how mad she is—the other's been that way
            since she was born.

ISMENE   My lord, whatever good sense
            people have by birth no longer stays with them
            once their lives go wrong—it abandons them.

CREON   In your case, that's true, once you made your choice
            to act in evil ways with wicked people.

ISMENE   How could I live alone, without her here?

CREON   Don't speak of her being here. Her life is over.

ISMENE   You're going to kill your own son's bride?   650

CREON   Why not? There are other fields for him to plough.

ISMENE   No one will make him a more loving wife
            than she will.

CREON   I have no desire my son should have an evil wife.

ANTIGONE   Dearest Haemon, how your father wrongs you.

CREON   I've had enough of this—you and your marriage.

ISMENE   You really want that? You're going to take her from him?

CREON   No, not me. Hades is the one who'll stop the marriage.

CHORUS LEADER   So she must die—that seems decided on.

CREON   Yes—for you and me the matter's closed.   660

[Creon turns to address his attendants]

            No more delay. You slaves, take them inside.
            From this point on they must act like women
            and have no liberty to wander off.
            Even bold men run when they see Hades   [580]
            coming close to them to snatch their lives.

[The attendants take Antigone and Ismene into the palace, leaving Creon and the Chorus on stage]

THIRD ODE

CHORUS – **Strophe 1**

Those who live without tasting evil
have happy lives—for when the gods
shake a house to its foundations,
then inevitable disasters strike,
670   falling upon whole families,
just as a surging ocean swell
running before cruel Thracian winds
across the dark trench of the sea
[590]   churns up the deep black sand
and crashes headlong on the cliffs,
which scream in pain against the wind.

Antistrophe 1

I see this house's age-old sorrows,
the house of Labdakos'[19] children,
sorrows falling on the sorrows of the dead,
680   one generation bringing no relief
to generations after it—some god
strikes at them—on and on without an end.
For now the light which has been shining
[600]   over the last roots of Oedipus' house
is being cut down with a bloody knife
belonging to the gods below—
for foolish talk and frenzy in the soul.

Strophe 2

Oh Zeus, what human trespasses
can check your power? Even Sleep,
690   who casts his nets on everything,
cannot master that—nor can the months,
the tireless months the gods control.
A sovereign who cannot grow old,
you hold Olympus as your own,
[610]   in all its glittering magnificence.
From now on into all future time,
as in the past, your law holds firm.
It never enters lives of human beings
in its full force without disaster.

700   **Antistrophe 2**

Hope ranging far and wide brings comfort
to many men—but then hope can deceive,
delusions born of volatile desire.
It comes upon the man who's ignorant
until his foot is seared in burning fire.
Someone's wisdom has revealed to us
this famous saying—sometimes the gods

---

[19] **Labdakos:** father to Laius, grandfather to Oedipus

lure a man's mind forward to disaster,
and he thinks evil's something good.
But then he lives only the briefest time
free of catastrophe.

[The palace doors open]

CHORUS LEADER   Here comes Haemon,   710
your only living son. Is he grieving
the fate of Antigone, his bride,
bitter that his marriage hopes are gone?   [630]

CREON   We'll soon find out—more accurately
than any prophet here could indicate.

[Enter Haemon from the palace]

My son, have you heard the sentence that's been passed
upon your bride? And have you now come here
angry at your father? Or are you loyal to me,
on my side no matter what I do?

HAEMON   Father, I'm yours. For me your judgments   720
and the ways you act on them are good—
I shall follow them. I'll not consider
any marriage a greater benefit
than your fine leadership.

CREON   Indeed, my son,
that's how your heart should always be resolved,
to stand behind your father's judgment   [640]
on every issue. That's what men pray for—
obedient children growing up at home
who will pay back their father's enemies,
evil to them for evil done to him,   730
while honouring his friends as much as he does.
A man who fathers useless children—
what can one say of him except he's bred
troubles for himself, and much to laugh at
for those who fight against him? So, my son,
don't ever throw good sense aside for pleasure,
for some woman's sake. You understand
how such embraces can turn freezing cold   [650]
when an evil woman shares your life at home.
What greater wound is there than a false friend?   740
So spit this girl out—she's your enemy.
Let her marry someone else in Hades.
Since I caught her clearly disobeying,
the only culprit in the entire city,
I won't perjure myself before the state.
No—I'll kill her. And so let her appeal

			to Zeus, the god of blood relationships.
			If I foster any lack of full respect
			in my own family, I surely do the same
750	[660]		with those who are not linked to me by blood.
			The man who acts well with his household
			will be found a just man in the city.
			I'd trust such a man to govern wisely
			or to be content with someone ruling him.
	[670]		And in the thick of battle at his post
			he'll stand firm beside his fellow soldier,
			a loyal, brave man. But anyone who's proud
			and violates our laws or thinks he'll tell
			our leaders what to do, a man like that
760			wins no praise from me. No. We must obey
			whatever man the city puts in charge,
			no matter what the issue—great or small,
			just or unjust. For there's no greater evil
			than a lack of leadership. That destroys
			whole cities, turns households into ruins,
			and in war makes soldiers break and run away.
			When men succeed, what keeps their lives secure
			in almost every case is their obedience.
			That's why they must support those in control,
770			and never let some woman beat us down.
			If we must fall from power, let that come
			at some man's hand—at least, we won't be called
	[680]		inferior to any woman.

CHORUS LEADER   Unless we're being deceived by our old age,
                what you've just said seems reasonable to us.

HAEMON   Father, the gods instill good sense in men—
                the greatest of all the things which we possess.
                I could not find your words somehow not right—
                I hope that's something I never learn to do.
780   But other words might be good, as well.
                Because of who you are, you can't perceive
                all the things men say or do—or their complaints.
[690]   Your gaze makes citizens afraid—they can't
                say anything you would not like to hear.
                But in the darkness I can hear them talk—
                the city is upset about the girl.
                They say of all women here she least deserves
                the worst of deaths for her most glorious act.
                When in the slaughter her own brother died,
790   she did not just leave him there unburied,
                to be ripped apart by carrion dogs or birds.
                Surely she deserves some golden honour?

	That's the dark secret rumour people speak.	[700]
	For me, father, nothing is more valuable	
	than your well being. For any children,	
	what could be a greater honour to them	
	than their father's thriving reputation?	
	A father feels the same about his sons.	
	So don't let your mind dwell on just one thought,	800
	that what you say is right and nothing else.	
	A man who thinks that only he is wise,	
	that he can speak and think like no one else,	
	when such men are exposed, then all can see	
	their emptiness inside. For any man,	[710]
	even if he's wise, there's nothing shameful	
	in learning many things, staying flexible.	
	You notice how in winter floods the trees	
	which bend before the storm preserve their twigs.	
	The ones who stand against it are destroyed,	
	root and branch. In the same way, those sailors	810
	who keep their sails stretched tight, never easing off,	
	make their ship capsize—and from that point on	
	sail with their rowing benches all submerged.	
	So end your anger. Permit yourself to change.	
	For if I, as a younger man, may state	
	my views, I'd say it would be for the best	[720]
	if men by nature understood all things—	
	if not, and that is usually the case,	
	when men speak well, it good to learn from them.	

CHORUS LEADER   My lord, if what he's said is relevant,   820
                 it seems appropriate to learn from him,
                 and you too, Haemon, listen to the king.
                 The things which you both said were excellent.

CREON   And men my age—are we then going to school
                 to learn what's wise from men as young as him?

HAEMON   There's nothing wrong in that. And if I'm young,
                 don't think about my age—look at what I do.

CREON   And what you do—does that include this,   [730]
                 honouring those who act against our laws?

HAEMON   I would not encourage anyone   830
                 to show respect to evil men.

CREON   And her—
                 is she not suffering from the same disease?

HAEMON   The people here in Thebes all say the same—
                 they deny she is.

Charting the Action

	CREON	So the city now will instruct me how I am to govern?
	HAEMON	Now you're talking like someone far too young. Don't you see that?
	CREON	Am I to rule this land at someone else's whim or by myself?
	HAEMON	A city which belongs to just one man is no true city.
840	CREON	According to our laws, does not the ruler own the city?
	HAEMON	By yourself you'd make an excellent king but in a desert.
[740]	CREON	It seems as if this boy is fighting on the woman's side.
	HAEMON	That's true— if you're the woman. I'm concerned for you.
	CREON	You're the worst there is—you set your judgment up against your father.
	HAEMON	No, not when I see you making a mistake and being unjust.
	CREON	Is it a mistake to honour my own rule?
850	HAEMON	You're not honouring that by trampling on the gods' prerogatives.[20]
	CREON	You foul creature— you're worse than any woman.
	HAEMON	You'll not catch me giving way to some disgrace.
	CREON	But your words all speak on her behalf.
	HAEMON	And yours and mine— and for the gods below.
	CREON	You woman's slave— don't try to win me over.
	HAEMON	What do you want— to speak and never hear someone reply?
[750]	CREON	You'll never marry her while she's alive.
	HAEMON	Then she'll die—and in her death kill someone else.

---

[20] **prerogatives**: exclusive rights or privileges

CREON   Are you so insolent you threaten me?   860

HAEMON   Where's the threat in challenging a bad decree?

CREON   You'll regret parading what you think like this—
you—a person with an empty brain!

HAEMON   If you were not my father, I might say
you were not thinking straight.

CREON   Would you, indeed?
Well, then, by Olympus, I'll have you know
you'll be sorry for demeaning me
with all these insults.

[Creon turns to his attendants]

                         Go bring her out—   [760]
that hateful creature, so she can die right here,
with him present, before her bridegroom's eyes.   870

HAEMON   No. Don't ever hope for that. She'll not die
with me just standing there. And as for you—
your eyes will never see my face again.
So let your rage charge on among your friends
who want to stand by you in this.

[Exit Haemon, running back into the palace]

CHORUS LEADER   My lord, Haemon left in such a hurry.
He's angry—in a young man at his age
the mind turns bitter when he's feeling hurt.

CREON   Let him dream up or carry out great deeds
beyond the power of man, he'll not save these girls—   880
their fate is sealed.

CHORUS LEADER   Are you going to kill them both?   [770]

CREON   No—not the one whose hands are clean. You're right.

CHORUS LEADER   How do you plan to kill Antigone?

CREON   I'll take her on a path no people use,
and hide her in a cavern in the rocks,
while still alive. I'll set out provisions,
as much as piety requires[21], to make sure
the city is not totally corrupted.
Then she can speak her prayers to Hades,
the only god she worships, for success   890
avoiding death—or else, at least, she'll learn,
although too late, how it's a waste of time
to work to honour those whom Hades holds.   [780]

---

[21] **piety**: devotion to religion; fulfillment of religious obligations

Charting the Action

FOURTH ODE

CHORUS – **Strophe**

O Eros[22], the conqueror in every fight,
Eros, who squanders all men's wealth,
who sleeps at night on girls' soft cheeks,
and roams across the ocean seas
and through the shepherd's hut—
no immortal god escapes from you,

900   nor any man, who lives but for a day.
[790]   And the one whom you possess goes mad.

Antistrophe

Even in good men you twist their minds,
perverting them to their own ruin.
You provoke these men to family strife.
The bride's desire seen glittering in her eyes—
that conquers everything, its power
enthroned beside eternal laws, for there

[800]   the goddess Aphrodite works her will,
whose ways are irresistible.

[Antigone enters from the palace with attendants who are taking her away to her execution]

910   CHORAL LEADER   When I look at her I forget my place.
I lose restraint and can't hold back my tears—
Antigone going to her bridal room
where all are laid to rest in death.

COMMOS

ANTIGONE – **Strophe 1**

Look at me, my native citizens,
as I go on my final journey,
as I gaze upon the sunlight one last time,
which I'll never see again—for Hades,
who brings all people to their final sleep,

[810]   leads me on, while I'm still living,
920   down to the shores of Acheron.[23]
I've not yet had my bridal chant,
nor has any wedding song been sung—
for my marriage is to Acheron.

CHORUS   Surely you carry fame with you and praise,
as you move to the deep home of the dead.
You were not stricken by lethal disease

[820]   or paid your wages with a sword.
No. You were in charge of your own fate.

---

[22] **Eros:** god of love and son of Aphrodite
[23] **Acheron:** a river in Hades across which the dead were ferried

So of all living human beings, you alone
make your way down to Hades still alive.   930

ANTIGONE – **Antistrophe 1**

I've heard about a guest of ours,
daughter of Tantalus²⁴, from Phrygia—
she went to an excruciating death
in Sipylus²⁵, right on the mountain peak.
The stone there, just like clinging ivy,
wore her down, and now, so people say,
the snow and rain never leave her there,   [830]
as she laments. Below her weeping eyes
her neck is wet with tears. God brings me
to a final rest which most resembles hers.   940

CHORUS

But Niobe²⁶ was a goddess, born divine—
and we are human beings, a race which dies.
But still, it's a fine thing for a woman,
once she's dead, to have it said she shared,
in life and death, the fate of demi-gods.

ANTIGONE – **Strophe 2**

Oh, you are mocking me! Why me—
by our fathers' gods—why do you all,
my own city and the richest men of Thebes,
insult me now right to my face,
without waiting for my death?   950
Well at least I have Dirce's springs,
the holy grounds of Thebes,
a city full of splendid chariots,
to witness how no friends lament for me
as I move on—you see the laws
which lead me to my rock-bound prison,
a tomb made just for me. Alas!
In my wretchedness I have no home,   [850]
not with human beings or corpses,
not with the living or the dead.   960

CHORUS

You pushed your daring to the limit, my child,
and tripped against Justice's high altar—
perhaps your agonies are paying back
some compensation for your father.

---

²⁴ **Tantalus**: son of Zeus who was punished by being "tantalized" by food and drink that were always just out of his reach

²⁵ **Sipylus**: mountain ruled by Tantalus; location of the weeping stone formation of Niobe

²⁶ **Niobe**: daughter of Tantalus; all her children were killed and she was turned to stone; her rock formation appears to weep tears for her children as it rains

Charting the Action

ANTIGONE – **Antistrophe 2**

Now there you touch on my most painful thought—
my father's destiny—always on my mind,
[860] along with that whole fate which sticks to us,
the splendid house of Labdakos—the curse
arising from a mother's marriage bed,
970 when she had sex with her own son, my father.
From what kind of parents was I born,
their wretched daughter? I go to them,
unmarried and accursed, an outcast.
Alas, too, for my brother Polyneices,
[870] who made a fatal marriage and then died—
and with that death killed me while still alive.

CHORUS

To be piously devout shows reverence,
but powerful men, who in their persons
incorporate authority, cannot bear
980 anyone to break their rules. Hence, you die
because of your own selfish will.

ANTIGONE – **Epode**[27]

Without lament, without a friend,
and with no marriage song, I'm being led
in this miserable state, along my final road.
[880] So wretched that I no longer have the right
to look upon the sun, that sacred eye.
But my fate prompts no tears, and no friend mourns.

CREON

Don't you know that no one faced with death
would ever stop the singing and the groans,
990 if that would help? Take her and shut her up,
as I have ordered, in her tomb's embrace.
And get it done as quickly as you can.
Then leave her there alone, all by herself—
she can sort out whether she wants suicide
or remains alive, buried in a place like that.
As far as she's concerned, we bear no guilt.
[890] But she's lost her place living here with us.

ANTIGONE

Oh my tomb and bridal chamber—
my eternal hollow dwelling place,
1000 where I go to join my people. Most of them
have perished—Persephone[28] has welcomed them
among the dead. I'm the last one, dying here
the most evil death by far, as I move down

---

[27] **Epode**: final stanza of the ode; follows the strophe and antistrophe
[28] **Persephone**: goddess of the underworld; she was abducted by Hades and forced to spend one third of each year there, which is the winter during which nothing blooms or grows

before the time allotted for my life is done.
But I go nourishing the vital hope
my father will be pleased to see me come,
and you, too, my mother, will welcome me,
as well as you, my own dear brother.
When you died, with my own hands I washed you.   [900]
I arranged your corpse and at the grave mound   1010
poured out libations. But now, Polyneices,
this is my reward for covering your corpse.
However, for wise people I was right
to honour you. I'd never have done it
for children of my own, not as their mother,
nor for a dead husband lying in decay—
no, not in defiance of the citizens.
What law do I appeal to, claiming this?
If my husband died, there'd be another one,
and if I were to lose a child of mine   1020
I'd have another with some other man.   [910]
But since my father and my mother, too,
are hidden away in Hades' house,
I'll never have another living brother.
That was the law I used to honour you.
But Creon thought that I was in the wrong
and acting recklessly for you, my brother.
Now he seizes me by force and leads me here—
no wedding and no bridal song, no share
in married life or raising children.   1030
Instead I go in sorrow to my grave,   [920]
without my friends, to die while still alive.
What holy justice have I violated?
In my wretchedness, why should I still look
up to the gods? Which one can I invoke
to bring me help, when for my reverence
they charge me with impiety? Well, then,
if this is something fine among the gods,
I'll come to recognize that I've done wrong.
But if these people here are being unjust   1040
may they endure no greater punishment
than the injustices they're doing to me.

CHORUS LEADER   The same storm blasts continue to attack
                 the mind in this young girl.   [930]

CREON   Then those escorting her
                 will be sorry they're so slow.

ANTIGONE   Alas, then,
                 those words mean death is very near at hand.

Charting the Action

CREON
> I won't encourage you or cheer you up,
> by saying the sentence won't be carried out.

ANTIGONE
1050
> O city of my fathers
> in this land of Thebes—
> and my ancestral gods,
> I am being led away.
> No more delaying for me.

[940]
> Look on me, you lords of Thebes,
> the last survivor of your royal house,
> see what I have to undergo,
> the kind of men who do this to me,
> for paying reverence to true piety.

[Antigone is led away under escort]

FIFTH ODE

CHORUS – **Strophe 1**

1060
> In her brass-bound room fair Danae[29] as well
> endured her separation from the heaven's light,
> a prisoner hidden in a chamber like a tomb,
> although she, too, came from a noble line.
> And she, my child, had in her care

[950]
> the liquid streaming golden seed of Zeus.
> But the power of fate is full of mystery.
> There's no evading it, no, not with wealth,
> or war, or walls, or black sea-beaten ships.

Antistrophe 1
> And the hot-tempered child of Dryas[30],
> king of the Edonians, was put in prison,

1070
> closed up in the rocks by Dionysus[31],
> for his angry mocking of the god.

[960]
> There the dreadful flower of his rage
> slowly withered, and he came to know
> the god who in his frenzy he had mocked
> with his own tongue. For he had tried
> to hold in check women in that frenzy
> inspired by the god, the Bacchanalian fire.
> More than that—he'd made the Muses angry,
> challenging the gods who love the flute.

1080 **Strophe 2**
> Beside the black rocks where the twin seas meet,
> by Thracian Salmydessos at the Bosphorus,

[970]
> close to the place where Ares dwells,

---

[29] **Danae**: daughter of a king; Zeus fell in love with her and they had a son, Perseus

[30] **child of Dryas**: Dryas' son, who objected to the worship of Dionysus, was imprisoned and driven mad; later he was blinded by Zeus as additional punishment.

[31] **Dionysus**: Greek god of wine and son of Zeus

the war god witnessed the unholy wounds
which blinded the two sons of Phineus[32],
inflicted by his savage wife—the sightless holes
cried out for someone to avenge those blows
made with her sharpened comb in blood-stained hands.

Antistrophe 2

In their misery they wept, lamenting
their wretched suffering, sons of a mother
 whose marriage had gone wrong. And yet,   1090   [980]
she was an offspring of an ancient family,
the race of Erechtheus, raised far away,
in caves surrounded by her father's winds,
Boreas' child, a girl who raced with horses
across steep hills—child of the gods.
But she, too, my child, suffered much
from the immortal Fates.

[Enter Teiresias, led by a young boy]

TEIRESIAS

Lords of Thebes, we two have walked a common path,
one person's vision serving both of us.
 The blind require a guide to find their way.   1100   [990]

CREON

What news do you have, old Teiresias?

TEIRESIAS

I'll tell you—and you obey the prophet.

CREON

I've not rejected your advice before.

TEIRESIAS

That's the reason why you've steered the city
on its proper course.

CREON

                              From my experience
I can confirm the help you give.

TEIRESIAS

                              Then know this—
your luck is once more on fate's razor edge.

CREON

What? What you've just said makes me nervous.

TEIRESIAS

You'll know—once you hear the tokens of my art.
As I was sitting in my ancient place
receiving omens from the flights of birds   1110
who all come there where I can hear them,
I note among those birds an unknown cry—   [1000]
evil, unintelligible, angry screaming.
I knew that they were tearing at each other
with murderous claws. The noisy wings
revealed that all too well. I was afraid.
So right away up on the blazing altar
I set up burnt offerings. But Hephaestus

---

[32] **Phineus**: King of Thrace, who imprisoned his first wife Cleopatra; his new wife blinded
Cleopatra's two sons out of jealousy.

1120	failed to shine out from the sacrifice—
	dark slime poured out onto the embers,
	oozing from the thighs, which smoked and spat,
[1010]	bile was sprayed high up into the air,
	and the melting thighs lost all the fat
	which they'd been wrapped in. The rites had failed—
	there was no prophecy revealed in them.
	I learned that from this boy, who is my guide,
	as I guide other men. Our state is sick—
	your policies have done this. In the city
1130	our altars and our hearths have been defiled,
	all of them, with rotting flesh brought there
	by birds and dogs from Oedipus' son,
	who lies there miserably dead. The gods
	no longer will accept our sacrifice,
[1020]	our prayers, our thigh bones burned in fire.
	No bird will shriek out a clear sign to us,
	for they have gorged themselves on fat and blood
	from a man who's dead. Consider this, my son.
	All men make mistakes—that's not uncommon.
1140	But when they do, they're no longer foolish
	or subject to bad luck if they try to fix
	the evil into which they've fallen,
	once they give up their intransigence.[33]
	Men who put their stubbornness on show
	invite accusations of stupidity.
	Make concessions to the dead—don't ever stab
	a man who's just been killed. What's the glory
[1030]	in killing a dead person one more time?
	I've been concerned for you. It's good advice.
1150	Learning can be pleasant when a man speaks well,
	especially when he seeks your benefit.

CREON	Old man, you're all like archers shooting at me—
	For you all I've now become your target—
	even prophets have been aiming at me.
	I've long been bought and sold as merchandise
	among that tribe. Well, go make your profits.
	If it's what you want, then trade with Sardis
	for their golden-silver alloy—or for gold
	from India, but you'll never hide that corpse
[1040] 1160	in any grave. Even if Zeus' eagles
	should choose to seize his festering body
	and take it up, right to the throne of Zeus,
	not even then would I, in trembling fear

---

[33] **intransigence**: being unwilling to agree or compromise

          of some defilement, permit that corpse
a burial. For I know well that no man
has the power to pollute the gods.
But, old Teiresias, among human beings
the wisest suffer a disgraceful fall
when, to promote themselves, they use fine words
to spread around abusive insults.   1170

TEIRESIAS   Alas, does any man know or think about . . .

CREON [*interrupting*]
        Think what? What sort of pithy common thought
are you about to utter?

TEIRESIAS [*ignoring the interruption*] . . . how good advice
    is valuable—worth more than all possessions.   [1050]

CREON   I think that's true, as much as foolishness
is what harms us most.

TEIRESIAS   Yet that's the sickness
now infecting you.

CREON   I have no desire
to denigrate[34] a prophet when I speak.

TEIRESIAS   But that's what you are doing, when you claim
my oracles are false.

CREON   The tribe of prophets—   1180
all of them—are fond of money

TEIRESIAS   And kings?
Their tribe loves to benefit dishonestly.

CREON   You know you're speaking of the man who rules you.

TEIRESIAS   I know—thanks to me you saved the city
and now are in control.

CREON   You're a wise prophet,
but you love doing wrong.

TEIRESIAS   You'll force me
to speak of secrets locked inside my heart.   [1060]

CREON   Do it—just don't speak to benefit yourself.

TEIRESIAS   I don't think that I'll be doing that—
not as far as you're concerned.

CREON   You can be sure   1190
you won't change my mind to make yourself more rich.

---

[34] **denigrate:** slander, criticize

	TEIRESIAS	Then understand this well—you will not see
		the sun race through its cycle many times
		before you lose a child of your own loins,
		a corpse in payment for these corpses.
		You've thrown down to those below someone
		from up above—in your arrogance
[1070]		you've moved a living soul into a grave,
1200		leaving here a body owned by gods below—
		unburied, dispossessed, unsanctified.
		That's no concern of yours or gods above.
		In this you violate the ones below.
		And so destroying avengers wait for you,
		Furies of Hades and the gods, who'll see
		you caught up in this very wickedness.
		Now see if I speak as someone who's been bribed.
		It won't be long before in your own house
		the men and women all cry out in sorrow,
[1080]		and cities rise in hate against you—all those
1210		whose mangled soldiers have had burial rites
		from dogs, wild animals, or flying birds
		who carry the unholy stench back home,
		to every city hearth. Like an archer,
		I shoot these arrows now into your heart
		because you have provoked me. I'm angry—
		so my aim is good. You'll not escape their pain.
		Boy, lead us home so he can vent his rage
		on younger men and keep a quieter tongue
		and a more temperate mind than he has now.

[1090] *[Exit Teiresias, led by the young boy]*

1220	CHORUS LEADER	My lord, my lord, such dreadful prophecies—
		and now he's gone. Since my hair changed colour
		from black to white, I know here in the city
		he's never uttered a false prophecy.
	CREON	I know that, too—and it disturbs my mind.
		It's dreadful to give way, but to resist
		and let destruction hammer down my spirit—
		that's a fearful option, too.
	CHORUS LEADER	Son of Menoikeos,
		you need to listen to some good advice.
	CREON	Tell me what to do. Speak up. I'll do it.
[1100] 1230	CHORUS LEADER	Go and release the girl from her rock tomb.
		Then prepare a grave for that unburied corpse.
	CREON	This is your advice? You think I should concede?

CHORUS LEADER   Yes, my lord, as fast as possible.
Swift footed injuries sent from the gods
hack down those who act imprudently.

CREON   Alas—it's difficult. But I'll give up.
I'll not do what I'd set my heart upon.
It's not right to fight against necessity.

CHORUS LEADER   Go now and get this done. Don't give the work
to other men to do.

CREON   I'll go just as I am.   1240
Come, you servants, each and every one of you.
Come on. Bring axes with you. Go there quickly—
up to the higher ground. I've changed my mind.   [1110]
Since I'm the one who tied her up, I'll go
and set her free myself. Now I'm afraid.
Until one dies the best thing well may be
to follow our established laws.

[Creon and his attendants hurry off stage]

SIXTH ODE

CHORUS – Strophe 1

    Oh you with many names,
    you glory of that Theban bride,
    and child of thundering Zeus,
    you who cherish famous Italy,   1250
    and rule the welcoming valley lands
    of Eleusian Deo—
    O Bacchus—you who dwell
    in the bacchants' mother city Thebes,
    beside Ismenus'[35] flowing streams,
    on land sown with the teeth
    of that fierce dragon.

Antistrophe 1   Above the double mountain peaks,
    the torches flashing through the murky smoke   1260
    have seen you where Corcyian nymphs
    move on as they worship you
    by the Kastalian stream.   [1130]
    And from the ivy-covered slopes
    of Nysa's hills, from the green shore
    so rich in vines, you come to us,
    visiting our Theban ways,
    while deathless voices all cry out
    in honour of your name, "Evoe."[36]

---

[35] **Ismenus**: river near Thebes, sacred to Apollo
[36] **Evoe**: similar to hallelujah, a cry of joy shouted by worshipers at festivals

Charting the Action

1270	**Strophe 2**	You honour Thebes, our city,
		above all others, you and your mother
		blasted by that lightning strike.
[1140]		And now when all our people here
		are captive to a foul disease,
		on your healing feet you come
		across the moaning strait
		or over the Parnassian hill.

Antistrophe 2

You who lead the dance,
among the fire-breathing stars,
1280   who guard the voices in the night,
[1150]   child born of Zeus, oh my lord,
appear with your attendant Thyiads,
who dance in frenzy all night long,
for you their patron, Iacchus.[37]

[Enter a Messenger]

MESSENGER

All you here who live beside the home
of Amphion and Cadmus—in human life
there's no set place which I would praise or blame.
The lucky and unlucky rise or fall
by chance day after day—and how these things
1290 [1160]   are fixed for men no one can prophesy.
For Creon, in my view, was once a man
we all looked up to. For he saved the state,
this land of Cadmus, from its enemies.
He took control and reigned as its sole king—
and prospered with the birth of noble children.
Now all is gone. For when a man has lost
what gives him pleasure, I don't include him
among the living—he's a breathing corpse.
Pile up a massive fortune in your home,
1300   if that's what you want—live like a king.
If there's no pleasure in it, I'd not give
[1170]   to any man a vapour's shadow for it,
not compared to human joy.

CHORUS LEADER   Have you come with news of some fresh trouble
in our house of kings?

MESSENGER   They're dead—
and those alive bear the responsibility
for those who've died.

CHORUS LEADER   Who did the killing?
Who's lying dead? Tell us.

---

[37] **Iacchus**: another name for Dionysus

MESSENGER	Haemon has been killed. No stranger shed his blood.
CHORUS LEADER	At his father's hand? Or did he kill himself?
MESSENGER	By his own hand—

angry at his father for the murder.   1310

CHORUS LEADER	Teiresias, how your words have proven true!
MESSENGER	That's how things stand. Consider what comes next.
CHORUS LEADER	I see Creon's wife, poor Eurydice— [1180]

she's coming from the house—either by chance,
or else she's heard there's news about her son.

[Enter Eurydice from the palace with some attendants]

EURYDICE   Citizens of Thebes, I heard you talking,
as I was walking out, going off to pray,
to ask for help from goddess Pallas.
While I was unfastening the gate,
I heard someone speaking of bad news   1320
about my family. I was terrified.
I collapsed, fainting back into the arms
of my attendants. So tell the news again—   [1190]
I'll listen. I'm no stranger to misfortune.

MESSENGER   Dear lady, I'll speak of what I saw,
omitting not one detail of the truth.
Why should I ease your mind with a report
which turns out later to be incorrect?
The truth is always best. I went to the plain,
accompanying your husband as his guide.   1330
Polyneices' corpse, still unlamented,
was lying there, the greatest distance off,
torn apart by dogs. We prayed to Pluto
and to Hecate, goddess of the road,
for their good will and to restrain their rage.   [1200]
We gave the corpse a ritual wash, and burned
what was left of it on fresh-cut branches.
We piled up a high tomb of his native earth.
Then we moved to the young girl's rocky cave,
the hollow cavern of that bride of death.   1340
From far away one man heard a voice
coming from the chamber where we'd put her
without a funeral—a piercing cry.
He went to tell our master Creon,
who, as he approached the place, heard the sound,
an unintelligible scream of sorrow.

Charting the Action

[1210]

He groaned and then spoke out these bitter words,
"Has misery made me a prophet now?
And am I travelling along a road

1350

that takes me to the worst of all disasters?
I've just heard the voice of my own son.
You servants, go ahead—get up there fast.
Remove the stones piled in the entrance way,
then stand beside the tomb and look in there
to see if that was Haemon's voice I heard,
or if the gods have been deceiving me."
Following what our desperate master asked,

[1220]

we looked. In the furthest corner of the tomb
we saw Antigone hanging by the neck,

1360

held up in a noose—fine woven linen.
Haemon had his arms around her waist—
he was embracing her and crying out
in sorrow for the loss of his own bride,
now among the dead, his father's work,
and for his horrifying marriage bed.
Creon saw him, let out a fearful groan,
then went inside and called out anxiously,
"You unhappy boy, what have you done?
What are you thinking? Have you lost your mind?

1370   [1230]

Come out, my child—I'm begging you—please come."
But the boy just stared at him with savage eyes,
spat in his face and, without saying a word,
drew his two-edged sword. Creon moved away,
so the boy's blow failed to strike his father.
Angry at himself, the ill-fated lad
right then and there leaned into his own sword,
driving half the blade between his ribs.
While still conscious he embraced the girl
in his weak arms, and, as he breathed his last,

1380
[1240]

he coughed up streams of blood on her fair cheek.
Now he lies there, corpse on corpse, his marriage
has been fulfilled in chambers of the dead.
The unfortunate boy has shown all men
how, of all the evils which afflict mankind,
the most disastrous one is thoughtlessness.

[Eurydice turns and slowly returns into the palace]

CHORUS LEADER   What do you make of that? The queen's gone back.
She left without a word, good or bad.

MESSENGER   I'm surprised myself. It's about her son—
she heard that terrible report. I hope

1390

she's gone because she doesn't think it right

to mourn for him in public. In the home,
surrounded by her servants, she'll arrange
a period of mourning for the house.
She's discreet and has experience—
she won't make mistakes. [1250]

CHORUS LEADER I'm not sure of that.
To me her staying silent was extreme—
it seems to point to something ominous,
just like a vain excess of grief.

MESSENGER I'll go in.
We'll find out if she's hiding something secret,
deep within her passionate heart. You're right— 1400
excessive silence can be dangerous.

[The Messenger goes up the stairs into the palace. Enter Creon from the side, with attendants.
Creon is holding the body of Haemon]

CHORUS LEADER Here comes the king in person—carrying
in his arms, if it's right to speak of this,
a clear reminder that this evil comes
not from some stranger, but his own mistakes. [1260]

CREON – **Strophe 1**
Aaiii—mistakes made by a foolish mind,
cruel mistakes that bring on death.
You see us here, all in one family—
the killer and the killed.
Oh the profanity of what I planned. 1410
Alas, my son, you died so young—
a death before your time.
Aaiii . . . aaiii . . . you're dead . . . gone—
not your own foolishness but mine.

CHORUS LEADER Alas, it seems you've learned to see what's right—
but far too late. [1270]

CREON Aaiiii . . . I've learned it in my pain.
Some god clutching a great weight struck my head,
then hurled me onto paths in wilderness,
throwing down and casting underfoot
what brought me joy. 1420
So sad . . . so sad . . .
the wretched agony of human life.

[The Messenger reappears from the palace]

MESSENGER My lord, you come like one who stores up evil,
what you hold in your arms and what you'll see
before too long inside the house. [1280]

Charting the Action

CREON   What's that?
Is there something still more evil than all this?

MESSENGER   Your wife is dead—blood mother of that corpse—
slaughtered with a sword—her wounds are very new,
poor lady.

CREON – **Antistrophe 1**

                         Aaiiii . . . . a gathering place for death . . .
1430   no sacrifice can bring this to an end.
Why are you destroying me? You there—
you bringer of this dreadful news, this agony,
what are you saying now? Aaiii . . .
You kill a man then kill him once again.
What are you saying, boy? What news?
[1290]   A slaughter heaped on slaughter—
my wife, alas . . . she's dead?

MESSENGER [*opening the palace doors, revealing the body of Eurydice*]
Look here. No longer is she concealed inside.

CREON   Alas, how miserable I feel—to look upon
this second horror. What remains for me,
1440   what's fate still got in store? I've just held
my own son in my arms, and now I see
right here in front of me another corpse.
[1300]   Alas for this suffering mother.
Alas, my son.

MESSENGER   Stabbed with a sharp sword at the altar,
she let her darkening eyesight fail,
once she had cried out in sorrow
for the glorious fate of Megareos,[38]
who died some time ago, and then again
1450   for Haemon, and then, with her last breath,
she called out evil things against you,
the killer of your sons.

CREON – **Strophe 2**

               Aaaii . . . My fear now makes me tremble.
Why won't someone now strike out at me,
pierce my heart with a double bladed sword?
[1310]   How miserable I am . . . aaiii . . .
how full of misery and pain . . .

MESSENGER   By this woman who lies dead you stand charged
with the deaths of both your sons.

---

[38] **Megareos**: youngest son of Creon and Eurydice; an inexperienced solder who died in battle

CREON   What about her?
How did she die so violently?

MESSENGER   She killed herself,   1460
with her own hands she stabbed her belly,
once she heard her son's unhappy fate.

CREON   Alas for me . . . the guilt for all of this is mine—
it can never be removed from me or passed
to any other mortal man. I, and I alone . . .
I murdered you . . . I speak the truth.
Servants—hurry and lead me off,   [1320]
get me away from here, for now
what I am in life is nothing.

CHORUS LEADER   What you advise is good—if good can come   1470
with all these evils. When we face such things
the less we say the better.

CREON – **Antistrophe 2**
Let that day come, oh let it come,
the fairest of all destinies for me,
the one which brings on my last day.   [1330]
Oh, let it come, so that I never see
another dawn.

CHORUS LEADER   That's something for the times ahead.
Now we need to deal with what confronts us here.
What's yet to come is the concern of those   1480
whose task it is to deal with it.

CREON   In that prayer
I included everything I most desire.

CHORUS   Pray for nothing.
There's no release for mortal human beings,
not from events which destiny has set.

CREON   Then take this foolish man away from here.
I killed you, my son, without intending to,   [1340]
and you, as well, my wife. How useless I am now.
I don't know where to look or find support.
Everything I touch goes wrong, and on my head
fate climbs up with its overwhelming load.   1490

[*The Attendants help Creon move up the stairs into the palace, taking Haemon's body with them*]

CHORUS   The most important part of true success
is wisdom—not to act impiously
towards the gods, for boasts of arrogant men   [1350]
bring on great blows of punishment—
so in old age men can discover wisdom.

Antigone in the Amphitheater

Choose one of the scenes from *Antigone* that you found appealing. Taking into consideration what you have learned about Greek performances, visualize what that scene would look like if it were performed on a stage, without sound or lighting devices or elaborate costumes or sets.

Scene: _____

Main characters: _____

What is the important action in this section? _____

_____

Pretend the circle below is an empty stage in a large amphitheater. Where will you place your actors? Why? What will the actors need to do to make the audience understand what is happening? Label your actors and any particular ways your Chorus moves.

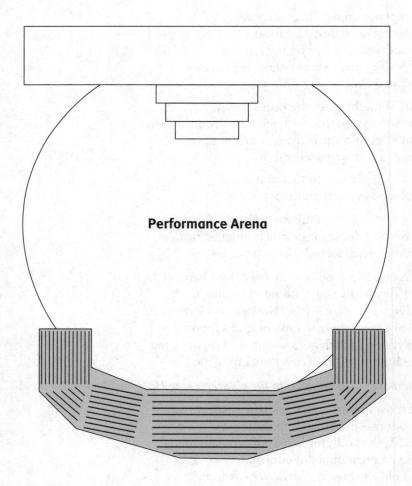

Performance Arena

Nonfiction

MAKING COMICS

by Scott McCloud

PUTTING **FACIAL EXPRESSIONS** TO USE IN **COMICS** REQUIRES YOU TO TACKLE **FOUR SUBJECTS:**

THE DIFFERENT **KINDS** OF FACIAL EXPRESSIONS AND WHERE THEY COME FROM.

HOW THOSE EXPRESSIONS ARE FORMED BY THE **MUSCLES** OF THE FACE.

THE VARIOUS STRATEGIES FOR **RENDERING** THOSE EXPRESSIONS **GRAPHICALLY.**

AND HOW FACIAL EXPRESSIONS WORK IN COMICS-STYLE **SEQUENCES.**

WHO?

OH!

HA! HA! HA! HA!

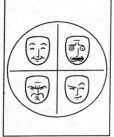

THE HUMAN FACE CAN TAKE ON ANY NUMBER OF SHAPES IN THE COURSE OF A DAY.

SOME INDICATE **PHYSICAL STATES** SUCH AS PAIN OR EXHAUSTION.

SOME ARE MEANT TO COMMUNICATE WITH OTHERS **DIRECTLY.**

BUT THE LION'S SHARE OF THE FACE'S POWER TO MOVE US LIES IN ITS ABILITY TO CONVEY **BASIC HUMAN EMOTIONS.**

THE RESULTS OF THAT PROCESS CAN BE VARIED AND COMPLEX, BUT AT ITS SOURCE ARE A FEW SIMPLE **BUILDING BLOCKS.**

IN 1872, DARWIN WROTE THAT SOME EXPRESSIONS MIGHT BE **UNIVERSAL,** A VIEW SHARED BY MODERN EXPRESSIONS EXPERTS LIKE PAUL EKMAN.*

THESE ARE THE **BASIC EMOTIONS** WHICH **ALL** HUMAN BEINGS EXHIBIT, REGARDLESS OF **CULTURE, LANGUAGE** OR **AGE,** A SMALL HANDFUL OF "PURE" EXPRESSIONS FROM WHICH OTHERS ARE DERIVED.

SIX OF THEM, TO BE EXACT.

Creon's Changing Character

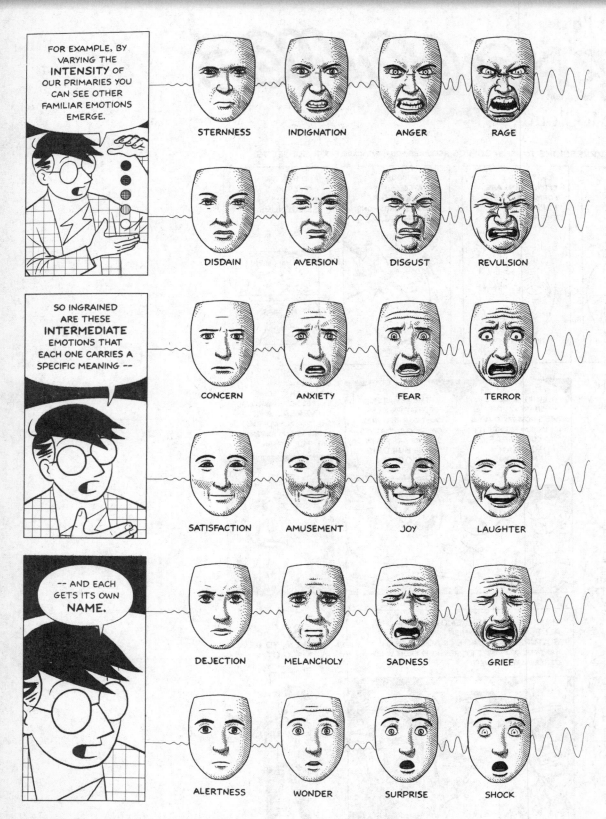

FOR EXAMPLE, BY VARYING THE **INTENSITY** OF OUR PRIMARIES YOU CAN SEE OTHER FAMILIAR EMOTIONS EMERGE.

STERNNESS   INDIGNATION   ANGER   RAGE

DISDAIN   AVERSION   DISGUST   REVULSION

SO INGRAINED ARE THESE **INTERMEDIATE** EMOTIONS THAT EACH ONE CARRIES A SPECIFIC MEANING --

CONCERN   ANXIETY   FEAR   TERROR

SATISFACTION   AMUSEMENT   JOY   LAUGHTER

-- AND EACH GETS ITS OWN **NAME.**

DEJECTION   MELANCHOLY   SADNESS   GRIEF

ALERTNESS   WONDER   SURPRISE   SHOCK

Draw a series of masks that record character changes in Creon, scene by scene. Your masks should express changes in his emotions and attitude. Below each mask, write words or lines from the play that support your interpretation. Also, explain how you think Creon would deliver these lines on stage. Space is provided for your work with the first two scenes; use your own paper for the third through seventh scenes.

First Scene (Ends with First Ode)

Mask	Emotions and Attitude

Textual Support	Delivery of Lines

Second Scene (Ends with Second Ode)

Mask	Emotions and Attitude

Textual Support	Delivery of Lines

Two Sides of the Coin

Is it ever justifiable to break the law? Examine that question by putting Antigone on trial for disobeying the king's order and by putting Creon on trial for condemning a woman to death for following her principles. You will be assigned a role in a courtroom and asked to use textual support as the basis for your performance when you speak during the trial.

After you are assigned a role, look through the text to formulate questions and find quotations that support your character's position in the play.

The major roles in Antigone's trial require you to do the following:

- Antigone: Plead not guilty; find textual support and cultural reasons for your position.

- Her lawyer: Formulate questions for your client and witnesses who will help her case. Prepare a closing argument that uses at least one persuasive appeal.

- Prosecutor: Formulate questions for Antigone and witnesses who will condemn her.

- Judge: Listen to all sides and be prepared to give orders as needed (be familiar with some judicial proceedings and terms).

- Jurors (chorus): Listen impartially, take notes, and be prepared to render a unanimous verdict based on evidence presented.

- Witnesses (Creon, Eurydice, Haemon, the guard, Ismene, messenger): Find textual support for testifying in court and be prepared to answer the lawyer's questions with appropriate lines from the play.

The major roles in Creon's trial require you to do the following:

- Creon: Plead not guilty; find textual support and cultural reasons for your position.

- His lawyer: Formulate questions for your client and witnesses who will help his case. Prepare a closing argument that uses at least one persuasive appeal.

- Prosecutor: Formulate questions for Creon and witnesses who will condemn him.

- Judge — Listen to all sides and be prepared to give orders as needed (be familiar with some judicial proceedings and terms).

- Jurors (chorus): Listen impartially, take notes, and be prepared to render a unanimous verdict based on evidence presented.

- Witnesses (Antigone, Eurydice, Haemon, the guard, Ismene, messenger): Find textual support for testifying in court and be prepared to answer the lawyer's questions with appropriate lines from the play.

Your role: _____

Lines you will use as textual support for your position: (Use questions if you are a lawyer.)

(Choose at least 10 lines to support your role.)

What was the outcome of the trial?

Who do you think was the most convincing and why?

How has the mock trial activity influenced your thinking about the essential questions in this unit? What have you learned about the nature of justice? What have you learned about constructing persuasive arguments?

Two Sides of the Coin

Now think back to the question: "Is it ever justifiable to break the law?"
How did you initially respond to that question?

What about now?

Describe your progress toward your goals for speaking and listening in
presentation situations like this one. Refine your goals as needed.

Imagine Antigone in other cultures and historical time periods. How might her fate be different if she committed the same crime in a different setting?

Place her in the times and places shown in the chart below and predict, based on the knowledge you have of that culture, what might happen to her. In the bottom row, add a time and place of your own choosing and make a prediction.

Time or Place	Punishment	Cultural Elements that Influence Your Opinion
Modern America		
Modern Singapore		
Nigeria in the late nineteenth century		

Think back to *Antigone* and Kohlberg's levels of moral development that you read about earlier in the unit.

Imagine the character of Antigone operating at each stage of moral development. How would her character respond to her dilemma? Use the space below to record your thoughts.

Level	Would she have gone against the king's order and buried her brother?	Why or Why Not?
Pre-conventional		
Conventional		
Post-conventional		

1. Work with a small group to come to a consensus on how a character in Antigone's situation might behave at each of the stages of moral development.

2. Next, create a series of tableaux that show a character at each stage of development. Remember that a tableau is like a snapshot or an action frozen in time. Also, keep in mind the analysis of art you completed in Activity 4.11 as you act out Antigone at different stages of her moral development.

Collaborative Chorus

SUGGESTED LEARNING STRATEGIES: Marking the Text, Summarizing, Graphic Organizer, Brainstorming, Notetaking, Discussion Groups, Rereading

The Chorus serves an important role in Greek theater, commenting on the issues relevant to the play. One of the important issues in *Antigone* is the power of love (Eros). Reread closely the lines of the Chorus in the Fourth Ode on page 310. Mark the text for these elements:

- Diction
- Allusions
- Figurative language
- Beliefs of the ancient Greeks

Summarize what the Chorus is saying about love. Be sure to find support in the text.

Compare and contrast the Chorus's belief about love with beliefs about love that your culture holds.

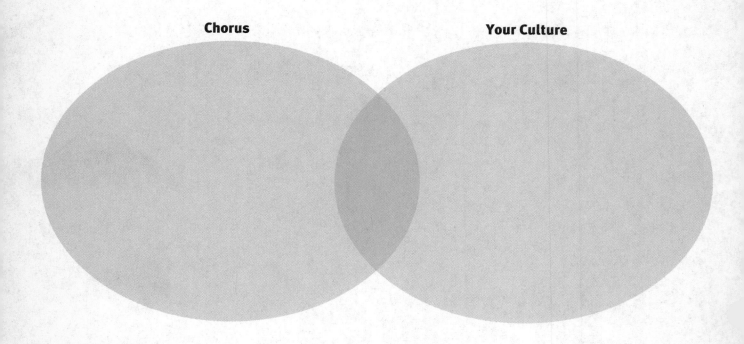

Chorus   **Your Culture**

How does the Chorus construct a persuasive argument?

Work with a small group to write an ode on the subject of love. Be sure to emulate the style of the Greek Chorus, including a Strophe and an Antistrophe, but make the content reflect your own beliefs. Use separate paper.

Writing a choral ode is one part of Embedded Assessment 2. With that in mind, consider the process you and your group used to write collaboratively. Write a reflection to guide your work later, including your thoughts on what worked and what you would do differently.

Brainstorm issues of justice in *Antigone*, listing as many as you can:

Choose one of these issues and connect it to modern thinking and beliefs.

Creating a Living Tableau

SUGGESTED LEARNING STRATEGIES: **Discussion Groups, Role Play, Notetaking**

Your assignment is to work with a group of six or seven other students to create a living tableau that presents an issue of justice and incorporates lines from *Antigone* and an original choral ode. Your tableau will reflect your understanding of the beliefs about justice reflected in *Antigone* and beliefs about justice reflected in your own culture.

Steps

Planning

1. With your group, identify an issue of justice in *Antigone*. Discuss the beliefs of ancient Greeks, providing textual support from the drama.

2. Find scenes in which this issue of justice is central. Highlight key lines that illustrate the issue of justice. Discuss the scenes and key lines as a group. Consider: Who speaks these lines? What is the subtext of these lines? What might the other characters be thinking and feeling in response to these lines? How does your group feel about these lines?

3. Build consensus about your group's collective stance on the issue, always maintaining respect for individuals' opinions. Analyze why your group responds as you do to the issue of justice.

4. Find what the chorus says about the issue, if they say anything.

5. Elect a director who will lead your group in rehearsals and introduce and conclude your presentation.

6. Choose roles for the presentation; except for the director, each student will play either a character or a member of the Chorus. Create a director's or actor's notebook. Take notes during discussions and rehearsals and save them in your notebook.

Creating

7. In your final presentation, you will play different roles (character, Chorus, director), but the whole group should contribute to the the presentation (introduction, tableau, ode, and conclusion).

8. Create masks that reflect analysis of the characters and the Chorus's responses to the issue of justice. Draft an explanation about the message you were trying to convey with your mask.

9. **Living tableau:** The group must agree on the key lines from the play each actor will bring to life. You may write lines for some characters if the need arises, but be sure to prepare a rationale for taking this liberty.

10. Think about the order of the delivery of lines and arrange them in a purposeful sequence.

11. Analyze how the subtext of each character's thoughts and feelings about the issue might be conveyed during the tableau presentation.

12. **Choral Ode:** The group will collaborate on writing a choral commentary (Strophe and Antistrophe) on the issue of justice that reflects your contemporary perspective. Emulate the style of the Chorus without copying the content.

13. **Introduction and conclusion:** Your group should collaborate on an introduction, which includes an engaging hook, and a conclusion that compares and contrasts the group's stance on the issue to the stance reflected in *Antigone*.

Refining and Presenting

14. The actors portraying characters should practice arranging themselves in a way that reflects the various characters' perspectives on the issue of justice. Consider overall aesthetic appeal, proximity of characters to each other, height of characters in relation to each other, body language, frozen gestures, and so on.

15. Rehearse delivering your assigned lines. When you say your line, you will "unfreeze," using gestures to enhance the delivery of your lines. Consider wearing name tags to help the audience recognize each character in the tableau.

16. The actors portraying the Chorus should rehearse the Choral Ode that your group has written. Practice using movement and choral chanting, demonstrating your understanding of the tradition of Greek theater.

17. The director should rehearse introducing your presentation with an engaging hook and concluding the presentation by comparing and contrasting your group's stance on the issue to the stance reflected in *Antigone*. The director should prepare to moderate a discussion about the presentation.

18. After the presentation, you will write a reflection on your experience and the audience will write a reflection on how this issue from an ancient play is relevant in modern times.

TECHNOLOGY TIP You may want to use software to create a multimedia presentation with graphics, images, and sound. Remember to convey a distinctive point of view with an appeal for your particular audience.

Creating a Living Tableau

SCORING GUIDE

Scoring Criteria	Exemplary	Proficient	Emerging
Ideas of Presentation	The group demonstrates a deep understanding of the drama by: • intentionally choosing lines that specifically represent an issue of justice; • expertly incorporating an introduction and conclusion that illuminate an understanding of beliefs in *Antigone* as well as modern beliefs; • seamlessly integrating masks that carefully analyze characters in relation to the issues of justice and are true to Greek theater.	The group demonstrates a clear understanding of the play by: • sufficiently choosing lines that represent an issue of justice; • adequately incorporating an introduction and conclusion that illuminate an understanding of beliefs in *Antigone* as well as modern beliefs; • smoothly integrating masks that carefully analyze characters in relation to the issues of justice and are true to Greek theater.	The group fails to demonstrate a complete understanding of the play by: • failing to choose lines that accurately represent an issue of justice; • ineffectively incorporating an introduction and conclusion that illuminate an understanding of beliefs in *Antigone* as well as modern beliefs; • awkwardly integrating masks that do not analyze characters in relation to the issues of justice and are not true to Greek theater.
Delivery of Presentation	The arrangement of the actors and delivery of lines are purposeful in reflecting various perspectives on the issue of justice. The overall organization of the tableau shows an impressive commitment to the acting and performance process.	The arrangement of the actors and delivery of lines adequately reflect the various perspectives on the issue of justice. The overall organization of the tableau shows sufficient commitment to the acting and performance process.	The arrangement of the actors and delivery of lines inadequately reflect the various perspectives on the issue of justice. The tableau is disorganized and shows little commitment to the acting and performance process.
Choral Odes	The written text and delivery of choral commentary skillfully emulate the tradition of Greek theater to exemplify a perspective on the issue of justice.	The written text and delivery of choral commentary emulate the tradition of Greek theater to show a perspective on the issue of justice.	The written text and delivery of choral commentary do not accurately emulate tradition of Greek theater and do little to show a perspective on the issue of justice.

SCORING GUIDE

Scoring Criteria	Exemplary	Proficient	Emerging
Reflective Texts	One text insightfully demonstrates the writer's metacognitive evaluation of his/her participation as a creator and presenter of the tableau. A second text demonstrates the writer's reflection on his/her role as an audience member by thoroughly analyzing how the issue of justice in an ancient play is relevant in modern times.	One text demonstrates the writer's metacognitive evaluation of his/her participation as a creator and presenter of the tableau. A second text demonstrates the writer's reflection on his/her role as an audience member by discussing how the issue of justice in an ancient play is relevant in modern times.	One text does little to evaluate the writer's metacognition of his/her participation as a creator and presenter of the tableau. A second text attempts to demonstrate the writer's reflection on his/her role as an audience member yet insufficiently analyzes how the issue of justice in an ancient play is relevant in modern times.
Additional Criteria			

Comments: _____

_____

_____

_____

_____

Reflection

An important aspect of growing as a learner is to reflect on where you have been, what you have accomplished, what helped you to learn, and how you will apply your new knowledge in the future. Use the following questions to guide your thinking and to identify evidence of your learning. Use separate notebook paper.

Thinking about Concepts

1. Using specific examples from this unit, respond to the Essential Questions:

   • What is the nature of justice?

   • How does one construct a persuasive argument?

2. Consider the new academic vocabulary from this unit (**Justice, Chorus**) as well as academic vocabulary from previous units, and select 3-4 terms of which your understanding has grown. For each term, answer the following questions:

   • What was your understanding of the word prior to the unit?

   • How has your understanding of the word evolved throughout the unit?

   • How will you apply your understanding in the future?

Thinking about Connections

3. Review the activities and products (artifacts) you created. Choose those that most reflect your growth or increase in understanding.

4. For each artifact that you choose, record, respond to, and reflect on your thinking and understanding, using the following questions as a guide:

   a. What skill/knowledge does this artifact reflect, and how did you learn this skill/knowledge?

   b. How did your understanding of the power of language expand through your engagement with this artifact?

   c. How will you apply this skill or knowledge in the future?

5. Create this reflection as Portfolio pages—one for each artifact you choose. Use the model in the box for your headings and commentary on questions.

Thinking About Thinking
Portfolio Entry

Concept:

Description of Artifact:

Commentary on Questions:

Building Cultural
Bridges

Essential Questions

? How do cultural
differences contribute
to conflicts over
environmental issues?

? What is the value of self-
reflection in preparing for
one's future?

Unit Overview

In previous units, you have learned that
literature can bring together people from
different cultures. Yet one viewing of the nightly
news proves that cultural harmony is far from
a reality. Cultural clashes continue to afflict
the world, and conflicts over environmental
resources are increasingly a source of such
conflicts. In this unit, you will examine one issue
in depth: global warming, or climate change,
and its causes and its effects. You will study
this issue with two purposes in mind: one, to
understand the issue and the conflicts to which
it contributes; and two, as a basis for a research
project that you will present to your classmates.
The project is a culmination of everything that
you have learned, so your final assessment
in this level will be a self-evaluation of your
current academic abilities—and a plan for how to
continue to improve them in the years to come.

Building Cultural Bridges
CONTENTS

Goals

▶ To examine how nonfiction texts (both print and non-print) construct our perceptions of what is true

▶ To analyze how writers and speakers use evidence to impact the persuasiveness of a claim

▶ To examine how perceptions of a writer or speaker's ethics affect the credibility of a text or its author

▶ To explore a complex issue or problem from multiple perspectives and to work with peers to present a solution

▶ To reflect on academic strengths and identify areas for further development

ACADEMIC VOCABULARY

Documentary Film

Objectivity

Subjectivity

*Texts not included in these materials.

Learning Focus:

Solving the World's Problems

From day one of this class, you have been examining what culture is and how it reflects and affects the ways we operate as a society and as individuals. But what happens when cultures come into conflict? What happens when the goals and values of various groups clash? And what happens when this clash involves real-world issues, like climate change or protecting endangered species in areas targeted for development?

Knowing how to explore an issue and to analyze the arguments presented by the various sides is an important skill. To analyze divergent arguments and opinions, you will read **nonfiction texts**—whether in print or nonprint formats—to identify how groups reveal the values and concerns that frame their perspectives on issues. You will also read these texts with an eye for the level of **subjectivity** they reveal, while also analyzing how authors and directors use **ethical appeals** to increase the credibility of their claims.

Evaluating sources is necessary if you wish to use them as supporting evidence. You will need supporting evidence as you become an advocate for a particular position within a dispute and then work to persuade your classmates to support your solution. With this goal in mind, you will revisit your work with the **components of argumentation** but move beyond them to develop a persuasive presentation that mediates rather than debates.

Independent Reading: In this unit, you will read both print and nonprint texts that deal with environmental issues as a source of cultural conflict. For independent reading, look for a nonfiction book, collection of articles and editorials, or a documentary film on an environmental or other major issue of interest to you.

Previewing the Unit

SUGGESTED LEARNING STRATEGIES: Close Reading, Marking the Text,
Summarizing/Paraphrasing, Graphic Organizer, Think-Pair-Share

Essential Questions

How do cultural differences contribute to conflicts over
environmental issues?

What is the value of self-reflection in preparing for one's future?

Unit Overview and Learning Focus

Predict what you think this unit is about. Use the words or phrases
that stood out to you when you read the Unit Overview and the
Learning Focus.

Embedded Assessment 1

What knowledge must you have (what do you need to know)? What
skills must you have (what will you need to do to complete the
Embedded Assessment successfully)? Write your responses below.

The Call to Act

My Notes

With your classmates, use the TP-CASTT strategy to analyze "I Need to Wake Up," writing your comments in the margin next to the song lyrics. Then, write a paragraph interpreting the theme of the song lyrics, citing specific lines for support.

Song

I NEED TO WAKE UP

by Melissa Etheridge

WORD CONNECTIONS

Comprehend contains the root *-prehend-*, from the Latin word *prehendere*, meaning "to seize." This root also appears in *reprehend, apprehend,* and *misapprehension*. The prefix *com-* means "with or together."

Have I been sleeping?
I've been so still
Afraid of crumbling
Have I been careless?
5   Dismissing all the distant rumblings
Take me where I am supposed to be
To comprehend the things that I can't see

Cause I need to move
I need to wake up
10   I need to change
I need to shake up
I need to speak out
Something's got to break up
I've been asleep
15   And I need to wake up
Now

And as a child
I danced like it was 1999
My dreams were wild
20   The promise of this new world
Would be mine
Now I am throwing off the carelessness of youth
To listen to an inconvenient truth

That I need to move
I need to wake up   25
I need to change
I need to shake up
I need to speak out
Something's got to break up
I've been asleep   30
And I need to wake up
Now

I am not an island
I am not alone
I am my intentions   35
Trapped here in this flesh and bone

And I need to move
I need to wake up
I need to change
I need to shake up   40
I need to speak out
Something's got to break up
I've been asleep
And I need to wake up
Now   45

I want to change
I need to shake up
I need to speak out
Oh, something's got to break up
I've been asleep   50
And I need to wake up
Now

GRAMMAR & USAGE

For style, rhythm, and emphasis, writers may use **anaphora** (the repetition of a word or words, at the beginning of sentences). Etheridge uses anaphora in the second verse of "I Need to Wake Up." Six of the lines include the words "I need" followed by an infinitive:

"Cause I need to move
I need to wake up
I need to change
I need to shake up
I need to speak out …
And I need to wake up …."

The repetition of "I need to" creates a pattern; as a result, the phrase emphasizes the urgency of the message.

The Call to Act

LITERARY TERMS

Dialogue is the words spoken by characters or participants in a film.

Narration is the act of telling a story.

The **theme** of a work is its message about life.

Diegetic sound is actual noises associated with the shooting of a scene, such as voices and background sounds.

Non-diegetic sound refers to voice-overs and commentary, sounds that do not come form the action on screen.

Etheridge's song won the 2002 Academy Award for Best Original Song for its use in the film *An Inconvenient Truth*, a film whose argument is that global warming poses a threat to humankind so severe that immediate action is needed. With that in mind, reread the text, looking for words or phrases that take on a specific meaning relevant to this context.

As you watch the video of the song, consider how the video's images affect your understanding of the lyrics. In particular, notice how the video uses the following film techniques:

- <u>primary footage</u>: scenes shot by the director specifically for the film, including interviews or footage of the performer/filmmaker
- <u>archival footage</u>: scenes taken from other sources, such as news broadcasts or home video
- <u>still images</u>: photographs as opposed to video footage, although the camera may pan or zoom on the photo
- <u>text</u>: subtitles, labels, graphics, etc. to help support the film's message.

Use the film viewing guide on the next page to take notes.

After watching, write a paragraph explaining how the video affected your understanding of what Etheridge means by "I Need to Wake Up."

Nonfiction Film Viewing Guide

Director: **Title:**   **Year:**

What Do You See? (primary or archival footage, interviews, still images, the filmmaker)

What Do You Hear? (dialogue, narration, diegetic and non-diegetic sound)

What Do You Read? (subtitles, graphics, labels)

How Is It Put Together? (editing sequence, transition devices)

What Is the Effect? (What is the **theme** of the video? What truth does it convey?)

ACADEMIC VOCABULARY

A documentary film is nonfiction that provides a visual record of actual events using photographs, video footage, and interviews.

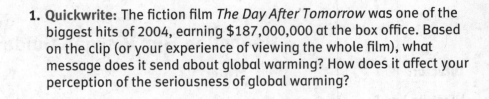

WORD CONNECTIONS

Documentary contains the root *-doc-*, from the Latin word *docere*, meaning "to teach." This root also appears in *document*, *docent*, *doctor*, *docile*, and *doctorate*. The suffix *-ary* indicates that the word is a noun.

1. **Quickwrite:** The fiction film *The Day After Tomorrow* was one of the biggest hits of 2004, earning $187,000,000 at the box office. Based on the clip (or your experience of viewing the whole film), what message does it send about global warming? How does it affect your perception of the seriousness of global warming?

2. *National Geographic* is one of the most respected popular media organizations devoted to science and nature. The organization has produced numerous documentary films. What message does the video clip you watched send about global warming? How does it affect your perception compared to *The Day After Tomorrow*?

3. After watching both clips, complete the Venn diagram below, comparing the genres. Consider how the presentation of the issue differs in the two films.

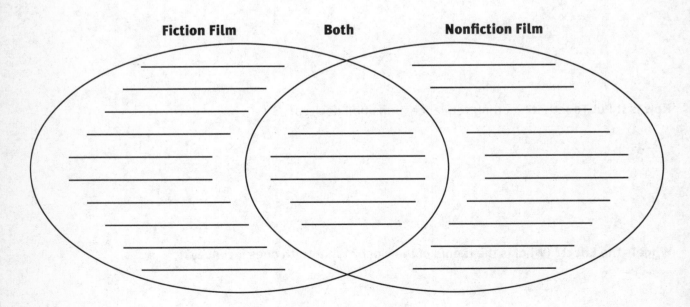

Fiction Film   **Both**   **Nonfiction Film**

4. Based on your comparison, define nonfiction or documentary film and identify its key characteristics.

That's Just the Way It Is

SUGGESTED LEARNING STRATEGIES: **Role Play, Marking the Text, Close Reading, Drafting**

1. Describe the role playing you have just witnessed. As you do so, choose one of three perspectives:

   - You are a "fly on the wall" merely trying to report the details of the confrontation.

   - You believe your teacher was overly aggressive in the situation and that the other person was a victim.

   - You believe the other person overreacted and your teacher was justified in his/her actions.

   Whatever perspective you choose, try to include specific details from the scene (dialogue, actions, etc.).

WORD CONNECTIONS

Objectivity and *subjectivity* contain the root *-ject-*, from the Latin word *jacere*, meaning "to throw." This root also appears in *reject, injection, project,* and *ejection.* The prefix *ob-* means "toward," and *sub-* means "under or from beneath."

2. After discussing the different paragraphs, define the following terms in the space provided.

Objectivity	
Subjectivity	

3. After listening to the paragraphs of your peers, underline or highlight the words, phrases, or details from your paragraph that might be considered subjective.

That's Just the Way It Is

Nonfiction Film Viewing Guide

Director: **Title:**   **Year:**

What Do You See? (primary or archival footage, interviews, still images, the filmmaker)

What Do You Hear? (dialogue, narration, diegetic and non-diegetic sound)

What Do You Read? (subtitles, graphics, labels, etc.)

How Is It Put Together? (editing sequence, transition devices, etc.)

What Is the Effect? (What is the level of subjectivity?)

Nonfiction Film Viewing Guide

Director: **Title:**   **Year:**

What Do You See? (primary or archival footage, interviews, still images, the filmmaker)

What Do You Hear? (dialogue, narration, diegetic and non-diegetic sound)

What Do You Read? (subtitles, graphics, labels)

How Is It Put Together? (editing sequence, transition devices)

What Is the Effect? (What is the level of subjectivity?)

That's Just the Way It Is

Nonfiction Film Viewing Guide

Director: **Title:**   **Year:**

What Do You See? (primary or archival footage, interviews, still images, the filmmaker)

What Do You Hear? (dialogue, narration, diegetic and non-diegetic sound)

What Do You Read? (subtitles, graphics, labels)

How Is It Put Together? (editing sequence, transition devices)

What Is the Effect? (What is the level of subjectivity?)

Previewing *The 11th Hour*

SUGGESTED LEARNING STRATEGIES: **SMELL**, Graphic Organizer

1. Your teacher will give you three note cards. Take the note cards and arrange them into every possible order of events. Write each variation below, and then identify what specific connotations or relationships are suggested by that particular sequence of statements.

2. As you watch the sequence of images in the first two minutes of the film *The 11th Hour*, write down each of the images you see. Then, working with classmates, write an explanation of what relationships are suggested between each image and the one that follows it. What does the meaning of the sequence as a whole seem to be?

> **LITERARY TERMS**
>
> **Juxtaposition** is the arrangement of ideas for the purpose of comparing or contrasting them.

3. Based on the two activities above, define the term **juxtaposition**:

> **WORD CONNECTIONS**
>
> *Juxtaposition* contains the Latin prefix *justa-*, meaning "near" or "beside," and the root *-pos-*, meaning "to place." The root also appears in *composition*, *compose*, *situation*, *positive*, and *opposition*.

Previewing *The 11th Hour*

As you watch the opening scenes of *The 11th Hour,* take notes in the SMELL graphic organizer below. Be sure to cite specific textual details.

Sender-Receiver Relationship: Who are the senders and receivers of the message and what is their relationship? (Consider the different audiences the film may be addressing.)

Message: What is a literal summary of the content? What is the meaning or significance of this information?

Emotional Strategies: What emotional appeals (*pathos*) does the director use? What seems to be their desired effect?

Logical Strategies: What logical arguments/appeals (*logos*) does the director use? What is their effect?

Language: What specific language supports the message? How does it affect the film's effectiveness? Consider both images and actual words.

The Nature of the Problem

SUGGESTED LEARNING STRATEGIES: Notetaking, Graphic Organizer, Questioning the Text, Drafting, Summarizing

Using the Cornell Notes system, record comments about the film, questions about its function as a text, and a summary of the effectiveness of the argument it makes.

Questions/Commentary	Notetaking Area

Summary Section

The Nature of the Problem

1. Using your notes on this section of the film, use the following model to create a chart identifying the various cause-effect claims made thus far.

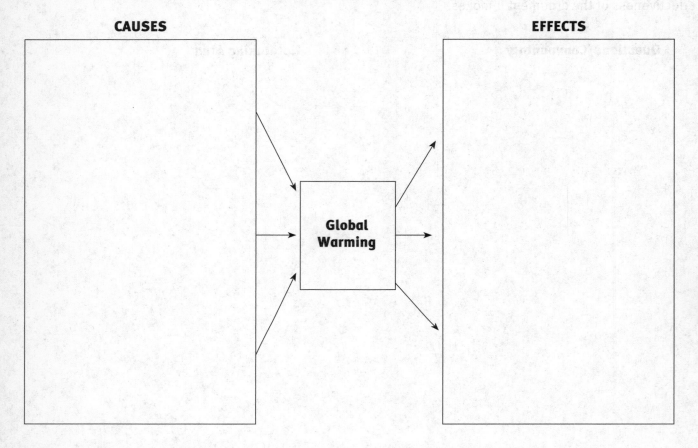

CAUSES   EFFECTS

Global
Warming

2. With your group, analyze three cause-effect links. How is each claim supported in the film (logos, ethos, pathos, empirical evidence, visual aids, and so on)? How persuasive is the claim as a result?

3. **Timed Writing Prompt:** Draft a response in which you analyze the purpose and effectiveness of one of the segments from today's viewing. Your teacher will specify the amount of time you will have to write your response. Remember to describe the cause-effect link(s) and to use effective transitions as you develop your analysis.

A Convergence of Crises

SUGGESTED LEARNING STRATEGIES: Summarizing, Drafting, Marking the Draft, Notetaking

You will be assigned one of the focus areas below. As you watch today's segment from *The 11th Hour*, fill out the viewing guide with details that connect to your focus area. After finishing the segment, summarize your findings.

ETHOS AND CREDIBILITY: This film relies on the testimony of experts to make its argument about sustainable development. Keep track of each person interviewed in this segment, and make notes to answer these questions.

- Which interviewees seem most or least credible, and why?

- What types of evidence do the most credible speakers present?

- How does their appearance and delivery affect credibility?

- Based on your responses, what can you conclude about how speakers make themselves credible to an audience?

EVIDENCE AND PERSUASION: This segment identifies a number of negative impacts of environmental development. Make a list of these as they are presented.

- How persuasive is evidence for each environmental impact that current approaches to development must end or be changed?

- How does visual information support the claims the speakers are making?

- What kinds of evidence and appeals (logical explanations, emotional appeals, the ethos of the speakers) make these claims persuasive?

- Based on your responses, what can you conclude about how to use visuals, documented evidence, and emotional appeals to support a claim?

VALUES AND PERSPECTIVES:

- What values does the film support? In other words, what does the film seem to support as the right way to feel about the issues?

- What perspectives does it criticize? What does it say, for example, about corporate and political attitudes in our culture?

- Is growth a means to an end, or an end in itself?

- What perspectives are NOT presented except through the filter of others who disagree with them?

- What biases dominate in the film? Does the film effectively speak to audience members who do not share those biases? Why or why not?

> **WORD CONNECTIONS**
>
> *Persuasion* contains the root *-suad-*, from the Latin word *suadere*, meaning "to advise or urge." This root also appears in *dissuade* and *persuadable*.

A Convergence of Crises

Nonfiction Film Viewing Guide

Director: **Title:**   **Year:**

What Do You See? (primary or archival footage, interviews, still images, the filmmaker)

What Do You Hear? (dialogue, narration, diegetic and non-diegetic sound)

What Do You Read? (subtitles, graphics, labels)

How Is It Put Together? (editing sequence, transition devices)

What Is the Effect? (What is the level of subjectivity?)

2. After sharing with the other members of your group, write a summary of the information presented by one of the other members. Be sure to answer the key questions for that person's topic (see previous page). Each member in your group should summarize the information presented by a different group member so that only one summary is written for each presentation.

3. Give your summary to the person whose presentation you summarized. Read through the summary you receive and mark the draft with feedback on three main criteria:

   • How effectively has the person summarized the main points?

   • Has any key information been omitted?

   • Is the summary objective or too subjective?

4. Based on these three criteria, how should the writer revise his or her summary to make it more comprehensive, accurate, and representative?

5. Revise your own paragraph to reflect the feedback you receive from your group member.

The Task of Our Generation

LITERARY TERMS

Logical appeal (logos) is the use of factual evidence and logical thought to appeal to an audience's sense of reason. **Emotional appeal** (pathos) is the use of emotional language or images to move audiences. **Ethical appeal** (ethos) works by establishing the writer as fair and open-minded. The writer tries to create a sense of trustworthiness and credibility.

1. Now that you have completed your viewing of the film, look back at your notes for this final segment. Then write at least five Level 2 questions about the effect or purpose of specific images and claims presented in the film's closing segment.

2. Working with classmates, identify several questions that effectively guide analysis of details in the segment you viewed. Be prepared to ask the class to respond to these questions and to respond to the questions of other students.

3. **Timed Writing Prompt:** Based upon your reaction to the film (and the class discussion), choose the quotation below that you think best articulates the film's call to action. Then write an analysis of how the film uses rhetorical devices such as **logical, emotional,** or **ethical appeals** to support this call to action. Include appropriate rhetorical devices and evidence from the film to support your analysis and to convey your intended meaning. Your teacher will specify the amount of time you have to write your analysis.

   - "All of these forces sweeping over the planet are the forces created by human beings. If human beings are the source of the problem, we can be the foundation of the solution."

   - "There's the model. In nature there is no waste. One organism's waste is another's food. That's the model for the industrial system that must eventually evolve."

   - "The direction to go is to decouple from our dependence on oil through efficient transportation, better-insulated houses, and the development of renewable alternatives like solar, wind and biomass and getting those to become the major part of the market. . ."

   - "Personal action is important. This problem of global warming is huge and tremendous and it may seem inconsequential to take your personal action but it is important for many reasons."

   - "We as citizens, leaders, consumers and voters have the opportunity to help integrate ecology into governmental policy and everyday living standards."

   - "During this critical period of human history, healing the damage of industrial civilization is the task of our generation."

SUGGESTED LEARNING STRATEGIES: **Summarizing, Drafting, Marking the Draft, Notetaking**

Article

DiCaprio Sheds Light on 11ᵗʰ Hour

by Scott Roxborough

May 20, 2007

My Notes

Leonardo DiCaprio sat down with The Hollywood Reporter and a handful of select film publications at the Hotel du Cap in Cannes on Saturday to discuss his upcoming environmental documentary "The 11th Hour." The film, which premiered in a special Out of Competition screening Saturday at the Festival de Cannes, uses a barrage of images and reams of interviews with the world's top environmental scientists to paint a bleak but still optimistic picture of the fate of our planet. "Hour" was directed by sisters Nadia Conners and Leila Conners Petersen, who wrote the script with DiCaprio.

Q: What was the most difficult thing for you in making this film?

DiCaprio: Trying to condense the vision of what these scientific experts are saying (about global warming) and trying to make it as clear and as emotionally moving as possible. Trying to condense a world of issues into an hour-and-a-half format in this film was the biggest challenge. But it was about giving them a platform where they didn't have to argue about the science. Because, and I keep stressing this, this is the overwhelming majority of the scientific community that believes in this. Not to have to be challenged about the science, about if their opinions were correct or if their opinions were valid. It was about them being able to express ideas and being able to give us, the public. Listen to the scientists and give us, the public, solutions for the future.

Q: With "The 11th Hour" are you hoping to reach a different audience than Al Gore's "An Inconvenient Truth" just because of who you are and the kind of attention this film will get because of your involvement with it?

A: "Yes, I guess you could call it a different audience. I mean, I didn't want to make this an overly political film, where just because of your political affiliation, you think you are somehow responsible for this and are somehow to blame. There are political overtones in the movie, we do point the finger. But ultimately, it is not about preaching to the choir, about reaching an audience that already gets it and already wants to become active. It's about, I suppose — and this is just about me following the lead of what the scientists and the experts have been saying — it's the cultural transformation that needs to happen. It's a swelling up from the ground level from people that are going to have to demand action. It goes beyond whether you are a democrat or republican in the United States. It goes beyond that. It goes into the realm of every politician having to be responsible because there is such a cultural awareness about global warming and environmental issues that they have to deal with it."

Q: Are you worried that, because you are a celebrity, people could dismiss this movie simply because of who you are?

A: "I am completely aware of the fact that being someone from quote-unquote Hollywood will garner a certain amount of skepticism and criticism as why should we listen to this person? I wanted to pose myself as a concerned citizen, not as an expert. I ask the questions and allow these people (the scientists) to give the answers. But you can also talk about the Hollywood community and about how they have traditionally been a part of a lot of great movements in the United States, going back to the civil rights movement or the peace movement. I don't think there's nothing wrong with that. As long as I don't pretend to be somebody who does have a degree, you know what I mean? But rather as a concerned citizen. Hopefully a larger audience will watch the film as opposed to if I wasn't involved with it.

Q: The film doesn't pander to a populist level. You get into a lot of pretty complicated detail in the film.

A: Well that comes down to the fact that these are extremely complicated issues and can't be put into a format of predigested baby food that is spoon-fed (the audience). These are complicated issues to wrap your head around, and we knew that. But ultimately the most important thing to us was whether you were emotionally moved at the end of the movie. And on a personal level, I believe that has been accomplished. Yes, a lot of the science is very hard to wrap your head around. But I was very clear in the movie. I want the public to be very scared by what they see. I want them to see a very bleak future. I want them to feel disillusioned halfway through and feel hopeless. And then when we get into the entire section in the second half when we talk about cultural transformation and a new way of looking at things and the alternatives or green technology and all these things, you realize there is great hope and there are options on the table. And hopefully the audience is moved and galvanized to do something about it. Hopefully.

As you view the film clip, focus carefully on how it portrays the threat posed by global warming. What cinematic techniques does the film use to support its claim? What rhetorical appeals?

Sender-Receiver Relationship: To whom are the filmmakers explicitly addressing their argument to here? How do they seem to feel about that target audience?

Message: What is the clip's central claim? What content does it use to support that claim?

Emotional Strategies: What emotional appeals does the director include? What seems to be their desired effect?

Logical Strategies: What logical arguments/appeals does the director include? What is their effect?

Language: What specific language is used in the clip to support the message? How does it impact the film's effectiveness and credibility? Consider both images and actual words.

Whose Truth Is True?

WORD CONNECTIONS

Refutation of an argument sometimes takes the form of an attack against the person rather than the message. The term *ad hominem* describes a personal attack. It is Latin for "against the man."

1. **Quickwrite:** After analyzing the clip, write a paragraph responding to the following questions:

   a. To what extent does media coverage appear biased in this sequence?

   b. What cinematic techniques do the directors use to establish the dramatic tone of the chapter?

   c. Does this sequence seem manipulative? If so, in what ways?

   d. Is it ethical for a filmmaker to emotionally manipulate an audience in order to be persuasive? Explain why or why not.

2. After you have written your paragraph, compare answers with your group members and then discuss the following questions:

   a. How persuasive is the film's depiction of the threat posed?

   b. How does presenting the threat in this way affect the film's credibility?

   c. As you compare answers, to what extent do you agree or disagree in your assessments? What explains any disagreements?

3. You will next read an article that presents a position about the
arguments made in *The 11th Hour*. Read your assigned article
individually, and complete the SMELL chart as you read. Highlight
evidence of the values and beliefs central to the writer's position.

Sender-Receiver Relationship: To whom is the writer explicitly addressing his or her argument?
How does the writer seem to feel about that target audience? What values does the writer (sender)
assume the reader shares or argue that they should share?

Message: What is a literal summary of the content? What is the article's ultimate thesis regarding
the subject?

Emotional Strategies: What emotional appeals does the writer include? What seems to be their
desired effect?

Logical Strategies: What logical arguments/appeals does the writer include? What is their effect?

Language: What specific language is used in the article to support the message or characterize the
opposition? How does it impact the writer's ethos and the article's effectiveness and credibility?

Whose Truth Is True?

4. After you and your group members finish evaluating your articles, present your conclusions to one another. Be sure to support your claims about the article's level of subjectivity by citing specific evidence from the text.

5. As a group, rank the four pieces based on how persuasive they are. You must come to a consensus on your ranking, so be prepared to justify your opinions, both with your group and with the class as a whole.

11th Hour	
Inhofe	
Michaels	
Marshall	

6. If you were writing a paper evaluating the claims about global warming presented in *The 11th Hour*, which of the three essays would be most or least credible if cited as a source and why? What is the relationship between the level of subjectivity in a source and its credibility with various audiences?

Speech

Inhofe slams DiCaprio and Laurie David for scaring kids in two-hour Senate speech debunking climate fears

Posted by Marc Morano

October 26, 2007

Senator James Inhofe (R-OK), Ranking Member of the Environment and Public Works Committee, delivered a more than two-hour floor speech today debunking fears of man-made global warming. Below is an excerpt of his remarks about how Hollywood, led by Leonardo DiCaprio and Laurie David, has promoted unfounded climate fears to children. Also, watch the video of Inhofe denouncing Hollywood on the Senate floor.

SENATOR INHOFE SPEECH EXCERPT:

We are currently witnessing an international awakening of scientists who are speaking out in opposition to former Vice President Al Gore, the United Nations, the Hollywood elitists and the media-driven "consensus" on man-made global warming.

We have witnessed Antarctic ice GROW to record levels since satellite monitoring began in the 1970's. We have witnessed NASA temperature data errors that have made 1934 — not 1998 — the hottest year on record in the U.S. We have seen global averages temperatures flat line since 1998 and the Southern Hemisphere cool in recent years.

These new developments in just the last six months are but a sample of the new information coming out that continues to debunk climate alarm.

But before we delve into these dramatic new scientific developments, it is important to take note of our pop culture propaganda campaign aimed at children.

HOLLYWOOD TARGETS CHILDREN WITH CLIMATE FEARS

In addition to (Al) Gore's entry last year into Hollywood fictional disaster films, other celebrity figures have attempted to jump into the game.

Hollywood activist Leonardo DiCaprio decided to toss objective scientific truth out the window in his new scarefest "The 11th Hour." DiCaprio refused to interview any scientists who disagreed with his dire vision of the future of the Earth.

In fact, his film reportedly features physicist Stephen Hawking making the unchallenged assertion that "the worst-case scenario is that Earth would become like its sister planet, Venus, with a temperature of 250 [degrees] centigrade."

GRAMMAR & USAGE

When writers quote from other sources, they must surround the borrowed words with quotation marks. Sometimes, however, a quotation includes words quoted from a different source or words already in quotation marks. These words should then be enclosed in single quotation marks (' '). For example: "In fact, his film reportedly features physicist Stephen Hawking making the unchallenged assertion that 'the worse-case scenario is that Earth would become like its sister planet, Venus, with a temperature of 250 [degrees] centigrade.'"

Whose Truth Is True?

I guess these "worst-case scenarios" pass for science in Hollywood these days. It also fits perfectly with DiCaprio's stated purpose of the film.

DiCaprio said on May 20th of this year: "I want the public to be very scared by what they see. I want them to see a very bleak future."

While those who went to watch DiCaprio's science fiction film may see his intended "bleak future," it is DiCaprio who has been scared by the bleak box office numbers, as his film has failed to generate any significant audience interest.

GORE'S PRODUCER TO KIDS: 'BE ACTIVISTS'

Children are now the number one target of the global warming fear campaign. DiCaprio announced his goal was to recruit young eco-activists to the cause.

"We need to get kids young," DiCaprio said in a September 20 interview with *USA Weekend*.

Hollywood activist Laurie David, Gore's co-producer of "An Inconvenient Truth" recently co-authored a children's global warming book with Cambria Gordon for Scholastic Books titled, *The Down-To-Earth Guide to Global Warming*.

David has made it clear that her goal is to influence young minds with her new book when she recently wrote an open letter to her children stating: "We want you to grow up to be activists."

Apparently, David and other activists are getting frustrated by the widespread skepticism on climate as reflected in both the U.S. and the UK according to the latest polls.

It appears the alarmists are failing to convince adults to believe their increasingly shrill and scientifically unfounded rhetoric, so they have decided kids are an easier sell.

But David should worry less about recruiting young activists and more about scientific accuracy. A science group found what it called a major "scientific error" in David's new kid's book on page 18.

According to a Science and Public Policy Institute release on September 13:

"The authors [David and Gordon] present unsuspecting children with an altered temperature and CO_2 graph that reverses the relationship found in the scientific literature. The manipulation is critical because David's central premise posits that CO_2 drives temperature, yet the peer-reviewed literature is unanimous that CO_2 changes have historically followed temperature changes."

David has now been forced to publicly admit this significant scientific error in her book.

NINE YEAR OLD: 'I DON'T WANT TO DIE' FROM GLOBAL WARMING

A Canadian high school student named McKenzie was shown Gore's climate horror film in four different classes.

"I really don't understand why they keep showing it," McKenzie said on May 19, 2007.

In June, a fourth grade class from Portland Maine's East End Community School issued a dire climate report: "Global warming is a huge pending global disaster" read the elementary school kids' report according to an article in the Portland Press Herald on June 14, 2007. Remember, these are fourth graders issuing a dire global warming report.

And this agenda of indoctrination and fear aimed at children is having an impact.

Nine year old Alyssa Luz-Ricca was quoted in the Washington Post on April 16, 2007 as saying:

"I worry about [global warming] because I don't want to die."

The same article explained: "Psychologists say they're seeing an increasing number of young patients preoccupied by a climactic Armageddon."

I was told by the parent of an elementary school kid last spring who said her daughter was forced to watch "An Inconvenient Truth" once a month at school and had nightmares about drowning in the film's predicted scary sea level rise.

The Hollywood global-warming documentary "Arctic Tale" ends with a child actor telling kids: "If your mom and dad buy a hybrid car, you'll make it easier for polar bears to get around."

Unfortunately, children are hearing the scientifically unfounded doomsday message loud and clear. But the message kids are receiving is not a scientific one, it is a political message designed to create fear, nervousness and ultimately recruit them to liberal activism.

There are a few hopeful signs. A judge in England has ruled that schools must issue a warning before they show Gore's film to children because of scientific inaccuracies and "sentimental mush."

In addition, there is a new kids book called "The Sky's Not Falling! Why It's OK to Chill About Global Warming." The book counters the propaganda from the pop culture.

OBJECTIVE, EVIDENCE BASED SCIENCE IS BEGINNING TO CRUSH HYSTERIA

My speech today and these reports reveal that recent peer-reviewed scientific studies are totally refuting the Church of Man-made Global Warming.

GLOBAL WARMING MOVEMENT 'FALLING APART'

Meteorologist Joseph Conklin who launched the skeptical website http://www.climatepolice.com/ in 2007, recently declared the "global warming movement [is] falling apart."

Whose Truth Is True?

All the while, activists like former Vice President Al Gore repeatedly continue to warn of a fast approaching climate "tipping point."

I agree with Gore. Global warming may have reached a "tipping point."

The man-made global warming fear machine crossed the "tipping point" in 2007.

I am convinced that future climate historians will look back at 2007 as the year the global warming fears began crumbling. The situation we are in now is very similar to where we were in the late 1970's when coming ice age fears began to dismantle.

Remember, it was *Newsweek Magazine* which in the 1970's proclaimed meteorologists were "almost unanimous" in their view that a coming Ice Age would have negative impacts. It was also *Newsweek* in 1975 which originated the eerily similar "tipping point" rhetoric of today:

Newsweek wrote on April 28, 1975 about coming ice age fears: "The longer the planners delay, the more difficult will they find it to cope with climatic change once the results become grim reality."

Of course *Newsweek* essentially retracted their coming ice age article 29 years later in October 2006. In addition, a 1975 National Academy of Sciences report addressed coming ice age fears and in 1971, NASA predicted the world "could be as little as 50 or 60 years away from a disastrous new ice age."

Today, the greatest irony is that the UN and the media's climate hysteria grow louder as the case for alarmism fades away. While the scientific case grows weaker, the political and rhetorical proponents of climate fear are ramping up to offer hefty tax and regulatory "solutions" both internationally and domestically to "solve" the so-called "crisis."

Skeptical Climatologist Dr. Timothy Ball formerly of the University of Winnipeg in Canada wrote about the current state of the climate change debate earlier this month:

"Imagine basing a country's energy and economic policy on an incomplete, unproven theory - a theory based entirely on computer models in which one minor variable (CO2) is considered the sole driver for the entire global climate system."

And just how minor is that man-made CO2 variable in the atmosphere?

Meteorologist Joseph D'Aleo, the first Director of Meteorology at The Weather Channel and former chairman of the American Meteorological Society's (AMS) Committee on Weather Analysis and Forecasting, explained in August how miniscule mankind's CO2 emissions are in relation to the Earth's atmosphere.

"If the atmosphere was a 100 story building, our annual anthropogenic CO2 contribution today would be equivalent to the linoleum on the first floor," D'Aleo wrote.

GRAMMAR & USAGE

Notice the writer's use of quotation marks around the words "solutions," "solve," and "crisis." Placing these words in quotation marks helps the writer suggest irony or sarcasm, which is intended to lead the reader to place less emphasis on the other side's claims.

Article

Global Warming:
No Urgent Danger; No Quick Fix

by Patrick J. Michaels
Atlanta Journal-Constitution
August 21, 2007

It's summer, it's hot and global warming is on the cover of *Newsweek*. Scare stories abound. We may only have 10 years to stop this! The future survival of our species is at stake!

OK, the media aren't exactly nonpartisan, especially on global warming. So what's the real story and what do we need to know?

Fact: The average surface temperature of the Earth is about 0.8° C warmer than it was in 1900, and human beings have something to do with it. But does that portend an unmitigated disaster? Can we do anything meaningful about it at this time? And if we can't, what should or can we do in the future?

These are politically loaded questions that must be answered truthfully, especially when considering legislation designed to reduce emissions of carbon dioxide, the main global warming gas.

Unfortunately, they'll probably be ignored. Right now there are a slew of bills before Congress, and many in various states, that mandate massively reducing carbon dioxide emissions. Some actually propose cutting our CO2 output to 80 percent or 90 percent below 1990 levels by the year 2050.

Let's be charitable and simply call that legislative arrogance. U.S. emissions are up about 18 percent from 1990 as they stand. Whenever you hear about these large cuts, ask the truth: How is this realistically going to happen?

I did that on an international television panel two weeks ago. My opponent, who advocated these cuts, dropped his jaw and said nothing, ultimately uttering a curse word for the entire world to hear. The fact of the matter is he had no answer because there isn't one.

Nor would legislation in any state or Washington, D.C., have any standing in Beijing. Although the final figures aren't in yet, it's beginning to look like China has just passed the United States as the world's largest emitter of carbon dioxide. Like the United States, China has oodles of coal, and the Chinese are putting in at least one new coal-fired power plant a month. (Some reports have it at an astonishing one per week.) And just as it does in the United States, when coal burns in China, it turns largely to carbon dioxide and water.

Whose Truth Is True?

My Notes

What we do in the United States is having less and less of an effect on the concentration of carbon dioxide in the world's atmosphere.

We certainly adapted to 0.8° C temperature change quite well in the 20th century, as life expectancy doubled and some crop yields quintupled. And who knows what new and miraculously efficient power sources will develop in the next hundred years.

The stories about the ocean rising 20 feet as massive amounts of ice slide off of Greenland by 2100 are also fiction. For the entire half century from 1915 through 1965, Greenland was significantly warmer than it has been for the last decade. There was no disaster. More important, there's a large body of evidence that for much of the period from 3,000 to 9,000 years ago, at least the Eurasian Arctic was 2.5° C to 7° C warmer than now in the summer, when ice melts. Greenland's ice didn't disappear then, either.

Then there is the topic of interest this time of year — hurricanes. Will hurricanes become stronger or more frequent because of warming? My own work suggests that late in the 21st century there might be an increase in strong storms, but that it will be very hard to detect because of year-to-year variability.

Right now, after accounting for increasing coastal population and property values, there is no increase in damages caused by these killers. The biggest of them all was the Great Miami Hurricane of 1926. If it occurred today, it would easily cause twice as much damage as 2005's vaunted Hurricane Katrina.

So let's get real and give the politically incorrect answers to global warming's inconvenient questions. Global warming is real, but it does not portend immediate disaster, and there's currently no suite of technologies that can do much about it. The obvious solution is to forgo costs today on ineffective attempts to stop it, and to save our money for investment in future technologies and inevitable adaptation.

Patrick J. Michaels is a senior fellow in environmental studies at the Cato Institute and is on leave as research professor of environmental sciences at the University of Virginia.

Article

Jeremy Clarkson and Michael O'Leary Won't Listen to Green Cliches and Complaints About Polar Bears

by George Marshall
The Guardian (UK)
March 9, 2009

Academics meeting in Bristol at the weekend for Britain's first conference on the psychology of climate change argued that the greatest obstacles to action are not technical, economic or political — they are the denial strategies that we adopt to protect ourselves from unwelcome information.

It is true that nearly 80% of people claim to be concerned about climate change. However, delve deeper and one finds that people have a remarkable tendency to define this concern in ways that keep it as far away as possible. They describe climate change as a global problem (but not a local one) as a future problem (not one for their own lifetimes) and absolve themselves of responsibility for either causing the problem or solving it.

Most disturbing of all, 60% of people believe that "many scientific experts still question if humans are contributing to climate change". Thirty per cent of people believe climate change is "largely down to natural causes", while 7% refuse to accept the climate is changing at all.

How is it possible that so many people are still unpersuaded by 40 years of research and the consensus of every major scientific institution in the world? Surely we are now long past the point at which the evidence became overwhelming?

If only belief formation were this simple. Having neither the time nor skills to weigh up each piece of evidence we fall back on decision-making shortcuts formed by our education, politics and class. In particular we measure new information against our life experience and the views of the people around us.

George Lakoff, of the University of California, argues that we often use metaphors to carry over experience from simple or concrete experiences into new domains. Thus, as politicians know very well, broad concepts such as freedom, independence, leadership, growth and pride can resonate far deeper than the policies they describe.

My Notes

GRAMMAR & USAGE

The **subjunctive mood** indicates an uncertainty or something that is not real. Marshall uses the subjunctive in his statement: "If only belief formation were this simple."

My Notes

None of this bodes well for a rational approach to climate change. Climate change is invariably presented as an overwhelming threat requiring unprecedented restraint, sacrifice, and government intervention. The metaphors it invokes are poisonous to people who feel rewarded by free market capitalism and distrust government interference. It is hardly surprising that political world view is by far the greatest determinant of attitudes to climate change, especially in the US where three times more Republicans than Democrats believe that "too much fuss is made about global warming".

An intuitive suspicion is then reinforced by a deep distrust of the key messengers: the liberal media, politicians and green campaign groups. As Jeremy Clarkson says, bundling them all together: "...everything we've been told for the past five years by the government, Al Gore, Channel 4 News and hippies everywhere is a big bucket of nonsense." Michael O'Leary, the founder of Ryanair, likens "hairy dungaree and sandal wearing climate change alarmists" to "the CND nutters of the 1970s". These cultural prejudices, however simplistic, align belief with cultural allegiance: "People like us," they say, "do not believe in this tripe."

However much one distrusts environmentalists, it is harder to discount the scientists… depending, of course, on which scientists one listens to. The conservative news media continues to provide a platform for the handful of scientists who reject the scientific consensus. Of the 18 experts that appeared in Channel 4's notorious skeptic documentary *The Great Global Warming Swindle*, 11 have been quoted in the past two years in the Daily and Sunday Telegraph, five of them more than five times.

Dr Myanna Lahsen, a cultural anthropologist at the University of Colorado, has specialised in understanding how professional scientists, some of them with highly respected careers, turn climate skeptic. She found the largest common factor was a shared sense that they had personally lost prestige and authority as the result of campaigns by liberals and environmentalists. She concluded that their engagement in climate issues "can be understood in part as a struggle to preserve their particular culturally charged understanding of environmental reality."

In other words, like the general public, they form their beliefs through reference to a world view formed through politics and life experience. In order to maintain their skepticism in the face of a sustained, and sometimes heated, challenge from their peers, they have created a mutually supportive dissident culture around an identity as victimised speakers for the truth.

This individualistic romantic image is nurtured by the libertarian right think tanks that promote the skeptic arguments. One academic study of 192 skeptic books and reports found that 92% were directly associated with right wing free market think tanks. It concluded that the denial of climate change had been deliberately constructed "as a tactic of an elite-driven counter-movement designed to combat environmentalism".

So, given that skepticism is rooted in a sustained and well-funded ideological movement, how can skeptics be swayed? One way is to reframe climate change in a way that rejects the green cliches and creates new metaphors with a wider resonance. So out with the polar bears and saving the planet. Instead let's talk of energy independence, and the potential for new enterprise.

And then there is peer pressure, probably the most important influence of all. So, when dealing with a skeptic, don't get into a head to head with them. Just politely point out all the people they know and respect who believe that climate change is a serious problem — and they aren't sandal-wearing tree huggers, are they?

• *George Marshall is founder of the Climate Outreach Information Network and the author of Carbon Detox and the blog climatedenial.org.*

My Notes

Why Do Reasonable People Disagree?

1. In Unit 1, you defined the term *culture*. Look back at your definition now, and rewrite it in the space below. You may revise it if you'd like, based on your experiences since Unit 1.

> Culture =

2. Read the following definitions of culture. Then, in your groups, discuss your reactions to each. In particular, consider what each reveals about the causes of cultural conflict.

   • "By definition, objective culture is comprised of artifacts and technology that produces them (e.g., tools, habitations, modes of transport, paintings, buildings, and so on) and observable human activities (e.g., behavioral norms, interpersonal roles, child-rearing practices, institutional structures, social and legal prescriptions, etc.). Subjective culture, on the other hand, consists of human cognitive processes (e.g., values, stereotypes, attitudes, feelings, motivations, beliefs, and most generally, meanings)." — Y. Tanaka, "Proliferating Technology and the Structure of Information-Space." *From Intercultural and International Communication*. Ed. F. L. Casmir. Washington, DC: University Press of America, 1978. pp. 185–212.

   • "Thus, we reject conceptions of culture as fixed, coherent, or 'natural' and instead view it as dynamically changing over time and space—the product of ongoing human interaction. . . . We recognize that there are ideas and practices which may be maintained over long periods of time, from generation to generation, but . . . It is also influenced by, influences and generally contradicts with, contemporary social, economic and political factors. Geography too is significant. It is not just about where you are on the world map, for example, but about the ways in which space and place interact with understandings about being a person. Moreover, any one individual's experience of culture will be affected by the multiple aspects of their identity—'race,' gender, sex, age, sexuality, class, caste position, religion, geography, and so forth—and it is likely to alter in various circumstances." –Skelton,

T. and T. Allen. "Introduction." From *Culture and Global Change*. Eds. T. Skelton and T. Allen. London: Routledge, 1999. pp. 1–10.

- "Culture [is] a contested zone. . . . Thinking about culture as a contested zone helps us understand the struggles of cultural groups and the complexities of cultural life. It also aids us in coming to understand and consider various cultural realities and perspectives of the diverse groups that reside within any cultural space. If we define culture as a contested zone in which different groups struggle to define issues in their own interests, we must also recognize that not all groups have equal access to public forums to voice their concerns, perspectives, and the everyday realities of their lives." –Moon, D. G. "Thinking about 'Culture' in Intercultural Communication." From *Readings in Intercultural Communication*. 2nd Ed. Eds. Martin, J.N.; T. K. Nakayama and L.A. Flores. Boston: McGraw Hill, 2002. pp. 13–21.

3. After having read these definitions, revise your own. How does each challenge, reinforce, or modify your understanding of what culture means? In the space provided, record your reaction.

Culture is ....

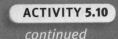

Why Do Reasonable People Disagree?

4. Once you have considered different perspectives, you can start to evaluate some realistic approaches to achieving change. Read through the UN Millennium Declaration and answer the following questions with your group members.

- <u>Topic:</u> Who is participating in establishing this declaration, and what is/are the problem(s) being addressed?

- <u>Policy Statement:</u> What is the declaration meant to accomplish?

- <u>Reason:</u> Why is the declaration needed?

- <u>Procedures:</u> How will the declaration be translated into action? What specific actions are described? When and where will they be implemented? What is not mentioned that could be done? What will not be done (that some nations may request), and why?

- <u>People:</u> Who will do what?

- <u>Impact:</u> What will be accomplished through these actions? How will action address the concerns of various nations?

Quickwrite: In a quickwrite, answer the following questions: What difficulties might you encounter when trying to resolve a complex issue such as an environmental conflict? What kinds of limitations do you have to accept when working toward a solution all groups will find acceptable?

Declaration

UNITED NATIONS MILLENNIUM DECLARATION

The General Assembly
Adopts the following Declaration:

United Nations Millennium Declaration

I. Values and principles

1. We, heads of State and Government, have gathered at United Nations Headquarters in New York from 6 to 8 September 2000, at the dawn of a new millennium, to reaffirm our faith in the Organization and its Charter as indispensable foundations of a more peaceful, prosperous and just world.

2. We recognize that, in addition to our separate responsibilities to our individual societies, we have a collective responsibility to uphold the principles of human dignity, equality and equity at the global level. As leaders we have a duty therefore to all the world's people, especially the most vulnerable and, in particular, the children of the world, to whom the future belongs.

3. We reaffirm our commitment to the purposes and principles of the Charter of the United Nations, which have proved timeless and universal. Indeed, their relevance and capacity to inspire have increased, as nations and peoples have become increasingly interconnected and interdependent.

4. We are determined to establish a just and lasting peace all over the world in accordance with the purposes and principles of the Charter. We rededicate ourselves to support all efforts to uphold the sovereign equality of all States, respect for their territorial integrity and political independence, resolution of disputes by peaceful means and in conformity with the principles of justice and international law, the right to self-determination of peoples which remain under colonial domination and foreign occupation, non-interference in the internal affairs of States, respect for human rights and fundamental freedoms, respect for the equal rights of all without distinction as to race, sex, language or religion and international cooperation in solving international problems of an economic, social, cultural or humanitarian character.

My Notes

Why Do Reasonable People Disagree?

5. We believe that the central challenge we face today is to ensure that globalization becomes a positive force for all the world's people. For while globalization offers great opportunities, at present its benefits are very unevenly shared, while its costs are unevenly distributed. We recognize that developing countries and countries with economies in transition face special difficulties in responding to this central challenge. Thus, only through broad and sustained efforts to create a shared future, based upon our common humanity in all its diversity, can globalization be made fully inclusive and equitable. These efforts must include policies and measures, at the global level, which correspond to the needs of developing countries and economies in transition and are formulated and implemented with their effective participation.

6. We consider certain fundamental values to be essential to international relations in the twenty-first century. These include:

- **Freedom.** Men and women have the right to live their lives and raise their children in dignity, free from hunger and from the fear of violence, oppression or injustice. Democratic and participatory governance based on the will of the people best assures these rights.

- **Equality.** No individual and no nation must be denied the opportunity to benefit from development. The equal rights and opportunities of women and men must be assured.

- **Solidarity.** Global challenges must be managed in a way that distributes the costs and burdens fairly in accordance with basic principles of equity and social justice. Those who suffer or who benefit least deserve help from those who benefit most.

- **Tolerance.** Human beings must respect one other, in all their diversity of belief, culture and language. Differences within and between societies should be neither feared nor repressed, but cherished as a precious asset of humanity. A culture of peace and dialogue among all civilizations should be actively promoted.

- **Respect for nature.** Prudence must be shown in the management of all living species and natural resources, in accordance with the precepts of sustainable development. Only in this way can the immeasurable riches provided to us by nature be preserved and passed on to our descendants. The current unsustainable patterns of production and consumption must be changed in the interest of our future welfare and that of our descendants.

- **Shared responsibility.** Responsibility for managing worldwide economic and social development, as well as threats to international peace and security, must be shared among the nations of the world and should be exercised multilaterally. As the most universal and most representative organization in the world, the United Nations must play the central role.

7. In order to translate these shared values into actions, we have identified key objectives to which we assign special significance. . . .

IV. Protecting our common environment

21. We must spare no effort to free all of humanity, and above all our children and grandchildren, from the threat of living on a planet irredeemably spoilt by human activities, and whose resources would no longer be sufficient for their needs.

22. We reaffirm our support for the principles of sustainable development, including those set out in Agenda 21, agreed upon at the United Nations Conference on Environment and Development.

23. We resolve therefore to adopt in all our environmental actions a new ethic of conservation and stewardship and, as first steps, we resolve:

- To make every effort to ensure the entry into force of the Kyoto Protocol, preferably by the tenth anniversary of the United Nations Conference on Environment and Development in 2002, and to embark on the required reduction in emissions of greenhouse gases.

- To intensify our collective efforts for the management, conservation and sustainable development of all types of forests.

- To press for the full implementation of the Convention on Biological Diversity and the Convention to Combat Desertification in those Countries Experiencing Serious Drought and/or Desertification, particularly in Africa.

- To stop the unsustainable exploitation of water resources by developing water management strategies at the regional, national and local levels, which promote both equitable access and adequate supplies.

- To intensify cooperation to reduce the number and effects of natural and man-made disasters.

- To ensure free access to information on the human genome sequence.

My Notes

Exploring One Conflict Together

The newspaper article "A Roaring Battle Over Sea Lions" presents a range of stakeholder interests. Stakeholders are those motivated by various concerns. Use the explanations below to help you analyze the interests, impact, and involvement of stakeholders as you read the article on sea lions.

- *Stakeholder Values and Interests* refers to the values that motivate the stakeholder, the project's benefit(s) to the stakeholder, the changes that the project might require the stakeholder to make, and the project activities that might cause damage or conflict for the stakeholder.

- *Stakeholder Impact* refers to how important the stakeholder's participation is to the success of the proposed project. Consider:

  - The role the key stakeholder must play for the project to be successful, and the likelihood that the stakeholder will play this role.

  - The likelihood and impact of a stakeholder's negative response to the project.

- *Stakeholder Involvement* refers to the kinds of things that could be done to enlist stakeholder support and reduce opposition. Consider how one might approach each of the stakeholders. What kind of information will they need? Is there a limit to what changes they would support? Are there other groups or individuals that might influence the stakeholder to support the initiative?

1. The article, "A Roaring Battle Over Sea Lions," presents multiple perspectives on a conflict about the management of sea lions that feed on endangered salmon at the Bonneville Dam in Oregon. Preview the article. Then, in the space below, identify as many stakeholder groups as you can—including those that are obvious and those that may be involved even if they don't seem to have a specific agenda.

A Roaring Battle Over Sea Lions

At a dam outside Portland, Oregon, a controversy heats up over whether the animals should be removed—and even killed—in order to save the salmon.

by Bill Hewitt

Along the Columbia River, between Oregon and Washington, the sea lion stirs strong emotions. For Andrea Kozil, who regularly hikes along the river, the creatures, sleek and playful, are more like old friends than ordinary animals. "You can recognize them," say Kozil. "Thousands of people come to see them; the kids name them." But for fishermen and tribal members of the region, the sea lions, protected by federal law, are anything but cuddly. Because they prey on endangered wild salmon that also inhabit the Columbia, many locals see them as a threat to their way of life. "The sea lions are pretty much out of control," complains Dennis Richey, executive director of Oregon Anglers. "Something has to be done."

Feelings, already running high, have lately hit a new and more rancorous phase. Earlier this year, after winning approval from the federal government, wildlife officials in the area began a five-year program to remove as many as 85 of the California sea lions each year—by killing them if need be—from the waters around the Bonneville Dam, 40 miles east of Portland, where the creatures gorge on fish swimming upstream to spawn. Animal rights activists, including the Humane Society of the United States, have filed suit to stop the program, which was just getting under way when, on May 4, six sea lions were found dead in traps near the dam. Authorities said on May 14 that the animals had apparently died of heatstroke, but how the gates slammed closed remained a mystery. "Whether it was vigilantes or negligence, humans killed them," says Sharon Young of the Humane Society.

Those in favor of ousting the sea lions insist that their measures are a modest response to a critical problem: The numbers of wild salmon are in sharp decline. Meanwhile, the California sea lion, hunted nearly to extinction in the last century, has made a remarkable recovery since being protected in 1972, now numbering 240,000. Sea lions have been drawn to the Bonneville Dam because the salmon must congregate around the fish ladders—a series of pools arranged like ascending steps—in order to proceed upriver, making them an easy lunch. The plan to remove the sea lions included the stipulation that efforts be made to find zoos or aquariums to take as many of the animals as possible. Only those left over could be euthanized—or shot if they eluded capture. "No one's suggesting a scorched-earth policy," says Charles Hudson, of the Columbia River Inter-Tribal Fish Commission. "There was no bloodlust."

My Notes

GRAMMAR & USAGE

Relative (adjective) clauses can be **restrictive** (essential) or **nonrestrictive** (nonessential). Notice the use and punctuation of the adjective clauses in the following examples:

Nonrestrictive: For Andrea Kozil, **who regularly hikes along the river,** the creatures are more like old friends....

Restrictive: Because they prey on endangered wild salmon **that also inhabit the Columbia,** many locals see them as a threat....

In your writing, consider whether your adjective clauses need commas.

My Notes

But animal rights activists maintain that the government's own statistics, based on limited observation, suggest that the sea lions consume a relatively small percentage of the salmon. (State officials contend that the real percentage is far higher—and growing.) "The salmon are not going extinct because of the sea lions, but because of pollution, dams and overfishing," says Kozil, who works for a great-ape rescue organization in Portland and is one of the plaintiffs in the pending lawsuit to block the removal. "The sea lions have been demonized."

Hudson argues that it is the activists who have let their emotions get away from them, favoring the cute sea lions over the less attractive fish. "There seems to be a picking and choosing of one species over another," he says. "It's maddening." After the six sea lion deaths, officials agreed to suspend the removal program for this season. But that will not lay to rest the strong emotions on either side. Says Young of the Humane Society: "This issue is not going to go away."

2. Make notes from information in the article, and conduct research on this topic using multiple, reliable sources. Organize your information using the form below. Choose three key stakeholders with different positions, and analyze their interests, impact, and involvement. When you review the stakeholders involved in the issue of the sea lions, assign A for extremely important, B for fairly important, and C for not very important. Record these letters in the column entitled "Assessment of Impact." Record strategies for obtaining support or reducing obstacles to your project in the last column in the matrix.

Stakeholder	Stakeholder's Values and Interest(s) in the Project	Assessment of Impact	Stakeholder Involvement

3. Based on the concerns of the stakeholders you and your classmates have identified, what are some possible steps that could be taken to solve the conflict at Bonneville Dam?

Exploring One Conflict Together

4. Once you have considered different perspectives, you can start to draft a policy proposal that suggests solutions. Use the following template to brainstorm and organize the elements of a policy proposal for the sea lion controversy.

   • <u>Topic:</u> Who are the stakeholders, and what problem is to be addressed?

   • <u>Policy Statement:</u> What will your proposal accomplish?

   • <u>Reason:</u> Why is your proposal needed?

   • <u>Procedures:</u> How will the proposal be translated into action? What specific actions are you proposing? When and where will they be implemented?

   • <u>People:</u> Who will do what? How will actions address the concerns of the stakeholders?

   • <u>Impact:</u> What will be accomplished through these actions?

5. **Quickwrite:** In a paragraph, answer the following questions:
   • What sort of difficulties arise when one tries to resolve a complex issue such as an environmental conflict?
   • How can a stakeholder analysis help you to evaluate potential solutions to the problem?
   • What kinds of limitations do you have to accept when working toward a solution acceptable to people with different cultural perspectives?

A World of Conflicts

SUGGESTED LEARNING STRATEGIES: Graphic Organizer, Think-Pair-Share, Brainstorming

Using the chart below, brainstorm with a partner some environmental issues in the world that are caused by or connected to cultural conflicts.

Environmental Issues that Link to Cultural Conflicts

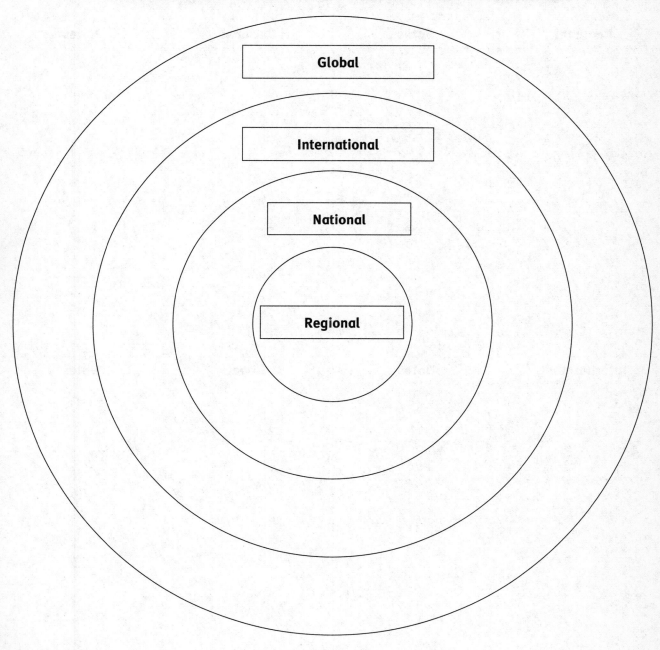

After the Gallery Walk, work with your group members to identify a few topics in each category that might be possible topics for your project. As a group, generate some notes on what you already know and would like to learn about each topic.

Regional	Notes	National	Notes

International	Notes	Global	Notes

- Looking over this list of issues, which ones do you think you might be interested in examining closely? Consult with your group members to discuss all opinions as you narrow your possible topics to choose a major research focus.

- Now, as a group, choose one of the above issues and brainstorm a preliminary list of stakeholders and their positions that may be involved in the conflict. Each group member can then conduct research with one stakeholder's position in mind, although your list may change as you research the conflict. Fill out the chart below and submit it to your teacher for approval.

Preliminary Topic Proposal Form

- **Topic:** What is the problem being addressed?

- **Rationale:** Why is your proposal needed?

- **Stakeholders:** What groups can you initially identify as involved in the conflict?

- **Research Assignments:**

- **Deadlines:**

- Source Evaluation Sheets: _____   Presentation Draft: _____

- Annotated Bibliography: _____   Formal Presentation: _____

- Individual Position Papers: _____   Personal Reflections: _____

- Structured Discussion _____

SUGGESTED LEARNING STRATEGIES: Graphic Organizer

Article

"Stay of Execution for Sea Lions at Bonneville Dam"

THE HUMANE SOCIETY OF THE UNITED STATES

1   On April 1, The HSUS negotiated a temporary stay of execution for sea lions with the National Marine Fisheries Service and the states of Washington and Oregon.

2   NMFS had authorized the states to begin shooting as many as 85 sea lions this April to prevent them from consuming a mere 0.4 to 4.2 percent of salmon and steelhead near Bonneville Dam, even though the states have recently proposed to increase fishing quotas by 33 percent (from 9 to 12 percent) in light of expected record Chinook salmon runs for 2008.

3   The HSUS and Wild Fish Conservation, along with individual citizens, have filed suit to block the 5-year program that could result in the deaths of 425 California sea lions.

4   Under the agreement reached this week, no sea lions will be killed until the court can hear arguments on The HSUS's request to halt the entire program. The Court is expected to make a decision on or before April 18, 2008.

5   **FACTS:**

While birds, other fish, sea lions, and fishermen all kill salmon, the primary threats are from loss of quality spawning habitat and dams blocking their normal migratory routes up and down river.

The major causes of salmon losses are:

- Dams: NMFS estimates the Federal Columbia River Power System kills 16.8 percent of adult Snake River Basin Steelhead and 59.9 percent of juveniles.

- Fishing: NMFS authorizes the incidental take of between 5.5 and 17 percent of the Upper Columbia spring Chinook and Upper Snake River spring/summer Chinook.

- Birds: NMFS estimated that avian predators consumed 18 percent of juvenile salmonids reaching the Columbia River estuary in 1998.

- Research: In 2003, NMFS authorized a research permit to take 4.8 percent of listed sockeye.

6   The plan to shoot sea lions coincides with estimates that this spring's Columbia River salmon run is likely to be the third largest in almost 30 years, and a likely 200 percent increase in total fish over 2007.

As you investigate the issue of your choice, you must evaluate your sources for subjectivity and types of appeals. Unlike most printed sources, information posted on Web sites is not always checked for factual accuracy. Be sure to use reliable and credible sites in your research.

Use the template below to **evaluate** a web site as your teacher guides you.

Topics and Questions	Responses
The URL: • What is the Web site's domain? (.com = for-profit organization; .gov, .mil, .us (or other country code) = a government site; .edu = an educational institution; .org = a nonprofit organization) • Is this URL a professional or personal page? • Why might using information from a personal page be a problem?	List Web site (title and URL). What can you tell from the URL?
Sponsor: • What organization or group sponsors the Web page? • If it has a link (often called "About Us") that leads you to that information, what can you learn about the sponsor?	What can you learn about the page's sponsor?
Timeliness: • When was the page last updated (usually posted at the top or bottom of the page)? A current date usually means the information is up-to-date.	What can you learn about the page's timeliness?
Purpose: • What is the purpose of the page? • Who is the target audience? • Does the page present information or opinion? Is the information objective or subjective? How do you know?	What can you tell about the page's purpose?
Author/Publisher: • Who publishes this page? If you don't know, try to find out whether the publisher is an expert on the topic. • What credentials does the author have? • Is this person or group considered an authority on the topic? How do you know?	What else can you learn about the author?
Links: • Does the page provide links that work? • Do the links go to authoritative sources? • Are they objective or subjective?	What can you tell from the links provided?

What's at Stake?

You and your group have selected a topic that you need to research in preparation for designing a presentation to your classmates. Your presentation for Embedded Assessment 2 will be a multimedia presentation with sound and graphics. As you research your topic, choose multiple sources that provide accurate, reliable information. Be sure to include materials from which you can create graphics or identify images you may want to use in your presentation. You will want to include a variety of graphics or images that represent the range of views from multiple sources, so organize your information by subtopic for each possible graphic or image. Also collect and organize information for creating charts or other visuals that would help your audience understand the topic or specific points you want to make. Be sure to identify sources clearly in case you need to revisit the source for additional information or images.

You will each find at least three sources, keeping in mind that you are trying to identify a broad range of stakeholder positions relative to your topic.

- For each source you collect, you will use the MLA format to create an annotated bibliography entry. Annotated bibliographies are tools for tracking and processing research work you do. (A form for creating your own annotated bibliography appears on page 398.)

- Entries typically consist of two parts: a complete bibliographic citation for the source and an annotation. For this task, the annotation will (1) summarize the information you found in the source, (2) assess the degree to which the source was helpful in your research and (3) reflect on how reliable the source is, given the level of subjectivity or the narrowness of the perspective it presents.

- On the next page, you will find sample entries. Your teacher will provide more examples.

Sample Magazine Entry

Author(s). "Title of Article." <u>Magazine Title</u>. Publication date or issue: page number.

Citation: Hewitt, Bill. "A Roaring Battle Over Sea Lions." <u>People</u>. June 8, 2008: 97–98.

Summary/Commentary: Hewitt presents a balanced perspective on the conflict, as well as a little history regarding the situation there. He identifies (and quotes) at least five major stakeholders and suggests many others as well. By quoting his sources, he presents their arguments without taking sides himself.

Sample Web Site Entry

Author(s). "Title of Article" (if it applies). Source of Article. Year/Date (of publication). Name of Institution/Organization/Publication. Date of access <URL>.

Citation: Humane Society of the United States. "Stay of Execution for Sea Lions at Bonneville Dam." 3 April 2008. Humane Society of the United States. 5 June 2008.
<u>http://www.hsus.org/marine_mammals/marine_mammals_news/</u>
<u>bonneville_suit_040308_1.html</u>

Summary/Commentary: This online article presents an objective account of the status of the legal suit objecting to the elimination of sea lions that were eating salmon at Bonneville Dam. While the language of the article is fairly unbiased, the writer uses facts to support a clear point of view—that the sea lions are not the problem, and that they are therefore victims. It reveals the Humane Society as a major stakeholder in the controversy. It also mentions the Wild Fish Conservation organization.

Use the annotated bibliography form on the following page to create your own entries.

Once you have completed your annotated entries, compile a complete annotated bibliography as a group. The bibliography should be in alphabetical order. You will also need to complete a source evaluation sheet for each online resource you use.

Source 1:

Annotation:

Source 2:

Annotation:

Source 3:

Annotation:

Evaluating Your Online Sources — Response Sheet

Using the response form below as a template, respond to the questions on page 395. Complete one form for each of your online sources.

List Web site (title and URL):

What can you tell from the URL?

What can you learn about the page's sponsor?

What can you learn about the page's timeliness?

What can you tell about the page's purpose?

What else can you learn about the author?

What can you tell from the links provided?

Creating and Delivering a Position Paper

1. Generate a list of major points in support of your stakeholder position. In particular, look for evidence to establish or refute key causal claims. Consider what information you may wish to quote in your paper. (Remember, you must cite at least three sources.) Be sure to document each piece of information you plan to use.

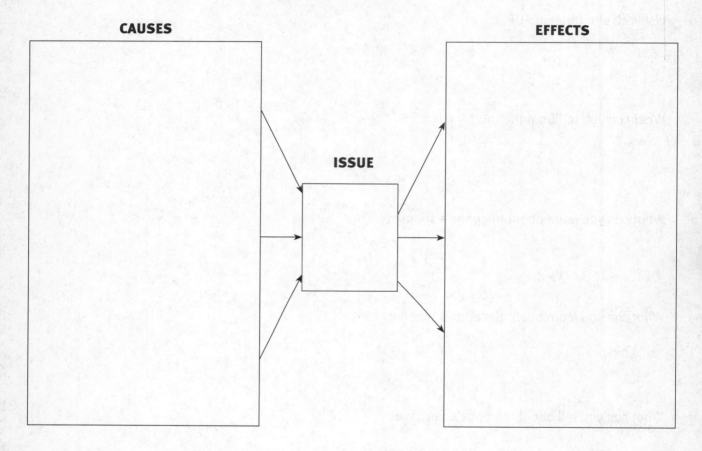

Writing Prompt: Based on what you have identified as your stakeholders' central concerns, organize your points into an outline that makes a case for their position on the issue. Use the Components of My Argument organizer on the next page as a general outline and for taking notes; however, because your work is to be delivered to your group, draft the paper as a speech. Analyze your purpose and your audience and address their needs accordingly. Be sure to include a formal introduction to establish your perspective. Use clear topic sentences to link each paragraph to your claim. Use direct quotes or paraphrased information (with credit to the source) to support your position. End with a formal conclusion that restates your claim and presents a call to action or a proposal for actions you would like listeners to take. Where appropriate, include graphics and illustrations to help you explain concepts or support your position.

Analyze the purpose and audience for your presentation, and base the development of your ideas on those needs. Use the following organizer to help you plan your presentation so that it reflects a logical progression of ideas, addresses the needs of the audience, clearly states your position and support, and defines the action you want your audience to take.

Components of My Argument

Element of Argument	Key Points or Information
Hook: Grab your audience's attention and establish your subject.	
Claim: State your basic position in a thesis statement.	
Support: Support your position/thesis statement to reflect a clear point of view for your audience on the issue with facts and other forms of information, and cite your sources, including background information that explains why you are concerned about the issue.	
Concessions / Refutations: • Build credibility by objectively discussing other sides or perspectives on the issue. • Identify common ground on which you and your opponents can agree.	
Call to Action: Propose the solutions you would like to see, and suggest what the benefits might be of adopting them.	

Creating and Delivering a Position Paper

Orally Citing Sources in a Speech

Doing the research is only part of the job in writing a speech. You must also incorporate your research into the speech itself through citation. You will be perceived as a more credible speaker when you use multiple sources and cite them in the body of your speech.

As you write your speech, summarize and paraphrase information from your sources rather than overusing verbatim quotes. Your goal is to incorporate your own viewpoint and support it by linking information from multiple sources into a cohesive speech. Use verbatim quotes to add emphasis to major points.

You cannot use information from a Web site, book, journal article, newspaper article, television program, radio broadcast, or any other written or spoken source, without giving credit to the source. Not providing this information is considered unethical and even an act of plagiarism.

Tips on citing sources within your speech or oral presentation:

- Do not say "quote, unquote" when you offer a direct quotation. Use brief pauses to frame the quotation instead. You may say "quote" if you're trying to emphasize the quotation.

- Provide enough information about each source so that your audience could, with a little effort, find it online or at the library.

- If your source is unknown to your audience, provide enough information to establish its credibility. Typically you should suggest the source's credentials by stating the expertise provided and the qualifications of the source's experts on the topic.

EXAMPLES

For a book with one author:

Mention: Author, brief credentials, date, and title.

Dr. Derek Bok, President Emeritus of Harvard University, wrote in his 2005 book, *Our Underachieving Colleges*, that ...

For a book with two or more authors:

Mention: Authors by last name, brief credentials, date, and title.

In the 1979 edition of *The Elements of Style*, renowned grammarians and composition stylists Strunk and White encourage every writer to "make every word tell."

For a Web site:

Mention: Site title, credentials, and date last updated

One of the most active developers of neurotechnology, Cyberkinetics, claims on its Web site, last updated on March 24, 2006, that...

For a TV or radio show:

Mention: Name of show, date it aired, title of story, and name of reporter

On March 24, 2006, National Public Radio's Morning Edition aired a story by reporter Christopher Joyce entitled, "Greenland glaciers moving more quickly to the ocean." In the story, experts claimed ....

For an interview you performed:

Mention: Name, date, and credentials.

In a personal interview conducted on February 12, 2006, with Charlotte Maddux, Director of the local chapter of the American Cancer Society, she told me....

For a print magazine:

Mention: Name of publication, name of reporter, and date.

According to a feature article written by reporter Kelli Brown about the rising costs of medicine in the March 27, 2006, issue of *Time* magazine ....

For a newspaper:

Mention: Name of reporter, name of publication, date, and version (print or electronic version). Providing additional information may give credibility to the source.

In a front page article in the January 17, 2006, edition of *The Washington Post*, reporter Dana Milbank quoted White House Chief of Staff, Andrew H. Card, Jr., who said, ...

For a reference work:

Mention: Title, credentials, and date of publication.

The 2005 edition of *Simmons Market Research*, considered the nation's leading authority on the behavior of the American consumer, notes....

Creating and Delivering Your Position Paper

Planning Citations:

Look at your outline, and for each section draft a source citation using the models on the previous page. Write the citations below, even though you may not use all of them. Remember, you must cite at least three sources in your individual position paper and in your group presentation.

Hook/Claim:

_____

_____

Supporting point 1:

_____

_____

Supporting point 2:

_____

_____

Supporting point 3:

_____

_____

Concession/refutation point:

_____

_____

Call to Action:

_____

_____

Presenting a Solution to an Environmental Conflict

SUGGESTED LEARNING STRATEGIES: **Discussion Groups, Drafting, Oral Presentation**

Assignment

Your assignment is to work with others to present a solution to an environmental conflict that has intercultural or international implications. As a group, you will deliver a multimedia presentation with sound, images, and graphics that contextualizes the conflict for your classmates and justifies your approach to resolving it. Consider your audience and include a range of appeals, such as case studies, anecdotes, images, analogies, and descriptions.

Steps

Planning

1. Present your position paper to your group. It should represent the best case for your position and advocate your stakeholder concerns. As each group member presents, record main points and any questions you have.

2. After the presentations, each group member should summarize another member's perspective and identify common ground or significant conflicts.

3. In an open discussion, engage in a conversation that identifies common ground, significant obstacles, and potential solutions. Then evaluate which solutions might actually work.

Drafting and Organizing

4. Consider the whole range of views on the topic and from a variety of reliable sources. Organize information, noting sources for quotations and visuals. Merge arguments from each position into one you all can accept. Use the solution/proposal structures modeled in Activities 5.10 and 5.11. Select arguments that bridge gaps and provide potential solutions to the problems and concerns. Using information from multiple sources, create graphics that support your arguments.

5. Following the discussion, group members should collaboratively create a multimedia presentation that proposes a solution to the problem, reflects a logical progression of ideas, and presents the range of stakeholders' views honestly and accurately.

6. Decide which position papers (if any) will be used as part of your presentation; use the Presentation Agenda on the next page to consider different organizational strategies.

Rehearsing and Delivering

7. Practice delivering your presentation. Use the assessment questions on page 407 to make sure you have considered all the key elements.

8. Deliver the presentation to the class. Listening students will complete evaluation forms.

9. After completing the presentation, use listening students' evaluation forms to write a reflection examining your process.

Presenting a Solution to an Environmental Conflict

Presentation Agenda

Once you and your group members have chosen three texts to present, create a presentation agenda showing the estimated time frame for each activity. Your teacher will assign a time frame for presentations. Break down each segment and estimate the time needed to present each portion to the class.

Estimated Presentation Time Frame: _____ minutes

I. Overview Presentation: _____ minutes
Group member/s:

Objective and Audience Connection:

II. First Piece: _____ minutes
Group member/s:

Objective and Audience Connection:

III. Second Piece: _____ minutes
Group member/s:

Objective and Audience Connection:

IV. Third Piece: _____ minutes
Group member/s:

Objective and Audience Connection:

V. Conclusion: _____ minutes
Group member/s:

Proposed resolution of the conflict:

Assessment Questions

Before you present your project, answer the following questions to be certain that you have fulfilled all the requirements:

▶ Do you have an engaging opening to grab your audience's attention?

▶ Have you provided enough historical overview and background information to help the class understand the conflict? Do your thesis and your analysis of the situation provide a clearly stated point of view for your audience? _____ Who is presenting this part?

▶ Have you chosen at least three stakeholder positions to present to the class?

▶ Have you organized how you will present the stakeholder positions to the class?

▶ Do you have an explanation of the possible solutions planned and their likely impact? _____ Who will present this?

▶ Do you cite at least three sources to increase your credibility and support your claims?

▶ Do you have a map or other graphics or illustrations to engage the audience and help you explain concepts?

▶ What other audience engagement techniques will you use?

▶ Do you have engaging speakers and speeches to keep the audience actively involved?

▶ Will all the group members be involved in the presentation?

▶ Do you have an effective conclusion?

If you answered "yes" to all of the above questions, you are ready for your presentation. If you answered "no" to any questions, revise your presentation to meet these guidelines.

Peer Evaluation

Fill out this form during your peers' presentation and use it to help you complete the Evaluative Feedback form on the next page.

Questions/Commentary	Notetaking Area

Summary Section

Evaluative Feedback

Complete this Evaluative Feedback form following each group's presentation.

Group members:

_____

Topic of the conflict presented:

_____

Create a graphic organizer that shows the causes of the conflict and the proposed solution(s). Then evaluate the group's proposed solution(s): Do you think the solution(s) will satisfy all stakeholders and resolve the issue effectively? Why or why not?

State two questions that you still have about this conflict.

How persuasive was the proposed solution? Identify the specific aspects of the presentation's content, organization, or delivery (including the use of media) that contributed to its credibility or most enhanced its persuasiveness.

Presenting a Solution to an Environmental Conflict

Self-Evaluation

Reflecting on My Group's Presentation

Complete this page reflecting on your group's presentation.

▶ How do you think your group's presentation went? Cite the Evaluative Feedback forms you received from your peers to support your answer.

▶ What turned out differently from what you expected? What went precisely as expected during your presentation?

▶ Describe the audience engagement strategies you and your group members used in your presentation. Were those strategies effective at teaching/presenting your conflict to your peers? Why or why not?

▶ What challenges did you and your group members face in either planning the presentation or presenting the information? How did you overcome those challenges?

▶ How did your engagement in this process affect your personal position on the topic you chose?

SCORING GUIDE

Scoring Criteria	Exemplary	Proficient	Emerging
Research Process	Students' selected sources indicate extensive research. The annotated bibliography and source sheets provide more than enough credible sources.	Students' selected sources indicate thorough research. The annotated bibliography and source sheets are completed and present all required information.	Students' selected sources fail to capture the essence of the cultural conflict. The annotated bibliography and source sheets are incomplete or show only cursory analysis of the sources.
Presentation	Students craft an engaging, well-organized presentation. Information from sources is effectively incorporated and correctly cited. Media (music, visual aids, etc.) effectively enhance audience appeal and persuasiveness. All members contribute.	Students craft an informative, well-organized presentation. Information from sources is incorporated and cited. Media (music, visual aids, etc.) enhance presentation of the content. All members contribute.	Students craft an uneven presentation. Information from sources may be absent or inadequately cited. Media (music, visual aids, etc.) distract or are underutilized. Not all members contribute.
Reflective Text	Students use the Evaluative Feedback forms to perceptively analyze how their own perspective on the issue was influenced. Specific and well-chosen examples are cited to support analysis.	Students use the Evaluative Feedback forms to thoroughly analyze how their own perspective on the issue was influenced. Relevant examples are cited to support the analysis.	Students fail to use the Evaluative Feedback forms to adequately analyze how their own perspective on the issue was influenced. Too few or no examples are cited to support analysis.
Additional Criteria			

Comments: _____

_____

_____

_____

_____

_____

Learning Focus:

Setting the Stage for Growth

Throughout the year, you have had opportunities to reflect on your learning as a result of your engagement in various activities. You have revisited the **essential questions** and **academic vocabulary** that are central to each unit—and to this course as a whole. But have you ever stopped to think about how what you do in this class links to what you might want to do in life? How might the skills and knowledge you develop in an English class be relevant to what goes on outside the hallowed halls of your school? In the remainder of this unit, you will have the opportunity to consider this, and you will even consult someone from the "real world" to see what insights they can provide.

This unit marks the culmination of your sophomore year, and you will have the opportunity to conduct an extensive self-evaluation of your current academic abilities as a reader, writer, researcher, collaborator, and presenter. It's a chance to reflect on where you are (in school and in life), where you want to go, and what skills you need to help you get there. Based on this reflection, you can craft a plan for your own academic future and share it with those people who might help you achieve the goals you set for yourself.

Mapping Expectations

SUGGESTED LEARNING STRATEGIES: **Quickwrite, Summarizing**

Revisit one of the Essential Questions for this unit and write your thoughts.

What is the value of self-reflection in preparing for one's future?

Quickwrite: Standards are common to everyday life. Schools, organizations, jobs, military, and other institutions rely on them. Why do we rely on standards, and how do they help both the learner and evaluator?

Mapping Expectations

Using the description of College Readiness Standards your teacher has given you, create a graphic or map that identifies key skills and knowledge you will need if you attend college. Use an image or approach that will help you to understand how the various standards fit together.

Summary of Standard: **Visual Representation:**

Reading

Writing

Speaking

Listening

Media Literacy

Reading the Signs

SUGGESTED LEARNING STRATEGIES: Graphic Organizer, Drafting, Sharing and Responding, Adding, Deleting, Rearranging

Look at the standards and your descriptions in Activity 5.15. Using different colors, code your summaries to identify areas you think are your strengths and those in which you think you need more experience and growth. Use a third color to indicate an area in which you have grown substantially this year.

Next, choose three or four standards in which you have grown substantially this year. Identify pieces of work from your portfolio: one showing your skills at the beginning of the year and the other demonstrating your growth this year. Draft a paragraph for each standard you chose. Use the following questions to guide your reflection.

- What skills did you possess at the beginning of the school year?
- How does the first piece reflect those skills?
- What activities or strategies from this year's work helped you improve?
- How does the second piece reflect your growth?
- What goals do you have in this area for next year?

Reading the Signs

Identify three standards you feel are in areas in which you need additional experience and growth. Identify artifacts from your portfolio that help you explain and support your self-evaluation.

Standard	Explain Why You Rated Your Performance as You Did

Off to See the Wizard

SUGGESTED LEARNING STRATEGIES: Role Playing, Notetaking

Levels of Questions

A successful interview hinges on questions that stimulate thoughtful responses. Levels of questions can be modified in order to help the interviewee reflect on his or her life. Be sure to ask open-ended questions and follow-up questions to encourage the best reflection.

Level of Questions	An Opportunity to Practice
Level 1 **Questions of Fact:** **What has the interviewee experienced?** Examples: What kind of writing do you do at work? What has helped you improve as a writer?	1 2 3
Level 2 **Questions of Inference:** **What has the interviewee learned?** Examples: How important are communication skills in your job? What was the most valuable thing you learned in your high school English classes?	1 2 3
Level 3 **Questions of Generalization: Why does it matter?** Examples: Why are listening skills important to college readiness? What advice do you have on how to improve my writing?	1 2 3

Plotting My Course

Combine insights you gained from your interviews with the strengths and weaknesses you identified in your self-assessments in Activities 5.15 and 5.16. Then develop an action plan for improving your academic readiness.

Explain your action plan:

Identify goals to support your action plan. Be specific and explain how they support the targeted standard.	How will you support each step to make that goal a reality?

An Academic Journey: Create a graphic of your goals that represents a pathway from the present to where you want to be in the future.

Essential Question: What is the value of self-reflection in preparing for one's future?

Presenting My Portfolio

SUGGESTED LEARNING STRATEGIES: **Drafting, RAFT**

Assignment

Your assignment is to write a letter in which you reflect on your growth as a student this year, identify areas you are going to target for future growth, and explain how you plan to address those areas in the future. You will need to choose an audience, collect your information and convey it accurately, organize the information effectively, anticipate and address your readers' potential questions, and format your letter to make it attractive and easy to read.

Steps

Planning

1. Review the list of skills necessary for college success. For each skill that you have identified and discussed in class, re-evaluate your level of readiness, keeping in mind what you have learned from your interview and from your reflection during the last few activities.

2. Select an audience for your letter and consider what role or voice you will assume in the letter.

Drafting and Organizing

3. Look carefully at those skills in which you feel you have a high degree of competence. Revisit your portfolio and select evidence to support your self-assessment. If some evidence is not reflected in your portfolio but in other achievements, write an explanation about how you have achieved readiness in this area.

4. Next, describe those areas in which you have grown significantly this year, citing evidence from your portfolio to support your assessment.

5. Now think about those areas you have identified where you are not yet at a level of academic readiness. Explain how you will target those areas in the future, keeping in mind what you learned from your interview and what your options are in your school.

6. Draft your letter to the audience you have selected.

Revising and Presenting

7. Present your portfolio and your revised letter to your teacher and another interested audience (parent, mentor, counselor, etc.) who will complete a portfolio response as you celebrate the work you have done to prepare for college success and the plans you have made to reach your goals.

8. Revise the final draft of your letter based on the feedback you receive from your teacher and your audience.

SCORING GUIDE

Scoring Criteria	Exemplary	Proficient	Emerging
Dear Reader Letter	Student crafts a Dear Reader letter that: • insightfully and descriptively discusses his or her own academic readiness; • clearly supports areas of competence and areas to target for future growth with reflective commentary and varied examples that directly connect to the writer's analysis; • demonstrates a clear and plausible plan describing strategies for reaching future goals.	Student crafts a Dear Reader letter that: • clearly addresses his or her own academic readiness; • supports areas of competence and areas to target for future growth with sufficient commentary and examples that directly connect to the writer's analysis; • demonstrates a plan describing strategies for reaching future goals.	Student attempts to craft a Dear Reader letter that: • addresses some of his or her own academic readiness of language art's skills; • supports areas of competence and areas to target for future growth with general commentary and limited examples that indirectly connect to the writer's analysis; • demonstrates an incomplete plan that may not describe strategies for reaching future goals.
Organization	The letter is multi-paragraphed and logically organized in a way that conveys the role of the author and enhances the understanding of the chosen audience.	The letter is multi-paragraphed and organized in a way that demonstrates the role of the author and shows an understanding of the chosen audience.	The letter may not be multi-paragraphed or organized in a way that conveys the role of the author or shows an understanding of the chosen audience.

SCORING GUIDE

Scoring Criteria	Exemplary	Proficient	Emerging
Presentation	The student skillfully and effectively uses the Dear Reader letter and portfolio artifacts to clearly communicate to his or her chosen audience. The student effectively revises his or her Dear Reader letter based on specific feedback provided by the audience.	The student uses the Dear Reader letter and portfolio artifacts to clearly communicate to his or her chosen audience. The student revises his or her Dear Reader letter based on general feedback provided by the audience.	The student attempts to use the Dear Reader letter and portfolio artifacts communicate to his or her chosen audience; however, the Dear Reader letter revision does little to respond to the feedback provided by the audience.
Additional Criteria			

Comments: _____

_____

_____

_____

_____

_____

Reflection

An important aspect of growing as a learner is to reflect on where you have been, what you have accomplished, what helped you to learn, and how you will apply your new knowledge in the future. Use the following questions to guide your thinking and to identify evidence of your learning. Use separate notebook paper.

Thinking about Concepts

1. Using specific examples from this unit, respond to the Essential Questions:

   • How do cultural differences contribute to conflicts over environmental issues?

   • What is the value of self-reflection in preparing for one's future?

2. Consider the new academic vocabulary from this unit (**Documentary Film, Objectivity, Subjectivity**) as well as academic vocabulary from previous units, and select 3–4 terms of which your understanding has grown. For each term, answer the following questions:

   • What was your understanding of the word prior to the unit?

   • How has your understanding of the word evolved throughout the unit?

   • How will you apply your understanding in the future?

Thinking about Connections

3. Review the activities and products (artifacts) you created. Choose those that most reflect your growth or increase in understanding.

4. For each artifact that you choose, record, respond to, and reflect on your thinking and understanding, using the following questions as a guide:

   a. What skill/knowledge does this artifact reflect, and how did you learn this skill/knowledge?

   b. How did your understanding of the power of language expand through your engagement with this artifact?

   c. How will you apply this skill or knowledge in the future?

5. Create this reflection as Portfolio pages—one for each artifact you choose. Use the model in the box for your headings and commentary on questions.

Thinking About Thinking
Portfolio Entry

Concept:

Description of Artifact:

Commentary on Questions:

Grammar Handbook

Part 1: Using Pronouns Clearly

Because a pronoun REFERS BACK to a noun or TAKES THE PLACE OF that noun, you have to use the correct pronoun so that your reader clearly understands which noun your pronoun is referring to. Therefore, pronouns should:

1. Agree in number

If the pronoun takes the place of a singular noun, you have to use a singular pronoun.

> If a student parks a car on campus, he or she has to buy a parking sticker.
> (**NOT:** If a student parks a car on campus, they have to buy a parking sticker.)

Remember: the words **everybody**, **anybody**, **anyone**, **each**, **neither**, **nobody**, **someone**, **a person**, etc. are singular and take singular pronouns.

> Everybody ought to do his or her best. (NOT: their best)
> Neither of the girls brought her umbrella. (NOT: their umbrellas)

NOTE: Many people find the construction "his or her" wordy, so if it is possible to use a plural noun as your antecedent so that you can use "they" as your pronoun, it may be wise to do so. If you do use a singular noun and the context makes the gender clear, then it is permissible to use just "his" or "her" rather than "his or her."

2. Agree in person

If you are writing in the "first person" (I), don't confuse your reader by switching to the "second person" (you) or "third person" (he, she, they, it, etc.). Similarly, if you are using the "second person," don't switch to "first" or "third."

> When a person comes to class, he or she should have his or her homework ready.
> (**NOT:** When a person comes to class, you should have your homework ready.)

3. Refer clearly to a specific noun.

Don't be vague or ambiguous.

> **NOT:** Although the motorcycle hit the tree, it was not damaged. (Is "it" the motorcycle or the tree?)
> **NOT:** I don't think they should show violence on TV. (Who are "they"?)
> **NOT:** Vacation is coming soon, which is nice. (What is nice, the vacation or the fact that it is coming soon?)
> **NOT:** George worked in a national forest last summer. This may be his life's work. (What word does "this" refer to?)
> **NOT:** If you put this sheet in your notebook, you can refer to it. (What does "it" refer to, the sheet or your notebook?)

Pronoun Case

Pronoun case is really a very simple matter. There are three cases.

- Subjective case: pronouns used as subject.
- Objective case: pronouns used as objects of verbs or prepositions.
- Possessive case: pronouns which express ownership.

Pronouns as Subjects	Pronouns as Objects	Pronouns that show Possession
I	me	my (mine)
you	you	your (yours)
he, she, it	him, her, it	his, her (hers), it (its)
we	us	our (ours)
they	them	their (theirs)
who	whom	whose

The pronouns **this, that, these, those,** and **which** do not change form.

Some problems of case:

1. **In compound structures, where there are two pronouns or a noun and a pronoun, drop the other noun for a moment. Then you can see which case you want.**

    Not: Bob and me travel a good deal.
    (Would you say, "me travel"?)
    Not: He gave the flowers to Jane and I.
    (Would you say, "he gave the flowers to I"?)
    Not: Us men like the coach.
    (Would you say, "us like the coach"?)

2. **In comparisons. Comparisons usually follow than or as:**

    He is taller than I (am tall).
    This helps you as much as (it helps) me.
    She is as noisy as I (am).

Comparisons are really shorthand sentences which usually omit words, such as those in the parentheses in the sentences above. If you complete the comparison in your head, you can choose the correct case for the pronoun.

    Not: He is taller than me.
    (Would you say, "than me am tall"?)

3. **In formal and semiformal writing:**

Use the subjective form after a form of the verb to be.

    Formal: It is I.
    Informal: It is me.

Use whom in the objective case.

    Formal: To whom am I talking?
    Informal: Who am I talking to?

Part 2: Appositives

An appositive is a noun or pronoun — often with modifiers — set beside another noun or pronoun to explain or identify it. Here are some examples of appositives (the **noun or pronoun will be in blue**, the **appositive will be in boldface**).

Your friend **Bill** is in trouble.
My brother's car, **a sporty red convertible with bucket seats**, is the envy of my friends.
The chief surgeon, **an expert in organ-transplant procedures**, took her nephew on a hospital tour.

An appositive phrase usually follows the word it explains or identifies, but it may also precede it.

A bold innovator, Wassily Kadinsky is known for his colorful abstract paintings.
The first state to ratify the U. S. Constitution, Delaware is rich in history.
A beautiful collie, Skip was my favorite dog.

Punctuation of Appositives

In some cases, the noun being explained is too general without the appositive; the information is essential to the meaning of the sentence. When this is the case, do not place commas around the appositive; just leave it alone. If the sentence would be clear and complete without the appositive, then commas are necessary; place one before and one after the appositive. Here are some examples.

The popular US **president John Kennedy** was known for his eloquent and inspirational speeches.

Here we do not put commas around the appositive, because it is essential information. Without the appositive, the sentence would be, "The popular US president was known for his eloquent and inspirational speeches." We wouldn't know which president was being referred to.

John Kennedy, **the popular US president**, was known for his eloquent and inspirational speeches.

Here we put commas around the appositive because it is not essential information. Without the appositive, the sentence would be, "John Kennedy was known for his eloquent and inspirational speeches." We still know who the subject of the sentence is without the appositive.

Part 3: What is the Difference Between Adjectives and Adverbs?

The Basic Rules: Adjectives

Adjectives modify nouns. To modify means to change in some way. For example:

- "I ate a meal." *Meal* is a noun. We don't know what kind of meal; all we know is that someone ate a meal.
- "I ate an enormous lunch." *Lunch* is a noun, and *enormous* is an adjective that modifies it. It tells us **what kind of** meal the person ate.

Adjectives usually answer one of a few different questions: "What kind?" or "Which?" or "How many?" For example:

- "The *tall* girl is riding a *new* bike." *Tall* tells us **which** girl we're talking about. *New* tells us **what kind of** bike we're talking about.
- "The *tough* professor gave us the *final* exam." *Tough* tells us **what kind of** professor we're talking about. *Final* tells us **which** exam we're talking about.
- "*Fifteen* students passed the midterm exam; *twelve* students passed the final exam." *Fifteen* and *twelve* both tell us **how many** students; *midterm* and *final* both tell us **which** exam.

So, generally speaking, adjectives answer the following questions: **Which? What kind of? How many?**

The Basic Rules: Adverbs

Adverbs modify verbs, adjectives, and other adverbs. (You can recognize adverbs easily because many of them are formed by adding *-ly* to an adjective, though that is not always the case.) The most common question that adverbs answer is **how**.

Let's look at verbs first.

- "She sang *beautifully*." *Beautifully* is an adverb that modifies *sang*. It tells us **how** she sang.
- "The cellist played *carelessly*." *Carelessly* is an adverb that modifies *played*. It tells us **how** the cellist played.

Adverbs also modify adjectives and other adverbs.

- "That woman is *extremely* nice." *Nice* is an adjective that modifies the noun *woman*. *Extremely* is an adverb that modifies *nice*; it tells us **how** nice she is. **How** nice is she? She's extremely nice.
- "It was a *terribly* hot afternoon." *Hot* is an adjective that modifies the noun *afternoon*. *Terribly* is an adverb that modifies the adjective *hot*. **How** hot is it? Terribly hot.

So, generally speaking, adverbs answer the question **how**. (They can also answer the questions **when**, **where**, and **why**.)

Part 4: Verbals

Gerunds

A gerund is a verbal that ends in *-ing* and functions as a noun. The term *verbal* indicates that a gerund, like the other two kinds of verbals, is based on a verb and therefore expresses action or a state of being. However, since a gerund functions as a noun, it occupies some positions in a sentence that a noun ordinarily would, for example: subject, direct object, subject complement, and object of preposition.

Gerund as subject:

- Traveling might satisfy your desire for new experiences. (**Traveling** is the gerund.)
- The study abroad program might satisfy your desire for new experiences. (The gerund has been removed.)

Gerund as direct object:

- They do not appreciate my singing. (The gerund is **singing**.)
- They do not appreciate my assistance. (The gerund has been removed)

Gerund as subject complement:

- My cat's favorite activity is sleeping. (The gerund is **sleeping**.)
- My cat's favorite food is salmon. (The gerund has been removed.)

Gerund as object of preposition:

- The police arrested him for speeding. (The gerund is **speeding**.)
- The police arrested him for criminal activity. (The gerund has been removed.)

A Gerund Phrase is a group of words consisting of a gerund and the modifier(s) and/or (pro)noun(s) or noun phrase(s) that function as the direct object(s), indirect object(s), or complement(s) of the action or state expressed in the gerund, such as:

The gerund phrase functions as the subject of the sentence.

Finding a needle in a haystack would be easier than what we're trying to do.

Finding (gerund) a needle (direct object of action expressed in gerund) in a haystack (prepositional phrase as adverb)

The gerund phrase functions as the direct object of the verb *appreciate*.

I hope that you appreciate <u>**my**</u> offering **you** *this opportunity*.

<u>**my**</u> (possessive pronoun adjective form, modifying the gerund)
offering (gerund)
you (indirect object of action expressed in gerund)
this opportunity (direct object of action expressed in gerund)

The gerund phrase functions as the subject complement.

Ned's favorite tactic has been <u>**lying to**</u> **his constituents**.

<u>**lying to**</u> (gerund)
his constituents (direct object of action expressed in gerund)

The gerund phrase functions as the object of the preposition *for*.

You might get in trouble for <u>**faking**</u> **an illness** *to avoid work*.

<u>**faking**</u> (gerund)
an illness (direct object of action expressed in gerund)
to avoid work (infinitive phrase as adverb)

The gerund phrase functions as the subject of the sentence.

<u>Being</u> **the boss** made Jeff feel uneasy.

Being (gerund)
the boss (subject complement for Jeff, via state of being expressed in gerund)

Punctuation
A gerund virtually never requires any punctuation with it.

Points to remember:
1. A gerund is a verbal ending in -ing that is used as a noun.
2. A gerund phrase consists of a gerund plus modifier(s), object(s), and/or complement(s).
3. Gerunds and gerund phrases virtually never require punctuation.

Participles
A participle is a verbal that is used as an adjective and most often ends in *-ing* or *-ed*. The term *verbal* indicates that a participle, like the other two kinds of verbals, is based on a verb and therefore expresses action or a state of being. However, since they function as adjectives, participles modify nouns or pronouns. There are two types of participles: present participles and past participles. Present participles end in *-ing*. Past participles end in *-ed*, *-en*, *-d*, *-t*, or *-n*, as in the words *asked*, *eaten*, *saved*, *dealt*, and *seen*.

- The *crying* baby had a wet diaper.
- *Shaken*, he walked away from the *wrecked* car.
- The *burning* log fell off the fire.
- *Smiling*, she hugged the *panting* dog.

A participial phrase is a group of words consisting of a participle and the modifier(s) and/or (pro)noun(s) or noun phrase(s) that function as the direct object(s), indirect object(s), or complement(s) of the action or state expressed in the participle, such as:

Example: Removing his coat, Jack rushed to the river.

The participial phrase functions as an adjective modifying *Jack*.

Removing (participle)
his coat (direct object of action expressed in participle)

> **Example:** Delores noticed her cousin **walking** along the shoreline.

The participial phrase functions as an adjective modifying *cousin*.
walking (participle)
along the shoreline (prepositional phrase as adverb)

> **Example:** Children **introduced to** music early develop strong intellectual skills.

The participial phrase functions as an adjective modifying *children*.
introduced (to) (participle)
music (direct object of action expressed in participle)
early (adverb)

> **Example: Having been a gymnast,** Lynn knew the importance of exercise.

The participial phrase functions as an adjective modifying *Lynn*.
Having been (participle)
a gymnast (subject complement for Lynn, via state of being expressed in participle)

Placement: In order to prevent confusion, a participial phrase must be placed as close to the noun it modifies as possible, and the noun must be clearly stated.

- *Carrying a heavy pile of books,* his foot caught on a step.
- *Carrying a heavy pile of books,* he caught his foot on a step.

In the first sentence there is no clear indication of who or what is performing the action expressed in the participle carrying. Certainly foot can't be logically understood to function in this way. This situation is an example of a <u>dangling modifier</u> error since the modifier (the participial phrase) is not modifying any specific noun in the sentence and is thus left "dangling." Since a person must be doing the carrying for the sentence to make sense, a noun or pronoun that refers to a person must be in the place immediately after the participial phrase, as in the second sentence.

Punctuation: When a participial phrase begins a sentence, a comma should be placed after the phrase.

- *Arriving at the store,* I found that it was closed.
- *Washing and polishing the car,* Frank developed sore muscles.

If the participle or participial phrase comes in the middle of a sentence, it should be set off with commas only if the information is not essential to the meaning of the sentence.

- Sid, *watching an old movie,* drifted in and out of sleep.
- The church, *destroyed by a fire,* was never rebuilt.

Note that if the participial phrase is essential to the meaning of the sentence, no commas should be used:

- The student *earning the highest grade point average* will receive a special award.
- The guy *wearing the chicken costume* is my cousin.

If a participial phrase comes at the end of a sentence, a comma usually precedes the phrase if it modifies an earlier word in the sentence but not if the phrase directly follows the word it modifies.

- The local residents often saw Ken wandering through the streets.
  (The phrase modifies *Ken*, not *residents*.)
- Tom nervously watched the woman, alarmed by her silence.
  (The phrase modifies *Tom*, not *woman*.)

Points to remember

1. A participle is a verbal ending in *-ing* (present) or *-ed*, *-en*, *-d*, *-t*, or *-n* (past) that functions as an adjective, modifying a noun or pronoun.

2. A participial phrase consists of a participle plus modifier(s), object(s), and/or complement(s).

3. Participles and participial phrases must be placed as close to the nouns or pronouns they modify as possible, and those nouns or pronouns must be clearly stated.

4. A participial phrase is set off with commas when it:
   (a) comes at the beginning of a sentence
   (b) interrupts a sentence as a nonessential element
   (c) comes at the end of a sentence and is separated from the word it modifies.

Infinitives

An infinitive is a verbal consisting of the word *to* plus a verb (in its simplest "stem" form) and functioning as a noun, adjective, or adverb. The term *verbal* indicates that an infinitive, like the other two kinds of verbals, is based on a verb and therefore expresses action or a state of being. However, the infinitive may function as a subject, direct object, subject complement, adjective, or adverb in a sentence. Although an infinitive is easy to locate because of the *to* + verb form, deciding what function it has in a sentence can sometimes be confusing.

- *To wait* seemed foolish when decisive action was required. (subject)
- Everyone wanted *to go*. (direct object)
- His ambition is *to fly*. (subject complement)
- He lacked the strength *to resist*. (adjective)
- We must study *to learn*. (adverb)

Be sure not to confuse an infinitive—a verbal consisting of *to* plus a verb—with a prepositional phrase beginning with *to*, which consists of *to* plus a noun or pronoun and any modifiers.

- **Infinitives:** to fly, to draw, to become, to enter, to stand, to catch, to belong
- **Prepositional Phrases:** to him, to the committee, to my house, to the mountains, to us, to this address

An Infinitive Phrase is a group of words consisting of an infinitive and the modifier(s) and/or (pro)noun(s) or noun phrase(s) that function as the actor(s), direct object(s), indirect object(s), or complement(s) of the action or state expressed in the infinitive, such as:

We intended **to leave** <u>early</u>.

The infinitive phrase functions as the direct object of the verb *intended*.

to leave (infinitive)
<u>early</u> (adverb)

I have a paper **to write** <u>before class</u>.

The infinitive phrase functions as an adjective modifying *paper*.

to write (infinitive)
<u>before class</u> (prepositional phrase as adverb)

Phil agreed **to give** <u>me</u> *a ride*.

The infinitive phrase functions as the direct object of the verb *agreed*.

to give (infinitive)
<u>me</u> (indirect object of action expressed in infinitive)
a ride (direct object of action expressed in infinitive)

They asked <u>**me**</u> **to bring** *some food*.

The infinitive phrase functions as the direct object of the verb *asked*.

> **me** (actor or "subject" of infinitive phrase)
> **to bring** (infinitive)
> *some food* (direct object of action expressed in infinitive)

Everyone wanted **Carol to be** <u>the captain</u> *of the team*.

The infinitive phrase functions as the direct object of the verb *wanted*.

> **Carol** (actor or "subject" of infinitive phrase)
> **to be** (infinitive)
> <u>the captain</u> (subject complement for Carol, via state of being expressed in infinitive)
> *of the team* (prepositional phrase as adjective)

Actors: In these last two examples the actor of the infinitive phrase could be roughly characterized as the "subject" of the action or state expressed in the infinitive. It is somewhat misleading to use the word *subject*, however, since an infinitive phrase is not a full clause with a subject and a finite verb. Also notice that when it is a pronoun, the actor appears in the objective case (*me*, not *I*, in the fourth example). Certain verbs, when they take an infinitive direct object, require an actor for the infinitive phrase; others can't have an actor. Still other verbs can go either way, as the charts below illustrate.

Verbs that take infinitive objects without actors:			
agree	begin	continue	decide
fail	hesitate	hope	intend
learn	neglect	offer	plan
prefer	pretend	promise	refuse
remember	start	try	

Examples:

- Most students *plan* to study.
- We *began* to learn.
- They *offered* to pay.
- They *neglected* to pay.
- She *promised* to return.

In all of these examples no actor can come between the italicized main (finite) verb and the infinitive direct-object phrase.

Verbs that take infinitive objects with actors:			
advise	allow	convince	remind
encourage	force	hire	teach
instruct	invite	permit	tell
implore	incite	appoint	order

Examples:

- He *reminded* me to buy milk.
- Their fathers *advise* them to study.
- She *forced* the defendant to admit the truth.
- You've *convinced* the director of the program to change her position.
- I *invite* you to consider the evidence.

In all of these examples an actor is required after the italicized main (finite) verb and before the infinitive direct-object phrase.

Verbs that use either pattern:				
ask	expect	(would) like	want	need

Examples:

- I *asked* to see the records.
- I *asked* him to show me the records.
- Trent *expected* his group to win.
- Trent *expected* to win.
- Brenda *likes* to drive fast.
- Brenda *likes* her friend to drive fast.

In all of these examples the italicized main verb can take an infinitive object with or without an actor.

Punctuation: If the infinitive is used as an adverb and is the beginning phrase in a sentence, it should be set off with a comma; otherwise, no punctuation is needed for an infinitive phrase.

- To buy a basket of flowers, John had to spend his last dollar.
- To improve your writing, you must consider your purpose and audience.

Points to remember:

1. An infinitive is a verbal consisting of the word *to* plus a verb; it may be used as a noun, adjective, or adverb.
2. An infinitive phrase consists of an infinitive plus modifier(s), object(s), complement(s), and/ or actor(s).
3. An infinitive phrase requires a comma only if it is used as an adverb at the beginning of a sentence.

Split infinitives

Split infinitives occur when additional words are included between *to* and the verb in an infinitive. Many readers find a single adverb splitting the infinitive to be acceptable, but this practice should be avoided in formal writing.

Examples:

- I like *to* on a nice day *walk* in the woods. (unacceptable)
  On a nice day, I like *to walk* in the woods. (revised)
- I needed *to* quickly *gather* my personal possessions. (acceptable in informal contexts)
  I needed *to gather* my personal possessions quickly. (revised for formal contexts)

Part 5: Prepositions for Time, Place, and Introducing Objects

One point in time

On is used with days:

- I will see you **on** Monday.
- The week begins **on** Sunday.

At is used with noon, night, midnight, and with the time of day:

- My plane leaves **at** noon.
- The movie starts **at** 6 p.m.

In is used with other parts of the day, with months, with years, with seasons:

- He likes to read **in** the afternoon.
- The days are long **in** August.
- The book was published **in** 1999.
- The flowers will bloom **in** spring.

Extended time

To express extended time, English uses the following prepositions: **since, for, by, from–to, from–until, during, (with)in**

- She has been gone **since** yesterday. *(She left yesterday and has not returned.)*
- I'm going to Paris **for** two weeks. *(I will spend two weeks there.)*
- The movie showed **from** August **to** October. *(Beginning in August and ending in October.)*
- The decorations were up **from** spring **until** fall. *(Beginning in spring and ending in fall.)*
- I watch TV **during** the evening. *(For some period of time in the evening.)*
- We must finish the project **within** a year. *(No longer than a year.)*

Place

To express notions of place, English uses the following prepositions: to talk about the point itself: **in**, to express something contained: **inside**, to talk about the surface: **on**, to talk about a general vicinity, **at**.

- There is a wasp **in** the room.
- Put the present **inside** the box.
- I left your keys **on** the table.
- She was waiting **at** the corner.

To introduce objects of verbs

English uses the following prepositions to introduce objects of the following verbs.

At: glance, laugh, look, rejoice, smile, stare
- She took a quick glance **at** her reflection.
  *(exception with **mirror**: She took a quick glance **in** the mirror.)*
- You didn't laugh **at** his joke.
- I'm looking **at** the computer monitor.
- We rejoiced **at** his safe rescue.
- That pretty girl smiled **at** you.
- Stop staring **at** me.

Of: approve, consist, smell
- I don't approve **of** his speech.
- My contribution to the article consists **of** many pages.
- He came home smelling **of** garlic.

Of (or about): dream, think
- I dream **of** finishing college in four years.
- Can you think **of** a number between one and ten?
- I am thinking **about** this problem.

For: call, hope, look, wait, watch, wish
- Did someone call **for** a taxi?
- He hopes **for** a raise in salary next year.
- I'm looking **for** my keys.
- We'll wait **for** her here.
- You go buy the tickets and I'll watch **for** the train.
- If you wish **for** an "A" in this class, you must work hard.

Part 6: Identifying Independent and Dependent Clauses

When you want to use commas and semicolons in sentences and when you are concerned about whether a sentence is or is not a fragment, a good way to start is to be able to recognize dependent and independent clauses. The definitions offered here will help you with this.

Independent Clause

An independent clause is a group of words that contains a subject and verb and expresses a complete thought. An independent clause is a sentence.

Jim studied in the Sweet Shop for his chemistry quiz.

Dependent Clause

A dependent clause is a group of words that contains a subject and verb but does not express a complete thought. A dependent clause cannot be a sentence. Often a dependent clause is marked by a **dependent marker word**.

When Jim studied in the Sweet Shop for his chemistry quiz . . . (What happened when he studied? The thought is incomplete.)

Dependent Marker Word

A dependent marker word is a word added to the beginning of an independent clause that makes it into a dependent clause.

When Jim studied in the Sweet Shop for his chemistry quiz, it was very noisy.

Some common dependent markers are: **after, although, as, as if, because, before, even if, even though, if, in order to, since, though, unless, until, whatever, when, whenever, whether,** and **while**.

Connecting Dependent and Independent Clauses

There are two types of words that can be used as connectors at the beginning of an independent clause: coordinating conjunctions and independent marker words.

1. Coordinating Conjunction

The seven coordinating conjunctions used as connecting words at the beginning of an independent clause are **and, but, for, or, nor, so,** and **yet**. When the second independent clause in a sentence begins with a coordinating conjunction, a comma is needed before the coordinating conjunction:

Jim studied in the Sweet Shop for his chemistry quiz, **but** it was hard to concentrate because of the noise.

2. Independent Marker Word

An independent marker word is a connecting word used at the beginning of an independent clause. These words can always begin a sentence that can stand alone. When the second independent clause in a sentence has an independent marker word, a semicolon is needed before the independent marker word.

Jim studied in the Sweet Shop for his chemistry quiz; **however**, it was hard to concentrate because of the noise.

Some common independent markers are: **also**, **consequently**, **furthermore**, **however**, **moreover**, **nevertheless**, and **therefore**.

Some Common Errors to Avoid

Comma Splices

A comma splice is the use of a comma between two independent clauses. You can usually fix the error by changing the comma to a period and therefore making the two clauses into two separate sentences, by changing the comma to a semicolon, or by making one clause dependent by inserting a dependent marker word in front of it.

Incorrect: I like this class, it is very interesting.

Correct: I like this class. It is very interesting.
- (or) I like this class; it is very interesting.
- (or) I like this class, and it is very interesting.
- (or) I like this class because it is very interesting.
- (or) Because it is very interesting, I like this class.

Fused Sentences

Fused sentences happen when there are two independent clauses not separated by any form of punctuation. This error is also known as a run-on sentence. The error can sometimes be corrected by adding a period, semicolon, or colon to separate the two sentences.

Incorrect: My professor is intelligent I've learned a lot from her.

Correct: My professor is intelligent. I've learned a lot from her.
- (or) My professor is intelligent; I've learned a lot from her.
- (or) My professor is intelligent, and I've learned a lot from her.
- (or) My professor is intelligent; moreover, I've learned a lot from her.

Sentence Fragments

Sentence fragments happen by treating a dependent clause or other incomplete thought as a complete sentence. You can usually fix this error by combining it with another sentence to make a complete thought or by removing the dependent marker.

Incorrect: Because I forgot the exam was today.

Correct: Because I forgot the exam was today, I didn't study.
- (or) I forgot the exam was today.

Part 7: Parallel Structure

Parallel structure means using the same pattern of words to show that two or more ideas have the same level of importance. This can happen at the word, phrase, or clause level. The usual way to join parallel structures is with the use of coordinating **conjunctions** such as "and" or "or."

Words and Phrases

With the -ing form (gerund) of words:

> **Parallel:** Mary likes hik**ing**, swimm**ing**, and bicycl**ing**.

With infinitive phrases:

> **Parallel:** Mary likes **to hike**, **to swim**, and **to ride** a bicycle.
> OR
> Mary likes to **hike**, **swim**, and **ride** a bicycle.

(Note: You can use "to" before all the verbs in a sentence or only before the first one.)

Do not mix forms.

Example 1

Not Parallel:
Mary likes hik**ing**, swimm**ing**, and **to ride** a bicycle.

Parallel:
Mary likes hik**ing**, swimm**ing**, and rid**ing** a bicycle.

Example 2

Not Parallel:
The production manager was asked to write his report quick**ly**, accurate **ly**, and **in a detailed manner**.

Parallel:
The production manager was asked to write his report quick**ly**, accurate**ly**, and thorough**ly**.

Example 3

Not Parallel:
The teacher said that he was a poor student because he wait**ed** until the last minute to study for the exam, complet**ed** his lab problems in a careless manner, and **his motivation was** low.

Parallel:
The teacher said that he was a poor student because he wait**ed** until the last minute to study for the exam, complet**ed** his lab problems in a careless manner, and lack**ed** motivation.

Clauses

A parallel structure that begins with clauses must keep on with clauses. Changing to another pattern or changing the voice of the verb (from active to passive or vice versa) will break the parallelism.

Example 1

Not Parallel:
The coach told the players **that they should get** a lot of sleep, **that they should not eat** too much, and <u>**to do**</u> some warm-up exercises before the game.

Parallel:
The coach told the players **that they should get** a lot of sleep, **that they should not eat** too much, and **that they should do** some warm-up exercises before the game.

OR

Parallel:

The coach told the players that they should **get** a lot of sleep, not **eat** too much, and **do** some warm-up exercises before the game.

Example 2

Not Parallel:

The salesman expected **that he would present** his product at the meeting, **that there would be** time for him to show his slide presentation, and **that questions would be asked** by prospective buyers. **(passive)**

Parallel:

The salesman expected **that he would present** his product at the meeting, **that there would be** time for him to show his slide presentation, and **that prospective buyers would ask** him questions.

Lists After a Colon

Be sure to keep all the elements in a list in the same form.

Example 1

Not Parallel:

The dictionary can be used for these purposes: to find **word meanings, pronunciations, correct spellings,** and **looking up irregular verbs**.

Parallel:

The dictionary can be used for these purposes: to find **word meanings, pronunciations, correct spellings,** and **irregular verbs**.

Proofreading Strategies to Try:

- Skim your paper, pausing at the words "and" and "or." Check on each side of these words to see whether the items joined are parallel. If not, make them parallel.
- If you have several items in a list, put them in a column to see if they are parallel.
- Listen to the sound of the items in a list or the items being compared. Do you hear the same kinds of sounds? For example, is there a series of "-ing" words beginning each item? Or do your hear a rhythm being repeated? If something is breaking that rhythm or repetition of sound, check to see if it needs to be made parallel.

Part 8: Introduction and General Usage in Defining Clauses

Relative pronouns are **that, who, whom, whose, which, where, when,** and **why.** They are used to join clauses to make a complex sentence. Relative pronouns are used at the beginning of the subordinate clause which gives some specific information about the main clause.

> This is the house *that* Jack built.
> I don't know the day *when* Jane marries him.
> The professor, *whom* I respect, was tenured.

In English, the choice of the relative pronoun depends on the type of clause it is used in. There are two types of clauses distinguished: *defining* (*restrictive*) relative clauses and *non-defining* (*non-restrictive*) relative clauses. In both types of clauses the relative pronoun can function as a subject, an object, or a possessive.

Relative Pronouns in Defining Clauses

Defining relative clauses (also known as *restrictive relative clauses*) provide some essential information that explains the main clause. The information is crucial for understanding the sentence correctly and cannot be omitted. Defining clauses are opened by a relative pronoun and **ARE NOT** separated by a comma from the main clause.

The table below sums up the use of relative pronouns in defining clauses:

Function in the sentence	Reference to				
	People	Things/concepts	Place	Time	Reason
Subject	who, that	which, that			
Object	(that, who, whom)	(which, that)	where	when	why
Possessive	whose	whose, of which			

Examples

Relative pronoun used as a subject:

This is the house *that* had a great Christmas decoration.
It took me a while to get used to people *who* eat popcorn during the movie.

Relative pronoun used as an object:

1. As can be seen from the table, referring to a person or thing, the relative pronoun **may be omitted** in the object position:

   This is the man (who / that) I wanted to speak to and whose name I'd forgotten.

   The library didn't have the book (which / that) I wanted.

   I didn't like the book (which / that) John gave me.

   This is the house *where* I lived *when* I first came to the US.

2. In American English, *whom* is not used very often. **Whom** is more formal than *who* and is very often omitted in **speech**:

   Grammatically Correct: The woman to *whom* you have just spoken is my teacher.

   Common in Speech: The woman (*who*) you have just spoken to is my teacher.

   However, *whom* may not be omitted if preceded by a preposition:

   I have found you the tutor <u>for</u> *whom* you were looking.

Relative pronoun used as a possessive:

Whose is the only possessive relative pronoun in English. It can be used with both people and things:

The family *whose* house burnt in the fire was immediately given a suite in a hotel.
The book *whose* author is now being shown in the news has become a bestseller.

General remarks: That, Who, Which compared

The relative pronoun *that* can only be used in defining clauses. It can also be substituted for *who* (referring to persons) or *which* (referring to things). *That* is often used in speech; *who* and *which* are more common in written English.

William Kellogg was the man *that* lived in the late 19th century and had some weird ideas about raising children. (spoken, less formal)

William Kellogg was the man *who* lived in the late 19th century and had some weird ideas about raising children. (written, more formal)

Although your computer may suggest to correct it, referring to things, *which* may be used in the defining clause to put additional emphasis on the explanation. Again, the sentence with *which* is more formal than the one with *that*: Note that since it is the defining clause, there is NO comma used preceding *which*:

The café *that* sells the best coffee in town has recently been closed. (less formal)
The café *which* sells the best coffee in town has recently been closed. (more formal)

Some special uses of relative pronouns in defining clauses

that / who
Referring to people, both *that* and *who* can be used. *That* may be used to refer to someone in general:

He is the kind of person *that/who* will never let you down.
I am looking for someone *that/who* could give me a ride to Chicago.

However, when a particular person is being spoken about, *who* is preferred:

The old lady *who* lives next door is a teacher.
The girl *who* wore a red dress attracted everybody's attention at the party.

that / which
There are several cases when *that* is more appropriate and is preferred to *which*.

After the pronouns *all, any(thing), every(thing), few, little, many, much, no(thing), none, some(thing)*:

The police usually ask for every detail *that* helps identify the missing person. (*that* used as the subject)
Marrying a congressman is *all* (that) she wants. (*that* used as the object)

After verbs that answer the question **WHAT?** For example, *say, suggest, state, declare, hope, think, write*, etc. In this case, the whole relative clause functions as the object of the main clause:

Some people *say* (that) success is one percent of talent and ninety-nine percent of hard work.
The chairman *stated* at the meeting (that) his company is part of a big-time entertainment industry.

After the noun modified by an adjective *in the superlative degree*:

This is the *funniest* story (that) I have ever read! (*that* used as the object)

After ordinal numbers, e.g., *first, second, etc.*:

The first draft (that) we submitted was really horrible. (*that* used as the object)

If the verb in the main clause is a form of *BE*:

This is a claim that has absolutely no reason in it. (*that* used as the subject)

Relative Pronouns in Non-Defining Clauses

Non-defining relative clauses (also known as non-restrictive, or parenthetical, clauses) provide some additional information which is not essential and may be omitted without affecting the contents of the sentence. All relative pronouns EXCEPT "that" can be used in non-defining clauses; however, the pronouns MAY NOT be omitted. Non-defining clauses ARE separated by commas.

The table below sums up the use of relative pronouns in non-defining clauses:

Function in the sentence	Reference to				
	People	Things/concepts	Place	Time	Reason
Subject	who	which			
Object	who, whom	which	where	when	why
Possessive	whose	whose, of which			

a. **Relative pronoun used as a subject:**

The writer, **who** lives in this luxurious mansion, has just published his second novel.

b. **Relative pronoun used as an object:**

The house at the end of the street, **which** my grandfather built, needs renovating.

c. **Relative pronoun used as a possessive:**

William Kellogg, **whose** name has become a famous breakfast foods brand-name, had some weird ideas about raising children.

Some Special Uses of Relative Pronouns in Non-Defining Clauses

a. **which**
If you are referring to the previous clause as a whole, use **which**:
My friend eventually decided to get divorced, **which** upset me a lot.

b. **of whom, of which**
Use **of whom** for persons and **of which** for things or concepts after numbers and words such as *most, many, some, both, none*:
I saw a lot of new people at the party, some **of whom** seemed familiar.
He was always coming up with new ideas, most **of which** were absolutely impracticable.

Part 9: Sentence Types and Punctuation Patterns

To punctuate a sentence, you can use and combine some of these patterns.

Pattern One: Simple Sentence
This pattern is an example of a simple sentence:

Independent clause [.]

Example: Doctors are concerned about the rising death rate from asthma.

Pattern Two: Compound Sentence
This pattern is an example of a compound sentence with a coordinating conjunction:

Independent clause [,] coordinating conjunction independent clause [.]

There are seven coordinating conjunctions: **and, but, for, or, nor, so, yet.**

Example: Doctors are concerned about the rising death rate from asthma, **but** they don't know the reasons for it.

Pattern Three: Compound Sentence

This pattern is an example of a compound sentence with a semicolon.

Independent clause [;] independent clause [.]

Example: Doctors are concerned about the rising death rate from asthma; they are unsure of its cause.

Pattern Four: Compound Sentence

This pattern is an example of a compound sentence with an independent marker.

Independent clause [;] <u>independent marker</u> [,] independent clause [.]

Examples of independent markers are the following: **therefore, moreover, thus, consequently, however, also.**

Example: Doctors are concerned about the rising death rate from asthma; <u>therefore</u>, they have called for more research into its causes.

Pattern Five: Complex Sentence

This pattern is an example of a complex sentence with a dependent marker.

<u>Dependent marker</u> dependent clause [,] Independent clause [.]

Examples of dependent markers are as follows: **because, before, since, while, although, if, until, when, after, as, as if.**

Example: <u>*Because*</u> doctors are concerned about the rising death rate from asthma, they have called for more research into its causes.

Pattern Six: Complex Sentence

This pattern is an example of a complex sentence with a dependent marker following the independent clause.

Independent clause <u>dependent marker</u> dependent clause [.]

Example: Doctors are concerned about the rising death rate from asthma <u>because</u> it is a common, treatable illness.

Pattern Seven

This pattern includes an independent clause with an embedded <u>non-essential</u> clause or phrase. A non-essential clause or phrase is one that can be removed without changing the meaning of the sentence or making it ungrammatical. In other words, the non-essential clause or phrase gives additional information, but the sentence can stand alone without it.

First part of an independent clause [,] non-essential clause or phrase, rest of the independent clause [.]

Example: Many doctors, including both pediatricians and family practice physicians, are concerned about the rising death rate from asthma.

Pattern Eight

This pattern includes an independent clause with an embedded <u>essential</u> clause or phrase. An essential clause or phrase is one that cannot be removed without changing the overall meaning of the sentence.

First part of an independent clause essential clause or phrase rest of the independent clause [.]

Example: Many doctors who are concerned about the rising death rate from asthma have called for more research into its causes.

Part 10: Making Subjects and Verbs Agree

1. When the subject of a sentence is composed of two or more nouns or pronouns connected by _and_, use a plural verb.

   She and **her friends** <u>are</u> at the fair.

2. When two or more singular nouns or pronouns are connected by _or_ or _nor_, use a singular verb.

   The book or **the pen** <u>is</u> in the drawer.

3. When a compound subject contains both a singular and a plural noun or pronoun joined by _or_ or _nor_, the verb should agree with the part of the subject that is nearer the verb.

   The boy or **his friends** <u>run</u> every day.
   His friends or **the boy** <u>runs</u> every day.

4. _Doesn't_ is a contraction of _does not_ and should be used only with a singular subject. _Don't_ is a contraction of _do not_ and should be used only with a plural subject. The exception to this rule appears in the case of the first person and second person pronouns _I_ and _you_. With these pronouns, the contraction _don't_ should be used. [Note that formal writing generally avoids the use of contractions.]

   He doesn't <u>like</u> it.
   They don't <u>like</u> it.

5. Do not be misled by a phrase that comes between the subject and the verb. The verb agrees with the subject, not with a noun or pronoun in the phrase.

   One of the boxes <u>is</u> open
   The people who listen to that music <u>are</u> few.
   The team captain, as well as his players, <u>is</u> anxious.
   The book, including all the chapters in the first section, <u>is</u> boring.
   The woman with all the dogs <u>walks</u> down my street.

6. The words _each_, _each one_, _either_, _neither_, _everyone_, _everybody_, _anybody_, _anyone_, _nobody_, _somebody_, _someone_, and _no one_ are singular and require a singular verb.

   Each of these hot dogs <u>is</u> juicy.
   Everybody <u>knows</u> Mr. Jones.
   Either <u>is</u> correct.

7. Nouns such as _civics_, _mathematics_, _dollars_, _measles_, and _news_ require singular verbs.

   The news <u>is</u> on at six.

   Note: The word **dollars** is a special case. When talking about an amount of money, it requires a singular verb, but when referring to the dollars themselves, a plural verb is required.

   Five dollars <u>is</u> a lot of money.
   Dollars <u>are</u> often used instead of rubles in Russia.

8. Nouns such as _scissors_, _tweezers_, _trousers_, and _shears_ require plural verbs. (There are two parts to these things.)

   These scissors <u>are</u> dull.
   Those trousers <u>are</u> made of wool.

9. In sentences beginning with _there is_ or _there are_, the subject follows the verb. Since _there_ is not the subject, the verb agrees with what follows.

There **are** many questions.
There **is** a question.

10. Collective nouns are words that imply more than one person but that are considered singular and take a singular verb, such as: *group*, *team*, *committee*, *class*, and *family*.

The team **runs** during practice.
The committee **decides** how to proceed.
The family **has** a long history.
My family **has never been able to agree**.

In some cases, a sentence may call for the use of a plural verb when using a collective noun.

The crew **are preparing** to dock the ship.

This sentence is referring to the individual efforts of each crew member.

11. Expressions such as *with*, *together with*, *including*, *accompanied by*, *in addition to*, or *as well* do not change the number of the subject. If the subject is singular, the verb is too.

The President, accompanied by his wife, **is** traveling to India.
All of the books, including yours, **are** in that box.

Sequence of Tenses

Simple Present: They walk.

Present Perfect: They have walked.

Simple Past: They walked.

Past Perfect: They had walked.

Future: They will walk.

Future Perfect: They will have walked.

Problems in sequencing tenses usually occur with the perfect tenses, all of which are formed by adding an auxiliary or auxiliaries to the past participle, the third principal part.

ring, rang, rung
walk, walked, walked

The most common auxiliaries are forms of "be," "can," "do," "may," "must," "ought," "shall," "will," "has," "have," "had," and they are the forms we shall use in this most basic discussion.

Present Perfect

The present perfect consists of a past participle (the third principal part) with "has" or "have." It designates action which began in the past but which continues into the present or the effect of which still continues.

1. Betty taught for ten years. (simple past)
2. Betty has taught for ten years. (present perfect)

The implication in (1) is that Betty has retired; in (2), that she is still teaching.

1. John did his homework. He can go to the movies.
2. If John has done his homework, he can go to the movies.

Infinitives, too, have perfect tense forms when combined with "have," and sometimes problems arise when infinitives are used with verbs such as "hope," "plan," "expect," and "intend," all of which usually point to the future (I wanted to go to the movie. Janet meant to see the doctor.) The perfect tense sets up a sequence by marking the action which began and usually was completed before the action in the main verb.

1. I am happy to have participated in this campaign!
2. John had hoped to have won the trophy.

Thus the action of the main verb points back in time; the action of the perfect infinitive has been completed.

The past perfect tense designates action in the past just as simple past does, but the action of the past perfect is action completed in the past before another action.

1. John raised vegetables and later sold them. (past)
2. John sold vegetables that he had raised. (past perfect)

The vegetables were raised before they were sold.

1. Renee washed the car when George arrived. (simple past)
2. Renee had washed the car when George arrived. (past perfect)

In (1), she waited until George arrived and then washed the car. In (2), she had already finished washing the car by the time he arrived.

In sentences expressing condition and result, the past perfect tense is used in the part that states the condition.

1. If I had done my exercises, I would have passed the test.
2. I think George would have been elected if he hadn't sounded so pompous.

Future Perfect Tense

The future perfect tense designates action that will have been completed at a specified time in the future.

1. Saturday I will finish my housework. (simple future)
2. By Saturday noon, I will have finished my housework. (future perfect)

Part 11: Using Active Versus Passive Voice

In a sentence using **active voice**, the subject of the sentence performs the action expressed in the verb.

The dog *bit* **the boy**.

The arrow points from the subject performing the action (the dog) to the individual being acted upon (the boy). This is an example of a sentence using the active voice.

Scientists *have conducted* **experiments** to test the hypothesis.

Sample active voice sentence with the subject performing the action described by the verb.

Watching a framed, mobile world through a car's windshield *reminds* me of watching a movie or TV.

The active voice sentence subject (watching a framed, mobile world) performs the action of reminding the speaker of something.

Each example above includes a sentence subject performing the action expressed by the verb.

Examples:

	Active	Passive
Simple Present	• The company ships the computers to many foreign countries.	• Computers are shipped to many foreign countries
Present Progressive	• The chef is preparing the food.	• The food is being prepared.
Simple Past	• The delivery man delivered the package yesterday.	• The package was delivered yesterday.
Past Progressive	• The producer was making an announcement.	• An announcement was being made.
Future	• Our representative will pick up the computer.	• The computer will be picked up.
Present Perfect	• Someone has made the arrangements for us.	• The arrangements have been made for us.
Past Perfect	• They had given us visas for three months.	• They had been given visas for three months.
Future Perfect	• By next month we will have finished this job.	• By next month this job will have been finished.

Part 12: Irregular Verbs: Overview and List

In English, regular verbs consist of three main parts: the root form (present), the (simple) past, and the past participle. Regular verbs have an *-ed* ending added to the root verb for both the simple past and past participle. Irregular verbs do not follow this pattern, and instead take on an alternative pattern.

The following is a partial list of irregular verbs found in English. Each listing consists of the present/root form of the verb, the (simple) past form of the verb, and the past participle form of the verb.

List of Irregular Verbs in English				Present	Past	Past Participle
Present	Past	Past Participle		deal	dealt	dealt
be	was, were	been		do	did	done
become	became	become		drink	drank	drunk
begin	began	begun		drive	drove	driven
blow	blew	blown		eat	ate	eaten
break	broke	broken		fall	fell	fallen
bring	brought	brought		feed	fed	fed
build	built	built		feel	felt	felt
burst	burst	burst		fight	fought	fought
buy	bought	bought		find	found	found
catch	caught	caught		fly	flew	flown
choose	chose	chosen		forbid	forbade	forbidden
come	came	come		forget	forgot	forgotten
cut	cut	cut				

Present	Past	Past Participle
forgive	forgave	forgiven
freeze	froze	frozen
get	got	gotten
give	gave	given
go	went	gone
grow	grew	grown
have	had	had
hear	heard	heard
hide	hid	hidden
hold	held	held
hurt	hurt	hurt
keep	kept	kept
know	knew	known
lay	laid	laid
lead	led	led
leave	left	left
let	let	let
lie	lay	lain
lose	lost	lost
make	made	made
meet	met	met
pay	paid	paid
quit	quit	quit
read	read	read
ride	rode	ridden
run	ran	run
say	said	said

Present	Past	Past Participle
see	saw	seen
seek	sought	sought
sell	sold	sold
send	sent	sent
shake	shook	sent
shine	shone	shone
sing	sang	sung
sit	sat	sat
sleep	slept	slept
speak	spoke	spoken
spend	spent	spent
spring	sprang	sprung
stand	stood	stood
steal	stole	stolen
swim	swam	swum
swing	swung	swung
take	took	taken
teach	taught	taught
tear	tore	torn
tell	told	told
think	thought	thought
throw	threw	thrown
understand	understood	understood
wake	woke (waked)	woken (waked)
wear	wore	worn
win	won	won
write	wrote	written

Commonly Confused Verbs

LIE versus LAY

Lie vs. Lay Usage		
Present	Past	Past Participle
lie, lying (to tell a falsehood)	I lied to my mother.	I have lied under oath.
lie, lying (to recline)	I lay on the bed because I was tired.	He has lain in the grass.
lay, laying (to put, place)	I laid the baby in her cradle.	We have laid the dishes on the table.

Example sentences:

After **laying** down his weapon, the soldier **lay** down to sleep.
Will you **lay** out my clothes while I **lie** down to rest?

SIT versus SET

Sit vs. Set Usage		
Present	Past	Past Participle
sit (to be seated or come to resting position)	I sat in my favorite chair.	You have sat there for three hours.
set (to put or place)	I set my glass on the table.	She has set her books on my desk again.

Example sentence:

Let's **set** the table before we **sit** down to rest.

RISE versus RAISE

Rise vs. Raise Usage		
Present	Past	Past Participle
rise (steady or customary upward movement)	The balloon rose into the air.	He has risen to a position of power.
raise (to cause to rise)	They raised their hands because they knew the answer.	I have raised the curtain many times.

Example sentence:

The boy **raised** the flag just before the sun **rose**.

Part 13: Capitalization and Punctuation

A Little Help with Capitals

If you have a question about whether a specific word should be capitalized that doesn't fit under one of these rules, try checking a dictionary to see if the word is capitalized there.

Use capital letters in the following ways:

The first words of a sentence

When he tells a joke, he sometimes forgets the punch line.

The pronoun "I"

The last time I visited Atlanta was several years ago.

Proper nouns (the names of specific people, places, organizations, and sometimes things)

Worrill Fabrication Company
Golden Gate Bridge
Supreme Court
Livingston, Missouri
Atlantic Ocean
Mothers Against Drunk Driving

Family relationships (when used as proper names)

I sent a thank-you note to Aunt Abigail, but not to my other aunts.
Here is a present I bought for Mother.
Did you buy a present for your mother?

The names of God, specific deities, religious figures, and holy books

God the Father
the Virgin Mary
the Bible
the Greek gods
Moses
Shiva
Buddha
Zeus

Exception: Do not capitalize the non-specific use of the word "god."

The word "polytheistic" means the worship of more than one god.

Titles preceding names, but not titles that follow names

She worked as the assistant to Mayor Hanolovi.
I was able to interview Miriam Moss, mayor of Littonville.

Directions that are names (North, South, East, and West when used as sections of the country, but not as compass directions)

The Patels have moved to the Southwest.
Jim's house is two miles north of Otterbein.

The days of the week, the months of the year, and holidays (but not the seasons used generally)

Halloween
October
Friday
winter
spring
fall

Exception: Seasons are capitalized when used in a title.

The Fall 1999 Semester

The names of countries, nationalities, and specific languages

Costa Rica
Spanish
French
English

The first word in a sentence that is a direct quote

Emerson once said, "A foolish consistency is the hobgoblin of little minds."

The major words in the titles of books, articles, and songs (but not short prepositions or the articles "the," "a," or "an," if they are not the first word of the title)

One of Jerry's favorite books is *The Catcher in the Rye*.

Members of national, political, racial, social, civic, and athletic groups

Green Bay Packers
African-Americans
Democrats
Friends of the Wilderness
Chinese

Periods and events (but not century numbers)

Victorian Era
Great Depression
Constitutional Convention
sixteenth century

Trademarks

Pepsi
Honda
IBM
Microsoft Word

Words and abbreviations of specific names (but not names of things that came from specific things but are now general types)

Freudian	UN
NBC	french fries
pasteurize	italics

Comma

Use a comma to join two independent clauses by a comma and a coordinating conjunction (*and, but, or, for, nor, so*).

Road construction can be inconvenient, but it is necessary.

The new house has a large fenced backyard, so I am sure our dog will enjoy it.

Use a comma after an introductory phrase, prepositional phrase, or dependent clause.

To get a good grade, you must complete all your assignments.

Because Dad caught the chicken pox, we canceled our vacation.

After the wedding, the guests attended the reception.

Use a comma to separate elements in a series. Although there is no set rule that requires a comma before the last item in a series, it seems to be a general academic convention to include it. The examples below demonstrate this trend.

On her vacation, Lisa visited Greece, Spain, and Italy.

In their speeches, many of the candidates promised to help protect the environment, bring about world peace, and end world hunger.

Use a comma to separate nonessential elements from a sentence. More specifically, when a sentence includes information that is not crucial to the message or intent of the sentence, enclose it in or separate it by commas.

John's truck, a red Chevrolet, needs new tires.

When he realized he had overslept, Matt rushed to his car and hurried to work.

Use a comma between coordinate adjectives (adjectives that are equal and reversible).

The irritable, fidgety crowd waited impatiently for the rally speeches to begin.

The sturdy, compact suitcase made a perfect gift.

Use a comma after a transitional element (*however, therefore, nonetheless, also, otherwise, finally, instead, thus, of course, above all, for example, in other words, as a result, on the other hand, in conclusion, in addition*)

For example, the Red Sox, Yankees, and Indians are popular baseball teams.

If you really want to get a good grade this semester, however, you must complete all assignments, attend class, and study your notes.

Use a comma with quoted words.

"Yes," she promised. Todd replied, saying, "I will be back this afternoon."

Use a comma in a date.

October 25, 1999
Monday, October 25, 1999
25 October 1999

Use a comma in a number.

15,000,000
1614 High Street

Use a comma in a personal title.

Pam Smith, MD
Mike Rose, Chief Financial Officer for Operations, reported the quarter's earnings.

Use a comma to separate a city name from the state.

West Lafayette, Indiana
Dallas, Texas

Avoid comma splices (two independent clauses joined only by a comma). Instead, separate the clauses with a period, with a comma followed by a coordinating conjunction, or with a semicolon.

Semicolon

Use a semicolon to join two independent clauses when the second clause restates the first or when the two clauses are of equal emphasis.

Road construction in Dallas has hindered travel around town; streets have become covered with bulldozers, trucks, and cones.

Use a semicolon to join two independent clauses when the second clause begins with a conjunctive adverb (*however, therefore, moreover, furthermore, thus, meanwhile, nonetheless, otherwise*) or a transition (*in fact, for example, that is, for instance, in addition, in other words, on the other hand, even so*).

Terrorism in the United States has become a recent concern; in fact, the concern for America's safety has led to an awareness of global terrorism.

Use a semicolon to join elements of a series when individual items of the series already include commas.

Recent sites of the Olympic Games include Athens, Greece; Salt Lake City, Utah; Sydney, Australia; Nagano, Japan.

Colon

Use a colon to join two independent clauses when you wish to emphasize the second clause.

Road construction in Dallas has hindered travel around town: parts of Main, Fifth, and West Street are closed during the construction.

Use a colon after an independent clause when it is followed by a list, a quotation, an appositive, or other idea directly related to the independent clause.

Julie went to the store for some groceries: milk, bread, coffee, and cheese.

In his Gettysburg Address, Abraham Lincoln urges Americans to rededicate themselves to the unfinished work of the deceased soldiers: "It is for us the living rather to be dedicated here to the unfinished work which they who fought here have thus far so nobly advanced. It is rather for us to be here dedicated to the great task remaining before us — that from these honored dead we take increased devotion to that cause for which they gave the last full measure of devotion — that we here highly resolve that these dead shall not have died in vain, that this nation under God shall have a new birth of freedom, and that government of the people, by the people, for the people shall not perish from the earth."

I know the perfect job for her: a politician.

Use a colon at the end of a business letter greeting.

To Whom It May Concern:

Use a colon to separate the hour and minute(s) in a time notation.

12:00 p.m.

Use a colon to separate the chapter and verse in a Biblical reference.

Matthew 1:6

Parentheses

Parentheses are used to emphasize content. They place more emphasis on the enclosed content than commas. Use parentheses to set off nonessential material, such as dates, clarifying information, or sources, from a sentence.

Muhammed Ali (1942-present), arguably the greatest athlete of all time, claimed he would "float like a butterfly, sting like a bee."

Use parentheses to enclose numbered items in a sentence.

He asked everyone to bring (1) a folding tent, (2) food and water for two days, and (3) a sleeping bag.

Also use parentheses for literary citations embedded in text or to give the explanation of an acronym.

Research by Wegener and Petty (1994) supports...
The AMA (American Medical Association) recommends regular exercise.

Dash

Dashes are used to set off or emphasize the content enclosed within dashes or the content that follows a dash. Dashes place more emphasis on this content than parentheses.

Perhaps one reason why the term has been so problematic—so resistant to definition, and yet so transitory in those definitions—is because of its multitude of applications.

In terms of public legitimacy—that is, in terms of garnering support from state legislators, parents, donors, and university administrators—English departments are primarily places where advanced literacy is taught.

The U.S.S. *Constitution* became known as "Old Ironsides" during the War of 1812—during which the cannonballs fired from the British H.M.S. *Guerriere* merely bounced off the sides of the *Constitution*.

To some of you, my proposals may seem radical—even revolutionary.

Use a dash to set off an appositive phrase that already includes commas. An appositive is a word that adds explanatory or clarifying information to the noun that precedes it.

The cousins—Tina, Todd, and Sam—arrived at the party together.

Quotation Marks

Use quotation marks to enclose direct quotations. Note that commas and periods are placed inside the closing quotation mark, and colons and semicolons are placed outside. The placement of question and exclamation marks depends on the situation.

He asked, "When will you be arriving?" I answered, "Sometime after 6:30."

Use quotation marks to indicate the novel, ironic, or reserved use of a word.

History is stained with blood spilled in the name of "justice."

Use quotation marks around the titles of short poems, song titles, short stories, magazine or newspaper articles, essays, speeches, chapter titles, short films, and episodes of television or radio shows.

"Self-Reliance," by Ralph Waldo Emerson
"Just Like a Woman," by Bob Dylan
"The Smelly Car," an episode of Seinfeld

Do not use quotation marks in indirect or block quotations. Indirect quotations are not exact wordings but rather rephrasings or summaries of another person's words. In this case, it is not necessary to use quotation marks. However, indirect quotations still require proper citations, and you will be committing plagiarism if you fail to do so.

Mr. Johnson, a local farmer, reported last night that he saw an alien spaceship on his own property.

Italics

Underlining and Italics are often used interchangeably. Before word-processing programs were widely available, writers would underline certain words to indicate to publishers to italicize whatever was underlined. Although the general trend has been moving toward italicizing instead of underlining, you should remain consistent with your choice throughout your paper. To be safe, you could check with your teacher to find out which he/she prefers. Italicize the titles of magazines, books, newspapers, academic journals, films, television shows, long poems, plays of three or more acts, operas, musical albums, works of art, websites, and individual trains, planes, or ships.

Time
Romeo and Juliet by William Shakespeare
The Metamorphosis of Narcissus by Salvador Dali
Amazon.com
Titanic

Italicize foreign words.

Semper fi, the motto of the U.S. Marine Corps, means "always faithful."

Italicize a word or phrase to add emphasis.

The *truth* is of utmost concern!

Italicize a word when referring to that word.

The word *justice* is often misunderstood and therefore misused.

Hyphen

Two words brought together as a compound may be written separately, written as one word, or connected by hyphens. For example, three modern dictionaries all have the same listings for the following compounds:

> hair stylist
> hairsplitter
> hair-raiser

Another modern dictionary, however, lists *hairstylist*, not *hair stylist*. Compounding is obviously in a state of flux, and authorities do not always agree in all cases, but the uses of the hyphen offered here are generally agreed upon.

1. Use a hyphen to join two or more words serving as a single adjective before a noun:

   > a one-way street
   > chocolate-covered peanuts
   > well-known author

   However, when compound modifiers come after a noun, they are not hyphenated:

   > The peanuts were chocolate covered.
   > The author was well known.

2. Use a hyphen with compound numbers:

   > forty-six
   > sixty-three
   > Our much-loved teacher was sixty-three years old.

3. Use a hyphen to avoid confusion or an awkward combination of letters:

   > re-sign a petition (vs. resign from a job)
   > semi-independent (but semiconscious)
   > shell-like (but childlike)

4. Use a hyphen with the prefixes *ex-* (meaning former), *self-*, *all-*; with the suffix *-elect*; between a prefix and a capitalized word; and with figures or letters:

   > ex-husband
   > self-assured
   > mid-September
   > all-inclusive
   > mayor-elect
   > anti-American
   > T-shirt
   > pre-Civil War
   > mid-1980s

5. Use a hyphen to divide words at the end of a line if necessary, and make the break only between syllables:

   > pref-er-ence
   > sell-ing
   > in-di-vid-u-al-ist

6. For line breaks, divide already hyphenated words only at the hyphen:

   > mass-
   > produced

Apostrophe

The apostrophe has three uses:

- to form possessives of nouns
- to show the omission of letters
- to indicate certain plurals of lowercase letters

Forming Possessives of Nouns

To see if you need to make a possessive, turn the phrase around and make it an "of the..." phrase. For example:

the boy's hat = the hat of the boy
three days' journey = journey of three days

If the noun after "of" is a building, an object, or a piece of furniture, then **no** apostrophe is needed!

room of the hotel = hotel room
door of the car = car door
leg of the table = table leg

Once you've determined whether you need to make a possessive, follow these rules to create one.

- **add 's to the singular form of the word (even if it ends in -s):**

  the owner's car
  James's hat (James' hat is also acceptable. For plural, proper nouns that are possessive, use an apostrophe after the 's': "The Eggles' presentation was good." The Eggles are a husband and wife consultant team.)

- **add 's to the plural forms that do not end in -s:**

  the children's game
  the geese's honking

- **add ' to the end of plural nouns that end in -s:**

  houses' roofs
  three friends' letters

- **add 's to the end of compound words:**

  my brother-in-law's money

- **add 's to the last noun to show joint possession of an object:**

  Todd and Anne's apartment

Showing omission of letters

Apostrophes are used in contractions. A contraction is a word (or set of numbers) in which one or more letters (or numbers) have been omitted. The apostrophe shows this omission. Contractions are common in speaking and in informal writing. To use an apostrophe to create a contraction, place an apostrophe where the omitted letter(s) would go. Here are some examples:

don't = do not
I'm = I am
he'll = he will
who's = who is
could've= could have (NOT "could of"!)
'60 = 1960

Don't use apostrophes for possessive pronouns or for noun plurals.

Apostrophes should not be used with possessive pronouns because possessive pronouns already show possession — they don't need an apostrophe. *His, her, its, my, yours, ours* are all possessive pronouns. Here are some examples:

wrong: his' book
correct: his book

wrong: The group made **it's** decision.
correct: The group made **its** decision.

(Note: *Its* and *it' s* are not the same thing. *It' s* is a contraction for "it is" and *its* is a possessive pronoun meaning "belonging to it." It's raining out= it is raining out. A simple way to remember this rule is the fact that you don't use an apostrophe for the possessive *his* or *hers*, so don't do it with *its*!)

wrong: a friend of **yours'**
correct: a friend of **yours**

Proofreading for apostrophes

A good time to proofread is when you have finished writing the paper. Try the following strategies to proofread for apostrophes:

- If you tend to leave out apostrophes, check every word that ends in *-s* or *-es* to see if it needs an apostrophe.
- If you put in too many apostrophes, check every apostrophe to see if you can justify it with a rule for using apostrophes.

Ellipsis

An ellipsis (a row of three dots: ...) must be used whenever anything is omitted from within a quoted passage—word, phrase, line, or paragraph-- regardless of its source or use. It would, therefore, apply to all usage, including technical, non-technical, medical, journalistic, fiction, etc. The usual form is a "bare" ellipsis (just the three dots, preceded and followed by a space), although the MLA Handbook for Writers of Research Papers recommends that the writer enclose an ellipsis in brackets [...] when omitting part of an original quotation, to differentiate instances of deleted text from ellipses included in the original text. In all cases, the entire quoted passage, including ellipses, is preceded and followed by quotation marks and the source properly cited.

Two things to consider: 1) using ellipses is a form of "editing" the source material, so be certain that the final outcome does not change the original meaning or intent of the quoted passage; and 2) if quoted text ends up with more ellipses than words, consider paraphrasing rather than using direct quotes.

Brackets

Brackets are most often used to clarify the meaning of quoted material. If the context of your quote might be unclear, you may add a few words to provide clarity. Enclose the added material in brackets.

Added Material: The quarterback told the reporter, "It's quite simple. They [the other team] played a better game, scored more points, and that's why we lost."

Resources

SpringBoard Learning Strategies

READING STRATEGIES

STRATEGY	DEFINITION	PURPOSE
Close Reading	Accessing small chunks of text to read, reread, mark, and annotate key passages, word-for-word, sentence-by-sentence, and line-by-line	To develop comprehensive understanding by engaging in one or more focused readings of a text
Diffusing	Reading a passage, noting unfamiliar words, discovering meaning of unfamiliar words using context clues, dictionaries, and/or thesauruses, and replacing unfamiliar words with familiar ones	To facilitate a close reading of text, the use of resources, an understanding of synonyms, and increased comprehension of text
Double-Entry Journal	Creating a two-column journal (also called Dialectical Journal) with a student-selected passage in one column and the student's response in the second column (e.g., asking questions of the text, forming personal responses, interpreting the text, reflecting on the process of making meaning of the text)	To respond to a specific passage with comments, questions, or insights to foster active involvement with a text and to facilitate increased comprehension
Graphic Organizer	Using a visual representation for the organization of information	To facilitate increased comprehension and discussion
KWHL Chart	Setting up discussion with use of a graphic organizer. Allows students to activate prior knowledge by answering "What do I *know*?" sets a purpose by answering "What do I *want* to know?" helps preview a task by answering "*How* will I learn it?" and reflects on new knowledge by answering "What have I *learned?*"	To organize thinking, access prior knowledge, and reflect on learning to increase comprehension and engagement
Marking the Text	Selecting text by highlighting, underlining, and/or annotating for specific components, such as main idea, imagery, literary devices, and so on	To focus reading for specific purposes, such as author's craft, and to organize information from selections; to facilitate reexamination of a text
Metacognitive Markers	Responding to text with a system of cueing marks where students use a **?** for questions about the text; a **!** for reactions related to the text; and an ***** for comments about the text and underline to signal key ideas	To track responses to texts and use those responses as a point of departure for talking or writing about texts
Predicting	Making guesses about the text by using the title and pictures and/or thinking ahead about events which may occur based on evidence in the text	To help students become actively involved, interested, and mentally prepared to understand ideas
Previewing	Examining a text's structure, features, layout, and so on, prior to reading	To gain familiarity with the text, make connections to the text, and extend prior knowledge to set a purpose for reading
QHT	Expanding prior knowledge of vocabulary words by marking words with a Q, H, or T (Q signals words students do not know; H signals words students have heard and might be able to identify; T signals words students know well enough to teach to their peers.)	To allow students to build on their prior knowledge of words, to provide a forum for peer teaching and learning of new words, and to serve as a pre-reading exercise to aid in comprehension

STRATEGY	DEFINITION	PURPOSE
Questioning the Text*	Developing literal, interpretive, and universal questions about the text while reading a text	To engage more actively with texts, read with greater purpose and focus, and ultimately answer questions to gain greater insight into the text
Quickwrite	Responding to a text by writing for a short, specific amount of time about a designated topic or idea related to a text	To activate background knowledge, clarify issues, facilitate making connections, and allow for reflection
RAFT	Responding to and analyzing text by brainstorming various roles (e.g., self, characters from other texts), audiences (e.g., a different character, a real person), formats (e.g., letter, brochure, essay, travel guide), and topics; readers may choose one particular role, audience, format, and topic to create a new text	To initiate reader response; to facilitate an analysis of a text to gain focus prior to creating a new text
Rereading	Encountering the same text with more than one reading	To identify additional details; to clarify meaning and/or reinforce comprehension of texts
SIFT*	Analyzing a fictional text by examining stylistic elements, especially symbol, images, and figures of speech, in order to show how all work together to reveal tone and theme.	To focus and facilitate an analysis of a fictional text by examining the title and text for symbolism, identifying images and sensory details, analyzing figurative language and identifying how all these elements reveal tone and theme
Skimming/Scanning	Skimming by rapid or superficial reading of a text to form an overall impression or to obtain a general understanding of the material; scanning by focusing on key words, phrases, or specific details to provide speedy recognition of information	To quickly form an overall impression prior to an in-depth study of a text; to answer specific questions or quickly locate targeted information or detail in a text

*AP strategy

READING STRATEGIES (Continued)

STRATEGY	DEFINITION	PURPOSE
SMELL*	Analyzing a persuasive speech or essay by asking five essential questions: • **S**ender-receiver relationship—What is the sender-receiver relationship? Who are the images and language meant to attract? Describe the speaker of the text. • **M**essage—What is the message? Summarize the statement made in the text. • **E**motional Strategies—What is the desired effect? • **L**ogical Strategies—What logic is operating? How does it (or its absence) affect the message? Consider the logic of the images as well as the words. • **L**anguage—What does the language of the text describe? How does it affect the meaning and effectiveness of the writing? Consider the language of the images as well as the words.	To analyze a persuasive speech or essay by focusing on five essential questions
SOAPSTone*	Analyzing text by discussing and identifying *Speaker, Occasion, Audience, Purpose, Subject,* and *Tone*	To use an analytical process to understand the author's craft
Summarizing/ Paraphrasing	Restating in one's own words the main idea or essential information expressed in a text, whether it be narration, dialogue, or informational text	To facilitate comprehension and recall of a text
Think Aloud	Talking through a difficult passage or task by using a form of metacognition whereby the reader expresses how he/she has made sense of the text	To reflect on how readers make meaning of challenging texts
TP-CASTT*	Analyzing a poetic text by identifying and discussing *Title, Paraphrase, Connotation, Attitude, Shift, Theme,* and *Title* again	To use an analytical process to understand the author's craft
Visualizing	Forming a picture (mentally and/or literally) while reading a text	To increase reading comprehension and promote active engagement with text
Word Maps	Using a clearly defined graphic organizer such as concept circles or word webs to identify and reinforce word meanings	To provide a visual tool for identifying and remembering multiple aspects of words and word meanings

*AP strategy

WRITING STRATEGIES

STRATEGY	DEFINITION	PURPOSE
Adding	Making conscious choices to enhance a text by adding additional words, phrases, sentences, or ideas	To refine and clarify the writer's thoughts during revision and/or drafting
Brainstorming	Using a flexible but deliberate process of listing multiple ideas in a short period of time without excluding any idea from the preliminary list	To generate ideas, concepts, or key words that provide a focus and/or establish organization as part of the prewriting or revision process
Deleting	Providing clarity and cohesiveness for a text by eliminating words, phrases, sentences, or ideas	To refine and clarify the writer's thoughts during revision and/or drafting
Double-Entry Journal	Creating a two-column journal (also called Dialectical Journal) with a student-selected passage in one column and the student's response in the second column (e.g., asking questions of the text, forming personal responses, interpreting the text, reflecting on the process of making meaning of the text)	To assist in organizing key textual elements and responses noted during reading in order to generate textual support that can be incorporated into a piece of writing at a later time
Drafting	Composing a text in its initial form	To incorporate brainstormed or initial ideas into a written format
Free writing	Using a fluid brainstorming process to write without constraints in order to solidify and convey the writer's purpose	To refine and clarify the writer's thoughts, spark new ideas, and/or generate content during revision and/or drafting
Generating Questions	Clarifying and developing ideas by asking questions of the draft. May be part of self-editing or peer editing	To clarify and develop ideas in a draft. Used during drafting and as part of writer response
Graphic Organizer	Representing ideas and information visually (e.g., Venn diagrams, flowcharts, cluster maps)	To provide a visual system for organizing multiple ideas, details, and/or textual support to be included in a piece of writing
Looping	Focusing on one section of a text and using that section to generate new ideas and then repeating the process with the newly generated segments	To refine and clarify the writer's thoughts, spark new ideas, and/or generate new content during revision and/or drafting
Mapping	Creating a graphic organizer that serves as a visual representation of the organizational plan for a written text	To generate ideas, concepts, or key words that provide a focus and/or establish organization during the prewriting, drafting, or revision process

WRITING STRATEGIES (Continued)

STRATEGY	DEFINITION	PURPOSE
Marking the Draft	Interacting with the draft version of a piece of writing by highlighting, underlining, color-coding, and annotating to indicate revision ideas.	To encourage focused, reflective thinking about revising drafts
Outlining	Using a system of numerals and letters in order to identify topics and supporting details and ensure an appropriate balance of ideas	To generate ideas, concepts, or key words that provide a focus and/or establish organization prior to writing an initial draft and/or during the revision process
Quickwrite	Writing for a short, specific amount of time about a designated topic related to a text	To generate multiple ideas in a quick fashion that could be turned into longer pieces of writing at a later time (May be considered as part of the drafting process)
RAFT	Generating and/or transforming a text by identifying and/or manipulating its component parts of *Role, Audience, Format,* and *Topic*	To consider the main elements of the writer's own work in order to generate a focus and purpose during the prewriting and drafting stages of the writing process
Rearranging	Selecting components of a text and moving them to another place within the text and/or modifying the order in which the author's ideas are presented	To refine and clarify the writer's thoughts during revision and/or drafting
Revisiting Prior Work	Looking through a collection of previously completed work to identify successes and challenges that may have been encountered with particular formats, conventions, style, word choice, and so on	To build on prior experience in preparation for a new piece of writing and/or to revise a previous piece of writing
Self-Editing/Peer Editing	Working with a partner to examine a text closely in order to identify areas that might need to be corrected for grammar, punctuation, spelling	To provide a systematic process for editing a written text to ensure correctness of identified components such as conventions of standard English
Sharing and Responding	Communicating with another person or a small group of peers who respond to a piece of writing as focused readers (not necessarily as evaluators)	To make suggestions for improvement to the work of others and/or to receive appropriate and relevant feedback on the writer's own work, used during the drafting and revision process
Sketching	Drawing or sketching ideas or ordering of ideas. Includes storyboarding, visualizing	To generate and/or clarify ideas by visualizing them; may be part of prewriting
Substituting	Replacing original words or phrases in a text with new words or phrases that achieve the desired effect	To refine and clarify the writer's thoughts during revision and/or drafting
Transformation of Text	Providing opportunities for students to create new text from a studied text by changing the genre, vernacular, time period, culture, point of view, and so on	To highlight the elements of a genre, point of view and so on; to illustrate how elements of style work together
TWIST*	Arriving at a thesis statement that incorporates the following literary elements: tone, word choice (diction), imagery, style and theme	To craft an interpretive thesis in response to a prompt about a passage
Webbing	Developing a graphic organizer that consists of a series of circles connected with lines to indicate relationships among ideas	To generate ideas, concepts, or key words that provide a focus and/or establish organization prior to writing an initial draft and/or during the revision process

*AP strategy

SPEAKING AND LISTENING STRATEGIES

STRATEGY	DEFINITION	PURPOSE
Notetaking	Creating a record of information while listening to a speaker	To facilitate active listening; to record and organize ideas that assist in processing information
Oral Interpretation	Reading a text orally while providing the necessary inflection and emphasis that demonstrate an understanding of the meaning of the text	To share with an audience the reader's personal insight into a text through voice, fluency, tone, and purpose
Oral Reading	Reading aloud one's own text or the texts of others (e.g., echo reading, choral reading, paired readings).	To share one's own work or the work of others; build fluency and increase confidence in presenting to a group
Role Playing	Assuming the role or persona of a character	To develop the voice, emotions, and mannerisms of a character to facilitate improved comprehension of a text
Rehearsal	Encouraging multiple practices of a piece of text prior to a performance	To provide students with an opportunity to clarify the meaning of a text prior to a performance as they refine the use of dramatic conventions (e.g., gestures, vocal interpretations, facial expressions)

COLLABORATIVE STRATEGIES

STRATEGY	DEFINITION	PURPOSE
Think-Pair-Share	Considering and thinking about a topic or question and then writing what has been learned; pairing with a peer or a small group to share ideas; sharing ideas and discussion with a larger group	To construct meaning about a topic or question; to test thinking in relation to the ideas of others; to prepare for a discussion with a larger group
Discussion Groups	Engaging in an interactive, small group discussion, often with an assigned role; to consider a topic, text, question, and so on	To gain new understanding or insight of a text from multiple perspectives

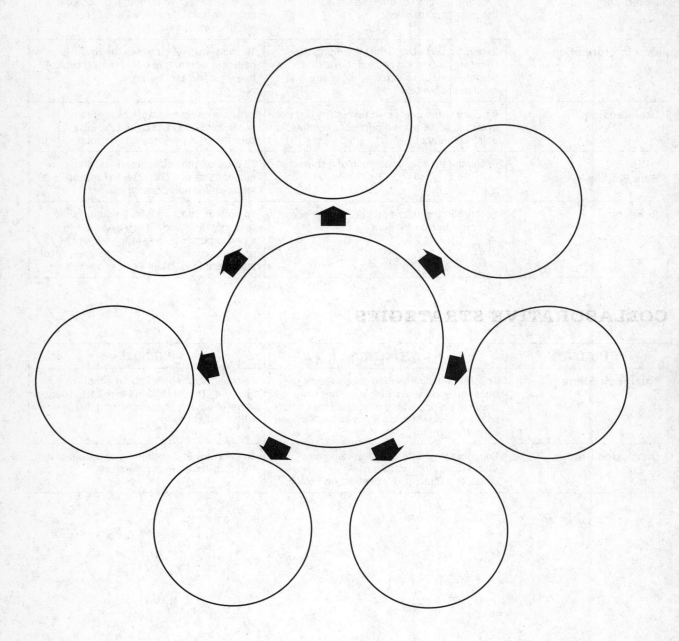

Word Map

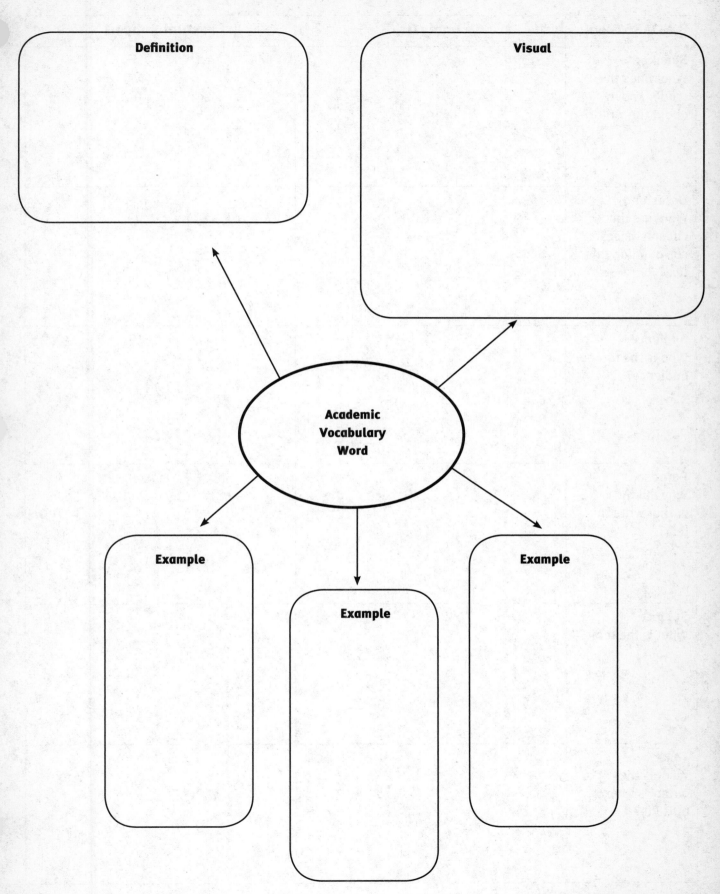

Definition

Visual

Academic
Vocabulary
Word

Example

Example

Example

SOAPSTone:

SOAPSTone	Analysis	Textual Support
Speaker: What does the reader know about the writer?		
Occasion: What are the circumstances surrounding this text?		
Audience: Who is the target audience?		
Purpose: Why did the author write this text?		
Subject: What is the topic?		
Tone: What is the author's tone, or attitude?		

TP-CASTT Analysis

Poem Title:

Author:

Title: Make a prediction. What do you think the title means before you read the poem?

Paraphrase: Translate the poem in your own words. What is the poem about? Rephrase difficult sections word for word.

Connotation: Look beyond the literal meaning of key words and images to their associations.

Attitude: What is the speaker's attitude? What is the author's attitude? How does the author feel about the speaker, about other characters, about the subject?

Shifts: Where do the shifts in tone, setting, voice, etc., occur? Look for time and place, keywords, punctuation, stanza divisions, changes in length or rhyme, and sentence structure. What is the purpose of each shift? How do they contribute to effect and meaning?

Title: Reexamine the title. What do you think it means now in the context of the poem?

Theme: Think of the literal and metaphorical layers of the poem. Then determine the overall theme. The theme must be written in a complete sentence.

Glossary
Glosario

A

active-voice verbs: a verb form indicating that the subject performs the action
verbos en voz activa: forma verbal que indica que el sujeto realiza la acción

advertising techniques: specific methods used in print, graphics, or videos to persuade people to buy a product or use a service
técnicas publicitarias: métodos específicos usados en impresos, gráfica o videos para persuadir a las personas a comprar un producto o usar un servicio

alliteration: the repetition of initial consonant sounds in words that are close together
aliteración: repetición de sonidos consonánticos iniciales en palabras cercanas

allusion: a reference to a well-known person, event, or place from history, music, art, or another literary work
alusión: referencia a una persona, evento o lugar muy conocidos de la historia, música, arte u otra obra literaria

anaphora: the repetition of the same word or group of words at the beginnings of two or more clauses or lines
anáfora: repetición de la misma palabra o grupo de palabras al comienzo de una o más cláusulas o versos

anecdotal evidence: evidence based on personal accounts of incidents
evidencia anecdótica: evidencia basada en relatos personales de los hechos

annotated bibliography: a list of sources used in research along with comments about each source
bibliografía anotada: lista de fuentes utilizadas en la investigación, junto con comentarios acerca de cada fuente

antagonist: the character who opposes or struggles again the main character
antagonista: personaje que se opone o lucha contra el personaje principal

aphorism: a succinct statement expressing an opinion or general truth
aforismo: afirmación breve que expresa una opinión o verdad general

archetypes: universal symbols—images, characters, motifs, or patterns—that recur in myths, art and literature through the world
arquetipos: símbolos universales —imágenes, personajes, motivos o patrones— reiterativos en los mitos, el arte y la literatura alrededor del mundo

archival footage: film footage taken from another, previously recorded, source
cortometraje de archivo: fragmento de película tomada de otra fuente grabada previamente

argument: a form of writing that presents a particular opinion or idea and supports it with evidence
argumento: forma de redacción que presenta una opinión o idea particular y la apoya con evidencia

argumentation: the structure of an argument includes the *hook* (quotation, example, or idea that catches readers' attention), *claim* (the opinion or thesis statement), *support* (evidence in the form of facts, statistics, examples, anecdotes, or expert opinions), *concession* (the writer's admission that the other side of the argument has a valid point), *refutation* (a well-reasoned denial of an opponent's point, based on solid evidence), and *call to action* (an inspired request of readers)
argumentación: la estructura de una argumentación incluye el gancho (cita, ejemplo o idea que capta la atención del lector), afirmación (declaración de opinión o tesis), apoyo (evidencia en forma de hechos, estadísticas, ejemplos, anécdotas u opiniones de expertos), concesión (admisión por parte del escritor de que la otra parte del debate tiene un punto válido), refutación (negación bien razonada de una opinión del oponente, basada en evidencia sólida) y llamado a la acción (petición inspirada de lectores)

argument by analogy: a comparison of two similar situations, implying that the outcome of one will resemble the outcome of the other
argumento por analogía: comparación de dos situaciones semejantes, infiriendo que el resultado de será parecido al resultado de la otra

aside: a short speech spoken by an actor directly to the audience and unheard by other actors on stage
aparte: alocución breve dicha por un actor directamente al público y que no escuchan los demás actores que están en el escenario

assonance: the repetition of similar vowel sounds in accented syllables, followed by different consonant sounds, in words that are close together
asonancia: repetición de sonidos vocálicos similares en sílabas acentuadas, seguida de diferentes sonidos consonánticos, en palabras que están cercanas

audience: the intended readers, listeners, or viewers of specific types of written, spoken or visual texts
público: lectores objetivo, oyentes o espectadores de tipos específicos de textos escritos, hablados o visuales

audience analysis: determining the knowledge, beliefs, and needs of a target audience in order to reach them successfully
análisis del público: determinar los conocimientos, creencias y necesidades de una audiencia objetivo de modo de llegar a ella con éxito

author's purpose: the specific reason or reasons for the writing; what the author hopes to accomplish
propósito del autor: razón específica para escribir; lo que el autor espera lograr

B

balanced sentence: a sentence that presents ideas of equal weight in similar grammatical forms to emphasize the similarity or difference between the ideas
oración balanceada: oración que representa ideas de igual peso en formas gramaticales similares para enfatizar la semejanza o diferencia entre las ideas

bias: an inclination or mental leaning for or against something, which prevents impartial judgment
sesgo: inclinación o tendencia mental a favor o en contra de algo, lo que impide una opinión imparcial

blank verse: unrhymed verse
verso libre: verso que no tiene rima

blocking: in drama, how actors position themselves in relation to one another, the audience, and the objects on the stage
bloqueo: en drama, el modo en que los actores se sitúan entre sí, con el público y los objetos en el escenario

C

caricature: a visual or verbal representation in which characteristics or traits are exaggerated or distorted for emphasis
caricatura: representación visual o verbal en la que las características o rasgos se exageran o se distorsionan para dar énfasis

characterization: the methods a writer uses to develop characters
caracterización: métodos que usa un escritor para desarrollar personajes

characters: people, animals, or imaginary creatures that take part in the action of a story. A short story usually centers on a *main character*, but may also contain one or more *minor characters*, who are not as complex, but whose thoughts, words, or actions move the plot along. A character who is *dynamic* changes in response to the events of the narrative; a character who is *static* remains the same throughout the narrative. A *round* character is fully developed—he or she shows a variety of traits; a *flat* character is one-dimensional, usually showing only one trait.
personajes: personas, animales o criaturas imaginarias que participan en la acción de un cuento. Un cuento corto normalmente se centra en un *personaje principal*, pero puede también contener uno o más *personajes secundarios*, que no son tan complejos, pero cuyos pensamientos, palabras o acciones hacen avanzar la trama. Un personaje que es *dinámico* cambia según los eventos del relato; un personaje que es *estático* permanece igual a lo largo del relato. Un personaje *complejo* está completamente desarrollado: muestra una diversidad de rasgos; un personaje *simple* es unidimensional, mostrando normalmente sólo un rasgo.

chorus: in traditional or classic drama, a group of performers who speak as one and comment on the action of the play
coro: en el drama tradicional o clásico, grupo de actores que hablan al unísono y comentan la acción de la obra teatral

cinematic elements: the features of cinema—movies, film, video—that contribute to its form and structure: *angles* (the view from which the image is shot); *framing* (how a scene is structured); *lighting* (the type of lighting used to light a scene); and *mise en scène* (the composition, setting, or staging of an image, or a scene in a film); *sound* (the sound effects and music accompanying each scene)
elementos cinematográficos: las características del cine—películas, filmaciones, video—que contribuyen a darle forma y estructura: *angulación* (vista desde la cual se toma la imagen); *encuadre* (cómo se estructura una escena); *iluminación* (tipo de iluminación que se usa para una escena); y *montaje* (composición, ambiente o escenificación de una imagen o escena en una película); *sonido* (efectos sonoros y música que acompañan cada escena)

claim: a position statement (or thesis) that asserts an idea or makes an argument
afirmación: declaración de opinión (o tesis) que asevera una idea o establece un debate

cliché: an overused expression or idea
cliché: expresión o idea que se usa en exceso

climax: the point at which the action reaches its peak; the point of greatest interest or suspense in a story; the turning point at which the outcome of the conflict is decided
clímax: punto en el que la acción alcanza su punto culminante; punto de mayor interés en un cuento; punto de inflexión en el que se decide el resultado del conflicto

coherence: the quality of unity or logical connection among ideas; the clear and orderly presentation of ideas in a paragraph or essay
coherencia: calidad de unidad o relación lógica entre las ideas; presentación clara y ordenada de las ideas en un párrafo o ensayo

commentary: in an expository essay or paragraph, the explanation of the importance or relevance of supporting detail and the way the details support the larger analysis
comentario: ensayo o párrafo expositivo, explicación de la importancia o relevancia de los detalles de apoyo, y la manera en que los detalles apoyan el análisis principal

complex sentence: a sentence containing one independent clause and one or more subordinate clauses
oración compleja: oración que contiene una cláusula independiente y una o más cláusulas subordinadas

complications: the events in a plot that develop the conflict; the complications move the plot forward in its rising action
complicaciones: sucesos de una trama que desarrollan el conflicto; las complicaciones hacen avanzar la trama en su acción ascendente

compound sentence: a sentence containing two independent clauses
oración compuesta: oración que contiene dos cláusulas independientes

concession: an admission in an argument that the opposing side has valid points
concesión: admitir en un debate que el lado opositor tiene opiniones válidas

conflict: a struggle or problem in a story. An *internal conflict* occurs when a character struggles between opposing needs or desires or emotions within his or her own mind. An *external conflict* occurs when a character struggles against an outside force. This force may be another character, a societal expectation, or something in the physical world.

conflicto: lucha o problema en un cuento. Un *conflicto interno* ocurre cuando un personaje lucha entre necesidades o deseos o emociones que se contraponen dentro de su mente. Un *conflicto externo* ocurre cuando un personaje lucha contra una fuerza externa. Esta fuerza puede ser otro personaje, una expectativa social o algo del mundo físico.

connotation: the associations and emotional overtones attached to a word beyond its literal definition or denotation. A connotation may be positive, negative, or neutral.

connotación: asociaciones y alusiones emocionales unidas a una palabra más allá de su definición literal o denotación. Una connotación puede ser positiva, negativa o neutra.

consonance: the repetition of final consonant sounds in stressed syllables with different vowel sounds

consonancia: repetición de sonidos consonánticos finales en sílabas acentuadas con diferentes sonidos vocálicos

context: the circumstances or conditions in which something takes place

contexto: circunstancias o condiciones en las que algo ocurre

conventions: standard practices and forms

convenciones: prácticas y formas usuales

couplet: two consecutive lines of verse with end rhyme; a couplet usually expresses a complete unit of thought

copla: dos líneas de versos consecutivos con rima final; una copla normalmente expresa una unidad de pensamiento completa

credibility: the quality of being trusted or believed

credibilidad: calidad de ser confiable o creíble

critical lens: a particular identifiable perspective as in Reader Response Criticism, Cultural Criticism, etc., through which a text can be analyzed and interpreted

ojo crítico: punto de vista particular identificable como por ejemplo Teoría de la recepción, Crítica sociocultural, etc., por medio del que se puede analizar e interpretar un texto

cultural conflict: a struggle that occurs when people with different cultural expectations or attitudes interact

conflicto cultural: lucha que ocurre cuando interactúan personas con diferentes expectativas o actitudes culturales

culture: the shared set of arts, ideas, skills, institutions, customs, attitude, values and achievements that characterize a group of people, and that are passed on or taught to succeeding generations

cultura: conjunto de artes, ideas, destrezas, instituciones, costumbres, actitud, valores y logros compartidos que caracterizan a un grupo de personas, y que se transfieren o enseñan a las generaciones siguientes

cumulative (or loose) sentence: a sentence in which the main clause comes first, followed by subordinate structures or clauses

oración acumulativa (o frases sueltas): oración cuya cláusula principal viene primero, seguida de estructuras o cláusulas subordinadas

D

deductive reasoning: a process of using general information from which to draw a specific conclusion

razonamiento deductivo: proceso en que se usa información general para sacar una conclusión específica

denotation: the exact literal meaning of a word

denotación: significado literal exacto de una palabra

detail: a specific fact, observation, or incident; any of the small pieces or parts that make up something else

detalle: hecho, observación o incidente específico; cualquiera de las pequeñas piezas o partes que constituyen otra cosa

dialect: the distinctive language, including the sounds, spelling, grammar, and diction, of a specific group or class of people

dialecto: lenguaje distintivo, incluyendo sonidos, ortografía, gramática y dicción, de un grupo o clase específico de personas

dialogue: the words spoken by characters in a narrative or film

diálogo: palabras que dicen los personajes en un relato o película

diction: the writer's choice of words; a stylistic element that helps convey voice and tone

dicción: selección de palabras por parte del escritor; elemento estilístico que ayuda a transmitir voz y tono

diegetic sound: actual noises associated with the shooting of a scene, such as voices and background sounds

sonido diegético: sonidos reales asociados con la filmación de una escena, como por ejemplo voces y sonidos de fondo

discourse: the language or speech used in a particular context or subject

discurso: lenguaje o habla usada en un contexto o tema en particular

documentary or nonfiction film: a genre of filmmaking that provides a visual record of factual events, using photographs, video footage, and interviews

documental o película de no-ficción: género cinematográfico que realiza un registro visual de sucesos basados en hechos por medio del uso de fotografías, registro en videos y entrevistas

drama: a play written for stage, radio, film, or television, usually about a serious topic or situation

drama: obra teatral escrita para representar en un escenario, radio, cine o televisión, normalmente sobre un tema o situación seria

E

editorial: an article in a newspaper or magazine expressing the opinion of its editor or publisher

editorial: artículo de periódico o revista, que expresa la opinión de su editor

effect: the result or influence of using a specific literary or cinematic device

efecto: resultado o influencia de usar un recurso literario o cinematográfico específico

empirical evidence: evidence based on experiences and direct observation through research
evidencia empírica: evidencia basada en experiencias y en la observación directa por medio de la investigación

epigram: a short witty saying
epigrama: dicho corto e ingenioso

ethos: (ethical appeal) a rhetorical appeal that focuses on ethics, or the character or qualifications of the speaker
ethos: (recurso ético) recurso retórico centrado en la ética o en el carácter o capacidades del orador

evidence: the information that supports or proves an idea or claim; forms of evidence include facts, statistics (numerical facts), expert opinions, examples, and anecdotes; *see also*, anecdotal, empirical, and logical evidence
evidencia: información que apoya o prueba una idea o afirmación; formas de evidencia incluyen hechos, estadística (datos numéricos), opiniones de expertos, ejemplos y anécdotas; *ver también* evidencia anecdótica, empírica y lógica

exaggeration: representing something as larger, better, or worse than it really is
exageración: representar algo como más grande, mejor o peor que lo que realmente es

explicit theme: a theme that is clearly stated by the writer
tema explícito: tema que está claramente establecido por el escritor

exposition: events that give a reader background information needed to understand a story. During exposition, characters are introduced, the setting is described, and the conflict begins to unfold.
exposición: sucesos que dan al lector los antecedentes necesarios para comprender un cuento. Durante la exposición, se presentan los personajes, se describe el ambiente y se comienza a revelar el conflicto.

extended metaphor: a metaphor extended over several lines or throughout an entire poem
metáfora extendida: metáfora que se extiende por varios versos o a través de un poema completo

F

falling action: the events in a play, story, or novel that follow the climax, or moment of greatest suspense, and lead to the resolution
acción descendente: sucesos de una obra teatral, cuento o novela posteriores al clímax, o momento de mayor suspenso, y que conllevan a la resolución

fallacy: a false or misleading argument
falacia: argumento falso o engañoso

figurative language: imaginative language not meant to be taken literally; figurative language uses figures of speech
lenguaje figurativo: lenguaje imaginativo que no pretende ser tomado literalmente; el lenguaje figurativo usa figuras literarias

flashback: an interruption in the sequence of events to relate events that occurred in the past
flashback: interrupción en la secuencia de los sucesos para relatar sucesos ocurridos en el pasado

fixed form: a form of poetry in which the length and pattern are determined by established usage of tradition, such as a sonnet
forma fija: forma de poesía en la que la longitud y el patrón están determinados por el uso de la tradición, como un soneto

foil: a character whose actions or thoughts are juxtaposed against those of a major character in order to highlight key attributes of the major character
antagonista: personaje cuyas acciones o pensamientos se yuxtaponen a los de un personaje principal con el fin de destacar atributos clave del personaje principal

folk tale: a story without a known author that has been preserved through oral retellings
cuento folclórico: cuento sin autor conocido que se ha conservado por medio de relatos orales

footage: literally, a length of film; the expression is still used to refer to digital video clips
metraje: literalmente, la longitud de una película; la expresión aún se usa para referirse a video clips digitales

foreshadowing: the use of hints or clues in a narrative to suggest future action
presagio: uso de claves o pistas en un relato para sugerir una acción futura

free verse: poetry without a fixed pattern of meter and rhyme
verso libre: poesía que no sigue ningún patrón, ritmo o rima regular

G

genre: a kind or style of literature or art, each with its own specific characteristics. For example, poetry, short story, and novel are literary genres. Painting and sculpture are artistic genres.
género: tipo o estilo de literatura o arte, cada uno con sus propias características específicas. Por ejemplo, la poesía, el cuento corto y la novela son géneros literarios. La pintura y la escultura son géneros artísticos.

genre conventions: the essential features and format that characterize a specific genre
convenciones genéricas: características básicas y el formato que caracterizan un género específico

graphics: images or text used to provide information on screen
gráfica: imágenes o texto que se usa para dar información en pantalla

graphic novel: a book-length narrative, or story, in the form of a comic strip rather than words
novela gráfica: narrativa o cuento del largo de un libro, en forma de tira cómica más que palabras

H

hamartia: a tragic hero's fatal flaw; an ingrained character trait that causes a hero to make decisions that ultimately lead to his or her death or downfall
hamartia: error fatal de un héroe trágico; característica propia de un personaje que causa que un héroe tome decisiones que finalmente llevan a su muerte o caída

hero: the main character or protagonist of a play, with whom audiences become emotionally invested
héroe: personaje principal o protagonista de una obra teatral, con el que el público se involucra emocionalmente

hook: an interesting quotation, anecdote, or example at the beginning of a piece of writing that grabs readers' attention
gancho: cita, anécdota o ejemplo interesante al comienzo de un escrito, que capta la atención del lector

humor: the quality of being amusing
humor: calidad de ser divertido

hyperbole: exaggeration used to suggest strong emotion or create a comic effect
hipérbole: exageración que se usa para sugerir una emoción fuerte o crear un efecto cómico

I

iamb: a metrical foot that consists of an unstressed syllable followed by a stressed syllable
yambo: pie métrico que consta de una sílaba átona seguida de una sílaba acentuada

iambic pentameter: a rhythmic pattern of five feet (or units) of one unstressed syllable followed by a stressed syllable
pentámetro yámbico: patrón rítmico de cinco pies (o unidades) de una sílaba átona seguida de una sílaba acentuada

image: a word or phrase that appeals to one of more of the five senses and creates a picture
imagen: palabra o frase que apela a uno o más de los cinco sentido y crea un cuadro

imagery: the verbal expression of sensory experience; descriptive or figurative language used to create word pictures; imagery is created by details that appeal to one or more of the five senses
imaginería: lenguaje descriptivo o figurativo utilizado para crear imágenes verbales; la imaginería es creada por detalles que apelan a uno o más de los cinco sentidos

implied theme: a theme that is understood through the writer's diction, language construction, and use of literary devices
tema implícito: tema que se entiende a través de la dicción del escritor, construcción lingüística y uso de recursos literarios

inductive reasoning: a process of looking at individual facts to draw a general conclusion
razonamiento inductivo: proceso de observación de hechos individuales para sacar una conclusión general

interior monologue: a literary device in which a character's internal emotions and thoughts are presented
monólogo interior: recurso literario en el que se presentan las emociones internas y pensamientos de un personaje

irony: a literary device that exploits readers' expectations; irony occurs when what is expected turns out to be quite different from what actually happens. *Dramatic irony* is a form of irony in which the reader or audience knows more about the circumstances or future events in a story than the characters within it; *verbal irony* occurs when a speaker or narrator says one thing while meaning the opposite; *situational irony* occurs

when an event contradicts the expectations of the characters or the reader.
ironía: recurso literario que explota las expectativas de los lectores; la ironía ocurre cuando lo que se espera resulta ser bastante diferente de lo que realmente ocurre. La *ironía dramática* es una forma de ironía en la que el lector o la audiencia saben más acerca de las circunstancias o sucesos futuros de un cuento que los personajes del mismo; la *ironía verbal* ocurre cuando un orador o narrador dice una cosa queriendo decir lo contrario; la *ironía situacional* ocurre cuando un suceso contradice las expectativas de los personajes o del lector.

J

justice: the quality of being reasonable and fair in the administration of the law; the ideal of rightness or fairness
justicia: calidad de ser razonable e imparcial en la administración de la ley; ideal de rectitud o equidad

juxtaposition: the arrangement of two or more things for the purpose of comparison
yuxtaposición: ordenamiento de dos o más cosas con el objeto de compararlas

L

literary theory: attempts to establish principles for interpreting and evaluating literary texts
teoría literaria: intento de establecer principios para interpretar y evaluar textos literarios

logical evidence: evidence based on facts and a clear rationale
evidencia lógica: evidencia basada en hechos y una clara fundamentación

logos: (logical appeal) a rhetorical appeal that uses logic to appeal to the sense of reason
logos: (apelación lógica) apelación retórica que usa la lógica para apelar al sentido de la razón

M

metacognition: the ability to know and be aware of one's own thought processes; self-reflection
metacognición: capacidad de conocer y estar consciente de los propios procesos del pensamiento; introspección

metaphor: a comparison between two unlike things in which one thing is spoken of as if it were another; for example, the moon was a crisp white cracker
metáfora: comparación entre dos cosas diferentes en la que se habla de una cosa como si fuera otra; por ejemplo, la luna era una galletita blanca crujiente

meter: a pattern of stressed and unstressed syllables in poetry
métrica: patrón de sílabas acentuadas y átonas en poesía

monologue: a dramatic speech delivered by a single character in a play
monólogo: discurso dramático que hace un solo personaje en una obra teatral

montage: a composite picture that is created by bringing together a number of images and arranging them to create a connected whole

montaje: cuadro compuesto que se crea al reunir un número de imágenes y que al organizarlas se crea un todo relacionado

mood: the atmosphere or general feeling in a literary work
carácter: atmósfera o sentimiento general en una obra literaria

motif: a recurrent image, symbol, theme, character type, subject, or narrative detail that becomes a unifying element in an artistic work.
motivo: imagen, símbolo, tema, tipo de personaje, tema o detalle narrativo recurrente que se convierte en un elemento unificador en una obra artística.

myth: a traditional story that explains the actions of gods or heroes or the origins of the elements of nature
mito: cuento tradicional que explica las acciones de dioses o héroes, o los orígenes de los elementos de la naturaleza

N

narration: the act of telling a story
narración: acto de contar un cuento

non-diegetic sound: voice-overs and commentary, sounds that do not come from the action on screen.
sonido no diegético: voces y comentarios superpuestos, sonidos que no provienen de la acción en pantalla.

O

objective: based on factual information
objetivo: basado en información de hechos

objectivity: the representation of facts or ideas without injecting personal feelings or biases
objetividad: representación de los hechos o ideas sin agregar sentimientos o prejuicios personales

ode: a lyric poem expressing feelings or thoughts of a speaker, often celebrating a person, event, or a thing
oda: poema lírico que expresa sentimientos o pensamientos de un orador, que frecuentemente celebra a una persona, suceso o cosa

onomatopoeia: words whose sound suggest their meaning
onomatopeya: palabras cuyo sonido sugiere su significado

oral tradition: the passing down of stories, tales, proverbs, and other culturally important stories and ideas through oral retellings
tradición oral: traspaso de historias, cuentos, proverbios y otras historias de importancia cultural por medio de relatos orales

oxymoron: words that appear to contradict each other; e.g., cold fire
oxímoron: palabras que parecen contradecirse mutuamente; por ejemplo, fuego frío

P

parallel structure (parallelism): refers to a grammatical or structural similarity between sentences or parts of a sentence, so that elements of equal importance are equally developed and similarly phrased for emphasis
estructura paralela (paralelismo): se refiere a una similitud gramatical o estructural entre oraciones o partes de una oración, de modo que los elementos de igual importancia se desarrollen por igual y se expresen de manera similar para dar énfasis

paraphrase: to briefly restate ideas from another source in one's own words
parafrasear: volver a presentar las ideas de otra fuente en nuestras propias palabras

parody: a literary or artistic work that imitates the characteristic style of an author or a work for comic effect or ridicule
parodia: obra literaria o artística que imita el estilo característico de un autor o una obra para dar un efecto cómico o ridículo

passive-voice verbs: verb form in which the subject receives the action; the passive voice consists of a form of the verb be plus a past participle of the verb
verbos en voz pasiva: forma verbal en la que el sujeto recibe la acción; la voz pasiva se forma con el verbo ser más el participio pasado de un verbo

pathos: (emotional appeal) a rhetorical appeal to readers' or listeners' senses or emotions
pathos: (apelación emocional) apelación retórica a los sentidos o emociones de los lectores u oyentes

periodic sentence: a sentence that makes sense only when the end of the sentence is reached; that is, when the main clause comes last
oración periódica: oración que tiene sentido sólo cuando se llega al final de la oración; es decir, cuando la cláusula principal viene al final

persona: the voice assumed by a writer to express ideas or beliefs that may not be his or her own
personaje: voz que asume un escritor para expresar ideas o creencias que pueden no ser las propias

personification: a figure of speech that gives human qualities to an animal, object, or idea
personificación: figura literaria que da características humanas a un animal, objeto o idea

persuasive argument: an argument that convinces readers to accept or believe a writer's perspective on a topic
argumento persuasivo: argumento que convence a los lectores a aceptar o creer en la perspectiva de un escritor acerca de un tema

perspective: a way of looking at the world or a mental concept about things or events, one that judges relationships within or among things or events
perspectiva: manera de visualizar el mundo o concepto mental de las cosas o sucesos, que juzga las relaciones dentro o entre cosas o sucesos

photo essay: a collection of photographic images that reveal the author's perspective on the subject
ensayo fotográfico: recolección de imágenes fotográficas que revelan la perspectiva del autor acerca del tema

plagiarism: the unattributed use of another writer's words or ideas
plagio: usar como propias las palabras o ideas de otro escritor

plot: the sequence of related events that make up a story or novel
trama: secuencia de sucesos relacionados que conforman un cuento o novela

poetic structure: the organization of words, lines, and images as well as ideas
estructura poética: organización de las palabras, versos e imágenes, así como también de las ideas

point of view: the perspective from which a narrative is told; i.e., first person, third person limited, third person omniscient
punto de vista: perspectiva desde la cual se cuenta un relato; es decir, primera persona, tercera persona limitada, tercera persona omnisciente

precept: a rule, instruction, or principle that guides somebody's actions and/or moral behavior
precepto: regla, instrucción o principio que guía las acciones y/o conducta moral de alguien

primary footage: film footage shot by the filmmaker for the text at hand
metraje principal: filmación hecha por el cineasta para el texto que tiene a mano

primary source: an original document containing firsthand information about a subject
fuente primaria: documento original que contiene información de primera mano acerca de un tema

prologue: the introduction or preface to a literary work
prólogo: introducción o prefacio de una obra literaria

prose: ordinary written or spoken language using sentences and paragraphs, without deliberate or regular meter or rhyme; not poetry or song
prosa: forma común del lenguaje escrito o hablado, usando oraciones y párrafos, sin métrica o rima deliberada o regular; ni poesía ni canción

protagonist: the central character in a work of literature, the one who is involved in the main conflict in the plot
protagonista: personaje central de una obra literaria, el que participa en el conflicto principal de la trama

Q
quatrain: a four-line stanza in a poem
cuarteta: en un poema, estrofa de cuatro versos

R
reasoning: the thinking or logic used to make a claim in an argument
razonamiento: pensamiento o lógica que se usa para hacer una afirmación en un argumento

refrain: a regularly repeated line or group of lines in a poem or song, usually at the end of a stanza
estribillo: verso o grupo de versos que se repiten con regularidad en un poema o canción, normalmente al final de una estrofa

refutation: the reasoning used to disprove an opposing point
refutación: razonamiento que se usa para rechazar una opinión contraria

reliability: the extent to which a source provides good quality and trustworthy information
confiabilidad: grado en el que una fuente da información confiable y de buena calidad

repetition: the use of any element of language—a sound, a word, a phrase, a line, or a stanza—more than once
repetición: uso de cualquier elemento del lenguaje—un sonido, una palabra, una frase, un verso o una estrofa—más de una vez

resolution (denouement): the end of a play, story, or novel in which the main conflict is finally resolved
resolución (desenlace): final de una obra teatral, cuento o novela, en el que el conflicto principal finalmente se resuelve

résumé: a document that outlines a person's skills, education, and work history
currículum vitae: documento que resume las destrezas, educación y experiencia laboral de una persona

rhetoric: the art of using words to persuade in writing or speaking
retórica: arte de usar las palabras para persuadir por escrito o de manera hablada

rhetorical appeals: the use of emotional, ethical, and logical arguments to persuade in writing or speaking
recursos retóricos: uso de argumentos emocionales, éticos y lógicos para persuadir por escrito o de manera hablada

rhetorical context: the subject, purpose, audience, occasion, or situation in which writing occurs
contexto retórico: sujeto, propósito, audiencia, ocasión o situación en que ocurre el escrito

rhetorical devices: specific techniques used in writing or speaking to create a literary effect or enhance effectiveness
dispositivos retóricos: técnicas específicas que se usan al escribir o al hablar para crear un efecto literario o mejorar la efectividad

rhetorical question: a question that is asked for effect or one for which the answer is obvious
pregunta retórica: pregunta hecha para producir un efecto o cuya respuesta es obvia

rhyme: the repetition of sounds at the ends of words
rima: repetición de sonidos al final de las palabras

rhyme scheme: a consistent pattern of rhyme throughout a poem
esquema de la rima: patrón consistente de una rima a lo largo de un poema

rhythm: the pattern of stressed and unstressed syllables in spoken or written language, especially in poetry
ritmo: patrón de sílabas acentuadas y no acentuadas en lenguaje hablado o escrito, especialmente en poesía

rising action: the movement of a plot toward a climax or moment of greatest excitement; the rising action is fueled by the characters' responses to the conflict
acción ascendente: movimiento de una trama hacia el clímax o momento de mayor emoción; la acción ascendente es impulsada por las reacciones de los personajes ante el conflicto

S

satire: a manner of writing that mixes a critical attitude with wit and humor in an effort to improve mankind and human institutions
sátira: manera de escribir que mezcla una actitud crítica con ingenio y humor en un esfuerzo por mejorar a la humanidad y las instituciones humanas

scenario: an outline, a brief account, a script, or a synopsis of a proposed series of events
escenario: bosquejo, relato breve, libreto o sinopsis de una serie de sucesos propuestos

secondary source: discussion about or commentary on a primary source; the key feature of a secondary source is that it offers an interpretation of information gathered from primary sources
fuente secundaria: discusión o comentario acerca de una fuente primaria; la característica clave de una fuente secundaria es que ofrece una interpretación de la información recopilada en las fuentes primarias

sensory details: details that appeal to or evoke one or more of the five senses--sight, sound, smell, taste, touch
detalles sensoriales: detalles que apelan o evocan uno o más de los cinco sentidos: vista, oído, gusto, olfato, tacto

sensory images: images that appeal to the reader's senses— sight, sound, smell, taste, touch
imágenes sensoriales: imágenes que apelan a los sentidos del lector: vista, oído, olfato, gusto, tacto

setting: the time and place in which a story happens
ambiente: tiempo y lugar en el que ocurre un relato

simile: a comparison of two or more unlike things using the words *like or as*; for example, the moon was as white as milk
símil: comparación entre dos o más cosas diferentes usando las palabras *como o tan*; por ejemplo, la luna estaba tan blanca como la leche

slanters: rhetorical devices used to present the subject in a biased way.
soslayo: recursos retóricos para presentar el tema de modo sesgado.

slogan: a short, catchy phrase used for advertising by a business, club, or political party
eslogan: frase corta y tendenciosa que usa como publicidad para un negocio, club o partido político

social commentary: an expression of an opinion with the goal of promoting change by appealing to a sense of justice
comentario social: expresión de una opinión con el objeto de promover el cambio al apelar a un sentido de justicia

soliloquy: a long speech delivered by an actor alone on the stage
soliloquio: discurso largo realizado por un actor sobre el escenario

sonnet: a fourteen-line lyric poem, usually written in iambic pentameter and following a strict pattern of rhyme
soneto: poema lírico de catorce versos, normalmente escrito en un pentámetro yámbico y que sigue un patrón de rima estricto

speaker: the imaginary voice or persona of the writer or author
orador: voz o persona imaginaria del escritor o autor

stakeholder: a person motivated or affected by a course of action
participante: persona motivada o afectada por el curso de una acción

stanza: a group of lines, usually similar in length and pattern, that form a unit within a poem
estrofa: grupo de versos, normalmente similares en longitud y patrón, que forman una unidad dentro de un poema

stereotype: an oversimplified, generalized conception, opinion, and/or image about particular groups of people.
estereotipo: concepto generalizado, opinión y/o imagen demasiado simplificada acerca de grupos específicos de personas.

structure: the way a literary work is organized; the arrangement of the parts in a literary work
estructura: manera en que la obra literaria está organizada; disposición de las partes en una obra literaria

style: the distinctive way a writer uses language, characterized by elements of diction, syntax, imagery, etc.
estilo: manera distintiva en que un escritor usa el lenguaje, caracterizada por elementos de dicción, sintaxis, lenguaje figurado, etc.

subculture: a smaller subsection of a culture; for example, within the culture of a high school may be many subcultures
subcultura: subsección más pequeña de una cultura; por ejemplo, dentro de la cultura de una escuela secundaria puede haber muchas subculturas

subjectivity: based on one's personal point of view, opinion, or values
subjetividad: en base en nuestro punto de vista, opinión o valores personales

subtext: the underlying or implicit meaning in dialogue or the implied relationship between characters in a book, movie, play or film. The subtext of a work is not explicitly stated.
subtexto: significado subyacente o implícito en el diálogo o la relación implícita entre los personajes de un libro, película, u obra teatral. El subtexto de una obra no se establece de manera explícita.

survey: a method of collecting data from a group of people; it can be written, such as a print or online questionnaire, or oral, such as an in-person interview
encuesta: método para recolectar datos de un grupo de personas; puede ser escrita, como un impreso o cuestionario en línea, u oral, como en una entrevista personal

symbol: anything (object, animal, event, person, or place) that represents itself but also stands for something else on a figurative level
símbolo: cualquier cosa (objeto, animal, evento, persona o lugar) que se representa a sí misma, pero también representa otra cosa a nivel figurativo

symbolic: serving as a symbol; involving the use of symbols or symbolism

simbólico: que sirve como símbolo; que implica el uso de símbolos o simbolismo

syntax: the arrangement of words and the order of grammatical elements in a sentence; the way in which words are put together to make meaningful elements, such as phrases, clauses, and sentences

sintaxis: disposición de las palabras y orden de los elementos gramaticales en una oración; manera en que las palabras se juntan para formar elementos significativos, como frases, cláusulas y oraciones

synthesis: the act of combining ideas from different sources to create, express, or support a new idea

síntesis: acto de combinar ideas de diferentes fuentes para crear, expresar o apoyar una nueva idea

T

target audience: the intended group for which a work is designed to appeal or reach

público objetivo: grupo al que se pretende apelar o llegar con una obra

thematic statement: an interpretive statement articulating the central meaning or message of a text

oración temática: afirmación interpretativa que articula el significado o mensaje central de un texto

theatrical elements: elements employed by dramatists and directors to tell a story on stage. Elements include *costumes* (the clothing worn by actors to express their characters), *makeup* (cosmetics used to change actors' appearances and express their characters), *props* (objects used to help set the scene, advance a plot and make a story realistic), *set* (the place where the action takes place, as suggested by objects, such as furniture, placed on a stage), *acting choices* (gestures, movements, staging, and vocal techniques actors use to convey their characters and tell a story).

elementos teatrales: elementos que utilizan los dramaturgos y directores para contar una historia en el escenario. Los elementos incluyen *vestuario* (ropa que usan los actores para expresar sus personajes), *maquillaje* (cosméticos que se usan para cambiar la apariencia de los actores y expresar sus personajes), *elementos* (objetos que se usan para ayudar a montar la escena, avanzar la trama y crear una historia realista), *plató* (lugar donde tiene lugar la acción, según lo sugieren los objetos, como muebles, colocados sobre un escenario), *opciones de actuación* (gestos, movimientos, representación y técnicas vocales que se usan para transmitir sus personajes y narrar una historia).

theme: a writer's central idea or main message about life; *see also*, explicit theme, implied theme

tema: idea central o mensaje principal acerca de la vida de un escritor; *véase también*, tema explícito, tema implícito

thesis: the main idea or point of an essay or article; in an argumentative essay the thesis is the writer's position on an issue

tesis: idea o punto principal de un ensayo o artículo; en un ensayo argumentativo, la tesis es la opinión del autor acerca de un tema

topic sentence: a sentence that states the main idea of a paragraph; in an essay, it also makes a point that supports the thesis statement

oración principal: oración que establece la idea principal de un párrafo; en un ensayo, también establece una proposición que apoya el enunciado de la tesis

tone: a writer's or speaker's attitude toward a subject

tono: actitud de un escritor u orador acerca de un tema

tragedy: a dramatic play that tells the story of a character, usually of a noble birth, who meets an untimely and unhappy death or downfall, often because of a specific character flaw or twist of fate

tragedia: obra teatral dramática que cuenta la historia de un personaje, normalmente de origen noble, que encuentra una muerte o caída imprevista o infeliz, con frecuencia debido a un defecto específico del personaje o una vuelta del destino

tragic hero: an archetypal hero based on the Greek concept of tragedy; the tragic hero has a flaw that makes him vulnerable to downfall or death

héroe trágico: héroe arquetípico basado en el concepto griego de la tragedia; el héroe trágico tiene un defecto que lo hace vulnerable a la caída o a la muerte

U

understatement: the representation of something as smaller or less significant than it really is; the opposite of exaggeration or hyperbole

subestimación: representación de algo como más pequeño o menos importante de lo que realmente es; lo opuesto a la exageración o hipérbole

V

valid: believable or truthful
válido: creíble o verídico

validity: the quality of truth or accuracy in a source
validez: calidad de verdad o precisión en una fuente

vignette: a picture or visual or a brief descriptive literary piece
viñeta: ilustración o representación visual o pieza literaria descriptiva breve

vocal delivery: the way words are expressed on stage, through volume, pitch, rate or speed of speech, pauses, pronunciation, and articulation

presentación vocal: manera en que se expresan las palabras en el escenario, por medio del volumen, tono, rapidez o velocidad del discurso, pausas, pronunciación y articulación

voice: the way a writer or speaker uses words and tone to express ideas as well as his or her personas

voz: manera en que el escritor u orador usa las palabras y el tono para expresar ideas, así como también su personaje

Index of Skills

Literary Skills

Academic voice, 163
Ad hominem, 368
Allusions, 101, 103, 107, 254
Analogies, 9, 40, 243
Anaphora, 22, 349
Antistrophe, 290, 337
Appeal types, 227, 234, 364
Archetypes, 149, 169
Artwork, analysis of, 262, 265
Audience
    definition of, 249
    for protest songs, 270
    selecting, 171
    voice and, 32, 48
Cause and effect, 360
Characters
    attitudes and beliefs of, 177
    comparing, 155
    gender ideas in, 173
    mask making for, 329
    moral development of, 257, 260, 334, 335
    point of view of, 276, 277, 278
    relationships of, 159, 160
    tragic heroes, 169, 174, 175
    traits of, 156, 157, 164
    on trial for actions, 330–331
    violent behavior of, 172
Choral odes, 290, 337
Chorus, 280, 284, 336
Circles of influence, 21
Claims, in an argument, 108, 360, 400, 401
Comics, 327–328
Conflict
    among subcultures, 92
    cultural, 58, 81, 88, 179, 380–381, 391
    definition of, 107
    environmental issues, 391, 392
    family, 89
    internal vs. external, 81, 88, 91, 93
    stakeholder interests in, 386, 389, 393, 396, 400
Cultural practices or beliefs, 178, 179
Culture Wheel, 154
Dialogue, definition of, 350
Diction, 9, 31, 32, 107, 163
Diegetic sound, 350
Documentary film, 352
Drama games, 282
Dramatic irony, 184
Editorials, 238
Emotional appeals, 364

Essays, 94, 266
Ethical appeals, 364
Ethos, 227, 361, 364
Exaggeration, 72
Figurative language, 79
Folk tales, 148–149
Gender roles, analysis of, 173
Genres, 269, 271
Good writing, characteristics of, 53
Greek theater, 280, 281–282, 284, 326, 336
Hamartia, 169, 174, 175
Heroes, tragic, 169, 174, 175
Hook, 99, 108, 114, 225, 401, 404
Humor, 58, 72, 115
Idioms, 185
Images
    associations evoked from, 16, 17
    definition of, 9
    juxtaposition of, 357
    photo essays, 266
Interviews, 403, 417
Irony, 72, 105, 184
Juxtaposition, 100, 357, 361
Kohlberg's stages of moral reasoning, 257, 260, 334, 335
Literary elements, 81, 88, 91, 93
Logical appeals, 364
Masks, 329
Logos, 227, 364
Metaphors, 67
Monologues, 36–41, 171
Moral reasoning, 257, 260, 334, 335
Narration, 350
Non-diegetic sound, 350
Nonfiction texts, perspectives in, 346
Novels, 146, 150, 151
Odes, 290, 337
Oral tradition, 148
Pathos, 227, 364
Persona, 104
Photo essays, 266
Plays
    Greek theater, 279–281, 284, 326, 336
    theatrical elements in, 80, 81, 88, 91, 93
    tragedy, 276, 279, 280
    visualizing, 326
Poetry
    anaphora in, 22
    SOAPSTone analysis of, 46
    TWIST analysis of, 20
    voice in, 30
Protagonists, 95

Proverbs, 148
Role playing, 47, 161
Sarcasm, 105
Satire, 58, 72, 116
Sequence of events, 357
Socratic Seminars, 162, 170, 179
Song lyrics, 33, 348, 350
Stereotypes, 43, 93
Stichomythia, 285
Strophe, 290, 337
Style, definition of, 29
Subcultures, 4, 21, 91, 92
Symbols, 16, 149
Synthesis essays, 94, 136–137
Tableaux, 161, 335
Theatrical elements, 80, 81, 88, 91, 93
Theme, 100, 107, 350
Thesis, 225
Tone, 4, 11, 20, 30, 33, 42, 46, 47, 48, 58, 66, 73, 125–126, 135, 169, 368
    in academic voice, 163
    character attitudes and, 58
    definition of, 32
    textual evidence, 66
    verbs and adjectives and, 69
Tragedy, 276, 279, 280
Tragic flaws, 169, 174, 175
Tragic heroes, 169, 174, 175
Understatement, 72
Voice
    academic, 163
    components of, 31
    crafting, 28, 29
    cultural, 4, 29
    definitions of, 11, 28
    describing, 48
    passive vs. active, 109, 219
    roles in life and, 47
    types of, 32

Reading Skills

Anticipation guides, 215, 271
Artwork, reading, 61, 62, 63
Close reading, 42, 46, 63, 180
Connotation, 9, 73, 263
Denotation, 9, 73, 263
Discussion groups, 115, 217, 226, 249, 261
Independent reading, 4, 58, 146, 200, 346
Notetaking, 210, 216, 235, 359
Paraphrasing, 151, 217
Prereading, 82, 216
Previewing, 5, 59, 146, 201, 347, 358

Questioning the text, 17, 162, 176, 178, 359, 364
RAFT, 171
SIFT analysis, 135, 180
Sketching, during reading, 216
Skimming, 210
SMELL strategy, 228, 358, 367, 369
SOAPSTone analysis, 42, 46, 125
Socratic Seminars, 107, 261
TP-CASTT analysis, 180, 348

Writing Skills

Active voice, 109, 219
Anecdotal evidence, 209
Annotated bibliographies, 396, 397, 398
Argument(s)
    ad hominem refutation of, 368
    appeal types in, 227, 234
    claims in, 108, 360, 401
    definition of, 234
    elements of, 108, 114, 401
    evidence in, 108, 209, 346, 361, 401
    persuasive language in, 200
    stakeholders in, 386, 389, 393, 396, 400
Block format, for compare/contrast response, 64
Body paragraphs, 64
Brainstorming
    art forms, 269, 270
    contexts, 151
    cultural issues, 236, 337, 391
    for group discussion questions, 136, 261
    lists, 6
    notetaking from, 14
    policy proposals, 390
    word webs, 6, 10
Call to action, 108, 400, 401
Cause-effect claims, 360, 400
Citations, 396, 397, 402, 404
Claims, in an argument, 108, 360, 400, 401
Compare and contrast, 63, 64, 83, 126, 155, 160, 336, 352
Concessions, in an argument, 108
Conclusions, 64, 400
Cornell Notes system, 359
Credibility
    ethos and, 361
    of Internet sources, 152, 395, 397, 399
    subjectivity and, 370
    in writing, 401
Discussion groups
    close reading in, 180
    evaluation in, 370, 382
    keeping on task in, 115

persuasion in, 217
RAFT activity in, 171
speaking and listening skills in, 226
Double-entry journals, 156
Drafting, 172, 236, 390, 400
Empirical evidence, 209
Essays, 67, 262
Evidence
    in documentary film, 361
    functions of, 108
    in position papers, 401
    source evaluation in, 346
    types of, 209
Hook, in an argument, 108, 225, 401
Internet sources, evaluating, 152, 395, 397, 398, 399
Introduction paragraph, 64, 400
KWL charts, 247
Logical evidence, 209
Magazines, as sources, 397, 403
MLA format, 396, 397
Norms for communication, 15
Objectivity, 353, 401
OPTIC strategy, 265, 266
Outlines, 172
Passive voice, 109, 219
Perspective
    changes over time, 65
    criticism of, 361
    cultural, 4, 29
    definition of, 29
Persuasion
    art forms in, 269
    cause-effect claims in, 360, 400
    in film, 361, 368, 370
    by a Greek Chorus, 337
    music in, 270
Plagiarism, 152
Policy proposals, 390, 393, 396
Portfolio entries, 53, 54, 142, 196, 342, 422
Position papers, 400–404
Prewriting strategies, 172
Quickwriting, 16, 32, 53, 60, 65, 72, 82, 114, 173, 184, 207, 208, 352, 368, 382, 390, 413
Reflection
    on cultural differences, 87
    on discussion groups, 226, 236, 261, 283
    on learning, 196
    on perception of others, 79
    on perspective, 66
    self-reflection, 413, 415, 418
    on thinking, 142
    on voice, 48
Refutations, in an argument, 108
Reliability. *See* Credibility

Revising, 380–381
Rhetorical questions, 240
Sentence variety, 106, 241
Source(s). *See also* Source evaluation
    annotated bibliographies of, 396, 397
    citations of, 396, 397, 402, 404
    Internet, 152, 395, 397, 398, 399
    plagiarism of, 152
    in speeches, 402–403, 404
Source evaluation
    in annotated bibliographies, 396, 397
    Internet sources, 152, 395, 397, 399
    subjectivity and, 370
Subjectivity, 353, 370
Summarizing, 361, 363, 396, 397
Support. *See* Evidence
Surveys, 256
Synthesis essays, 136–137
Synthesis prompt, 99
Thesis, 225
Thesis statements, 64, 80, 155, 160
Tone
    definition of, 32
    textual evidence of, 66
    verb tense and voice, 109
    in word arrays, 33
Topic sentence, 62, 64, 400
Transitions, 64, 66, 160
TWIST, 20
URLs, 152, 395, 399
Validity. *See* Credibility
Visualization, 262, 414
Web page sponsors, 152, 395, 399
Writing prompts, 23, 48, 81, 88, 93, 95, 160, 164, 170, 175, 177, 184, 227, 360, 364, 400
    basic parts of, 94

Media Skills

Film
    cultural conflict in, 81
    documentary, 352
    juxtaposition in, 361
    persuasion in, 361, 368, 370
    SMELL analysis of, 367, 369
    techniques in, 350
    theatrical elements in, 80, 81, 88, 91, 93
    viewing guide, 351, 354, 362
Newspaper articles, 386, 403
Oral citation of sources, 403
Painting, OPTIC analysis of, 265
Photo essays, 266
Protest music, 270
TV and radio shows, 403

Listening and Speaking Skills

Chorus, 285
Communication norms, 15
Group discussions, 115, 217, 226
Oral tradition, 148
Role playing, 161, 171, 330, 353
Source citations, in speeches, 402–403, 404
Stichomythia, 285
Summarizing presentations, 363
Trials for characters, 330–332

Language Skills

Active voice, 443
Adjective clauses, 177, 387
Adjectives, 69
    basic rules, 425
    versus adverbs, 425
Adverbial clauses, 11, 177, 241
Adverbial phrases, 241
Adverbs, 241
    basic rules, 426
Anaphora, 22
Appositives, 11, 425
    punctuation of, 425
Apostrophe, 453
Brackets, 454
Capitalization, rules for, 446
Clauses, defining, 436
Colon, 450
    lists after, 436
Commas, 113, 130, 387, 448
    splices, 434
Commonly confused verbs, 445
Comparison and contrast, 64
Complex sentences, 11, 84, 177
Compound sentences, 84
Conjunctions, 64
    coordinating, 433
Contrasting expressions, 113
Coordinating conjunctions, 64
Dashes, 186, 450
Dependent clauses, 433
    connecting with independent clauses, 433
Dependent marker word, 433
Ellipsis, 454
Fused sentences, 434
Gerunds, 73, 426
    phrases, 426–427
    punctuation with, 427
Hyphen, 452
Independent clauses, 433
Independent marker word, 434
Idioms, 185
Infinitive phrases, 73, 264

Infinitives, 73, 429
    phrases, 429
    split, 431
    verbs that take infinitive objects, 430–431
Irregular verbs, 444
Italics, 451
Metaphors, 67
Nonrestrictive clauses, 387
Nonrestrictive phrases, 130
Noun clauses, 177
Parallel structure, 264, 435
    clauses, 435
    lists after a colon, 436
    words and phrases, 435
Parentheses, 450
Participial phrases, 74, 130, 241
Participles, 74, 427
    phrases, 428
    punctuation with, 428
Passive voice, 443
Past perfect tense, 109
Periodic sentences, 11
Prepositional phrases, 210
Prepositions, 210, 432
    for time, place, and introducing objects, 432–433
Pronouns, 423
    agreement in number and person, 423
    avoiding vague referents and ambiguity, 423
    case, 424
    in comparisons, 424
    in compound structures, 424
    in formal and semiformal writing, 424
    in non-defining clauses, relative, 438
    as objects, 424
    relative, 436–437
    showing possession, 424
    special uses of, 438–439
    as subjects, 424
Proofreading strategies, 436
Punctuation, expressing oneself with, 35
Quotation marks, 105, 371, 451
Relative clauses, 387
Restrictive clauses, 387
Restrictive phrases, 130
Semicolon 449
Sentences
    complex, 11, 84, 177, 440
    compound, 84, 439
    fragments, 434
    parallel structure in, 264
    periodic, 11
    simple, 84, 439

    types of, 439
Simple sentences, 84
Single quotation marks, 371
Split infinitives, 431
Subject-verb agreement, 441
Subjunctive form, 123
Subordinating conjunctions, 64
Syntax, 11, 30, 32, 107
Verbal phrases, 73
Verbals, 73, 74, 426
    gerunds, 426
    participles, 427
    infinitives, 429
Verbs
    active vs. passive voice of, 109, 219
    commonly confused, 445
    irregular, 444
    subjunctive form of, 123
    tenses of, 109, 442–444
    tone and, 69
Word choice, 30

Vocabulary Skills

Academic vocabulary, 16, 21, 29, 43, 72, 80, 81, 94, 100, 104, 108, 175, 284
Connotation, 9, 67, 68
Context clues, 102, 202
Cue words, 64
Culture vocabulary, 10
Denotation, 9, 67, 68
Derivations, 6, 12, 29, 36, 43, 68, 69, 70, 86, 95, 119, 150, 154, 156, 173, 180, 181, 204, 205, 209, 217, 230, 232, 249, 254, 348, 352, 353, 357, 361
Foreign words, 31, 85, 117, 161
Multiple meanings, 284
Word associations, 206
Word sort, 10
Word webs, 6, 10, 284

Index of Authors and Titles